CAMPAIGN AND ELECTION REFORM

Selected Titles in ABC-CLIO's
CONTEMPORARY
WORLD ISSUES
Series

For a complete list of titles in this series, please visit
www.abc-clio.com.

Books in the Contemporary World Issues series address vital issues in today's society, such as genetic engineering, pollution, and biodiversity. Written by professional writers, scholars, and nonacademic experts, these books are authoritative, clearly written, up-to-date, and objective. They provide a good starting point for research by high school and college students, scholars, and general readers as well as by legislators, businesspeople, activists, and others.

Each book, carefully organized and easy to use, contains an overview of the subject, a detailed chronology, biographical sketches, facts and data and/or documents and other primary-source material, a directory of organizations and agencies, annotated lists of print and nonprint resources, and an index.

Readers of books in the Contemporary World Issues series will find the information they need to have a better understanding of the social, political, environmental, and economic issues facing the world today.

CAMPAIGN AND ELECTION REFORM

A Reference Handbook

Second Edition

Glenn H. Utter and Ruth Ann Strickland

CONTEMPORARY WORLD ISSUES

A B C  C L I O

Santa Barbara, California
Denver, Colorado
Oxford, England

Library of Congress Cataloging-in-Publication Data
Utter, Glenn H.
    Campaign and election reform : a reference handbook / Glenn H.
Utter and Ruth Ann Strickland. — 2nd ed.
        p.   cm. — (Contemporary world issues)
    Includes bibliographical references and index.
    ISBN 978-1-59884-069-8 (hard copy : alk. paper) —
    ISBN 978-1-59884-070-4 (ebook)
    1. Elections—United States.   2. Election law—United States.   3. Po-
litical campaigns—United States.   4. Campaign funds—United States.
5. Political participation—United States.   I. Strickland, Ruth Ann.   II.
Title.

JK1976.U88   2008
324.70973-dc22

                                                           2008011881

12   11   10   09   08   1   2   3   4   5   6   7   8   9   10

ABC-CLIO, Inc.
130 Cremona Drive, P.O. Box 1911
Santa Barbara, California 93116–1911

This book is also available on the World Wide Web as an e-Book.
Visit abc-clio.com for details.

This book is printed on acid-free paper ∞
Manufactured in the United States of America

Contents

Preface

Citizens have often reacted with a certain level of cynicism to campaigns and elections. H. L. Mencken, the noted curmudgeon of American journalism, once compared a national campaign to "the best circus ever heard of, with a mass baptism and a couple of hangings thrown in," an event better even than war. And George Bernard Shaw commented that an election is "a moral horror," a battle without blood, and a mud bath for all those involved in it. Despite such evaluations, voting has come to signify the very essence of democracy. This is true in part because the term "democracy" is now used primarily to refer to representative democracy.

When the United States first became a nation, many prominent Americans still regarded democracy with suspicion. Political parties, a major component of representative democracy, had not yet been invented. According to the newly adopted national Constitution, U.S. senators were to be selected by state legislatures, and the president was to be chosen by a group of individuals, called the electoral college, who were appointed by state legislatures. Only members of the House of Representatives were to be elected by the citizens according to electoral rules determined by the respective states. From that inauspicious beginning, the history of campaigns and elections is an account of various reforms intended to provide for more honest and fair electoral procedures and to extend the right to vote. Various measures, such as the elimination of property qualifications for voting, granting women the right to vote, introducing the secret ballot, guaranteeing voting rights to minorities, and providing for the regulation of campaign practices have significantly altered the campaign and election process.

At times so-called reforms, rather than expanding the franchise, established significant restrictions on the right to vote. Most obviously, the election laws introduced in Southern states following Reconstruction severely limited the voting rights of minorities. Stringent registration requirements, introduced in the late nineteenth century and intended to limit voter fraud, undoubtedly discouraged many Americans from voting. Since the passage of the Voting Rights Act in 1965 and the Federal Election Campaign Act in 1974, much greater attention has been given to facilitating voting. However, despite the many recent reforms, there has been a gradual decline in voter turnout over the last three decades. Troubled by this trend, reformers have offered their favored explanations and solutions. For instance, in the early 1990s Frances Fox Piven and Richard Cloward campaigned vigorously for voter registration reform, claiming that overly strict registration laws prevented many Americans, especially the less well-to-do, from participating in the electoral process. They argued that the National Voter Registration Act, which President Bill Clinton signed into law in May 1993 and which went into effect in January 1995, would significantly increase voter participation. However, the disappointing turnout rate in the 1996 presidential election did not support their optimism.

Given the charges of inefficiency and inaccuracies in vote counting following the 2000 presidential election, Congress in 2002 passed the Help America Vote Act, which created the Election Assistance Commission to assist in improving federal election administration and to help states in replacing old voting equipment with more technically advanced systems. Voting technology remains a controversial issue, especially regarding the verifiability of election results with the use of electronic voting.

Although various measures, such as election day registration, voting assistance for the disabled, and early voting, have contributed to making the campaign and election process fairer, they are responsible primarily for making the voting procedure more convenient for those who already are inclined to participate. Nearly 50 percent of eligible citizens remain aloof from electoral politics. In a continuing effort to deal with this situation, recent proposals call for an alteration in electoral mechanics. For instance, in place of the single-member district plurality system, some argue that a variation of proportional representation, such as cumulative voting, should be introduced. Such alternatives would give citizens a greater sense of the importance of their vote and would grant minority group members a greater opportunity to be elected to office. However, a proportional system, which would also increase the influence of minor parties, has not gained much support from Democratic and Republican party leaders.

Laws relating to campaign finance, one of the most difficult reform issues to resolve, have so far been ineffective in controlling the use of money in politics. While some point to the corrupting influence of money and the need for stricter regulations, others argue that the constitutional protection of free speech includes the right to use one's resources freely to affect the political process. In contrast to proposals further limiting the amount that individuals may contribute to political campaigns, some recommend that limits on donations and spending should be greatly eased or even eliminated and that at the same time strong disclosure legislation should be enacted allowing citizens to gain information about the sources of candidates' campaign funding. In 2002 Congress passed the Bipartisan Campaign Reform Act (BCRA), which was intended to prohibit national political party committees' use of unrestricted funds in state and local campaigns and to regulate the many issues ads funded by independent groups during the period just before an election. The U.S. Supreme Court in *Federal Election Commission v. Wisconsin Right to Life, Inc.* (2007) ruled that such restrictions on ads were unconstitutional as applied to issue ads and not explicit political advocacy, thus raising doubts about the effectiveness of the BCRA.

Clearly, reform proposals are often guided by considerations of political advantage. The rules and regulations governing campaigns and elections are seldom neutral. Whether intentionally or not, they almost inevitably advantage some political interests and disadvantage others. However, while admitting that political reform is itself a part of the political process, we believe that any treatment of campaign and election reform must be guided ultimately by considerations of fairness and a clear understanding of democratic principles.

We wish to express our sincere appreciation to Bob Lyman, dean of the College of Arts and Sciences, Stan Aeschleman, provost at Appalachian State University, Brenda Nichols, dean of the College of Arts and Sciences, Cruse Melvin, associate dean of the College of Arts and Sciences, and Stephen Doblin, provost and vice president for academic affairs at Lamar University, for the generous support they provided in helping us complete this volume. Of course, we accept full responsibility for any errors of fact or judgment.

Glenn H. Utter and Ruth Ann Strickland

1

Background and History

Suffrage Expansion and Voting Rights

Throughout U.S. history many changes in the electoral system have been classified as campaign and election reforms. The most basic type of reform, however, involved the expansion of the right to vote, and the history of voting in the United States is truly a history of suffrage expansion. When delegates from 12 of the 13 states met in Philadelphia in the summer of 1787 to write a new constitution, voting rights in the states generally were restricted to white males who owned property. The new constitution said little about voting, other than providing for the popular election of members of the House of Representatives. Voting qualifications were left to the individual states because regulations varied widely among them and the delegates thought it prudent not to attempt a resolution of the differences (Wright 1967, 26–27).

In the first half of the 19th century, property qualifications steadily disappeared in all of the states, except for certain elections dealing, for instance, with tax issues. Following the Civil War, ratification of the Thirteenth, Fourteenth, and Fifteenth Amendments amounted to a constitutional revolution in which the federal government received significantly greater authority to ensure the rights of citizens in the several states. The Fifteenth Amendment specifically guaranteed the right to vote for former male slaves. The national Constitution notwithstanding, Southern states were able to deny voting rights to African Americans during the later years of the 19th century and the first decades of the twentieth by instituting what many Southern whites considered voter registration reforms. Such strategies as the literacy test, good character requirements that disfranchised those convicted of certain crimes, the grandfather clause that exempted many whites from voter registration requirements, and intimidation virtually eliminated minority voting in Southern states.

At the same time that black men were being denied the right to vote, women were crusading for the franchise. To a certain extent, the women's rights movement in the United States grew out of the antislavery cause. Elizabeth Cady Stanton, the wife of an abolitionist leader, organized the first women's rights convention in Seneca Falls, New York, in 1848. During the Civil War, Stanton and Susan B. Anthony established the National Woman's Loyal League to lobby for what became the Thirteenth Amendment, ratified in December 1865, which prohibited slavery. Following the Civil War, many in the women's rights movement expected that women would be granted the franchise along with black men. However, the more cautious supporters of black suffrage believed that combining their goal with the push for woman suffrage would jeopardize both causes. In 1869 rival woman suffrage organizations were established: the more radical National Woman Suffrage Association, based in New York, which called for immediate nationwide enfranchisement of women, and the more conservative American Woman Suffrage Association, headquartered in Boston, which was more willing to accept the precedence of black suffrage. The two organizations combined in 1890 to form the National American Woman Suffrage Association. The fight for woman suffrage continued for over 50 years before final victory was achieved in 1920 with ratification of the Nineteenth Amendment. There had been successes along the way, especially in Western states, but they were few as the frustrating struggle dragged on year after year. In 1904, two years before her death, Anthony made her final appearance before a Senate committee considering a woman suffrage amendment. She reminded the senators that she was the only surviving member of a group that, 35 years before, had appealed to Congress for the franchise (Lutz 1959, 298). The early advocates did not live to see the end result of their efforts, but they had prepared the way for a new generation who made the final push for woman suffrage.

The United States traveled a tortuous road of reform to remedy the injustices that denied the franchise to minorities. The

U.S. Supreme Court, in *Smith v. Allwright* (1944), declared unconstitutional the white primary, which had prohibited blacks in Southern states from voting in the Democratic primary. However, Southern states continued to employ other methods of discrimination to discourage minority voter registration and voting. The Civil Rights Act of 1957, the first civil rights legislation since 1875, authorized the U.S. attorney general to file suits in federal district court to gain injunctions against violations of the Fifteenth Amendment. This act failed to bring about significant reforms. The Attorney General's Office filed only four suits in the three years following the act's passage (Grofman, Handley, and Niemi 1992, 13). Attempting to remedy some of the weaknesses of the 1957 legislation, Congress passed another civil rights act in 1960. Although the new legislation authorized federal district court judges to appoint federal referees to replace state election officials and required local election administrators to store voting records for 22 months after an election, it ultimately had little more effect than its predecessor. By 1965 only 35.5 percent of eligible African Americans were registered to vote in the South, compared to 73.4 percent of eligible whites (Grofman, Handley, and Niemi 1992, 20). In 1964 Congress had passed a significant new civil rights act. Although it focused primarily on questions of public accommodation, school funding, and employment, one section placed limitations on the use the literacy test as a qualification for voter registration.

The use of the poll tax—the payment of a fee as a prerequisite for voting—was a common practice when the Constitution was written, but by the middle of the 19th century states generally had ceased using it. However, following ratification of the Fifteenth Amendment in 1870, which prohibited denying the right to vote on the basis of race, color, or previous condition of servitude, Southern states revived the poll tax as a means of denying the right to vote to African Americans, the majority of whom were poor, as well as to poor whites (Stephens and Scheb 1999, 352). In 1937, in *Breedlove v. Suttle,* the U.S. Supreme Court ruled that the poll tax by itself violated neither the Fourteenth nor the Fifteenth Amendment. By 1960 just five Southern states continued to use the poll tax. In 1964 three-fourths of the states finally ratified the Twenty-fourth Amendment, which prohibited the use of the poll tax as a prerequisite for voting in presidential or congressional elections, and in 1966 the U.S. Supreme Court in *Harper v. Virginia State Board of Elections* overruled the *Breedlove* decision, declaring unconstitutional the use of the poll tax in state elections. At that time only two states—Virginia and Texas—still had a poll tax for state elections (Schmidt et al. 2006, 707).

The 1964 Civil Rights Act soon was followed by the Voting Rights Act of 1965 (VRA), Section 2 of which reinforced the Fifteenth Amendment, prohibiting any voting qualifications, standards, or procedures that denied or abridged the right to vote because of race or color. The act bolstered the attorney general's suit-filing authority, but most importantly it authorized the Justice Department to circumvent the judiciary in Southern states to intervene in the interest of blacks who had been denied the right to vote. In certain jurisdictions, the literacy test was suspended for five years and voting regulations were to remain unaltered unless the attorney general or the district court of the District of Columbia approved any application to change the voting system, a process known as preclearance. The act provided for federal registration examiners and election observers to ensure that voting procedures would remain fair and nondiscriminatory. By 1966 only 4 out of the 13 Southern states had fewer than 50 percent of blacks registered to vote, and, just two years following passage of the bill, at least 50 percent of blacks in each of the states targeted by the act were registered. The overall proportion of eligible blacks registered to vote increased to over 52 percent (Grofman, Handley, and Niemi 1992, 20). In 2000 African American registration rates trailed white registration rates by only 2 percent ("ACLU Voting Rights: About the VRA" 2006). The VRA demonstrated how effective reform legislation can be in bringing about increased voter participation if it targets a specific problem.

Although the number of minority elected officials in the South has increased dramatically in recent years—from less than 100 before passage of the VRA to more than 3,000 by 1994 (Engstrom 1994, 687) and more than 9,000 in 2005 (Will 2005)—many have contended that an even greater number of minority officials should be elected to public office. Representatives in the United States for the most part are elected through the single-member district plurality system, which generally is considered to favor the major parties and the dominant groups.

The 1970 revisions to the VRA continued the strict provisions of the 1965 act. Literacy tests were suspended in all states for an additional five years. In 1975 Congress extended the act once more and expanded its provisions to cover language minorities. The newly added section 203 required election administrations to provide bilingual election materials if 5 percent of the jurisdiction's voting age population constituted a single-language minority and if the illiteracy rate in that group exceeded the national rate. Literacy tests were prohibited permanently rather than simply suspended. In 1982 Congress extended the VRA for an additional 25 years. Amendments required states to redistrict to increase the likelihood that minorities would gain representation. However, the Justice Department's efforts to increase minority representation in Congress met a potential obstacle when the U.S. Supreme Court limited the ability of states to redistrict for this purpose. Remanding North Carolina's redistricting plan, which had resulted in an oddly shaped congressional district, members of the Court in *Shaw v. Reno* (1993) expressed concern about the formation of districts that segregate, or "balkanize," citizens by race and ruled that race cannot be the sole factor in creating legislative districts. Some students of elections advocated the adoption of a system of proportional representation to replace the single-member legislative districts in order to assure minority representation, but overall states maintained the traditional legislative districts, facing subsequent charges of both political and racial gerrymandering, which involves the drawing of legislative district lines in such a way as to advantage a particular political interest or ethnic group.

When the VRA, called the Fannie Lou Hamer, Rosa Parks, and Coretta Scott King Voting Rights Act Reauthorization and Amendments Act of 2006, came before Congress for an additional 25-year extension, a small number of conservative members raised objections to some of the act's provisions. Some objectors claimed that the preclearance provision wrongly punished states and localities that long ago had eliminated any discriminatory actions. Representative Louie Gohmert (R-TX) introduced an amendment, ultimately defeated, that would have reduced the extension period from 25 to 10 years (Levine 2006). Others objected to the section 5 provision requiring multilingual ballots. Those supporting the act argued that its provisions were still needed, pointing to such instances as the U.S. Supreme Court's decision in *League of United Latin American Citizens v. Perry*, which was announced as Congress debated the VRA renewal. In that case, the Court found that the 2003 Texas redistricting plan violated the VRA to the extent that a southwest Texas district's boundary lines split the Hispanic population, thus diluting that group's vote strength. The VRA renewal act passed in the House by a vote of 390 to 33 and unanimously in the Senate. Just days after President George W. Bush signed the legislation, a municipal utility district north of Austin, Texas, filed a lawsuit over the preclearance provision, claiming that the district was being unfairly punished for conditions that never existed in its jurisdiction. In 2002 the district had spent $1,250 in legal fees to file for approval from the U.S. Department of Justice to move its one polling place from a residential garage to a school. Observers expected that other small jurisdictions would file suits objecting to the preclearance provision (Elliot 2006).

Since passage of the Voting Rights Act of 1965, which effectively ensured the right of minorities to register and vote, concern gradually shifted to questions of the effectiveness of the franchise. For instance, at-large elections at the local level came under attack for their tendency to deny minority candidates representation on governing bodies. Originally a progressive reform measure, at-large elections were geared to encourage residents and their representatives to focus on citywide policy concerns rather than parochial interests. But one result of such elections was the inability of minority groups to gain sufficient support citywide to elect favored candidates. After 1965 a number of dilution methods, such as the introduction of at-large elections and the annexation of areas with large white populations, were used to ensure majority white voting strength in local jurisdictions. Gerrymandered districts also guaranteed victories for white candidates (Engstrom 1994, 685). The preclearance provisions of the VRA helped to stem the tide of proposals to alter voting systems. In *Allen v. State Board of Elections* (1969) the U.S. Supreme Court identified vote dilution as an unallowable limitation on the right to vote and hence subject to the preclearance provisions of the VRA. In addition, the so-called results test, added as part of the 1982 amendments to the VRA, stipulated that, regardless of motivation, changes in election laws that cause the dilution of minority vote strength are invalid (Engstrom 1994, 687).

Another expansion of voting rights was the ratification of the Twenty-sixth Amendment in 1971, which granted to those at least 18 years old the right to vote in federal elections. Prior to 1971 states tended to limit voting to those at least 21 years of age. The civil rights movement and widespread youth protests against the Vietnam War undoubtedly spurred the adoption of this amendment. However, subsequent turnout data indicated that the youngest age group had the lowest voter turnout rate in the United States.

Term Limits

Another electoral reform issue, term limits, occupied the attention of many political activists in the 1990s. By 1996, 21 states had adopted some form of term limits for state legislators. According to Maine's stringent requirement, adopted in a 1993 referendum, the time incumbent legislators already had served counted toward the limit of four consecutive two-year terms. Louisiana, Nevada, Oklahoma, and Utah approved a 12-year cap on state legislators (Chada and Bernstein 1996, 363). The appeal of term limits resulted in part from the success incumbents experienced in gaining reelection and in part from the perception of a disaffected public that long-term career politicians could not be trusted. Although many Republicans supported term limits in the early 1990s, a Republican-controlled Congress from 1995 to 2007 failed to pass a term limit proposal. Despite Congress's failure to act, at least 15 states approved initiatives to limit the length of service of their members of Congress. However, the U.S. Supreme Court in *U.S. Term Limits, Inc., v. Thornton* (1995) ruled that states could not impose term limits on members of the U.S. House of Representatives because such limits introduced a qualification for election to Congress not found in the Constitution. Therefore, establishing term limits for members of Congress would require a constitutional amendment.

In the 1990s Mark Petracca (1993, 703), a supporter of term limits, argued that rotation in office represented a fundamental part of republican government and the rights of citizenship. On the other hand, opponents argued for prudence, claiming that term limits would result in a less professional legislature, which would mean even greater dominance by professional staff and special interests in Congress and greater influence for the executive branch. More recently Alan Greenblatt (2006), opposing term limits for members of state legislatures, has argued that such limits created a discontinuity in policy making and policy application in the states that had established them. However, with the exception of two states that repealed term limits—Idaho in 2002 and Utah in 2003—state legislators have tended to shy away from attempts to remove such limits in the face of their continuing popularity among the electorate.

Ballot Fraud and Voter Fraud

For democratic elections to acquire sufficient legitimacy, voters must be assured that the electoral process has been justly administered and their votes honestly counted. Reformers have attempted to control vote fraud, which can take various forms but falls into two basic categories: (1) voter fraud, which occurs when an individual casts a ballot illegally, and (2) ballot fraud, which usually takes place after votes have been cast and involves the dishonest counting of ballots. During the early years of the nation, voters simply registered their preferences orally. Subsequently, political parties and candidates printed their own ballots, distinguishing them by color or special symbol. Voters were provided the ballot of the preferred party. Because voters could not conceal how they voted, these systems at times led to intimidation and violence. The introduction of the secret, or Australian, ballot (so-called because it was used first in Australia beginning in the 1850s before being adopted in the United States), occurred in the 1880s and eliminated much of the opportunity either to threaten or to promise rewards to voters. The Australian ballot called for the preparation of ballots at public expense instead of distribution by political parties, the presentation of all candidates' names on each ballot, the distribution of ballots only at official polling places, and the secret marking of ballots.

To evade the secret ballot, unscrupulous politicians introduced various vote fraud techniques, including repeat voting and casting an already prepared ballot (called the Tasmanian dodge, possibly because the Australian ballot was first introduced in the Australian territory of Tasmania). In this technique, which circumvented the secret ballot, a candidate or group hired a person to go to the polling place as a voter and get a ballot. Instead of casting the ballot, the person took the ballot back to headquarters, where he was paid for getting it. Those at headquarters completed the ballot, selecting the desired candidates. Another person went to the polling place with the already prepared ballot, received a new one, cast the prepared ballot, and returned to headquarters with the new blank ballot. The process continued throughout election day with various workers. As the opportunity arose, corrupt election officials could use other techniques, such as defacing ballots cast for opposition candidates, correcting favorable but spoiled ballots, substituting premarked ballots, stuffing ballot boxes with additional ballots, and simply misreporting vote totals (Benson 1978, 173). To discourage fraud, various actions were specifically prohibited under federal statute (18 U.S.C. 241 and 242), including preventing a qualified citizen from casting a ballot, stuffing ballot boxes, impersonating a qualified voter, altering ballots, registering voters illegally, fraudulently casting absentee ballots, and voting more than once in the same election (Kimberling and Sims 1996, 18). Federal statutes forbade any act that could broadly be construed as vote buying, such as offering payment for voting or registering to vote. In 1980 the Election Crimes Branch (ECB) of the Public Integrity Section of the U.S. Department of Justice's Criminal Division was established (Donsanto 1989, 20). The ECB focuses on prosecuting criminal violations of federal election law. Such criminal offenses include stuffing ballot boxes, intimidating voters, destroying ballots, falsifying voter registrations, impersonating voters, paying citizens to vote, and falsifying election returns.

The introduction of computer technology represented the opportunity to cast and count ballots even more quickly and accurately. By 1992 nearly two-thirds of the electorate cast ballots that were counted mechanically or electronically (Garber 1995, 7–15). In the 2004 presidential election, 32.2 percent of voters used optical scan machines; 28.9 percent used electronic touch screen, or direct recording electronic (DRE) machines; 18.6 percent voted with punch cards; 12.8 percent used lever machines; and fewer than 1 percent voted with paper ballots ("Counting the

Number of Ways We Can Vote" 2004). Although many saw electronic voting systems as major improvements over previous procedures, others remained less certain that electronic counting represented progress, claiming instead that new systems provided opportunities for vote fraud on a grand scale. Computer-tabulated voting in most cases required the production of machine-readable punch card ballots that allowed officials to maintain a paper trail to document security at the various stages, from production and storage prior to use to accounting for unvoted and spoiled ballots, and finally to the storage of voted ballots in anticipation of any challenge to the vote outcome (Garber 1995, 3). However, the 2000 presidential election revealed critical flaws in this voting system, which could fail to count ballots due to problems with the chads, the areas that are punched out of the cards to register a vote choice. With hanging chads, some of the punched areas remained attached to the cards, and with dimpled chads, a voter failed to punch through the card, leaving instead an indentation.

James Condit Jr., head of Cincinnatus News Service and an early critic of electronic voting, claimed that the computerized vote tallying of Voter News Service, located in New York City, possibly denied Pat Buchanan a 1996 Arizona Republican presidential primary victory. Condit pointed to other possible examples of vote fraud via computer high jinks and urged a return to the paper ballot that precinct workers count by hand after the polls close on election day (Condit 1996, 17). More recently, many have raised doubts especially about DRE machines, even those equipped with printers to produce a paper trail, and advocate a return to some version of the paper ballot. However, others have emphasized that the traditional voting and counting procedure itself proved notoriously inaccurate and allowed many opportunities for fraud. Poll officials, who often worked a 12-hour day, were required to count by hand a large number of ballots quickly and accurately. Rather than returning to this system, reforms will more likely focus on tighter computer security, more stringent voting machine certification, and improved procedures for auditing vote totals. Crucially, election officials must establish some valid procedure to assure voters that their ballots have been honestly and expeditiously recorded and counted. Otherwise, doubts can easily be raised about the honesty and accuracy of election results, and hence the authority of elected officials ultimately can be put into question.

The Electoral College

Critics of the constitutionally prescribed procedure for electing the president had long warned that the system could lead to a crisis in U.S. democracy because, due largely to the extraconstitutional winner-take-all (unit rule) policy, whereby all of a state's electoral votes are awarded to the popular vote winner, the nationwide popular vote winner may not receive a majority of the electoral votes. Critics argue that the system for electing the president represents an 18th-century device that fails to meet the needs of a modern governing system. During an era in which democratic principles prevail, the United States still allows the most powerful political official in the world to be selected via the creaking machinery of the electoral college. Not since 1804, when ratification of the Twelfth Amendment provided for separate ballots for president and vice president, has the presidential election system been significantly altered, although informal modifications have occurred.

In 1961 the electoral college was modified slightly when the states ratified the Twenty-third Amendment, granting to the District of Columbia a number of electors to which it would be entitled were it a state, but in any event no more electoral votes than the least populous state. Prior to ratification of this amendment, people living in the District, not being residents of a state, could not vote in presidential elections. Since the 1964 presidential election, District voters have selected three presidential electors, which have consistently gone to the Democratic candidate. Residents of the District still lack representation in Congress. Granting such representation through an additional constitutional amendment has been a politically controversial issue because any representatives from the District would undoubtedly add to the Democratic Party congressional delegation.

The 1800 presidential election made clear that the electoral college, as originally established, would not work. As the original Constitution mandated, each elector voted for two candidates for president. The top vote getter, assuming the candidate received a majority of the electoral votes, was elected president, and the candidate receiving the second highest number of votes was elected vice president. The framers of the constitution failed to foresee the development of a political party system in which presidential and vice presidential candidates would run together on a party ticket. When Thomas Jefferson, the Democratic-Republican Party presidential candidate, and Aaron Burr, that party's vice presidential candidate, received identical numbers of electoral votes, the House of Representatives had to decide the presidential election winner.

The Constitution did not specify how a state's electors should be chosen, leaving the decision to the state legislatures. However, by 1836 all states except one had adopted selection by popular vote. Today 538 electors choose the president, and these individuals are determined by the voters in each of the 50 states and the District of Columbia who cast their ballots for presidential candidates. Each state has a number of electors equal to its representation in Congress (House and Senate). Only two states—Maine and Nebraska—allow for electoral vote distribution according to popular vote totals within their congressional districts; they do not award all electoral votes to the statewide popular vote winner.

The 1800 election was one of three occasions when the electoral college failed to provide a winner. In 1824 the U.S. House of Representatives again selected the president when no candidate received a clear majority of the electoral votes. In that year the electoral vote was divided among four candidates—John Quincy Adams, Henry Clay, William H. Crawford, and Andrew Jackson—with Jackson receiving the most electoral votes but falling short of the necessary majority. With Clay supporting Adams, the House elected Adams president, a decision that Jackson and his supporters bitterly resented, given Jackson's early electoral lead.

In addition to the possibility that no candidate receives a majority of the electoral vote, which would result in the U.S. House of Representatives choosing the president, the candidate who did not receive a plurality of the popular votes could win a majority of the electoral college vote. In the 1876 election, Democratic candidate Samuel Tilden received 250,000 more popular votes than Republican Rutherford B. Hayes, but, because of disputed electoral votes from Florida, Louisiana, South Carolina, and Oregon, Congress established an electoral commission composed of five senators, five representatives, and five Supreme Court justices, seven of whom were Democrats and eight were Republicans. On March 2, 1877, by a strict party vote, the commission awarded all disputed electoral votes to Hayes, thus giving the Republican a one-vote victory (185 to 184) over Tilden (Morison 1965, 733–34). The difficulties of 1824 and 1876 notwithstanding, no electoral college reform occurred. The electoral college caused a further embarrassment in the 1888 election when

Benjamin Harrison won a majority of the electoral vote even though Grover Cleveland, the incumbent president, received 100,000 more popular votes. Harrison received 233 electoral votes to Cleveland's 168 (Barbour and Wright 2003, A-19). Sanford Levinson (2006, 82–83) claims that the 1960 election is yet another example of electing a minority president, with Richard M. Nixon actually receiving more popular votes than John F. Kennedy (34,108,147 votes for Nixon and 34,049,976 for Kennedy), even though Kennedy defeated Nixon in the electoral college (303 to 219, with Harry Byrd receiving 13 votes).

A circumstance in which the popular vote winner lost in the electoral college did not occur again for more than 100 years, when in the 2000 election Republican George W. Bush won the electoral college vote (271 to 266), even though Albert Gore received 544,000 more popular votes than Bush out of more than 104 million votes nationwide. The election occurred on November 7, but the final outcome was not determined until December 12, when the U.S. Supreme Court, in *Bush v. Gore*, ruled in favor of George W. Bush, ordering that any further vote counts ordered by the Florida supreme court should cease. Therefore, the Bush victory that Katherine Harris, Florida's secretary of state, had certified on November 26, finally went into effect, with Bush leading Gore by 537 votes out of a total of almost six million votes cast in the state (Saltman 2006, 2). That the race depended on the vote outcome of a single state, in which the voting system and procedures were strongly challenged—particularly the use of a confusing punch card ballot in some areas of the state as well as a poorly maintained voter registration system that inaccurately identified those eligible to vote—added mightily to the controversy over the presidential election. The 2000 election led to calls for reforms both in the electoral college and in voter registration and voting systems.

In summer 2007, Thomas Hiltachk, a lawyer associated with the California Republican Party, began sponsoring a ballot initiative for the June 3, 2008 California primary. The initiative would change how California distributed its 55 electoral votes from a winner-take-all basis to awarding electoral votes by congressional districts, with the statewide winner receiving two additional electoral votes associated with the state's two U.S. senators. If such a system had been in effect in 2004, George W. Bush, who lost California to Democratic candidate John Kerry, would have won 22 of the state's electoral votes. Democrats strongly objected to placing the measure on the ballot, calling the proposed alteration in allocating electoral votes a partisan proposal masquerading as electoral reform and a way to provide the Republican Party with an automatic bonus of electoral votes in the November 2008 election. Democrats noted that, if the proposal passed, the measure would be challenged in federal court as a violation of the U.S. Constitution, which states that state legislatures (not voters on a ballot measure) are to determine the method of selecting presidential electors. Others observed that, even if electoral votes in all states were allocated by presidential candidate winners in congressional districts rather than statewide, the system would not be improved because the vast majority of congressional districts are the product of partisan gerrymandering (Alter 2007).

Candidate Nominations

As suffrage expanded to greater numbers of citizens early in U.S. history, controversies arose over just how candidates would be nominated as representatives of a political party to seek public office. In 1796 the Federalist Party and the Democratic-Republican Party each used a congressional party caucus to nominate their presidential candidate (Dahl 1967, 211–12). Parties also used the caucus at the state and local levels to nominate other candidates. The parties employed the caucus until 1824, when that nomination procedure fell into disrepute. Opponents, who used the term "King Caucus," objected to this nomination process for several reasons: for being controlled by a small group within the party and thus failing to represent the party membership, for violating the principle of separation of powers by allowing the legislative branch to select candidates for the executive branch, and for secret deals involved in manipulating nominations (Plano and Greenberg 1997, 64–65). In 1831 the Anti-Masonic Party initiated the convention method of nomination, and the Jacksonian Democrats followed with a nominating convention in 1832. By 1835 the legislative caucus method of nomination had virtually disappeared.

The nominating convention, used at the national, state, and local levels, was considered a significant democratic reform because convention delegates were considered representatives of the general membership of the party. However, the convention method in practice proved to be far from democratic because state and local party leaders exercised ultimate control over the convention procedures (Dahl 1967, 246). Due to disillusionment with the party convention as a system of representative democracy and general concern over corrupt political practices, advocates of democratization urged the adoption of the primary method of nomination in which the general membership of the parties and their supporters would participate in an election to nominate candidates. By the first decade of the 20th century, the party primary had become the overwhelmingly favored method of nomination. Although many considered the primary a significant election reform, others saw the adoption of the primary as an unfortunate development for representative democracy. Those holding this position have argued that political parties perform crucial functions in a democratic system, one of which is to nominate candidates to campaign on the party platform. However, the primary took the nomination process out of the hands of the parties and gave it to the general electorate. Especially in those states that adopted the open primary, voters could choose the primary in which to vote without previously declaring a party preference. Because party membership in the United States involves simply an expression of individual preference, even in states with a closed primary, the nomination process was taken from the formal party structure. Although the introduction of the primary to nominate candidates was considered an electoral reform, others concluded that parties, considered an important element in the democratic electoral process, were thereby seriously weakened.

After 1968 the presidential primary became the crucial element in the presidential nomination process. If candidates were to win the party nomination, they had to demonstrate their ability to attract votes and to accumulate sufficient numbers of delegates in the primaries to win the nomination at the national convention. Of special importance in measuring a candidate's viability was performing well in the early contests, particularly the New Hampshire primary and the Iowa caucuses. In the 1980s Southern states collaborated to hold their presidential primary elections earlier in the season on the same day in March, called Super Tuesday, in order to increase their influence on the nomination process. This tendency, called front-loading, involved states' moving their primaries to earlier dates to increase their influence on the presidential nomination. Since then, individual states became increasingly concerned about scheduling their primaries so that their voters would have a real influence on the nomination before the de facto winner had been determined. In an attempt to control the state parties' scheduling of presidential primaries and caucuses, in 2006 the Democratic National Committee (DNC) decided to permit Nevada and South Carolina to hold presidential nominating events early, along with the traditionally first states of Iowa and New Hampshire, and that no other state could hold such events as early. The Republican National Committee (RNC) made a similar ruling (Zuckerman 2007, 72). However, many states, maneuvering their primaries for maximum influence on the presidential nomination, scheduled primary dates much earlier in the election cycle.

By May 2007 it was estimated that as many as 25 states would hold primaries no later than February 5, 2008. Florida, in a bill passed by the state legislature and signed by Governor Charlie Crist, subsequently moved its party primaries to January 29. The DNC threatened that any candidate who campaigned in a state that violated the primary election rules would not be eligible to win any of that state's convention delegates (Walsh 2007, 28). In August the DNC's rules and bylaws committee voted to deny Florida all delegates to the 2008 Democratic National Convention if the state party did not agree to change the primary date. However, Florida Democratic Party chair, Karen Thurman, gave no indication that such a change would occur. South Carolina Republicans decided to move their primary to January 19, the same day chosen by Florida (Hoffman 2007, A12). In August the Wyoming Republican Party announced that they were moving the delegation selection process to January 5 (Gruver 2007, A7). In September the Michigan legislature approved and the governor signed a bill moving the state's presidential primaries to January 15. The RNC had threatened to deny to early primary states half of their convention delegates for moving up their primaries, but to no avail (Ohlemacher 2007, A8). The process of leapfrogging to an earlier time in the primary and caucus season led political analysts to speculate that electoral events would occur in December 2007, an unprecedented situation in which party presidential nominations could be determined as early as six months before the party conventions and ten months before the general election. However, by February the primaries had not indicated an obvious Democratic presidential nominee and speculation increased that the nearly 800 super delegates—party professionals and elected officials who gain delegate status automatically—might become the ultimate key to the nomination.

National party leaders called for order to be restored in the chaotic nomination process in which candidates were uncertain about strategy, particularly regarding the raising and spending of campaign funds and the most effective way of using such funds. To establish greater order in the process, various alternative reforms were suggested, such as establishing regional primaries to be held at intervals throughout the primary period. However, there appeared to be little initiative to establish such a system, which would require the cooperation of all states holding presidential primaries (Calabresi 2007, 47).

Progressive Era Reforms

The use of party primaries was just one of the reforms that the Progressive Movement advocated in the late 19th and early 20th centuries. Progressives, concerned with the ill effects of the rapid industrialization that followed the Civil War, the resulting concentration of wealth in the hands of a relatively small number of industrialists, and the corrupt practices of many state and local politicians and political parties, supported various social and economic reforms, including worker's compensation, laws restricting child labor, and minimum wage legislation. The political reforms that the movement advocated included the adoption of the secret ballot and the direct election of U.S. senators, the latter of which was achieved in 1913 with adoption of the Seventeenth Amendment.

Other Progressive reforms included the initiative and referendum, which allowed voters to approve or reject substantive legislation in elections. The referendum is a procedure by which a state legislature proposes legislation that must receive the approval of the electorate in a general or specially called election. In a constitutional referendum, voters determine the fate of proposed amendments to the state constitution. The initiative differs from the referendum in that the citizens themselves propose the legislation through the petition procedure, which requires the signature of a certain percentage of registered voters, varying from 5 to 15 percent, depending on the state (Plano and Greenberg 1997, 151).

The Progressive Movement, seeking to reduce the influence of political party machines at the local level, introduced the use of nonpartisan ballots for municipal elections, thus turning elections into nonpartisan local contests that kept the national parties at bay. Seeing the party labels as symbols of narrow interests and graft, Progressives believed citizens could agree on matters of public interest if these divisive labels were taken out of local politics. However, nonpartisan elections further weakened the political parties' role in U.S. politics, and some regarded them as a further blow to democratic politics.

Although supporters considered the initiative and referendum important democratic reforms begun during the Progressive era, their use has brought mixed results. Unless a controversial issue appears on the ballot, referenda tend to attract only a small percentage of voters. Many states require state constitutional amendments to be ratified by voters, but often such amendments are technical in nature and citizens fail to see the relevance of them to their own lives. Therefore, turnout in such elections tends to be very low. The recall is an initiative to remove an elected official from office. Its use in California in 2003 to remove Governor Gray Davis from office and replace him with Arnold Schwarzenegger in a simultaneous special election raised discussions about the effects of such a process on the stability of the governing process.

Low Voter Turnout

In the 1950s and early 1960s, political scientists such as Seymour Martin Lipset (1960, 181, 219) suggested that high proportions of nonvoters could be attributed to system stability and to a decline in major social conflicts and that higher levels of turnout could threaten the stability of the political system. However, many of those who advocated election reform considered low voter turnout in the United States a serious problem for democracy that needed to be addressed. Despite the Voting Rights Act of 1965 and other legislation intended to ensure the right to vote for all eligible Americans, the rate of turnout in national elections steadily declined in the three decades following the 1960 presidential election. Curtis Gans (1989, 9) noted two discrete problems: low voter turnout and declining turnout over three decades. He associated declining voter turnout with such possible causes as diminished feelings of political efficacy, weakened political party identification among citizens, and less dependence on newspapers as the prime source of political news (Gans 1989, 10). Reformers such as Frances Fox Piven and Richard Cloward (1996), who focused attention on institutional barriers to higher voter turnout, became major supporters of legislation that would facilitate voter registration. They noted that the single best predictor of voting is whether a person is registered and that low turnout results from the continued presence of registration and voting regulations that discourage potential voters from exercising the franchise, and they reasoned that the turnout rate would rise as the proportion of registered Americans increased.

In 1993 Congress passed the National Voter Registration Act (NVRA), which requires states to offer the opportunity for citizens to register at driver's license offices and other agencies, including offices where individuals apply for welfare, food stamps, Medicaid, and disability services (Piven and Cloward 1996, 39). The legislation also required all states to institute a system of mail-in registration. Before passage of the NVRA, several state governments had initiated motor-voter laws in the 1970s. By 1992, 27 states had some type of motor-voter registration program. Allowing individuals to register to vote when they applied for or renewed their driver's license made voter registration part of a routine activity that required no additional effort, thus lowering the individual costs of registering. Some states used a more active approach that combined registration and licensing forms or that required department of motor vehicles (DVM) officials to ask people if they wished to register. Other states instituted a more passive strategy in which voter registration was not integrated into everyday DVM transactions; individuals could register by using forms available at the bureau, but no prompting occurred. Investigations indicated that active programs raised voter turnout by 5 percent but passive programs had little or no effect (Highton 2004, 510). When the NVRA went into effect in 1995, the law applied to 44 states and the District of Columbia. Idaho, Minnesota, New Hampshire, North Dakota, Wisconsin, and Wyoming were exempt because those states had no voter registration requirements or allowed for election-day registration at polling places. Other states, such as Arkansas, Vermont, and Virginia, were given additional time to comply because they needed to amend their state constitutions to accommodate the new law (U.S. Department of Justice 2006).

Piven and Cloward anticipated major reforms in political party platforms as registration rates across race, income, and age became more equalized and turnout rates increased. They expected the registration rolls to swell by 40 million from January 1995, when the law took effect, to the 1998 midterm elections. However, the NVRA's effects on voter turnout have been uncertain. Voter registration rates rose slightly from 71.6 percent in 1992 to 73.8 percent in 2000, and voter turnout rates in 1996, 1998, and 2002 were not substantially higher than pre-NVRA turnout levels. Nonetheless, in the 2004 presidential election, turnout rose to 60.7 percent, the highest level since 1968. In addition, registration increased 3 percent over the 2000 figure to 71 percent (Young 2006). The increased registration and voter turnout, however, may have been attributable more to the efforts of partisan groups than to the effects of the NVRA.

Although a large percentage of registrants vote, this inclination may not apply as readily to those who previously have not taken an active part in politics but now find themselves registered to vote. As Jerry Calvert and Jack Gilchrist (1993, 696) have suggested, voter turnout may not increase among traditional nonvoters who have disproportionately low incomes, who are unemployed, who are members of minority groups, or who are young. There is some evidence that election law reforms such as the NVRA that expedite the registration and voting process can mobilize young people. When asked directly to vote, young people are more likely to become politically active (Hansen 2001; Kirby and Lopez 2004). Nonetheless, members of these groups, who have historically low voter turnout rates, will not necessarily demonstrate increased voting levels simply because more of them have registered to vote.

Calvert and Gilchrist (1993, 697) cited evidence that registration deadlines of fewer than 30 days before the election and election day registration are associated with higher voter turnout levels. In contrast, they cited evidence that in states that had instituted postcard registration, turnout actually declined, and of ten states that enacted motor-voter registration prior to the national legislation, eight experienced declining voter turnout averaging nearly 6 percent. As of 2006, six states (Idaho, Maine, Minnesota, New Hampshire, Wisconsin, and Wyoming) had instituted election day registration, allowing any eligible citizen to register and vote on election day (Hill 2006, 36). However, this reform appeared to offer added incentive for those already predisposed to vote and did not significantly increase the turnout rates among the less advantaged. According to Gans (1989, 10), the solution to low voter turnout, and especially to declining turnout, lay with a series of variables not directly related to election regulations. He blamed declining voter turnout on such things as inadequate civic training for youth, the lack of a sense of civic virtue, the declining importance of political parties in mobilizing voters, and vituperative campaign tactics that alienate voters. Given the complex reasons for the failure to vote, perhaps it should not have been expected that reducing the individual costs of voter registration would increase turnout among people who fail to see how participation benefits them and who are alienated from the political process (Hill 2006; Martinez and Hill 1999). David Hill (2006, 7), on the other hand, focused his analysis of low voter turnout on institutional arrangements. The U.S. electoral system increases the costs of voting, making participation in elections more difficult than in other Western democracies.

Elections in a Crisis

Absentee and early voting played a significant role in the New Orleans, Louisiana, election following Hurricane Katrina, which devastated the city in August 2005. The election machinery, adapted to the unique circumstances of a hurricane-ravaged city, enabled residents to select their political leaders. Originally scheduled for February, the local election was postponed until April 22, and U.S. district judge Ivan Lemell refused on two occasions—in February and again in March—to grant a further postponement (McGill 2006). With as many as two-thirds of New Orleans's 300,000 registered voters having evacuated the city, election officials had to plan for ways in which all qualified residents could have the opportunity to participate in the election. In addition to voting in the city itself, officials provided a liberalized absentee voting process that would permit individuals who never had voted in person at a precinct to cast an absentee ballot by mail. New Orleans residents also could vote at remote polling places established in 10 parishes around the state. In February, Louisiana secretary of state Al Ater announced that as many as a million mailers would be sent to evacuees who had filed change-of-address forms with the U.S.

Post Office; the mailers would explain voting procedures for the upcoming election, including how to request an absentee ballot (White 2006).

The New Orleans mayoral contest had attracted more than 20 candidates, but the two most prominent hopefuls were the incumbent, Mayor Ray Nagin, and Louisiana lieutenant governor Mitch Landrieu. These two candidates campaigned in various cities—including Houston, Dallas, Atlanta, Memphis, and Baton Rouge—to which New Orleans residents had moved to escape the devastation of the hurricane (Mack 2006). In the April 22 election approximately 110,000 votes were cast, an 18 percent decrease from the 2002 turnout. More than 16,000 voters requested an absentee ballot, and many voters were reported to have cast ballots at the remote sites, with many traveling back to Louisiana to vote early at these sites rather than entering the city or filing for an absentee ballot (CNN 2006). Ray Nagin and Mitch Landrieu were the top vote getters, with 38 percent and 29 percent respectively. On May 20 Nagin won the runoff election with 52 percent of the vote to Landrieu's 48 percent. Thirty-eight percent of the city's registered voters participated, with approximately 25 percent of them casting absentee ballots or voting at remote sites (PBS 2006).

Legislative Apportionment and Gerrymandering

The gerrymander has been a focus of political controversy throughout American history. Drawing district lines to benefit a political party or faction predates the term "gerrymander," which was coined in 1811 when Governor Elbridge Gerry of Massachusetts was associated with an attempt by the Democratic-Republican Party to gain an advantage in state legislative elections. Redistricting inevitably involves conscious decisions about just where district boundaries are drawn and hence opens the door for partisan bias. The problem is as real today as it was in the 19th century, and the opportunity for gerrymandering has been enhanced by the use of sophisticated computer software programs such as Caliper's Maptitude for Redistricting (Toobin 2003, 75). Malapportionment, a closely related issue, involves the failure to redraw district lines according to shifts in population. In the landmark decision *Baker v. Carr* in 1962, the U.S. Supreme Court ruled that federal courts have jurisdiction in cases concerning the apportionment of legislative districts because malapportionment may deny equal protection of the law mandated by the Fourteenth Amendment.

The *Baker* case led to several other challenges to state and local government districting policies. In *Gray v. Sanders* (1963) the Court, overruling the county unit system in Georgia, declared that each person's vote must have equal weight in primary elections for U.S. senators and state executive officers. In yet another case (*Reynolds v. Sims,* 1964), the Court ruled that seats in both houses of a state legislature must be apportioned on the basis of population. Like the U.S. Congress, state legislatures often contained one chamber that was apportioned according to population whereas a second provided equal representation to geographical areas. Ruling that the dual system of representation at the national level resulted from the special constitutional arrangements of federalism, the Court denied the validity of providing for representation in state legislatures on the basis of geographical areas rather than people.

In 1964 the Supreme Court ruled in *Wesberry v. Sanders* that state legislative and congressional districts must be drawn in such a way as to assure approximately equal populations in all districts. Another case before the Court (*Avery v. Midland County,* 1968) involved the huge population inequalities that had developed in local jurisdictions. One commissioner precinct in Midland County, Texas, which included the city of Midland, contained 97 percent of the residents of the county, and the other three precincts shared the remaining 3 percent. The Supreme Court applied the rule that representative districts must be of approximately equal size. Today any representative body that derives its members from districts must abide by the equal population rule.

Gerrymandering in recent years has continued to be a controversial issue. In *Veith et al. v. Jubelirer* (2004), the U.S. Supreme Court, in a 5-to-4 ruling, declared that although redistricting could exceed the boundaries of acceptability due to bias in favor of one political group, the majority was unable to establish any guidelines for determining when such a circumstance has occurred; hence the Court allowed the Pennsylvania redistricting plan, which was highly favorable to Republicans, to stand. Another case, *League of United Latin American Citizens et al. v. Perry*

(2006), involved a highly unusual redistricting plan approved by the Texas legislature and governor in 2003. Following the 2000 census, the Texas legislature, then divided between Democratic and Republican control, could not agree to a redistricting plan. Therefore, a court-ordered strategy was instituted that maintained the status quo between the two parties, with each electing 16 members of Congress. However, when Republicans gained a majority in both houses of the state legislature in 2003, they took the highly unusual step of initiating another redistricting plan with the assistance of Rep. Tom DeLay (R-TX). Following a contentious legislative battle in which Democratic legislators twice fled the state capital to deny Republicans a quorum during two special sessions, a new plan that favored Republicans was passed in a third special session. Republicans gained five U.S. House seats in the 2004 election. In the 2006 Supreme Court decision, just one of the new districts was ruled a violation of the Voting Rights Act because the vote strength of Latinos in that southwest Texas district had been diluted. Once again, the Court majority was unwilling to reject a redistricting plan as inordinately political. Critics of the Court's decision conjectured that partisan gerrymandering would become a more frequent occurrence. Largely due to gerrymandering, the number of safe seats in the U.S. House of Representatives for either major party prior to the 2006 election was estimated to be 400 out of a total of 435 (Frost 2006). Some called for states to establish bipartisan or nonpartisan redistricting commissions to do the job now performed by partisan legislatures, arguing that the establishment of such commissions would lead to greater competition between the two major parties.

Campaign Finance, the Federal Election Campaign Act, and the Bipartisan Campaign Reform Act

Five years before the passage of the Bipartisan Campaign Reform Act (BCRA, 2002), Kathleen Sullivan (1997) presented several common arguments made in favor of campaign finance reforms that would further limit contributions and expenditures. First, private campaign contributions violate the principle of suffrage equality because those able to contribute more resources have a greater opportunity to have their voices heard in the political process. Second, private contributions distort the election process by possibly assisting the wrong people to become candidates— that is, those who have attracted campaign contributions but not necessarily wide popular support. Third, money may lead to the corruption of public officials because they are likely to base their decisions on the urgings of campaign contributors. Fourth, a type of carpetbagging—intervention from outside a political jurisdiction to influence local politics—may occur when individuals contribute to candidates in districts throughout the nation, a practice that raises questions about whether legislators truly represent their constituents. Fifth, a private system of campaign finance is said to require candidates to spend far too much time and energy in raising campaign funds. A system of public financing would increase the opportunity to confront the issues in a public forum rather than searching for campaign donations. Sixth, large amounts of money in campaigns may reduce the quality of debate by allowing candidates to focus their campaigns on the expensive medium of television, where brief presentations replace genuine discussions of issues. Even though television has become a more difficult medium to use, given the proliferation of cable and satellite networks and the increased use of the Internet, it still remains a primary tool for campaigning. Finally, the candidate with the most funds can take an anticompetitive advantage in the campaign. For instance, in the 2000 race for the Republican presidential nomination, George W. Bush achieved such an overwhelming advantage in campaign fund-raising that other potential nominees simply could not compete effectively. Congressional incumbents, even if they are essentially assured of little opposition in the next election, often raise large amounts of campaign funds to prepare themselves for any eventuality or to discourage even further any competition (Linden 2005).

In 1972 Congress passed the Federal Election Campaign Act to regulate donations to U.S. House and Senate campaigns, including primaries, and to provide for the regulation of corporate and individual participation in federal election campaigns. A reaction to heavy campaign spending and the potential influence of personal wealth on the electoral process, the new legislation replaced previous federal corrupt practices acts. Following the Watergate revelations, which included charges of illegal activities during the 1972 presidential campaign, Congress enacted the Federal Election Campaign Act of 1974. This act provided for public funding of presidential elections and partial funding of presidential primaries and caucuses through a system of matching payments supported with funds to be provided by a voluntary checkoff—initially one dollar—on income tax returns. Among other provisions, the legislation held individuals to a maximum $1,000 contribution to a candidate and a total of $25,000 in donations to political campaigns in any election year. Interest groups and political action committees were limited to a contribution of $5,000 to a candidate in a primary or general election. The act also created the Federal Election Commission (FEC), an independent regulatory agency assigned the responsibility of administering federal campaign finance laws, including provisions for the public funding of presidential elections, regulation of contributions and expenditures to candidates for federal office, and reception of campaign finance disclosure reports from political action committees (Whiting et al. 1990, 14).

Many reformers concluded that the operation of the FEC was a major disappointment. They charged that Congress had not provided the agency with sufficient appropriations to handle its large workload and that the commission lacked a staff to conduct investigations of financial reports. The requirement setting the number of commissioners at six (three Democrats and three Republicans) resulted in tie votes and hence stalemate and inaction. In 1979 Congress refused to grant the FEC the authority to conduct random audits of congressional campaigns, further weakening the agency's ability to deter violations of campaign finance regulations. Because a chairperson can serve for only one year, the FEC lacked the leadership potential that a long-term chair could provide. Violators of campaign laws had little to fear from the FEC, for the lengthy investigation procedures often forced delays, and civil penalties could not exceed $5,000 or the amount of the contested contribution, whichever is greater. In 2006 the commission levied fines totaling more than $600,000 on three independent fund-raising organizations for spending millions of dollars in the 2004 presidential campaign that were raised illegally from large donors and corporations ("3 Groups Fined for Violating Campaign Laws" 2006). In February 2008 Senator John McCain's presidential campaign faced uncertainty when the FEC chair suggested that McCain was legally obligated to abide by primary election and caucus season spending limits even though a definitive ruling was not possible because four of the six places on the commission were unfilled. Although the creation of the FEC was part of a major attempt to reform the campaign finance

system, serious limitations on its operation led to recommendations for additional reform. Many proposals focused on the question of soft money contributions that went virtually uncontrolled
and unreported. The recommendations ranged from forbidding
national party committees from using soft money to finance federal campaign activities to prohibiting nationally organized soft
money fund-raising campaigns.

After the 2000 election, reform advocates intensified their
efforts to establish further limitations on campaign funding. Although previous attempts to pass legislation had been blocked
in the U.S. Senate with filibusters organized mainly by Republicans, the misdeeds of the Houston-based Enron Corporation
and the company's ultimate disintegration led to renewed reform efforts. Enron had contributed nearly $2.5 million to the
two major parties during the 1999–2000 election cycle. In 2002
Christopher Shays (R-CT) and Marty Meehan (D-MA) in the
House, and John McCain (R-AZ) and Russell Feingold (D-WI)
in the Senate, introduced the Bipartisan Campaign Reform Act
to ban soft money (unregulated) contributions to the national
political parties. The BCRA was intended to address the increased reliance on soft money in campaign financing, the proliferation of issue advertisements, and the generally perceived
corruption of the political process. By March 20 the bill had
passed the House and Senate, and President Bush signed the
bill into law on March 27.

The BCRA consists of several major provisions, including
bans on:

1. Raising or spending of soft money contributions by
    national political party organizations;
2. Soft money contributions to, and expenditures by, state
    and local parties engaged in federal election activities;
3. Raising or spending soft money by federal
    officeholders or candidates;
4. Nonpartisan issue ads funded from corporations and
    labor unions 30 days before a primary election and 60
    days before a general election;
5. Political party transfer to, or solicitation of soft money
    from, politically active, tax-exempt groups; and
6. State candidates' use of soft money in public
    communications that support or attack federal
    candidates.

In addition, the act increased the individual donation limit to a candidate during an election from $1,000 to $2,000 and the total yearly limit on individual contributions to federal candidates, political parties, and PACs from $25,000 to $37,500. The BCRA required that individuals disclose the sources of election communication funds and how much they spend on these communications.

Senator Mitch McConnell (R-KY) quickly mounted a legal challenge to the Bipartisan Campaign Reform Act. Following a divided ruling by a three-judge panel, the U.S. Supreme Court heard arguments in *McConnell v. Federal Election Commission* on September 8, 2003. The justices issued a ruling in December, holding that the soft money ban constituted a minor limitation on free speech and hence was justified by the legitimate government interest in preventing actual corruption or its appearance that could result from large financial contributions. The Court struck down two of the law's provisions: the prohibition on those under the age of 18 from making political contributions and the requirement that political parties in a general election must choose between making independent or coordinated expenditures on a candidate's behalf.

Applicable to two election cycles—2004 and 2006—the BCRA appeared to have encouraged an increase in small contributions of $200 or less to the political parties and presidential candidates. Although political parties could no longer use soft money, the presidential election committees raised more hard money, enabling them to play a major role in the 2004 election. House and Senate campaign committees were not as successful in 2004, failing to raise enough hard money to replace the soft money receipts they had lost. Table 1.1 compares the pre-BCRA contribution limits with the post-BCRA limits.

In spite of the new legislation and the Supreme Court decision upholding most of its provisions, campaign finance remained an area of concern for reform advocates, primarily due to the section 527 groups, named after the section of the Internal Revenue code under which they are established. Such groups as MoveOn.org Voter Fund, League of Conservative Voters, and Swiftboat Veterans and POWs for Truth, accepting unlimited donations from corporations, labor unions, and individuals, played a significant role in the 2004 presidential election. The FEC failed to take a definitive stand regarding the applicability of contribution limits to section 527 groups. Only when a group unmistak-

TABLE 1.1
Pre– and Post–Bipartisan Campaign Reform Act Contribution Limits.

Donors	Candidate Committee per Election	Political Action Committee (PAC) per Year	State, Local, and District Political Parties per Year	National Political Party per Year	Aggregate Total
Individual (pre-BCRA)	$1,000	$5,000	$5,000	$20,000	$25,000 per year
2005–2006 cycle	$2,100	$5,000	$10,000	$26,700	$101,400 biennially
State, local, and district political parties (pre-BCRA)	$5,000	$5,000	$5,000	$15,000	No limit
2005–2006 cycle	$5,000 combined limit	$5,000 combined limit	Unlimited transfers	Unlimited transfers	
National Party Committee (pre-BCRA)	$5,000	$5,000	$5,000	$15,000	No limit
2005–2006 cycle	$5,000	$5,000	Unlimited transfers	Unlimited transfers	$37,000 to Senate candidate per campaign
PAC (multi-candidate, pre-BCRA)	$5,000	$5,000	$5,000	$15,000	No limit
2005–2006 cycle	$5,000	$5,000	$5,000	$15,000	No limit
PAC (not multi-candidate, pre-BCRA)	$2,000	$5,000	$5,000	$20,000	No limit
2005–2006 cycle	$2,100	$5,000	$10,000 combined limit	$26,700	No limit

Source: Federal Election Commission (2007).

ably advocated the election or defeat of a candidate would the FECA and BCRA rules apply.

In June 2007 the U.S. Supreme Court issued an opinion in *Wisconsin Right to Life, Inc., Appellant v. Federal Election Commission* that involved a challenge to the BCRA prohibition on issues ads 30 days before a primary election and 60 days before a general election. The 5-to-4 majority, citing First Amendment protection of free speech, ruled that such a prohibition was too restrictive. Chief Justice John Roberts, speaking for the majority, commented that, "Where the First Amendment is implicated, the tie goes to the speaker, not the censor." Justice David Souter, dissenting, declared that, "After today, the ban on contributions by corporations and unions and the limitation on their corrosive spending when they enter the political arena are open to easy circumvention, and the possibilities for regulating corporate and union campaign money are unclear" (Sherman 2007).

In September 2007 the troubling issue of campaign finance resurfaced with the case of Norman Hsu, a Democratic fundraiser and a fugitive who had skipped sentencing in a 1991 grand theft conviction. Hsu, who had raised $850,000 in donations to Senator Hillary Clinton's presidential campaign, was under federal investigation for allegedly violating election statutes. The Clinton campaign decided to return the funds to approximately 260 donors and to review their fund-raisers more thoroughly, including making criminal background checks (Kuhnhenn 2007, A7).

The Help America Vote Act and Beyond

The 2000 presidential election revealed serious problems with the general administration of elections and specifically with the use of punch cards for voting. The possibility of overvoting (voting for more than one candidate for the same office) could occur without the voter being aware of the mistake, thus invalidating the vote. Undervoting (failing to vote for any candidate for an office) also could occur simply from oversight, but also from a failure to punch through the chad (the so-called dimpled chad) or from the chad remaining attached to the punch card (the hanging chad). If either circumstance arose, the computer system would likely fail to count the vote. These weak links in the voting process led to a major predicament in the 2000 presidential election when it came down to which candidate—George W. Bush or Albert Gore—won the popular vote in Florida and hence that state's 25 electoral votes. After intense maneuvering by both political parties over the extent to which recounts should be conducted, on December 12 the U.S. Supreme Court finally ruled that the recount ordered by the Florida supreme court should cease. Thus, Bush was declared the winner of the Florida electoral votes and gained a majority (271) of the total electoral votes. An estimated 180,000 Florida ballots had been ruled invalid due to undervotes and overvotes attributed to the use of punch card voting and the confusing ballot format (Saltman 2006, 33).

Due largely to the embarrassing problems with voting in Florida and other states in the 2000 election, Congress in 2002 passed the Help America Vote Act (HAVA), authorizing $3.86 billion in federal aid to help states improved election administration. The main goal of the HAVA is to ensure the uniform and nondiscriminatory administration of federal elections. States accepting HAVA funds were required to update voting equipment, mandate that first-time voters who register by mail show photo identification, offer provisional ballots to voters whose eligibility is in question, post voting information at polling locations, maintain statewide voter registration lists, and establish complaint procedures for those who experience problems in voting. The HAVA also provided for assistance to the disabled by requiring states that accept HAVA funds to make available a way for the hearing and vision impaired to cast secret ballots. The new law mandated accessibility for those with disabilities, including the blind and visually impaired (Saltman 2006, 199). In addition, polling jurisdictions must provide potential voters with the opportunity to cast a provisional ballot if their names do not appear on the official voter registration list. The HAVA also mandated that states establish a statewide computerized list of registrants and give all state and local election officials access to the list. The law established requirements for voter identification, which involved the presentation of a current driver's license or the last four digits of the prospective voter's social security number (Saltman 2006, 199). Individuals who register for the first time by mail must present a valid photo identification or other proof of identification and residence. If voting by mail, new registrants must include with the ballot the same identification required if they voted in person. The act authorized funding for states and localities to improve election equipment and procedures. Table 1.2 summarizes the HAVA provisions.

The act established the U.S. Election Assistance Commission (EAC), composed of four commissioners, two to be selected from each major political party. After the initial appointments in which two commissioners served for two years and two for four years, each commissioner would serve a four-year term. The

TABLE 1.2
Help America Vote Act Provisions.

Section	Purpose
Title I (Election Administration)	Provides payments to states to improve election administration and to replace punch card and lever machines.
Title II (Election Assistance Commission)	Establishes the Election Assistance Commission (EAC); the EAC issues voluntary guidelines for voting systems and meeting HAVA requirements, provides testing and certification of voting systems, and offers grants to states to help them meet requirements.
Title III (State Requirements)	Establishes requirements for states that include providing voters the opportunity to check for and correct ballot errors; requiring voter identification for first-time mail registrants; instituting voting systems with independent verification capacity; establishing provisional voting and posting voting information; providing voting devices for the disabled; ensuring minority language accessibility; and implementing a single centralized, computerized statewide voter registration list.
Title IV (Enforcement)	Provides for the Department of Justice enforcement; each state must establish a state-based administrative grievance procedure to hear voter complaints.
Title V (Help America Vote College Program)	Encourages college students to participate in the political process by volunteering as poll workers.
Title VI (Help America Vote Foundation)	Encourages high school students to participate in the political process by volunteering as poll watchers.
Title VII (Military and Overseas Voters)	Improves ballot access for military and overseas voters by the postmarking and timely delivery of ballots; not refusing ballots due to early submission; establishing a central state office for information on registration and absentee ballots; and issuing state reports on the number of ballots transmitted and returned.
Title VIII (Transition)	Transfer of responsibilities and oversight from Federal Election Commission to Office of Election Administration.
Title IX (Miscellaneous)	The EAC may conduct audits of grant recipients and if grants are not used to meet requirements, states may be required to make repayments; establishes criminal penalties for a conspiracy to deprive voters of a fair election and for providing false information in registering and voting; defines the circumstances in which registrars may remove names from registration lists.

Sources: Montjoy (2005); Secretary of State Office, Mississippi (n.d.).

chair and vice chair of the commission, who serve one-year terms, are chosen by the commissioners themselves from among their membership. An executive director reports directly to the commission. The act created a Standards Board, composed of 55 state and 55 local officials who meet at least once every two years to determine the nine members of the Executive Board. A Board of Advisors is composed of 37 members, 25 of whom are selected from state and local government organizations and federal agencies, 4 are science and technology specialists, and 8 are appointed by the chair and ranking member of House and Senate committees responsible for election administration (Saltman 2006, 197).

The HAVA requires that voters be able to verify privately and independently the vote choices made and alter selections or correct any errors before the ballot is finally cast; be able to alter or correct any errors before the ballot is cast; and be informed of any possible overvote and be given the opportunity to correct the ballot. In fiscal year 2004, the EAC distributed $1.3 billion to 42 states, American Samoa, and the District of Columbia (Saltman 2006, 200). The financial assistance provided to states was used largely to acquire new voting machines that would meet heightened standards and to establish state-level voter registration and identification procedures (Hall and Wang 2004). States replaced lever voting machines and punch card voting procedures with more advanced technology, including direct recording electronic (DRE) machines and marksense ballots. The federal government allocated $850 million to the states over three years for the purchase of voting systems that are accessible to the disabled (Schneider 2005).

Several difficulties have blocked the full implementation of HAVA requirements. For instance, the use of provisional balloting has been problematic in several jurisdictions. Prior to the 2004 election, some states, including Colorado, Florida, Michigan, Missouri, and Ohio, announced that they would not count provisional ballots of eligible voters who voted at the wrong polling place (Cooper 2004). In 2004, 1.9 million voters nationwide cast provisional ballots. Of those, approximately 1.2 million (64.5 percent) were ultimately counted. Although provisional balloting provided a safety net to hundreds of thousands of voters, over half a million ballots were not counted and procedures for handling such ballots varied greatly from state to state. Of complaints registered by voters in 2004, those related to the administration of provisional ballots were most frequent. Voters complained that ballots were not available, that poll workers did not provide access to them or refused voter requests for provisional ballots, and that poll workers appeared to misunderstand provisional balloting procedures. Due to inconsistent and unclear rules on provisional balloting, many eligible voters may have been disfranchised in 2004 (Weiser 2006).

The requirement of a computerized, statewide registration list has encountered difficulties, due partly to the mobility of

Americans. The National Voter Registration Act (NVRA) mandates that states regularly update voter registration lists to assure their accuracy, identifying registrants who have died or moved away from the jurisdiction. States have used different mechanisms for making their registration lists accurate and current. In Washington State, for example, the legislature ordered the secretary of state to remove voters from the registration list if their first or last names did not match driver's license records and entries in other public databases. Consequently, in May 2006, 55,000 registrants were purged from the state's new centralized voter registration list. Subsequently, a U.S. district court judge issued an injunction blocking enforcement of this HAVA provision, arguing that the procedure sanctioned by the legislature was not relevant to determining whether a person was qualified to vote. In 2006 many states were only in the initial stages of developing compliance mechanisms, and they anticipated finding that name changes due to marriage and divorce would further complicate attempts to update registration lists (Katel 2006).

The initial implementation of the HAVA has had at least one positive effect: the reduction in the proportion of voters using the notoriously unreliable punch card voting equipment from 31 percent in 2000 to 13 percent in 2004. Using HAVA money, 30 states by 2006 had upgraded their voting systems, moving away from punch card and lever voting machines. Despite this trend, numerous states have experienced difficulty in achieving such objectives as making voting equipment accessible to the disabled; maintaining voter privacy and secret ballots; creating auditable, verifiable voting results; and avoiding software errors or manipulation potentially attributable to electronic voting. Many concluded that state and local governments would require additional assistance to avoid voting machine and software pitfalls.

Uniform implementation of HAVA provisions across the states so far has not occurred. A lack of funding and administrative structure limit the ability of states to respond in a timely manner. The money authorized to the states was not appropriated by the deadlines set for implementation, and the members of the Election Assistance Commission who were to review and approve state election administration grant requests were not confirmed until December 2003. Therefore, in general, state and local implementation of the act was slow and delayed due to the lack of funding and guidance from the EAC. Without more coordination and cooperation between federal and state officials, the right to vote in the United States will be less than optimal ("Is America Ready to Vote? Election Readiness Briefing Paper" 2004). As state and local governments continue to struggle with implementing the HAVA, many voters may be disfranchised due to irregularities in voter registration procedures and problems with election hardware and software.

As states began to replace old voting systems, many, including computer scientists, raised questions about the dependability and security of DRE machines. Even before the extensive push to adopt electronic voting systems, Howard Strauss, a computer scientist at Princeton University, was quoted as saying that computerized election security is "not a door without locks, it's a house without doors" (Condit 1996, 15). Some feared that a small group of individuals could gain, or already had gained, access to the computer programs employed to tally votes, manipulating the results for a favored candidate in a sufficiently large number of election jurisdictions to alter the election results. As computerized vote counting procedures become more centralized, concerns continue to be raised about such possibilities as computer operator misconduct, remote entry into the computer counting process, inputting of false data, sabotage for political reasons, malicious mischief, and simple computer breakdowns that could have dire consequences for the legitimacy of the election process. William Kimberling (1986, 11) has noted that traditional safeguards against fraud—the decentralization of election administration, the system of checks whereby the two major political parties monitor each other's electoral behavior, and public accountability made possible by a paper trail—are all weakened by the major advantage of computer systems: the achievement of a highly centralized procedure for the swift counting of large numbers of ballots.

Because they record votes electronically, DRE voting machines by themselves leave no paper trail at all. While some believe DREs resolve the problems of ballot accountability, others argue that they lead to significant new problems due to lack of verifiability. A summary of a symposium on voting and vote counting held at the Kennedy School of Government (Camp, Friedman, and Bowman 2004, 20) concluded that DRE systems could not meet the criteria for an adequate vote audit: a recount of ballots, an examination of the systems employed, a transparent electoral process, and monitored possession and treatment of ballots. According to critics, such voting systems should not be used without the creation of a paper trail that would allow voters to compare their on-screen choices with a paper printout. The paper trail could be employed in an audit of the vote to check the accuracy of the electronic vote totals and perhaps in a recount. By the 2006 midterm election, at least 23 states required that electronic voting machines provide a voter-verified paper trail (Duffy 2006). The extremely close 2006 Florida congressional race between Republican Vern Buchanan and Democrat Christine Jennings, in which 18,000 votes allegedly were lost, raised additional fears about unverifiable electronic voting. In January 2007 newly elected Florida governor Charlie Crist announced that his state would seriously consider abandoning touch screen voting machines and instead adopt paper ballots counted by optical scanners (Goodnough and Drew 2007). However, groups representing the disabled have expressed support for electronic machines, claiming that they provide the best accessibility for persons with disabilities (Schneider 2005; Zambon 2007).

Reports during the 2006 election of vote switching—voters selecting one candidate but the confirmation screen registering a vote for another candidate—led to heightened calls for paper verification (Seligson 2006). Computer science researchers at Princeton University and Carnegie Mellon University claimed that the touch screen voting machines of certain companies could be fairly easily hacked (Stewart 2007). Supporters of such machines have responded that hacking would be very difficult to accomplish and that the present system is far more resistant to fraud than previous voting procedures, including the paper ballot (Arrison and Vasquez 2005).

Concern for adequate security of electronic voting machines led members of Congress to propose changes to the HAVA to require some type of paper trail to allow for voter verification of individual vote decisions and to allow for genuine audits of election results and the possibility of recounts. In 2007 Rep. Rush Holt (D-NJ) became one of the more vocal supporters of a verifiable vote, introducing the Voter Confidence and Increased Accessibility Act. If passed, the bill would require a voter-verified paper audit trail (VVPAT) for electronic voting systems, establish state audit boards to inspect election results, and provide assurances of disability access to polling places (Smolka and Smolka 2007). Objections to Holt's bill came from those who believed that electronic voting machines were sufficiently accurate and dependable to obviate the need for the generation of a paper trail, which was considered confusing to the voter and cumbersome for election officials, especially if intended for recounts. Political commentator David Broder (2007) expressed reservations about the bill, citing criticisms issued by the National Conference of State Legislatures and the National Association of Counties that the legislation would add to the difficulties of administering elections and produce serious unintended consequences in future elections.

Those who objected to electronic voting machines argued that mandating a paper trail was not a sufficient safeguard and that paper ballots should be reintroduced. In 2007 other members of Congress proposed bills to ensure fair and accurate procedures and that the vote results coincide with the individual choices of voters. For instance, Sen. Barack Obama (D-IL) introduced the Deceptive Practices and Voter Intimidation Prevention Act, which would add additional protections against deceptive practices regarding the presentation of information about the voting process. Those concerned with voter fraud continued to push for legislation requiring more stringent requirements for voter identification. However, the U.S. Justice Department in April 2007 reported discovering few cases of organized attempts to vote illegally (Lipton and Urbina 2007).

Disagreements between those whose primary objective is encouraging greater voter turnout and those who express intense concern about possible voter fraud are likely to continue. The introduction of new technologies makes anticipating the substance of election reform a highly uncertain enterprise. New technologies can present novel problems that improved technologies possibly can resolve, perhaps obviating the many proposed bills in Congress intended to ensure accurate vote choices and vote counts. The history of campaigns and elections indicates that the maintenance of a fair election system in such a large country requires the continued diligence of public officials at all levels of government and the willingness to consider innovative reforms to ensure a most important component of democratic government.

References

"ACLU Voting Rights: About the VRA." Voting Rights Act: Renew. Restore. 2006. www.votingrights.org/more.php

Alter, Jonathan. "A Red Play for the Golden State." *Newsweek,* August 13, 2007: 33

Arrison, Sonia, and Vince Vasquez. "Clear Up Misinformation about Electronic Voting." *Houston Chronicle,* June 30, 2005: B11

Barbour, Christine, and Gerald C. Wright. *Keeping the Republic: Power and Citizenship in American Politics.* Boston: Houghton Mifflin, 2003

Benson, George C. S. *Political Corruption in America.* Lexington, MA: Lexington Books, 1978

Broder, David S. 2007. "A Paper Trail Toward Chaos?" *Washington Post National Weekly Edition,* May 21–27, 2007: 4

Calabresi, Massimo. "Election Chaos." *Time,* May 14, 2007: 47

Calvert, Jerry W., and Jack Gilchrist. "Suppose They Held an Election and Almost Everybody Came!" *PS: Political Science and Politics* 26 (December 1993): 695–700

Camp, Jean, Allan Friedman, and Warigia Bowman. *Voting, Vote Capture and Vote Counting Symposium.* Cambridge, MA: Kennedy School of Government, 2004

Chada, Anita, and Robert A. Bernstein. "Why Incumbents Are Treated So Harshly: Term Limits for State Legislators." *American Politics Quarterly* 24 (July 1996): 363–76

Condit, James J. "A House without Doors: Vote Fraud in America." *Chronicles* (November 1996): 15–17

Cooper, Mary H. "Voting Rights." *CQ Researcher* 14 (October 29, 2004): 901–24. CQ Researcher Online. www.cqpress.com/product/Researcher-Online.html

"Counting the Number of Ways We Can Vote." *Houston Chronicle,* March 16, 2004: A7

Dahl, Robert A. *Pluralist Democracy in the United States: Conflict and Consent.* Chicago: Rand McNally, 1967

Donsanto, Craig. "The Election Crimes Branch." *Journal of Election Administration* 16 (Summer 1989): 20–21

Duffy, Michael. "Can This Machine Be Trusted?" *Time,* November 6, 2006: 38

Elliot, Janel. "Voting Rights Statute Tested." *Houston Chronicle,* September 8, 2006: B1

Engstrom, Richard L. "The Voting Rights Act: Disfranchisement, Dilution, and Alternative Election Systems." *PS: Political Science and Politics* 27 (December 1994): 685–88

Frost, Martin. "Thanks to Supreme Court, It's Wild West All over Again." *Houston Chronicle,* July 6, 2006: B9

Gans, Curtis. "Voter Participation Revisited." *Journal of Election Administration* 16 (Summer 1989): 8–11

Garber, Marie. *Innovations in Election Administration 10: Ballot Security and Accountability.* Washington, DC: National Clearinghouse on Election Administration, 1995

Goodnough, Abby, and Christopher Drew. "Florida Plans to Return to Paper Ballot System." *Houston Chronicle,* February 2, 2007: A3

Greenblatt, Alan. "The Truth about Term Limits." *Governing* (January 2006): 24, 26–28

Grofman, Bernard, Lisa Handley, and Richard G. Niemi. *Minority Representation and the Quest for Voting Equality.* Cambridge, UK: Cambridge University Press, 1992

Gruver, Mead. "Wyoming GOP Leapfrogs Iowa and New Hampshire." *Houston Chronicle,* August 30, 2007: A7

Hall, Thad, and Tova Andrea Wang. "USA: Will the State-Run Electoral Process Work This Time?" *Federations,* July 2004: 6

Hansen, John Mark. "Voter Registration." The Twentieth Century Fund. July 2001. tcf.org/Publications/ElectionReform/NCFER/Hansen_chap2 _voter.pdf

Highton, Benjamin. "Voter Registration and Turnout in the United States." *Perspectives on Politics* 2, 3 (September 2004): 507–14

Hill, David. *American Voter Turnout: An Institutional Perspective.* Boulder, CO: Westview Press, 2006

Hoffman, Kathy Barks. "Michigan Gazing at Front of Primaries' Line." *Houston Chronicle,* August 23, 2007: A12

Katel, Peter. "Voting Controversies." *CQ Researcher* 16 (September 15, 2006): 745–68. CQ Researcher Online. www.cqpress.com/product ?Researcher-Online.html

Kimberling, William. "Secure against What? An Approach to Computer Security." *Journal of Election Administration* 13 (Winter 1986): 11–14

Kimberling, William, and Peggy Sims. *Federal Election Law 96: A Summary of Federal Laws Pertaining to Registration, Voting, and Public Employee Participation.* Washington, DC: Office of Election Administration, 1996

Kirby, Emily Hoban, and Mark Hugo Lopez. 2004. "State Voter Registration and Election Day Laws." Fact Sheet, Center for Information and

Research on Civic Learning and Engagement. www.civicyouth.org /PopUps/FactSheets/FS_StateLaws.pdf, posted June 2004

Kuhnhenn, Jim. "Clinton Camp Sets Bar in Handling Fundraiser Furor." *Houston Chronicle,* September 12, 2007: A7

Levine, Samantha. "Texan Loses Bid to Alter Ballot Law." *Houston Chronicle,* July 14, 2006): A8

Levinson, Sanford. *Our Undemocratic Constitution: Where the Constitution Goes Wrong (and How We the People Can Correct It).* New York: Oxford University Press, 2006.

Linden, Seth. "Running on Plenty: Why Well-Entrenched Congressional Incumbents Continue to Build Big Campaign War Chests." *Campaigns and Elections,* August 2005: 21

Lipset, Seymour Martin. *Political Man.* Garden City, NY: Doubleday, 1960

Lipton, Eric, and Ian Urbina. "Fears of Widespread Voter Corruption Unfounded, Justice Department Finds." *Houston Chronicle,* April 12, 2007: A5

Lutz, Alma. *Susan B. Anthony: Rebel, Crusader, Humanitarian.* Boston: Beacon Press, 1959

Mack, Kristen. "Seeking New Orleans Votes around Houston." *Houston Chronicle,* March 14, 2006: B1.

Martinez, Michael D., and David Hill. "Assessing the Impact of the National Voter Registration Act on Midterm Elections." Paper presented at the annual meeting of the American Political Science Association, 1999

McGill, Kevin. "Judge Won't Postpone N. O. Mayoral Election." *Houston Chronicle,* February 25, 2006: A10.

Morison, Samuel Eliot. *The Oxford History of the American People.* New York: Oxford University Press, 1965

"New Orleans Election in 'Uncharted Waters.'" Cable News Network. April 22, 2006. www.cnn.com/2006/POLITICS/04/21/nola.elections /index.html

Ohlemacher, Stephen. "Primary Scramble under Way." *Houston Chronicle,* September 5, 2007: A8

PBS News Hour. pbs.org/newshour/extra/features/jan-june06/nola _5-22.html

Petracca, Mark P. "A New Defense of State-Imposed Congressional Term Limits." *PS: Political Science and Politics* 26 (December 1993): 700–705

Piven, Frances Fox, and Richard A. Cloward. "Northern Bourbons: A Preliminary Report on the National Voter Registration Act." *PS: Political Science and Politics* 29 (March 1996): 39–42

Plano, Jack C., and Milton Greenberg. *The American Political Dictionary,* 10th ed. New York: Harcourt Brace, 1997

Saltman, Roy G. *The History and Politics of Voting Technology.* New York: Palgrave Macmillan, 2006

Schmidt, Steffen W., Mack C. Shelley, Barbara A. Bardes, William Earl Maxwell, and Ernest Crain. *American Government and Politics Today, Texas Edition.* Belmont, CA: Thomson/Wadsworth, 2006

Schneider, Elizabeth. "Voting Machines and the Disabled." *Campaigns and Elections,* May 2005: 35

Seligson, Dan. "Election 2006: No Breakdowns, but Questions Remain." *Campaigns and Elections,* December 2006: 101

Shear, Michael D. 2007. "Democrats Crack Down on Florida over Primary." *Houston Chronicle,* August 26, 2007: A4

Sherman, Mark. "Justices' Scales May Be Tipping to the Right." *Houston Chronicle,* June 26, 2007: A1

Smolka, Richard G., and David Smolka. "House Plans to Mark Up Holt Bill After Returning from Spring Recess." *Election Administration Reports* 37 (April 2, 2007): 1–2

Stephens Jr., Otis H., and John M. Scheb II. *American Constitutional Law,* 2nd ed. Belmont, CA: West/Wadsworth, 1999

Stewart, Warren. "Our Election System Is Broken: Can Congress Fix It?" *The Washington Spectator,* January 15, 2007: 1

Sullivan, Kathleen. "Political Money and Freedom of Speech." Unpublished speech presented at the University of California at Davis, February 13, 1997

"3 Groups Fined for Violating Campaign Laws," *Houston Chronicle,* December 14, 2006: A10

Toobin, Jeffrey. "The Great Election Grab: When Does Gerrymandering Become a Threat to Democracy?" *The New Yorker,* December 8, 2003: 63–66, 75–76, 78, 80

U.S. Commission on Civil Rights, Office of Civil Rights Evaluation. "Is America Ready to Vote? Election Readiness Briefing Paper." April 2004. www.thememoryhole.org/usccr/usccr_is_america_ready_to_vote.htm

U.S. Department of Justice, Civil Rights Division—Voting Section Home Page. 2006. "About the National Voter Registration Act." www.usdoj.gov /crt/voting/nvra/activ_nvra.htm

Walsh, Kenneth T. "Florida's Primary Flap." *U.S. News and World Report,* August 6, 2007: 28

Weiser, Wendy R. "Are HAVA's Provisional Ballots Working?" Paper presented at the Center for Democracy and Election Management Conference at American University, March 29, 2006

White, Elizabeth. "Louisiana Prepares to Send Instructions to Displaced Voters." *Houston Chronicle,* February 5, 2006: A7

Whiting, Meredith, E. Patrick McGuire, Catherine Morrison, and Jessica Shelly. *Campaign Finance Reform.* New York: The Conference Board, 1990

Will, George F. "VRA, All of It, Forever?" *Newsweek,* October 10, 2005: 70

Wright, Benjamin Fletcher. *Consensus and Continuity, 1776–1787.* New York: W. W. Norton, 1967

Young, John. "There Is Still Room for Improvement in America's Voting." *Beaumont Enterprise,* October 24, 2006: 11A

Zambon, Kat. "Push for Paper-Based Voting Divides Advocates." *Campaigns and Elections,* January 2007: 56

Zuckerman, Mortimer B. "The Primary Experiment." *U.S. News and World Report,* May 7, 2007: 72

2

Problems, Controversies, and Solutions

In focusing on the efforts, both historical and contemporary, to reform the U.S. electoral system, this book raises a key question. Precisely what constitutes reform? What represents reform to one person amounts to antidemocratic reaction to someone else, and what some consider an advancement in the right to vote, in the eyes of others only increases the opportunities for fraud. The term might qualify as an essentially contested concept, for there has often been fundamental disagreement over the reform status of specific measures. For instance, the introduction of voter registration arguably decreased the amount of vote fraud but also discouraged many eligible Americans from voting. Like an athletic event, the electoral process is composed of a combination of cooperative and competitive elements. The participants must adhere to certain rules while competing for votes so that the process can result in a legitimate winner whom all can acknowledge. However, unlike the typical athletic contest, participants in the political game may compete to alter the rules in their favor, at the same time labeling the new regulations as reform. We touch on many changes that could be termed reforms at least from a particular ideological or partisan perspective. Among such changes we include measures that extend the right to vote, enhance the security of the electoral process by limiting the opportunity for fraud, increase the convenience of—or possibly eliminate—voter registration requirements, streamline voting procedures for the average voter, improve the efficient operation of the election system, help ensure that elections accurately reflect the choices of the electorate, and eliminate systemic biases in favor of or against specific individuals or groups.

Sometimes well-intentioned proposals to increase voter registration and turnout can be interpreted as instances of inappropriate intervention in the electoral process. For instance, in 2006 a proposition appeared on the Arizona ballot that, if approved, would have created a $1 million lottery prize for voters. Each person casting a ballot in the state election would be assigned a number, and the prizewinner would be selected at random. Although the objective of the lottery was to increase voter turnout, critics of the proposal questioned the legality of such a policy at both the federal and state levels. According to Arizona law, it is a misdemeanor to "treat, give, pay, loan, contribute, offer or promise money or other valuable consideration" to encourage a person to vote (Davenport 2006). Arizona voters rejected the ballot measure in the November election, so the legality of the proposal was not tested.

We begin by examining the fundamental procedures the various states have used to record and count ballots, moving from paper ballots that must be counted by hand to reliance on machines that counted ballots mechanically and ultimately to computer-assisted means of voting and vote counting.

Electoral Mechanics

With state governments being primarily responsible for election administration, a variety of balloting procedures and voting hardware have been used, including paper ballots, mechanical lever machines, punch card systems, marksense (optical scanning) ballots, and electronic systems. The oldest voting procedure—the paper ballot—allows voters to mark boxes next to the preferred candidates' names. These ballots must be hand counted and are readily available for recounting if the outcome is contested. Because a manual count is time-consuming and can require many people to participate in the process, paper ballots are used primarily in less populous counties with relatively few election contests. By 1998 paper ballots were used in about 13 percent of all counties, constituting about 1.4 percent of the population (Knack and Kropf 2002, 541–43). In 2006 paper ballot use had declined to approximately 2 percent of all counties and covered less than 0.2 percent of the voting age population (Knack and Kropf 2002).

Mechanical voting systems allow voters to indicate their voting decisions by pulling a lever near a candidate's name. The levers are connected to counting wheels that maintain a running tally of the votes cast for each candidate. Introduced in 1892, mechanical lever voting machines have not been manufactured since 1982. These machines were criticized for being inaccessible to voters with disabilities and for not producing a paper record of votes cast. By 1998 only about 15 percent of counties still used mechanical lever machines, affecting about 18 percent of the voting population. In 2006 mechanical voting systems were used in just 62 counties (1.99 percent) and covered less than 7 percent of the nation's voting age population (Knack and Kropf 2002).

Beginning in the mid-1960s and continuing throughout the 1970s, punch card systems became more widely used than paper ballots or mechanical voting systems. Punch card systems employ two types of ballots. The simpler ballot design—Datavote—allows voters to punch a hole on a card beside the candidate's name using a punching tool with a metal shaft. The second type provides the candidate's names in a booklet attached to a mechanical holder under which voters insert a prescored punch card. Each hole on the punch card has a corresponding number. Voters punch a hole corresponding to the number of the candidate they wish to support. With a stylus or other device, voters punch holes at the appropriate spots on the card, forcing out the marked areas (the chads). In comparison to paper ballots and mechanical voting systems, punch card machines are less expensive and, due to the ease of use, help reduce long lines at the polls. In 1998 about 20 percent of counties comprising almost 35 percent of the population used punch card technology. Following the 2000 election, the use of punch cards rapidly declined, and by 2006 only 13 counties used punch card systems affecting less than 0.5 percent of voters (Saltman 2006).

Marksense, or optical scan, ballots emerged at the same time as punch card technology but spread more slowly. Similar to paper ballots, marksense ballots require voters to use a black marker to fill in a circle or box beside the names of preferred candidates. A scanning machine is used to read the dark marks on ballots and record the results. Although like paper ballots, a marksense ballot is larger, allowing jurisdictions to provide information about candidates directly on the ballot rather than in a separate booklet. Two types of optical scanners are in use. Precinct-count optical scanning equipment allows voters to feed ballots directly into the reader, which can be programmed to return the ballot to the voter if the voter has mistakenly selected more than one candidate for the same office (Saltman 2006, 13). With central-count marksense equipment, on the other hand, voters drop ballots into a box, and election officials then feed the ballots into the counting machine. With this system, voters do not have a chance to correct faulty ballots. Optical scan equipment grew in popularity in the 1990s, and by 1998 this technology was in use in 39 percent of all counties, representing about 27 percent of the population. By 2006, 56 percent of all counties had embraced optical scan technology, covering almost 50 percent of the voting age population in the United States.

Use of direct recording electronic (DRE) systems began in the mid-1970s. DRE system voting machines show the candidates' names on a computer screen. Voters push a button on the computer or a spot on the surface of the computer screen to record their votes. Voters may write in a candidate, using a keyboard to type the name. Vote choices are stored electronically, and, if the machine is programmed correctly, voters have no chance to vote more than once. DRE systems can be programmed to display ballots in any language to accommodate minority voters for whom English is a second language. These systems also can be designed to aid the disabled, granting improved access to those with disabilities and auditory assistance to the blind (Fischer 2001, 17). Compared to such voting systems as punch cards and lever machines, DRE systems are claimed to reduce voter rolloff—the failure to register a vote choice for all offices and measures on the ballot—by up to 26 percent in judicial elections (Fischer 2001). Flashing lights prompt a voter to continue making vote choices until the ballot is complete. Reduced voter rolloff means that more voter choices are reflected in the vote outcome. The use of DRE systems increased from 2 percent of all counties in 1988 to 8 percent in 1998, representing about 9 percent of the population. In 2006 over 36 percent of all counties embraced electronic voting equipment, constituting nearly 39 percent of the voting age population (Fischer 2001).

More than 90 percent of counties in the United States use either marksense or DRE systems. The shift to these systems was driven by problems voters had with using punch card systems. The 2000 election in particular raised the specter that many vote choices may have been recorded incorrectly or not at all because voters did not insert cards into the holder correctly, because they did not use sufficient force to punch out chads or did not punch holes in the correct place, or because chads remained attached to the cards. Reportedly, voter confusion in certain Florida counties resulted from poor ballot design and inadequate instructions to poll workers. The butterfly ballot, a type of punch card ballot, proved most problematic in Florida, a key state in determining the presidential election results in 2000. Voters could not tell whether they had made mistakes after removing the punch card from the holder, and recounts were difficult because no candidate information was printed on the punch card. In Palm Beach, a dual-column butterfly ballot was used listing George W. Bush first (with the corresponding first punch hole), Albert Gore second (corresponding to the third place to be punched), and third-party candidate Pat Buchanan's name at the top of the second column (with his place on the punch card appearing second). Subsequent investigation indicated that voters found the dual butterfly ballot confusing (Davis 2000).

As an additional limitation to punch card voting, researchers have found that voting equipment may influence the racial gap in the proportion of voided ballots. African Americans cast invalid ballots more frequently than whites. Voting records from Louisiana and South Carolina, the only states to report voter turnout by race, indicate that punch card voting systems produce a wider gap in frequency of voided ballots between blacks and whites than do mechanical lever and electronic machines. These findings added further incentive to upgrade voting systems (Tomz and Houweiling 2003, 58–60).

Given the highly negative media reporting on punch card technology after the 2000 elections, many assumed that simply replacing punch card systems with alternatives would correct the problem. However, replacing punch cards has not resolved the problem because each system has its peculiar weaknesses. For example, mechanical lever machines may disconnect from the counter mechanism, leaving a vote uncounted with no possibility of recovering it. Marksense systems can produce inaccurate results if voters attempt to erase a vote choice but do not completely remove the mark or if they mistakenly circle the name of the candidate rather than filling in the circle or box with a black mark. DRE systems are widely criticized for failing to produce an auditable, verifiable voting record. Computerized or electronic voting in general, including DRE and optical scanning as well as punch cards, may experience either security problems or programming errors (Knack and Kropf 2002, 543–44).

Election Ballots

Ballot format varies from state to state and may influence vote decisions. Some states list candidates by office, and others list them by political party affiliation. The party column ballot—also called the Indiana ballot—lists candidates of a given party, usually alphabetically, under the party's name. By emphasizing candidates' party affiliation, the party column ballot promotes straight ticket voting and even allows voters to select all of one party's candidates collectively—known as straight-ticket voting. The office block ballot—also called the Massachusetts ballot—lists candidates alphabetically in columns under the office for which they are nominated. This ballot format was intended to reduce the role of party affiliation and to prompt voters to consider the candidates for each office on their individual merits or issue stances. Research indicates that the office block ballot not only increases split ticket voting but also increases voter rolloff (Walker 1966, 462–463).

The order in which the candidates' names are listed on the ballot may influence voting decisions and has raised questions about fairness. A relationship may exist between the order of names and voter bias in that voters are more likely to vote for the first-named candidate, especially if they are unfamiliar with the candidates. Some states require the listing of candidates alphabetically by last name, whereas others list candidates by party affiliation, with the candidate of the party winning the last general election presented first. Still other states list candidates through a random procedure. Some state ballots provide an array of information on candidates, such as their incumbency status, occupation, party affiliation, and city of residence. In low-information contests such as judicial races, revealing a candidate's party affiliation increases the likelihood that voters will complete the ballot by voting for one of the candidates (Miller and Krosnick 1998).

Party tends to serve as a cue for many voters and affects whether they choose to vote for a candidate for a particular office (Klein and Baum 2001, 720). In 2001, 77 percent of American cities made use of nonpartisan elections and the rest held partisan elections, indicating the success of Progressive Movement reforms of the early 20th century. The nonpartisan ballot does reduce partisan considerations in voter decisions, but there is evidence that it also depresses voter turnout. When left with no partisan labels, voters often are forced to rely on other voting cues such as name recognition or incumbency (Klein and Baum 2001; Schaffner, Streb, and Wright 2001, 25–27).

The Electoral College

The original Constitution of 1787, modified by the Twelfth Amendment that was ratified in 1804, established the method of electing the U.S. president. State legislatures determine the method of selecting electors, who then vote for a presidential and vice presidential candidate. Early in U.S. history, states determined that electors would be selected by the popular vote. Each state has as many electoral votes as it has members of Congress in the House of Representatives and the Senate (the number of representatives plus two). Presently there are 538 electors, corresponding to the 435 members of the U.S. House of Representatives and the 100 senators, plus three electors for the District of Columbia.

Those who advocate reforming the method of electing the president note several weaknesses of the electoral college. Some observe that the electors chosen through popular vote have no constitutional obligation to cast their votes for the candidate they pledged themselves to support. Occasionally faithless electors cast votes for a candidate other than the one to whom they are pledged. This action could lead to a constitutional crisis if only a handful of electoral votes separate the two major candidates. David Hill (2006, 90) notes that, in the history of presidential elections, there have been 156 "faithless electors" who voted for someone other than their party's official candidate. The most recent case occurred in 2000 when an elector pledged to Democratic candidate Albert Gore cast a blank ballot. Seventeen states have enacted legislation that prohibits electors from voting for anyone other than the popular vote winner. Although such laws apparently never have been challenged in the courts, they may be of questionable constitutionality because the U.S. Constitution itself contains no such limitation on an elector's voting decision.

To win the presidency, a candidate must receive a majority (at least 270) of the electoral votes. Should no candidate receive a majority (a situation that could occur if more than two candidates receive electoral votes), the House of Representatives is to select the next president from among the top three electoral vote recipients. However, in the House, each state would cast just one vote. Therefore, states with small populations, such as Arizona, New Mexico, and Montana, would have as much say in the election of the president as large states like California, Texas, and New York. Such a system contradicts the fundamental democratic principle of one person, one vote; a citizen in California would have a small fraction of the influence in the selection of the president that a resident of Arizona would have.

Perhaps the most serious charge against the electoral college is that the popular vote winner may not win in the electoral college, a situation that has occurred at least twice (1888 and 2000) in the nation's history. The minority candidate in the popular vote may be elected if he or she wins narrowly in large states but loses in smaller states by larger vote margins. Given the greater contemporary commitment to democracy, such an event represents a significant threat to the legitimacy of the political process.

Critics of the electoral college argue that the present method of electing the president contributes to low voter turnout. A person's vote for president counts not at the national level, but only toward determining which candidate receives the electoral votes for the state in which the voter casts a ballot. In recent elections the major party candidates have concentrated their campaign efforts and resources only in the states—called battleground or swing states—where each candidate has a realistic chance of winning the popular vote. In the 2004 presidential campaign, 18 states were considered competitive and therefore received the overwhelming attention of the two major candidates (Schaller 2004, 1). In the 2004 election, voters in Texas who supported Democratic candidate John Kerry had little incentive to cast a ballot for president because George W. Bush's lead was insurmountable in that state. Similarly, Bush supporters in California could have concluded that a vote for their candidate would have no effect on the election outcome because Kerry was highly favored to—and did—win the state.

These and other criticisms of the electoral college have led to several reform proposals. To counter the faithless elector problem, a so-called automatic plan could be established. Rather than choosing a group of individuals to elect the president, the popular vote in each state would be translated directly into electoral votes. Another possible reform involves instituting the procedure now used by Maine and Nebraska: Electoral votes would be allocated by vote outcomes in each congressional district rather than statewide. A state's two additional electoral votes corresponding to its two senators would be awarded to the statewide popular vote winner. This plan would assure a more accurate translation of popular votes into electoral votes. A more sweeping reform would completely scrap the electoral college and introduce direct popular election. Given the perception that the present electoral system is outmoded and undemocratic, this alternative is the most obvious successor to the electoral college. However, instituting the popular election of the president would require the ratification of a constitutional amendment, a highly difficult procedure requiring a two-thirds vote in each house of Congress to propose the amendment, followed by ratification by three-fourths of the state legislatures. Smaller states, which are advantaged in the current system, would likely oppose popular election. Therefore, although popular election is the most obvious reform, there appears to be little chance that a push for such an amendment would succeed, even in light of the difficulties experienced in the 2000 election.

Those who defend the present system focus their arguments on the weaknesses of direct popular election. They maintain that, compared to popular election, the electoral college more likely assures that the winning candidate will receive a geographically broad distribution of support. A popular vote proportion greater than a bare majority in any state adds nothing to a candidate's electoral college votes; candidates must win in several states to accumulate the necessary majority of electoral votes. Further, it is claimed that the present system augments the position of minorities, who may have greater influence over the vote outcome in individual states than in the nation as a whole. Finally, many admit that the electoral college in its winner-take-all form encourages the continuation of the two-party system and hence reinforces the stability of the political process (Kimberling 1988a). Direct popular election could encourage several candidates to enter the race, possibly dividing the vote broadly among them and thereby considerably complicating what at first appeared to be a very simple electoral process. A minimum percentage of the vote required for election (possibly 40 percent) would need to be established, as would provision for a runoff election in case no candidate wins a majority on the first ballot. However, to avoid a runoff election, the single transferable vote procedure could be introduced, in which voters indicate more than one choice for president in descending order of preference. If no candidate receives a majority of the popular vote on the first ballot, the votes of those indicating a first-choice preference for the candidate with the least number of votes would be transferred to their second choices. The process would continue until one candidate received a majority.

Yet another reform proposal was originally suggested in 1978 by the 20th Century Fund Task Force on Reform of the Presidential Election Process (Schlesinger Jr. 2000). Called the national bonus plan, this procedure maintains the electoral college but advocates a constitutional amendment that would add 102 bonus electoral votes to be awarded to the popular vote winner. The popular vote winner thus would be assured of receiving a majority in the electoral college. With one candidate being virtually guaranteed an electoral vote majority, the embarrassment of presidential selection by the House of Representatives would be eliminated. If combined with the automatic plan, the national bonus plan would resolve many of the criticisms of the electoral college. Supporters argue that a chief virtue of the national bonus plan is that it would resolve the difficulties of the electoral college while maintaining its claimed advantages and avoiding possible unexpected consequences of more extensive change. However, this proposal also would require the arduous process of constitutional amendment and would not address the criticism that the electoral college dampens voter turnout due to the winner-take-all procedure.

A recent proposal, called the National Popular Vote Plan, involves states agreeing to an interstate compact, pledging to cast the electoral votes of the state to the nationwide popular vote winner. The compact would become operational when a sufficient number of states to constitute a majority of the electoral college vote (at least 270) have approved the measure (Peirce 2006). Those supporting electoral college reform prefer this plan because it does not require a constitutional amendment but simply action by enough states to represent a majority of the electoral college. Critics of the plan, including columnist David S. Broder (2006) recommend caution, commenting that criticisms of direct popular election also apply to the National Popular Vote Plan. Broder suggests that direct popular election would increase the costs of campaigning because major party candidates could no longer depend on what have come to be known as safe states in the electoral college. In addition, wealthy independent candidates could attract significant popular vote support (Broder 2007), thus increasing even further the role of money in elections. Critics also mention that the 11 largest states could approve the proposal and hence alter the presidential election system for all 50 states, although supporters note that those 11 states would represent a majority of the U.S. population. A further difficulty might be that, with the electoral college still formally in effect, the wishes of the majority of voters in a state would be ignored; the electoral votes of a state could be awarded to a candidate who lost the popular vote in that state. Supporters of the plan respond that such an outcome is preferable to one in which the popular vote winner nationally loses in the electoral college.

Voter Turnout

Any reform recommended to deal with low voter turnout varies with the perspective embraced to explain the low levels of voting in the United States. Kimberling (1988b) summarizes 10 not necessarily mutually exclusive perspectives. First, those who focus on the need for greater learning recommend voter education programs. Second, those who identify apathy as a major cause of low voter turnout support motivational campaigns: Many citizens require the equivalent of cheerleaders to encourage them to become politically active. Third, others point to the strong relationship between voting and participation in other community affairs. For instance, Robert D. Putnam (2000) has chronicled declining social capital, which is the decreasing willingness of Americans to engage in community organizations and activities, including electoral participation. A fourth perspective emphasizes an individual's stage of life: Strong interest in public affairs develops only as individuals mature. Fifth, a constitutional approach focuses on the basic structure of government: Centralized parliamentary systems experience greater voter turnout than the U.S. separation of powers system because they offer simpler vote choices and because the more disciplined political parties in these systems provide stronger incentives for citizens to vote (i.e., voters perceive government under the control of a single party to be more responsive). Sixth, an administrative approach identifies regulations that discourage registration and voting. A closely related seventh explanation holds that Americans often lack the necessary information about registering and voting. Eighth, the assimilation perspective associates voting with the degree to which a group has been integrated into the mainstream of American political culture; those failing to participate have not yet entered the mainstream of political life. Ninth, class struggle theory attributes low voter turnout to the conscious efforts of the upper classes to discourage participation by the poor. Finally, critical realignment theory suggests that turnout rates tend to vary over time, depending on the level of competition between the political parties and the stakes involved.

Some of these approaches to turnout offer very specific reforms, especially the administrative perspective, which counsels modification in election laws to encourage greater registration and voting rates. Others, such as the stage-of-life viewpoint, offer few obvious solutions to low turnout rates. None of the approaches does very well by itself in explaining the declining voter turnout that the United States has experienced since the 1960s. David Hill (2006, 144–46) concludes that sizable increases in voter turnout could be achieved through reforms that would be very difficult to introduce: eliminating the electoral college, moving from the single-member plurality district system to proportional representation for congressional and state legislative elections, and transforming the separation of powers system into a parliamentary form of government. Hill suggests several more easily introduced reforms, each of which may have a modest positive effect on turnout: election day registration; weekend voting or creation of a national holiday for voting; increased opportunity for early voting or mail-in voting; Internet voting (although the drawbacks presently appear to outweigh the benefits); proportional allocation of votes in the electoral college; and public financing of congressional campaigns (Hill 2006, 144–45).

Early and Absentee Voting

A specific reform measure designed to encourage voting participation is early voting, a procedure that allows citizens to vote in person during extended hours on weekdays and weekends for a period before election day. Unlike absentee voting, a person need not apply to vote early, and ballots cast early do not differ from those cast on election day and cannot be challenged individually, as can absentee ballots. Texas, the first state to establish early voting, began its program gradually. In 1987 the state legislature passed a measure eliminating the requirement that individuals voting absentee must state a reason for doing so. Absentee voting had come to be known as the liar's ballot because the reasons given often were considered simply excuses for being permitted to vote early by mail. In 1989 the state legislature enacted legislation that required the most populous counties to offer extended voting hours for the final week of absentee voting. In 1991 the legislature took the final step toward early voting, allowing any eligible voter to cast an early ballot during a period generally beginning 17 days before the election and ending on the fourth day before the election at designated locations (Rosenfield 1994, 7). Those who are away from their county on election day or during early voting, who are sick or disabled, who are at least 65 years of age, who are confined to jail but still eligible to vote, or who are in the military and previously resided in Texas may vote early by mail (Brown et al. 2005, 186).

Although critics of early voting argue that the program increases the costs of campaigns and elections and provides greater opportunities for fraud and voter intimidation, supporters believe that the program gives more options to voters, thus encouraging higher levels of turnout. Critics also argue that with early voting the symbolic importance of all voters taking time to cast their ballot on the same day is lost. However, Roy Saltman (2006, 43) notes that various states throughout U.S. history did not always use a single election day. In some states voters were permitted to cast ballots over several days. Regardless of the criticisms, voters, who can avoid long lines and cast their ballots more conveniently, have found early voting appealing. In some areas, from 20 to 50 percent of voters have taken advantage of the chance to vote early.

A possible consequence of early voting may be altered campaign strategy. With a large proportion of voters going to the polls before election day, candidates may find it necessary to shift campaign spending away from the last few days before the election to appeal to early voters (Nordlinger 2003). The program's effects on overall turnout is uncertain. Three researchers at the Reed College Early Voting Center (Paul Gronke, Eva Galanes-Rosenbaum, and Peter Miller) reported at the conference "2008 and Beyond: The Future of Elections and Ethics Reform in the States," sponsored by Kent State University, that the introduction of no-fault early voting had a positive but minor effect on voter turnout compared to such factors as level of interest in the election and political mobilization efforts by political parties and other groups (Smolka and Smolka 2007a). As with election day registration, early voting probably represents a convenience for those already inclined to vote, but it does not act as a significant spur to those who traditionally have failed to participate in the electoral process.

Simplifying Election Forms

States have attempted to simplify election forms as another way to encourage registration and voting. Document revision definitely can have a positive effect on voter registration, election participation, and the accuracy of election results. Ballot format and the positioning of candidates must be tested for usability to avoid the sort of confusion attributed to Florida's butterfly ballot in 2000. Traditionally, materials often have been verbose, formal, and filled with bureaucratic and legal jargon. A study sponsored by the U.S. Department of Education estimated that 90 million Americans might find it difficult to read and understand printed information that appears on official forms such as those distributed by election officials (Fox 1996, 1). To make election forms less forbidding, Mike Fox (1996) has recommended various word substitutions. For instance, use "so" rather than "accordingly," "you/your" instead of the impersonal "applicant/applicant's," "here is" rather than "attached herewith is," "quickly" rather than "expeditiously," "give up" rather than "forfeit," and "asked" rather than "propounded." In addition, Fox has recommended that election materials provide only enough information necessary for the voter to comply with election procedures. Forms also can include clear definitions of key words with which voters should be familiar, such as "absentee voter," "eligible voter," "precinct," and "ballot." Any extraneous content adds to the probability of misunderstandings and failure to read and complete the forms. Fox has suggested that election officials test revised forms with focus groups to determine the level of readability and understanding.

Voting and the Disabled

As with many other areas of activity, individuals with disabilities have received increased consideration in recent years with regard to their access to polling places. An estimated 50 million people in the United States have disabilities (Access for Disabled Americans 2007), including impairment to vision, mobility, communication, and dexterity, that require special provision to ensure them access to the electoral process. With such a large proportion of the population experiencing some form of disability, measures to increase physical accessibility to the polling place represent significant election reforms. The Voting Accessibility for the Elderly and Handicapped Act of 1984 was the first federal attempt to ensure accessible voting facilities. Because certain features of the polling place that present no difficulties for the average voter may represent serious obstacles to the disabled, election officials are required to take steps to ensure that disabled persons can exercise the right to vote. The Americans with Disabilities Act (ADA) of 1990 expanded the responsibility of election officials to provide accessibility to registration offices and polling places. In addition, amendments to the Voting Rights Act of 1965 specify that voters needing assistance due to blindness, disability, or the inability to read or write may receive assistance if they wish (Paradigm Design Group 1996, 5). The 1993 National Voter Registration Act, which provides for registration by mail and at various public agencies, also mandates registration at "any office in the State that provides State funded programs primarily engaged in providing services to persons with disabilities" (Paradigm Design Group 1996, 7). ADA guidelines mandate appropriate automobile accessibility, passenger loading zones, public transportation stops, temporary ramps, and wheelchair accessibility to polling places and booths. Election officials and poll workers should be sensitive to the existence of physical barriers and to other special needs of voters with disabilities, particularly those with impaired communication. Those with poor vision might need better lighting, large type, or assistance in reading the ballot while maintaining the secret ballot; those with impaired mobility cannot travel long distances from the street to the polling place in the building and may require seats while voting; and those with limited dexterity may require such special help as levered doorknobs and appropriate ballot marking devices (Paradigm Design Group 1996, 36). The Help America Vote Act of 2002 mandated that states provide at least one voting machine in each polling place that can be accessed by disabled persons (Schneider 2005). Maine, New Hampshire, Oklahoma, and Vermont have instituted a vote-by-phone system for the disabled.

Mail-Ballot Elections

Some states have introduced all-mail-ballot elections, in which official ballots are mailed to all registered voters, typically two or three weeks prior to the deadline set for their return. Usually such elections have involved referenda and nonpartisan candidates (Rosenfield 1995). Sixteen states (Alaska, California, Colorado, Florida, Kansas, Minnesota, Missouri, Montana, Nebraska, Nevada, New Mexico, New York, North Dakota, Oregon, Utah, and Washington) have adopted some variation of the mail-ballot election. Surveys of election officials in those states indicate that one perceived advantage of such elections is increased voter participation. Critics argue that the use of all-mail ballots in a state considerably larger than Oregon would open the door to extensive vote fraud opportunities and unforeseen administrative difficulties in statewide mailed balloting. Although fraud, including the possibility of bribery and intimidation, could be considered a real concern, election officials tend to regard mail-ballot elections as being just as free from dishonesty as polling place and absentee ballot voting. To avoid fraud, signature verification becomes an important procedure.

The first all-mail-ballot election occurred in Monterey, California, on a ballot measure for a flood control district with approximately 45,000 eligible voters (Rosenfield 1995, 1). Although postage costs can be high, this expense apparently compares favorably to the costs of establishing polling places and hiring and training poll workers and all the other expenses associated with traditional elections. All-mail-ballot elections are an interesting innovation whose popularity may spread and possibly significantly increase voter turnout, especially in local referenda and nonpartisan elections that generally do not attract high voter participation. However, increased turnout may have resulted from the novelty of the voting procedure, and any initial positive effect on turnout might subside. Nonetheless, other benefits of the all-mail-ballot election, such as cost-effectiveness and convenience, may lead to its continued use and to adoption by additional jurisdictions. If the security concerns regarding Internet voting can be adequately addressed, this voting procedure may become a significant complement to mailed balloting, especially for overseas military personnel and civilians.

In December 1995 Oregon held the first all-mail-ballot party primaries and in January 1996 conducted the first all-mail-ballot election to fill a U.S. Senate seat following the resignation of Sen. Robert Packwood (R-OR) (Southwell and Burchett 1997). The election was conducted efficiently and apparently at reduced costs. In 2000 Oregon began conducting presidential elections entirely by mail. David Hill (2006, 139) cites studies indicating that, although voter turnout may increase overall, the greatest effect of the all-mail ballot may be in local elections that ordinarily do not attract much voter interest.

Voting Assistance Programs

Concern that every eligible citizen, regardless of circumstance, has the opportunity to cast a ballot in an election led to the passage of the 1955 Federal Voting Assistance Act, which established the Federal Voting Assistance Program (FVAP), located in the Office of the Secretary of Defense. The original intent of the legislation was to assist members of the armed forces to register and vote in their home jurisdictions (Valentino 1989, 28). The responsibilities of the program specified in the original act were expanded in 1968 and 1975 by the Overseas Citizens Voting Rights Act and in 1986 by the Uniformed and Overseas Citizens Absentee Voting Act. The FVAP now assists not only members of the armed forces and their families, but also those in the merchant marine and any U.S. citizen who is living abroad. Citizens may register and vote if they meet voter requirements in the last place they lived before moving to another country. The program assists those residing overseas in communicating with local election officials and works with officials to promote more efficient absentee registration and voting procedures. The office's publication, *Voting Assistance Guide,* provides prospective overseas voters with registration and absentee voting information about the procedures of individual states. The FVAP also distributes materials that encourage U.S. citizens to register and vote and has cooperated with the Advertising Council and the National Association of Secretaries of State in a national media campaign to encourage voting. The FVAP prescribes to the states an official postcard form (Federal Post Card Application), available by mail as well as online, that facilitates overseas registration and voting. Provisions of the Help America Vote Act of 2002 called for additional funding for voting assistance personnel in the military. Each state is required to specify an office responsible for providing voter registration information and absentee ballot procedures to military and overseas voters (Saltman 2006, 200). The active role that the FVAP plays in facilitating and encouraging voting may serve as a model for a more generalized reform program that initiates efforts to encourage Americans' participation in the electoral process.

Public Employees

Public employees have often been the focus of campaign and election reform. Traditionally they were pressured to donate a portion of their salaries to a political party or candidate as a condition for continued employment. The Political Activities Act (Hatch Act), passed in 1939, prohibited employees of the federal government from contributing to political parties or candidates. Under the 1993 amendments to the act, federal government employees may participate in political activities such as signing petitions for candidates or ballot issues, assisting in partisan and nonpartisan voter registration drives, and serving as poll workers in a partisan or nonpartisan election. However, a federal employee may not run for public office in partisan elections, wear political buttons while on the job, receive political contributions, or engage in partisan political activity involving anyone who interacts with the employee's government agency. Members of the armed forces are also prohibited by statute from campaigning for a candidate or issue or from soliciting contributions from others while on active duty (Kimberling and Sims 1996, 25, 30).

The reforms initiated by the Hatch Act have been effective in protecting federal employees from pressures to make campaign contributions. Although the 1993 provisions eased restrictions somewhat, the act's regulations remain largely intact. Despite criticisms that the Hatch Act denies federal employees the right to participate in the democratic process, the U.S. Supreme Court upheld the legislation, ruling in 1947 (*United Public Workers v. Mitchell*) that a person may be removed from employment for taking part in political management or political campaigns. In 1973, in *Broadrick v. Oklahoma*, the Court ruled that the country's best interest required a system of federal service dependent on merit rather than on political service. The restrictions assured job security, thus attracting larger numbers of qualified people, and protected them from "political extortion." The reforms instituted by the Hatch Act will continue to be examined, but the legislation undoubtedly has improved the conditions of federal employment and helped to establish a system of public employee hiring based on merit, not political loyalty.

Representation Systems

Municipal election systems vary from city to city in the United States. Some localities elect representatives by district, some have at-large elections, and others combine both systems. More rarely, some jurisdictions use proportional election systems such as cumulative, limited, or choice voting. Nearly two-thirds of all municipalities use at-large elections. Typically, at-large elections are used in small cities and affluent communities. Only 14 percent of municipalities rely totally on district elections. Cities with populations of 200,000 or more are likelier than smaller municipalities to use district elections. Some cities (approximately 21 percent) use both at-large and district elections. A limited number of jurisdictions in the United States use semiproportional representation plans. The single-member district plurality system is the predominant voting system for electing state legislators and members of the U.S. House of Representatives

At-Large Elections

Introduced in the early part of the 20th century, at-large elections allow voters to select candidates who run city- or countywide, with each voter casting a single vote for each contested office. For example, if four city council seats are up for election, each voter can vote for four candidates. In some cases, all candidates may actually run against one another with the top vote getters winning the seats. In other cases, a runoff election between the two top vote getters may be used to ensure that the winner of the seat obtains majority support. At-large elections may decrease representation for an ethnic, racial, or political group, especially if the group is concentrated in a small geographic area or does not have a citywide presence. If the dominant group votes as a bloc, they may defeat minority group candidates. Justice William O. Douglas noted in *Kilgarlin v. Hill* (1967) that at-large elections allow "the majority to defeat the minority on all fronts." The courts have struck down some at-large systems as unconstitutional and as a violation of the

Voting Rights Act for failure to provide fair representation to minority populations (Donovan and Smith 1994).

District Elections

Prior to the introduction of the at-large election in the Progressive era, most cities used winner-take-all district elections. District elections allow for selecting a single representative from each of the geographic areas in the city. District, or precinct, elections are generally thought to grant racial, ethnic, or political groups, especially those that are geographically concentrated, greater opportunity to gain representation. In some cases, the adoption of district elections in local jurisdictions has increased representation for minorities in local governments, particularly African Americans. Yet district elections are not a panacea and have also faced court challenges. The system may create problems in multiethnic, multiracial communities where drawing district lines benefits one group but overlooks others, such as Latinos. Donovan and Smith (1994) concluded that majority–minority districts created by racial gerrymandering as a means to increase minority representation may not have a positive effect on turnout when minority registration rates are already low.

At the federal level and in most states, the single-member district plurality system is used to elect legislators. Single-member plurality (SMP) elections allow populations in geographically defined districts to elect one representative to the legislature. The candidate receiving a plurality of the votes wins the election. SMP does not require a runoff election between the two top vote getters if no candidate receives a majority. The single-member plurality voting system was mandated by federal law in 1967 for use in electing members of the U.S. Congress. Proportional representation and semiproportional voting systems tend to have higher voter turnout rates than SMP systems ("Single Member Plurality Systems" 2006), arguably because the former allow ethnic, racial, and political minorities greater opportunity to gain election.

Multimember Districts

In contrast to single-member district elections, some states have relied on multimember districts (MMDs), allowing two or more persons to represent a legislative district. As of 1998 13 states had multimember districts in state legislative elections. The use of MMDs has declined substantially. In the 1980s, 66 state senate and 576 state house districts were multimember, but by 1998, 40 state senate and 440 state house districts were multimember. Beginning in 1982, MMDs were challenged under the Voting Rights Act and the equal protection clause of the U.S. Constitution, as well as section 2 of the Voting Rights Act of 1965, for disadvantaging minority candidates who found it difficult to gain election from such districts. Although the U.S. Supreme Court has invalidated some multimember districts [for instance, in *Thornburg v. Gingles* (1986), a case involving a challenge to six multimember state legislative districts in North Carolina] for diluting minority vote strength, it has not declared the use of multimember legislative districts unconstitutional. Until 1967 many states used multimember districts to elect members of Congress. The change from MMD to single-member districts provided the opportunity to determine whether the latter increased the diversity of state delegations to Congress. An examination of all the MMD congressional races indicated that the diversity of a state's congressional delegation increased when states changed from multimember district systems to single-member district systems (Calabrese 2000, 611; Wasserman 1999).

The effects of multimember districts on diversity have also been examined at the state and local levels. Although women candidates are more successful in multimember districts and are more likely to represent multimember districts in state legislatures, black candidates have greater success in single-member district systems (Montcrief and Thompson 1992, 254). Multimember districts also influence legislative decision making; in state legislatures, they often produce more ideologically extreme legislators as they try to stake out and appeal to a particular constituency (Richardson, Russell, and Cooper 2004, 340).

Proportional Representation

Although rare in the United States, a variety of proportional voting systems are in place across the country. Choice voting, also known as preference voting, allows voters to rank their preferences for candidates. For example, assuming five seats are to be filled in a city council election and several more candidates than seats, each voter ranks his or her most preferred candidates from first to fifth choice. Any candidate receiving a certain minimum percentage of first-preference votes is declared a winner. If all seats are not filled after the first tally, the candidate with the fewest votes is eliminated and the second choices on the eliminated candidate's ballots are transferred to the remaining candidates. This procedure, called the single transferable vote, is continued until all seats are filled. This voting system helps to ensure that voter preferences are not "wasted" and that various groups are represented at the end of the voting process. Joseph Zimmerman (1994, 675) has suggested that, if enough representatives are elected (at least five) in a multimember district, the single transferable vote can provide greater opportunities for women and minorities to gain office. One jurisdiction—Cambridge, Massachusetts—uses choice voting ("Semiproportional Voting Systems n.d.;" "Choice Voting—The Optimal Full Representation Election Method" 2006).

In cumulative voting, instead of voting for one candidate to fill a single legislative seat, citizens are responsible for electing several representatives. In a multimember district, each voter has as many votes as there are seats to be filled. If there are seven seats, the voter can cast all seven votes for one candidate, one each for seven candidates, or any other combination. A minority group may concentrate votes on one candidate to increase the chance of gaining representation. Cumulative voting was used to elect the Illinois state house from 1870 to 1980, resulting in many more victories for African American candidates than in the winner-take-all elections used at the same time to elect the state senate. Promoted by Lani Guinier (1994) as a means of obtaining fair minority representation, cumulative voting is used by 62 jurisdictions (including city councils and school boards), with most of them concentrated in Texas ("Communities in America Currently Using Proportional Voting" 2006).

Limited voting usually occurs in a multimember district, and voters cast more than one vote but fewer votes than the total number of seats to be filled. The winners are the candidates who receive the most votes. Limited voting is similar to preference voting with one major difference: Voters have fewer votes to cast than the number of contested seats. For example, in a six-seat district, voters could have four votes, three votes, or even one. When voters have just one vote, the procedure is known as the one-vote system or the single nontransferable vote. In most cases, voters have one or two fewer votes than seats. School boards, county commissions, and city councils in 36 localities use limited voting. Its use is heavily concentrated in North Carolina and Alabama ("Limited Voting—A Simple, Compromise Full Representation Method" 2006).

While the preceding voting plans can be called semiproportional, many supporters of proportional representation recommend the introduction of a more direct proportional representation system (Richie and Hill 1999). In one version, the list system, each political party presents a list of candidates and voters vote for a political party. The parties win seats in proportion to their share of the total vote, and winners are selected from the party lists.

Generally, proportional voting systems encourage increased voter turnout. When voter turnout in Cambridge, Massachusetts, was compared to three other Massachusetts cities with similar demographics, results indicated that Cambridge had the smallest decline in voter turnout during a time when turnout had fallen generally across the United States and in Massachusetts (Pillsbury 2006). Many jurisdictions adopted cumulative voting (for instance, the lower house of the Illinois legislature), which allows voters more than one vote in the election of several officials and permits each voter to cast all votes for one candidate or to distribute the votes among several, thus, as a modified proportional representation system, fostering greater representation for minority groups. Findings indicate that cumulative voting is associated with higher voter turnout than SMP elections in the United States. The estimated boost in participation is 4 to 5 percent. Proportional voting systems likely increase voter participation in local elections because voters perceive that they have an increased chance of electing the candidate of their choice and therefore their votes will not be wasted. Also in cumulative voting, unlike single-member districts, more candidates may enter the race, making elections more competitive (Bowler, Brockington, and Donovan 2001).

The results of using different methods of electing representatives indicate how important electoral systems are to the outcome of elections. Alternatives to the single-member district system can achieve the same objectives as redrawing district lines to favor minority groups, a procedure the courts have found questionable.

Campaign Advertising and the Mass Media

The strong focus in recent decades on television campaign advertising has raised concerns about the costs of campaigning and the altered character of election campaigns. Campaign ads have become professionally produced equivalents to product advertising, often lasting no longer than 30 seconds. A study of the 1988 presidential campaign discovered that fewer than 13 percent of television ads lasted more than 60 seconds (West 1992, 76). Research has not led to definitive conclusions regarding the effects of advertising on voter turnout, although campaign advertising in general appears to increase turnout, and negative advertising apparently has a dampening effect on voter participation (Hill 2006, 20, 31). Many media researchers have concluded that such brief messages cannot adequately present positions on national issues. In the early 1990s, Darrell West (1992, 76) presented several possible proposals to reform media campaign practices. If, as some researchers conclude, ads contribute little to citizen knowledge, campaigns could be shortened considerably, thus supposedly decreasing the requirements for media advertising. Because the decline of political parties has been identified as a reason for the increased use of media advertising, some suggest that strengthening parties may help to limit media influence. With parties having an increased impact on voting behavior, the ephemeral influences of advertising supposedly would play a lessened role in vote choices. However, the popularity of past electoral reforms, such as the use of primaries to nominate candidates, that have weakened party organization might limit the extent to which parties can be revitalized. In addition, voters may be unwilling to offer their loyalty to parties, given the general trend toward declining party identification.

A more direct strategy for controlling media advertising involves structuring the format for ads. One proposal would require candidates to appear in any advertisement that refers to the opponent. Another would mandate tightened regulations about disclosing the sponsors of media ads, and yet another would require candidates to appear in ads at least 50 percent of the time (West 1992, 75). Critics of media advertising express their greatest displeasure with negative and misleading advertising, which they consider not only ethically questionable but also a discouragement to voter turnout. The Bipartisan Campaign Reform Act required candidates to state in their ads that they have approved the content of the message. However, so far the evidence is scant that requiring candidates to make such declarations in ads reduces negative advertising.

West recommended an oversight strategy dependent on the willingness of journalists to monitor campaign ads and evaluate them for truthfulness. Despite the possibility that journalists might be criticized for cynicism and could come under attack by the candidates who may wish to blame the messenger rather than the message, West argued that journalists could improve the political process by encouraging candidates to focus on substantive issues. For West's idea to work effectively, the possibility of journalistic exposure must act as a deterrent to false, misleading, or extremely negative ads. In recent elections the news media have evaluated candidates' television spots, conducting reality checks or adwatches that point to inaccuracies and exaggerations, as well as reporting on accurate communications. The effectiveness of such a watchdog role can only be determined by monitoring future campaign advertising for possible decreases in rates of misleading or negative statements (Jamieson and Waldman 2000).

Nontraditional Voters

Issues have been raised about the registration of so-called nontraditional voters, including college students living away from home and individuals who lack a traditional address (e.g., the homeless). Voter registration for college-age citizens is a major concern. In the 2004 presidential election, 41.9 percent of the youngest age group (18 to 24) reported voting, the lowest rate of any age group (U.S. Census Bureau 2004). Elfi Blum-Page has observed that roughly half the states use a no-gain, no-lose policy whereby students do not lose residency in their home state by attending school elsewhere, nor do they gain residency in the state where they are presently living (Blum-Page 1996, 24; Eshleman 1989). To ensure an effective franchise for students, it has been suggested that they be given the opportunity to vote in their college communities. However, concerns have been raised about potential election fraud or the prospect that students may outvote residents, especially in small college towns. In many states, due to reforms in election laws and litigation, students increasingly have been able to register and vote in the locations they prefer.

The Urban Institute has estimated that there are as many as 750,000 sheltered and unsheltered homeless people in the United States (U.S. Department of Housing and Urban Development 2007, iii), many of whom are eligible voters except for the lack of a permanent address. Should a homeless person be denied the right to vote for what may amount to economic reasons? Denying the vote to the homeless might be justified as the price of protecting the electoral process against vote fraud. The argument has also been made that the right to vote should be limited to those with a genuine stake in the community, and permanent residence serves as a principal criterion for community membership (Sims 1996, 6). However, Margaret Sims (1996, 15) suggests that a nontraditional address does not necessarily indicate a lack of commitment to the community. As a result of a campaign by the National Coalition for the Homeless, in tandem with provisions of the National Voter Registration Act and court rulings that permanent address requirements disfranchise the homeless as a class and violate the equal protection clause of the Fourteenth Amendment, many states have enacted legislation and revised voter registration regulations to accommodate homeless citizens. The NVRA's requirement for registration programs at government offices serving those on public assistance may be a major way of registering the homeless. The recent trend toward requiring photo identification to register and vote may prove to be an added hurdle for this group of people. Prior to the 2006 election, voter identification statutes—supported primarily by Republicans and opposed by Democrats—in at least nine states were challenged in the courts with varying results (Wallsten 2006).

In March 1996 an interesting piece of reform legislation was introduced into the U.S. House of Representatives. Titled the "Voting Rights of Former Offenders Act," the measure was geared to limit or eliminate provisions that deny the franchise to convicted felons. Data from 1995 indicated that approximately 5.3 million people were in federal, state, or local jails, on probation, or on parole. This number represented 2.8 percent of the adult population (Hancock 1996, 39). Congress failed to pass the legislation. In 2004 an estimated 4.7 million citizens were formally excluded from voting in that year's election because they had felony records. Forty-eight states prohibit prison inmates from voting, 33 states exclude parolees, and 29 states deny the right to probationers. Given that incarceration increased 600 percent from 1974 to 2004, some consider disfranchisement based on conviction for committing a criminal act a significant factor in low voter participation (Krajick 2004). In the 2004 Florida election, 8 percent of adults could not vote—including 25 percent of black males—because felons residing in that state are denied the right to vote indefinitely. Those who defend such disfranchisement argue that felons cannot be trusted to make responsible vote choices. However, those advocating a change in disfranchisement policy claim that it violates the Fourteenth Amendment's equal protection clause, the Fifteenth Amendment's prohibition against denying the right to vote based on "previous condition of servitude," and the Eighth Amendment's constraint on cruel and unusual punishment. So far these arguments have been unpersuasive. The Fourteenth Amendment allows states to deny the vote to those who participate "in rebellion or other crime," and no federal court has ruled unconstitutional any state laws that disfranchise felons. Kevin Krajick argues that Republicans, fearing the addition of significant numbers of Democratic voters, have been hesitant to alter such restrictions and that Democrats, concerned about being labeled soft on crime, have been unwilling to support change. Nonetheless, in April 2006 Florida governor Charlie Crist, a Republican, and a majority of the state's clemency board agreed to a plan to restore civil rights, including the right to vote, to felons (Royse 2007).

Campaign Spending

Some reform advocates have recommended that the practice of bundling, which involves the collection of contributions from several individuals to be passed on to a candidate, be prohibited. Another reform proposal of dubious constitutionality involves the continued call for spending limits on U.S. House and Senate campaigns. Public financing of congressional elections has gained some support as a means of limiting the potential dangers of special interest funding of campaigns. Although public financing could provide an increased opportunity to candidates who otherwise lack financial resources, opponents of the proposal contend that public financing actually would limit the ability of challengers to raise the money needed to compete effectively against incumbents.

Other proposals call for granting the Federal Election Commission authority to conduct random audits and to inspect a candidate's campaign contributions and receipts if there is evidence of a violation (Whiting et al. 1990, 17). Although some individuals focus on strengthening the FEC, others doubt the potential effectiveness of the commission, and still others express concern about granting a government agency significant new powers at a time when government downsizing and deregulation have become popular objectives. Larry Sabato and Glenn Simpson (1996, 330) have recommended reforms that emphasize more stringent disclosure with increased penalties for noncompliance, a proposal they call deregulation plus. They note that, unlike attempts to limit contributions and expenditures, disclosure legislation has fared well in legal challenges. Sabato and Simpson also recommend that each state establish stringent disclosure laws and penalties that they believe will serve as genuine deterrents to misconduct. To counteract somewhat the advantage of incumbents, Sabato and Simpson suggest the creation of discounts on mail and media time for challengers. Kathleen Sullivan (1997) also has supported the elimination of contribution and spending limits, along with a vigorous system of disclosure, arguing that an increased supply of money would mean less influence for any individual contributor and that disclosure rules would allow voters to retaliate against those accepting large donations from questionable sources.

At the state level, the practice of electing judges has raised concerns among reformers because of increased campaign spending in such races. Four states—Alabama, Louisiana, Texas, and West Virginia—elect all judges, with the exception of municipal court judges (Brown et al. 2005, 354). Ten states use some form of partisan election of judges, and 20 states hold nonpartisan judicial elections. The remaining 20 states use either the Missouri Plan (recommendation by a nominating commission and appointment by the governor, also called merit selection), gubernatorial appointment, or legislative appointment. During the last two decades the costs of campaigning for judicial candidates increased significantly as the competitiveness of judicial races intensified. Robert A. Carp, Ronald Stidham, and Kenneth L. Manning (2007, 103) note that the average expenditures for Texas supreme court candidates increased from less than $200,000 before 1984 to more than $2 million in 2004. Total expenditures for state supreme court races around the nation in 2004 approached $47 million. Critics of judicial selection through elections suggest that lawyers may contribute to a candidate's campaign expecting to receive a friendlier hearing in the courtroom. Alternatively, lawyers who are asked to make a contribution may feel pressure to do so. Interest groups, including unions and corporations, may contribute to campaigns expecting to influence court decisions by helping to elect judges favorable to their cause.

In 2002 the Brennan Center for Justice at New York University School of Law reported that 10 interest groups financed issues ads that mentioned 11 candidates for state supreme courts that year (Salant 2002). Candidates for supreme court places in nine states ran media ads. In 2000 state supreme court candidates raised $45.6 million, a 61 percent increase from 1998. Reformers argue that the best reform for campaign spending in judicial elections is the adoption of some form of merit appointment with retention elections—in other words, some variant of the Missouri plan.

Efforts to reform various aspects of the campaign and election process will certainly continue. The furor over campaign finance improprieties following the 1996 and 2000 presidential elections gave new urgency to campaign finance reform and the revamping of other aspects of the campaign and election process. Revelations of illegal contributions surfaced regularly, with the Democratic and Republican parties exchanging charges of misconduct. Reports that 938 people, among them several hundred contributors to Democratic Party campaign coffers, had been President Bill Clinton's overnight guests at the White House, disturbed many Washington insiders and aides to former presidents, who saw the practice as misuse of a government office to raise campaign funds (Balz and Cannon 1997).

By early 2007 the public financing system for presidential elections appeared to be on the verge of collapse. Senator Hillary Clinton (D-NY) seemed intent on raising sufficient campaign funds to allow her to reject not only matching funds in the party primaries—something that both major party candidates did in 2004—but also, if she gained the Democratic nomination, funding for the general election. In February 2007 the FEC acquiesced to a request from Sen. Barack Obama (D-IL), another Democratic presidential hopeful, that he be permitted to collect private contributions for the general election, should he be chosen the party's nominee. If his Republican opponent agreed to public financing, Obama then would return the general election funds to donors (*Houston Chronicle* 2007). The prospects for continuing campaign finance reform depend on the willingness of Congress to grant the

FEC or another agency the authority and resources to enforce any new regulations, as well as on Congress's ability to circumvent any threat to free speech that will catch the eye of the courts.

References

Access for Disabled Americans. 2007. www.accessfordisabled.com

Balz, Dan, and Lou Cannon. "Under Clinton, Old Practices on a New Scale." *Washington Post National Weekly Edition*, March 10, 1989: 8–9

Blum-Page, Elfi. "The Effects of Residence on Student Voting Rights." *Journal of Election Administration* 17 (1996): 24–34

Bowler, Shaun, David Brockington, and Todd Donovan. "Election Systems and Voter Turnout: Experiments in the United States." *Journal of Politics* 63 (August 2001): 902–15

Broder, David S. "End Run around the Constitution." *Washington Post*, March 26, 2006: B7

Broder, David S. "Let's Be Cautious about Changing Presidential Vote." *Houston Chronicle*, April 9, 2007: B9

Brown, Lyle C., Joyce A. Langenegger, Sonia R. García, and Ted A. Lewis. *Practicing Texas Politics*, 8th ed. Boston: Houghton Mifflin, 2005

Calabrese, Stephen. "Multimember District Congressional Elections." *Legislative Studies Quarterly* 25 (November 2000): 611–43

Carp, Robert A., Ronald Stidham, and Kenneth L. Manning. *Judicial Process in America*, 7th ed. Washington, DC: CQ Press, 2007

"Choice Voting—The Optimal Full Representation Election Method." FairVote. 2006. www.fairvote.org/?page=225

"Communities in America Currently Using Proportional Voting."FairVote. 2006. www.fairvote.org/?page=243

Cooper, Mary H. "Voting Rights." *CQ Researcher* 14 (October 29, 2004): 901–24. CQ Researcher Online. www.cqpress.com/product/Researcher-Online.html

Davenport, Paul. "Arizona Could Soon Award Random Voter." *Houston Chronicle*, August 4, 2006: A13

Davis, Jeanie Lerche. "Studies Show Butterfly Ballots Really Are Confusing." WebMd Medical News. 2000. www.webmd.com/news/20001130/studies-show-butterfly-ballots-really-are-confusing

Donovan, Todd, and Heather Smith. "Proportional Representation in Local Elections: A Review." Washington State Institute for Public Policy, 1994. www.wsipp.wa.gov/rptfiles/Localelections.pdf

Donsanto, Craig. "The Election Crimes Branch." *Journal of Election Administration* 16 (Summer 1989): 20–21

Eshleman, Kenneth. *Where Should Students Vote?* Lanham, MD: University Press of America, 1989

Fischer, Eric A. "RL 30733: Voting Technology in the United States: Overview and Issues for Congress." Congressional Research Service Report for Congress. March 21, 2001. usa.usembassy.de/etexts/gov/voting .pdf

Fox, Mike. *Innovations in Election Administration 13: Simplifying Election Forms and Materials.* Washington, DC: Office of Election Administration, 1996

Guinier, Lani. *The Tyranny of the Majority: Fundamental Fairness in Representative Democracy.* New York: Free Press, 1994

Hall, Thad, and Tova Andrea Wang. "USA: Will the State-Run Electoral Process Work This Time?" *Federations,* July 2004: 6

Hancock, Brian J. "The Voting Rights of Convicted Felons." *Journal of Election Administration* 17 (1996): 35–42

Hill, David. *American Voter Turnout: An Institutional Perspective.* Boulder, CO: Westview Press, 2006

Houston Chronicle. "Election Panel Cracks Door to Funding Options," March 2, 2007: A2

Jamieson, Kathleen Hall, and Paul A. Waldman. "Watching the Adwatches." In Larry M. Bartels and Lynn Vavreck, eds. *Campaign Reform: Insights and Evidence.* Ann Arbor: University of Michigan Press, 2000: 106–21

Kimberling, William. "Electing the President: The Genius of the Electoral College." *Journal of Election Administration* 15 (Autumn 1988a): 12–20

Kimberling, William. "Voting for President: Participation in America." *Journal of Election Administration* 15 (Autumn 1988b): 21–28

Kimberling, William, and Peggy Sims. *Federal Election Law 96: A Summary of Federal Laws Pertaining to Registration, Voting, and Public Employee Participation.* Washington, DC: Office of Election Administration, 1996

Klein, David, and Lawrence Baum. "Ballot Information and Voting Decisions in Judicial Elections." *Political Research Quarterly* 54 (December 2001): 709–28

Knack, Stephen, and Martha Kropf. "Who Uses Inferior Voting Technology?" *PS: Political Science and Politics* 35 (September 2002): 541–48

Krajick, Kevin. "Why Can't Ex-Felons Vote?" *Washington Post National Weekly Edition,* August 23–29, 2004: 27

Levinson, Sanford. *Our Undemocratic Constitution: Where the Constitution Goes Wrong (And How We the People Can Correct It).* New York: Oxford University Press, 2006

"Limited Voting—A Simple, Compromise Full Representation Method." FairVote. 2006. www.fairvote.org/?page=227

Lipton, Eric, and Ian Urbina. "Fears of Widespread Voter Corruption Unfounded, Justice Department Finds." *Houston Chronicle,* April 12, 2007: A5

Mack, Kristen. "Seeking New Orleans Votes around Houston." *Houston Chronicle,* March 14, 2006: B1

Miller, Joanne M., and Jon A. Krosnick. "The Impact of Candidate Name Order on Election Outcomes." *Public Opinion Quarterly* 62 (Autumn 1998): 291–330

Montcrief, Gary F., and Joel A. Thompson. "Electoral Structure and State Legislative Representation: A Research Note." *Journal of Politics* 54 (February 1992): 246–56

Nordlinger, Gary. "Early Voting: How It's Changing Campaign Strategies, Timing and Costs." *Campaigns and Elections* (June 2003): 27–29

Paradigm Design Group/Paralyzed Veterans of America. *Innovations in Election Administration 15: Ensuring the Accessibility of the Election Process.* Washington, DC: Federal Election Commission, 1996

Peirce, Neal R. "At Long Last: A Truly Fair Popular Presidential Vote?" *Houston Chronicle,* March 6, 2006: B9

Pillsbury, George. "Preference Voting and Voter Turnout: The Case of Cambridge, MA." FairVote. 2006. www.fairvote.org/?page=254

Putnam, Robert D. *Bowling Alone: The Collapse and Revival of American Community.* New York: Simon & Schuster, 2000

Richardson Jr., Lilliard E., Brian E. Russell, and Christopher A. Cooper. "Legislative Representation in a Single-Member versus Multiple-Member District System: The Arizona State Legislature." *Political Research Quarterly* 57 (June 2004): 337–44

Richie, Robert, and Steven Hill, eds. *Reflecting All of Us: The Case for Proportional Representation.* Boston: Beacon Press, 1999

Rosenfield, Margaret. *Innovations in Election Administration 9: Early Voting.* Washington, DC: National Clearinghouse on Election Administration, 1994

Rosenfield, Margaret. *Innovations in Election Administration 11: All-Mail-Ballot Elections.* Washington, DC: National Clearinghouse on Election Administration, 1995

Royse, David. "Florida Clears Way for Cons to Vote Again." *Houston Chronicle,* April 6, 2007: A9

Sabato, Larry J., and Glenn R. Simpson. *Dirty Little Secrets: The Persistence of Corruption in American Politics.* New York: Times Books, 1996

Salant, Jonathan D. "Money Flows into Judge Races." *Houston Chronicle,* November 21, 2002: A7.

Saltman, Roy G. *The History and Politics of Voting Technology.* New York: Palgrave Macmillan, 2006

Schaffner, Brian F., Matthew Streb, and Gerald Wright. "Teams without Uniforms: The Nonpartisan Ballot in State and Local Elections." *Political Research Quarterly* 54 (March 2001): 7–30

Schaller, Thomas F. "The Electoral College Is Seen by Many as the Deplorable College." *The Washington Spectator,* June 15, 2004: 1

Schlesinger, Arthur Jr. "Fixing the Electoral College." *Washington Post,* December 19, 2000: A39.

Schneider, Elizabeth. "Voting Machines and the Disabled." *Campaigns and Elections* (May 2005): 35.

"Semiproportional Voting Systems." Department of Politics, Mount Holyoke College. No date. www.mtholyoke.edu/acad/polit/damy /BeginningReading/semiproportional.htm

"Single Member Plurality Systems." FairVote—Factsheet No. 2. 2006. www.fairvote.org/?page=400

Sims, Margaret. "Voter Registration for the Homeless." *Journal of Election Administration* 17 (1996): 6–15

Smolka, Richard G., and David Smolka. "Scholars Report Early Voting Has Very Limited Effect on Turnout." *Election Administration Reports* 37 (February 2007a): 5–6

Smolka, Richard G., and David Smolka. "House Plans to Mark Up Holt Bill after Returning from Spring Recess." *Election Administration Reports* 37 (April 2, 2007b): 1–2

Southwell, Priscilla L., and Justin Burchett. "Survey of Vote-by-Mail Senate Election in the State of Oregon." *PS: Political Science and Politics* 30 (March, 1997): 53–57

Sullivan, Kathleen. "Political Money and Freedom of Speech." Unpublished speech presented at the University of California at Davis. February 13, 1997.

Tomz, Michael, and Robert P. Houweiling. "How Does Voting Equipment Affect the Racial Gap in Voided Ballots?" *American Journal of Political Science* 47 (January 2003): 46–60

U.S. Census Bureau. "Voting and Registration in the Election of November 2004." 2004. www.census.gov/population/www/socdemo/voting /cps2004.html

U.S. Department of Housing and Urban Development Office of Community Planning and Development. 2007. *The Annual Homeless Assessment Report to Congress.* www.huduser.org/Publications/pdf/ahar.pdf

Valentino, Henry. "The Federal Voting Assistance Program." *Journal of Election Administration* 16 (Summer 1989): 28–29

Walker, Jack L. "Ballot Forms and Voter Fatigue: An Analysis of the Office Block and Party Column Ballots." *Midwest Journal of Political Science* 10 (November 1966): 448–63

Wallsten, Peter. "Voting-Law Disputes Being Fought in Court." *Houston Chronicle* (September 13, 2006): A3

Wasserman, Scott. "Multimember Districts." In *Redistricting Law 2000.* National Conference of State Legislatures. 1999. www.senate.leg.state .mn.us/departments/scr/redist/red-tc.htm

West, Darrell M. "Reforming Campaign Ads." *PS: Political Science and Politics* 25 (March 1992): 74–77

Whiting, Meredith, E. Patrick McGuire, Catherine Morrison, and Jessica Shelly. *Campaign Finance Reform.* New York: The Conference Board, 1990

Zambon, Kat. "Push for Paper-Based Voting Divides Advocates." *Campaigns and Elections* (January 2007): 56.

Zimmerman, Joseph F. "Alternative Voting Systems for Representative Democracy." *PS: Political Science and Politics* 27 (December 1994): 674–77

3

Campaigns and Elections in Selected Western European Democracies

ince the end of World War II, many European nations have experienced a significant change in their economic and political relationships to each other, with increasingly cooperative interaction leading ultimately to the creation of the European Union (EU), now composed of 25 countries. With the advent of the EU, the electoral system of each of the countries was altered to the extent that its citizens can now select not only representatives to their individual national and subnational representative bodies, but also to the European Parliament. Such an election would be unheard-of in the United States, where even the president is not popularly elected, and the president, with the advice and consent of the U.S. Senate, appoints representatives to international organizations. Although the extent to which these European countries ultimately will form a government that significantly limits the sovereignty of national governments remains indeterminate, still they have introduced a system far beyond the present capabilities of the United States. The turnout for European Parliament (EP) elections in many countries has been very low. Gallagher, Laver, and Mair (2006, 126–27) note that voter turnout in the 2004 elections for the European Parliament was less than 40 percent in 11 countries and less than 30 percent in five.

When the U.S. Constitution was written in 1787, each state already had some form of representative government and at least limited suffrage rights. However, the countries treated in this

77

chapter have far longer and more varied histories that include periods when monarchs and aristocracies held the dominant position in government. For instance, Germany, which established a highly democratic regime (the Weimar Republic) following World War I, had by 1933 descended into dictatorship under Adolph Hitler and the Nazi Party. Under its earlier monarchs, England was ruled with few limitations on the sovereign. Powerful monarchs also ruled in France prior to the revolution of 1789. Before the fall of the Soviet Union, Poland was ruled by an autocratic regime that was strongly influenced by its communist neighbor to the east. These European countries experienced significant political transformations that involved the development of representative bodies and the expansion of the right to vote to increasing proportions of the population. We examine eight countries (Denmark, England, France, Germany, Italy, Norway, Poland, and Sweden), focusing on such topics as the type and frequency of elections, the level of voter turnout, the degree of party competition, the extent of suffrage rights, and recent electoral reforms. This discussion offers an overview of the electoral systems in these eight countries, along with their electoral reforms and alternative procedures for conducting democratic elections that provide a comparison and contrast with the U.S. electoral system and that possibly can contribute to campaign and election reform in the United States.

With the exception of England, these countries have had extensive experience with proportional representation, an electoral system with which the United States is largely unfamiliar. Proportional representation provides each political party with a proportion of legislative seats commensurate with the proportion of the total vote received. Various relatively complex methods have been devised to apportion representation among political parties. For instance, the d'Hondt method, named after the Belgian mathematician Victor d'Hondt, provides a formula for allocating seats using party list proportional representation. The Sainte-Laguë method, named for the French mathematician André Sainte-Laguë, involves a calculation that results in greater proportionality than the d'Hondt formula, thus benefiting small parties. In the Hare-Niemeyer method, used in Germany, the seat allocation for a party is determined by multiplying the number of votes a party receives by the number of seats to be filled and then dividing the result by the total number of votes cast. Whichever method a political system uses, the fundamental objective is to assure that election results reflect fairly closely the representation that political parties receive in the legislature. However, as the following discussion indicates, different political interests have preferred particular representation systems based on based on their ability to be important factors in determining the success of parties and other interests in a society.

Denmark

Denmark is a constitutional monarchy and parliamentary democracy governed under a constitution adopted in 1953. Queen Margrethe II has been on the throne since 1972. A politically influential monarchy ruled Denmark until 1849, when a new constitution established a limited monarchy governed by a two-house legislature. Only males who met a property qualification had the right to vote. The franchise was gradually extended, and ultimately, in 1915, all adults received the right to vote. Denmark was governed democratically until the German invasion in 1940 and remained an occupied country until 1945.

Jørgen Elklit (2002) identifies six Danish electoral systems. In the first, beginning in 1849, approximately 73 percent of men who were at least 30 years old possessed the right to vote. The rest were denied the vote either because they did not own a household, did not satisfy a one-year residence requirement in constituencies outside the capital, or were receiving or had received poor relief (Elklit 2002, 22). Automatic registration of voters was introduced within this system. From 1849 until 1915, Denmark employed the single-member district plurality system for electing members of the Folketing (People's Chamber), the lower house of the Danish parliament. By the beginning of the second electoral system in 1915, the percentage of men at least 30 years of age who had acquired voting rights had risen to 90 percent. During this period women also achieved the right to vote. A restriction on dependents and long residency requirements were eliminated, although the poor relief disqualification remained. The voting age was lowered to 29, with the understanding that in the future it would be further reduced. The plurality system of election was abolished in favor of a mixed-member proportional system—a combination of plurality and proportional systems—that Denmark used in only one election (1918).

With the beginning of the third electoral system in 1920, the voting age was lowered to 25. An electoral law enacted in 1920 provided for multimember districts and a nationwide district for the proportional distribution of seats (Elklit and Pade 1996, 10). In the 1930s a debate began over a proposal to abolish the Landsting, the upper house of the parliament. However, a proposed amendment to the constitution in 1939 to bring about electoral reforms failed to achieve approval in a referendum (Elklit 2002, 39). In 1950 Denmark entered a fourth electoral system, which included the passage of the 1948 Electoral Act that increased the number of compensatory seats in the proportional representation system from 21 to 30 percent, thus expanding the opportunity for greater proportionality of seat distribution in the parliament. Problems with gerrymandering were eliminated in the late 1940s with the establishment of a system of automatic allocation of seats to regions and multimember districts (Elklit 2002, 54–55).

The fifth electoral system, from 1953 to 1960 included the elimination of the Landsting and the formation of a unicameral legislature. The size of the Folketing was increased to 175, plus two seats each from Greenland and the Faeroe Islands, which are two self-governing provinces of Denmark. Although a change in the procedure for allocating seats increased the opportunity for smaller parties to win direct representation from the 23 multimember constituencies (Elklit 2002, 44), an increase in the electoral threshold (the minimum proportion of the vote qualifying a party for representation) tended to disadvantage the smallest parties. Subsequent legislation passed in 1961 lowered the threshold by more than 20 percent, from an absolute figure (60,000 votes) to 2.0 percent of the vote. The voting age was reduced to 23, and the last restrictions regarding poor relief were eliminated.

During the sixth electoral system, beginning in 1964, the voting age was further reduced: to 21 in 1961, to 20 in 1971, and ultimately to 18 in 1978. Elklit (2002, 47) notes that a major objective of changes in the Danish electoral system during the 20th century was to increase the level of proportionality between the popular vote and the seat allocations for political parties. However, Elklit contends that, rather than electoral law changes, including a lower electoral threshold, changes in the party system occurred due to shifts in the electorate and in the relationships among the political parties in parliament (2002, 50).

The allocation of the 175 seats occurs through a two-tier process similar to that of Sweden and other European countries.

The lower level involves the allocation of seats from multimember constituencies. The higher, national level comprises adjustment, or compensatory, seats that are allocated to the political parties to assure a close correspondence between the proportion of votes that a party receives and the proportion of seats allocated to it (Elklit and Pade 1996, 3). Denmark has a low level of disproportionality in the representation that political parties receive (1.8 on a scale from 0 to 100) (Gallagher, Laver, and Mair 2006, 364). Of the 175 national seats, 135 are distributed among 17 multimember districts, and 40 are compensatory seats that are distributed at the higher tier. Elections to parliament must occur at least once every four years but may occur more frequently if the prime minister decides to call an election. If this happens, then a new four-year period begins until a new election must be called. Denmark continues to employ a threshold rule to determine whether a political party is to receive compensatory seats in parliament. To gain representation, a party may either win a seat in any of the 17 multimember districts or receive at least 2 percent of the national vote. Measures either to raise or lower the threshold have failed to gain passage in the Folketing.

In election campaigns, the national radio and television service guarantees to all registered political parties equal access to preelection programs. Although political advertisements are not allowed on radio and television stations, all parties may present their platforms to the general public without charge. Public opinion polls may be conducted and published up to election day with no restrictions. The government provides financial support for all political parties and independent candidates who obtain at least 1,000 votes in the last parliamentary election (Elklit and Pade 1996, 18). Each year, parties and independent candidates are required to submit to the Ministry of the Interior a statement certifying that the funds were spent for political purposes within the country. In addition, parties must provide a yearly account of their income from membership fees and other sources (Elklit and Pade 1996, 19).

Following the transition from a single-member plurality to a multimember proportional representation system in the early 20th century, Denmark maintained the single-member constituencies as nomination districts, which remain important to the administration of elections at the subnational level (Elklit and Pade 1996, 10). Individuals vote on paper ballots by placing an "X" by the name of a political party, by the name of a party candidate (a personal, or preferential, vote), or by the name of an independent candidate. By voting for a party candidate, the individual is voting at the same time for the candidate's party (Elklit and Pade 1996, 20). Voters are guaranteed a secret ballot. Voters may be asked to provide some form of identification, such as a passport or driver's license. The election committees in the 103 nomination districts provide the results of elections to the Ministry of Interior, which calculates the final vote totals for the nation and allocates the compensatory seats to the political parties (Elklit and Pade 1996, 25).

The push to introduce technologically more sophisticated voting equipment is far less intense in Denmark, with a population of fewer than six million, than in the United States. Although the Danish government has not introduced computerized voting, computers are used to calculate vote totals and to allocate to the parties and independent candidates the 135 seats from the 17 multimember constituencies, to distribute the 40 compensatory seats to parties, and particularly to determine whether parties that failed to win a seat in the multimember constituencies are eligible for the compensatory seats. The maintenance of the list of eligible voters and the issuance of poll cards, which are distributed to prospective voters, also are computerized.

Political parties select the type of list they prefer to use in presenting candidates. The standing by district type has traditionally been used. In this type, one candidate, whose name is placed at the top of the party list in the nomination district, runs in each district. The candidate receives all the party votes in that district, in addition to the personal votes for the candidate in that and in the other nomination districts in the multimember constituency. In the second type of list, called standing in parallel, the names of all of a party's candidates in the multimember constituency are included on the ballot in each nomination district. Votes for the party are distributed among the candidates in proportion to the personal (preference) votes they receive (Elklit and Pade 1996, 17).

As in the United States, the provision of polling places generally is the responsibility of local authorities. Municipalities furnish polling booths, ballot boxes, ballot papers, and other necessary material in preparation for an election (Elklit and Pade 1996, 19). Unlike the United States, registering voters is a government, not an individual, responsibility. All citizens are included on the electoral register. Voter qualifications as stated in the constitution include Danish citizenship, permanent residence in the country, and a minimum age of 18. In addition, a prospective voter must not have been declared legally incompetent (Elklit and Pade 1996, 13). Government employees and employees of private companies who are working abroad, as well as those employed in international organizations, are regarded as having satisfied the residence requirement for voting. Danish voters living or traveling outside the country may cast an early vote at any of the country's diplomatic or consular missions (Elklit and Pade 1996, 13). Municipal election law allows not only Danish citizens but also foreign citizens who are residents of Denmark for three years prior to the election to vote and to become a candidate for municipal office. One week before the election, municipal authorities mail to each voter a poll card that is used in the voting process. The poll card contains information about the election, including the election date, the location at which voters are to cast their ballots, and the hours during which polling places will be open (Elklit and Pade 1996, 14). Due to the proportional representation system and the number of parties voters support, generally no one party is able to receive a majority of seats in the Folketing, and hence a coalition of parties tends to govern.

Those unable to travel to a polling place on election day—for instance, those confined to hospitals, nursing homes, or prisons—may cast an early vote. Officials selected by municipal councils collect advance votes from private homes and nursing homes. Hospitals and prisons can appoint staff members to collect the votes of those confined to such institutions (Elklit and Pade 1996, 21). Those not confined who wish to vote early must appear in person to cast their ballots. On election day the identities of advance voters are compared with the electoral register, and the vote is considered invalid if the voter's name does not appear on the register. If the voter has died in the period between casting a ballot and election day, that person's vote is considered invalid (Elklit and Pade 1996, 23).

The four parties that had long dominated Danish politics—the Social Democrats, Conservatives, Liberals, and Social Liberals—declined in their combined electoral support from 84 percent of the popular vote in 1971 to 58.3 percent in 1973. The number of parties achieving parliamentary representation increased from 5 to 10. Although the electoral support for the Democratic and Republican parties in the United States may fluctuate considerably over time, the single-member district plurality electoral system tends to prevent alternative political factions from gaining election to Congress.

Voter turnout in Denmark has been relatively high. The turnout rate in the 1950s was 81.8 percent, and from 2000 to 2004 the turnout rate was 87.1 percent (Gallagher, Laver, and Mair 2006, 291).

Denmark joined the European Union in 1973 (Gallagher, Laner, and Mair 2006, 117) and has been allotted 14 seats in the European Parliament. Distribution of seats among the member countries is not strictly proportional to population. If it were, Denmark would be awarded just 9 seats (Gallagher, Laver, and Mair 2006, 125). As in other European Union member countries, citizens from other EU countries residing in Denmark have the right to vote in elections to select representatives to the European Parliament, and citizens from other EU countries may become candidates from Denmark for the European Parliament. In 2004 Danish turnout for European Parliament elections was 47.9 percent, which was a rate similar to the generally low voter turnout among EU countries.

England

In 1800 fewer than three adults out of every 100 were granted the right to vote. In 1832 the franchise was extended to previously disfranchised groups. The Representation of the People Act of 1832 (also known as the Reform Act of 1832) allocated more seats in the House of Commons to large urban areas and granted the vote to select male leaseholders and householders, but excluded women. Under this act, five adults out of every 100 were enfranchised. Voter registration was required, and multiple polling places were set up within the same constituency. Polling was limited to two days, whereas previously polls had been open for up to 40 days.

The Second Reform Act (Reform Act of 1867) further increased the number of men who could vote by enfranchising all adult male urban householders and those who paid £10 per year for unfurnished lodging. With the passage of this act, the electorate more than doubled, to include 13 out of every 100 adults. In 1884 the Representation of the People Act continued the expansion of the vote to include all adult males who lived in a dwelling or house as an employee and those who occupied land or property with an annual rated value of £10. The size of the electorate again more than doubled to include 24 adults out of every 100.

In 1918 passage of another Representation of the People Act instituted suffrage to all males over the age of 21, regardless of wealth. Women over the age of 30 received the right to vote, provided they met some minimum property ownership qualifications. The 1918 act also created the current system of holding general elections on one day and established an annual electoral register. As a result of this act, 75 adults out of every 100 had achieved the right to vote. Not until the 1928 Representation of the People Act were women who were at least 21 years of age granted the right to vote. This act resulted in the expansion of the franchise to 99 adults out of every 100. By 1969 the voting age had been reduced to 18 for all men and women.

The Representation of the People Act of 1981 disqualified those who had been detained for an offense for more than one year. A 1983 act held that a convicted person could not vote while in prison, and a 1985 act allowed British citizens who at the time of an election were either working or vacationing abroad to vote by mail. Initially, British citizens could qualify for this privilege for up to five years after leaving the country, but this time period subsequently was extended to 15 years.

One of the more comprehensive voting reforms—the Electoral Administration Act of 2006—reduced the age of voter eligibility to 18. This act generally sought to address voter fraud issues in two ways: (1) by making it illegal to give false electoral registration details or to fail to provide this information, requiring local authorities to review polling stations and present reports to the Electoral Commission, and (2) by establishing an identification check on mailed vote applications. The act provided for the creation of new ballot designs, including ballots with bar codes or even photographs on ballots, and prohibited certain descriptive statements on ballots, such as "don't vote for them" or "none of the above."

Currently all legal residents qualify to vote in elections if they are citizens, are at least 18 years old, and have registered. Those imprisoned for a crime, the mentally impaired who are unable to exercise reasoned judgment, those with unsettled bankruptcies, and those convicted of corrupt electoral practices within five years of an election are not eligible. Citizens who move abroad may vote for 15 years after taking up residency in another country. Voters may participate in numerous types of elections, including general elections to select the members of Parliament (MPs), the European Parliament, and local administrations.

In each polling district a presiding officer and clerks administer the voting process. Voters are given a paper ballot. Although England does not use voting machines or any type of electronic voting, the country has experimented with electronic voting. In May 2002, voting systems by phone, by touch screen kiosks, and even by text message were used in pilot programs to increase voter participation in elections. No decision has been made regarding the extensive use of these technologies.

In 2000 modifications of the electoral process allowed for postal voting on demand, permitted the use of psychiatric hospitals for use as registration addresses, and required polling assistance for the disabled (BritainUSA: Britain at Your Fingertips n.d.). Before ballots are moved from a polling district to a central location for counting, all ballots from the same constituency or geographic location are combined. Therefore, it is not possible to analyze voting patterns by district. Ballot boxes are sealed prior to the move to prevent tampering. During the counting process, ballots may be voided if they do not have the official mark of the polling station, if the number of votes exceeds that of the candidates one may vote for, if the ballot has marks on it that identify the voter, if the voter's choice is unclear due to confusing marks, or if the ballot is left unmarked (BritainUSA: Britain at Your Fingertips n.d.; "How British Elections Work" 1951).

From 1945 until 1997, voter turnout averaged more than 70 percent. In 1970 voter turnout declined for the first time, possibly due to the eligibility of 18-, 19-, and 21-year-olds, who were granted the right to vote for the first time but many of whom abstained from voting. After 1970, with universal suffrage well established, voter turnout increased but then declined in 1997 (71.5 percent) and fell even more dramatically in 2001 (59.4 percent). One factor contributing to the decline was a perception that few differences separated the Labour and Conservative parties. Of those surveyed, only 17 percent in 2001 and 21 percent in 2005 perceived a "great deal of difference" between the major parties. Another suggested reason for lowered voter turnout was the apparent assumption on the part of many voters that the Labour Party had become dominant and would win the majority of the parliamentary seats. In addition, a study conducted by the Electoral Commission in 2005 found that the electorate was largely uninformed about politics and political party stances, could not decide for whom to vote, were disillusioned with politics, and found the campaigns insufficiently spontaneous and too negative (Norton 2007, 184–85).

Average voter turnout remained high from the 1950s (79.1 percent) to the 1990s (74.4 percent) but fell significantly (to 59.4 percent) in the period 2000–2004 (Gallagher, Laver, and Mair 2006, 291).

Prior to the 1980s, voters elected only the members of parliament and local government councillors. In the 21st century, in addition to members of parliament, voters elect a wide array of positions, including local authorities (council election), the mayor of London (greater London authority election), the European Parliament, the Scottish Parliament, the Welsh National Assembly, and the Northern Ireland Assembly. In addition, by-elections may be held to replace those who resign or die in office. England also employs the referendum, which allows voters to express their preferences on specific issues (Norton 2007, 154–55).

England employs the first-past-the-post (FPTP) system—also called the single-member district plurality system—in contrast to proportional representation. FPTP systems give the popular vote winner the sole victory; the person with the highest number of votes within a constituency wins the election. The FPTP system is claimed to have contributed to political stability in England because it allows a new government to assume the reins of government quickly, provides for swift continuity in day-to-day political life, and presents a clear mandate to the new government. Although minority governments—in which no party commands a majority in parliament—have been formed, their duration has been limited. Another claimed advantage of the FPTP system is that constituents may contact a specific representative with their concerns ("First Past the Post" n.d.). The two major parties are advantaged by the FPTP system. For instance, in the 2001 election the Labour Party won 40.7 percent of the vote and 64.2 percent of seats in Parliament, and the Conservative Party received 31.7 percent of the vote and 25.9 percent of seats, whereas the third-party Liberal Democrats obtained 18.3 percent of the vote but just 8.1 percent of seats (Norton 2007, 180).

Reform groups, such as Charter 88 and the Electoral Reform Society, have called for instituting proportional representation. Arguing that the lack of representation afforded to a widened array of parties is undemocratic, reformers claim that the will of the people is not truly reflected in the national vote. In 1951 (Conservative) and 1974 (Labour), the ruling governments received fewer popular votes but still won more seats than their opponents. In 1997 the Labour Party, with 43.2 percent of the vote, won more than 63 percent of the seats, whereas the Conservatives and Liberal Democratics received 47.5 percent of the vote but just 32 percent of the seats. These trends continued in the 2001 and 2005 elections, with the ruling party winning less than 50 percent of the popular vote but still maintaining a dominant position in Parliament.

Elections are held 17 working days after the date of the proclamation announcing the dissolution of Parliament. Therefore, campaigns last just three to four weeks, an extremely short period compared to the marathon campaigns in the United States. Television and radio advertising by political candidates is prohibited, but newspaper or poster advertising is unregulated, except that these advertisements must supply the name and address of the printer, the candidate's campaign manager, and the person who is supposed to benefit from the material. Radio and television stations make available time free of charge for political party and election broadcasts. To obtain free airtime, a party not currently represented in Parliament must contest one-sixth or more of election seats. The time allocated depends on the percentage of votes that the party won in previous elections and on the level of electoral support experienced in the past. News programs provide extensive coverage of all major party political activities during campaigns and provide for discussions and debates among rival candidates as well as phone-in question-and-answer sessions between the public and political candidates (BritainUSA: Britain at Your Fingertips n.d.).

Candidates for parliamentary elections are subject to expenditure limits, and disclosure of all personal expenses is required. Candidates for Parliament are granted a franking privilege that allows them to send free of charge one postal communication weighing no more than 2 ounces to each elector in the constituency. With the passage of the Political Parties, Elections and Referendums Act of 2000, political parties, which may accept unlimited contributions, became subject to campaign expenditure limits. They must disclose contributions larger than £5,000 to the Electoral Commission. Limits on expenditures apply to advertising, the production of party campaign broadcasts, direct mail, the development and production of the party's manifesto (platform), canvassing the electorate, and sponsoring election rallies.

France

The French electoral process resembles that of the United States in some notable respects (for instance, the use of the single-member district system to elect representatives) but not in others (for instance, while France elects a president by direct popular vote, the United States uses the indirect method of the electoral college). The histories of the two democracies also vary considerably. Although the United States periodically experienced deep crises such as the Civil War and the Great Depression, the governing document written in 1787 remained in effect, with amendments infrequently added. In contrast, since the 1789 revolution France has experienced various governing systems, including five republics.

In 1791 a constitutional monarchy was created, followed quickly by the First Republic in 1792. Republican government ended in 1804 when Napoleon Bonaparte became emperor. With Napoleon's final defeat by other European powers, the Congress of Vienna (1814–1815) recognized Louis XVIII, grandson of Louis XV, as the legitimate sovereign. The 1830 revolution resulted in the replacement of Louis XVIII's successor, Charles X, by Louis Philippe, who ruled until the 1848 revolution and the creation of the Second Republic. Louis Napoleon Bonaparte, nephew of Napoleon Bonaparte, was elected president, but in 1852 he proclaimed himself emperor (Napoleon III), thus ending the Second Republic and instituting the Second Empire. With France's defeat in the 1870–1871 Franco-Prussian War, the Third Republic was established. Internal scandal and the costly world war of 1914–1917 notwithstanding, the Third Republic survived until Germany's quick victory over France at the beginning of World War II. Following the war, France established the Fourth Republic, which varied little from the governing structure of the Third Republic. The country experienced political instability, with the constant reformation of governing coalitions. When France's attempt to maintain control of Algeria led to the collapse of the Fourth Republic, Charles de Gaulle, a leader of the free French during World War II, reentered the public realm to form the Fifth Republic, becoming its first president. De Gaulle successfully defended the new regime against radical military personnel who opposed independence for France's colonial holdings, especially Algeria.

The Fifth Republic's governing system combines elements of the parliamentary and presidential systems, which is termed a semipresidential system (Gallager, Laver, and Mair 2006, 26). Originally the president was elected by popular vote for a seven-year term, and the members of parliament served five-year terms. This arrangement could lead to a situation, called cohabitation (a condition similar to divided government in the United States), in which different political parties or coalitions control the presidency and the parliament (National Assembly). A newly elected president is responsible for selecting the prime minister from the members of the Assembly. However, if another party controls the Assembly, the president has no realistic alternative but to choose a prime minister from the opposition to gain the approval of the members of the Assembly. For instance, following the 1997 parliamentary election, conservative president Jacques Chirac was forced to select a socialist, Lionel Jospin, as the new prime minister (Gallager, Laver, and Mair 2006, 27). Subsequently the presidential term was reduced to five years so that presidential and parliamentary elections are held at the same time, thus increasing the probability that the president may select a political ally as prime minister.

The multiparty system characteristic of the Fourth Republic continued in the Fifth Republic, but two major party blocs—one on the left and the other on the right—emerged, in part due to the adoption of a single-member district system with a two-round majority election, called the double-ballot system. This system increased the likelihood that two candidates would compete in the second round in each electoral district (Gallagher, Laver, and Mair 2006, 207, 348). The nation is divided into 555 single-member districts, each of which elects a deputy to the National Assembly. Twenty-two additional deputies are elected from overseas territories and departments. If a candidate receives a majority of the vote in the first-round election, that person wins the seat; if not, a runoff election is held a week later. Candidates receiving at least 12.5 percent of the vote in the first round are eligible to run in the second round. If fewer than two candidates achieve eligibility, then the top two first-round vote getters compete in the second round. The plurality winner in the second round wins the election. Disproportionality between election results and seat allocation among the political parties is high. Gallagher, Laver, and Mair (2006, 368) note that, although the right-wing parties received 38 percent of the vote in the 1993 parliamentary election, they nonetheless won 466 (nearly 81 percent) of the 577 seats.

The 321 members of the second house of the French parliament, the Senate, are chosen indirectly by an electoral college composed of deputies, general councillors, regional councillors, and representatives of municipal councils in each department. Each senator serves a nine-year term, with one-third of the senators selected every three years ("Elections and Referenda" 2002).

Today all French citizens at least 18 years of age have the right to vote. Exceptions include those mentally dependent on others and those who have been convicted of certain crimes. Candidates for office must submit their intention to run in the election at least 21 days before the election and submit a deposit of 1,000 French francs, which is reimbursed if the candidate receives at least 5 percent of the votes cast in one of the two voting rounds ("France: Electoral System" 2007).

Voter participation since the 1950s has remained high in France compared to the United States. In the 1980s the average participation rate was 71.9 percent, which nonetheless was more than 10 percent lower than the average for 16 Western European nations (82.6 percent). In the 1990s the average was 68.9 percent, contrasted to a 16-nation average of 78.6 percent (Gallagher, Laver, and Mair 2006, 291). However, in the 2007 presidential runoff election, turnout reached 84 percent, which may be attributed in part to the clear choice between a conservative and a socialist candidate.

In addition to elections to the National Assembly, France holds local elections in which voters select members of the municipal council. The municipal council then chooses one of its members to serve a six-year term as mayor. In each department, voters participate in so-called cantonal elections to select the members (councillors) of the General Council, who serve a six-year term. One councillor is elected from each canton through the two-ballot system. The members of the regional council, a level of the electoral system created in 1982, are elected for six-year terms through a system of proportional representation ("Elections and Referenda" 2002).

The French president is also elected through a two-round procedure, in which a runoff election is held if no candidate receives a majority of the popular vote in the first round. In the

2002 presidential election, 16 parties ran presidential candidates, and the top two vote getters, Jacques Chirac (19.88 percent) and right-wing candidate Jean-Marie Le Pen (16.86 percent) competed in the second round, with Chirac receiving 82.2 percent of the vote and Le Pen 17.8 percent. In the first round of the 2007 presidential election, 12 candidates competed, with Nicolas Sarkozy of the Union for a Popular Majority Party receiving 31 percent of the popular vote and Ségolèn Royal, the Socialist Party candidate, garnering nearly 26 percent. In the runoff election, Sarkozy received 53 percent of the vote and Ségolène 47 percent.

Some, including Steven Hill and Guillaume Serina (2007), have argued that, instead of a two-round election, France should institute instant runoff voting in which voters can rank their choices for the office. Hill and Serina claim that instant runoff voting, if used in past elections, could have produced different results more in line with voter preferences because it allows voters to register their second choices. The third-place candidate in 2007, François Bayrou, the candidate of the Union for French Democracy Party, supposedly was the second choice of many Sarkozy and Ségolène supporters and therefore may have won under an instant runoff procedure. In the 2000 election, Le Pen, the right-wing candidate, was able to receive a larger percentage of the votes than any of the more liberal candidates (17 percent) because supporters of those candidates split their support among them. Thus, Le Pen qualified for the runoff, in which he ultimately received just 18 percent of the vote. Again, with an instant runoff, the results might have been very different.

Party nominations are often controlled by small influential groups within the parties, although local influence can play a part in the nomination process. Therefore, central party officials must take into account the preferences of local party members when deciding on nominees (Gallagher, Laver, and Mair 2006, 324). Political campaigning in France is more limited than in the United States. Political advertising on radio and television is prohibited, although each candidate or political party receives free time on radio stations and television channels. Publication of the results of public opinion polls is prohibited in the week before an election to prevent the polls from influencing the election outcome. Restrictions have been placed on billboard advertising four months prior to the election campaign. Businesses may not provide funds to political parties. Laws passed in the 1990s require political parties and committees to publish reports of campaign spending. Candidates are limited in the amount they may spend in the first and second rounds. The government compensates candidates for a portion of campaign expenses depending on the proportion of the vote received in the election. Presidential candidates receiving more than 5 percent of the vote receive 36 percent of expenses ("Elections and Referenda" 2002).

In contrast to the United States, where only state and local governments use the referendum, France has employed this electoral device at the national level for more than 200 years. In 1958 voters in a referendum approved the establishment of the Fifth Republic, and four years later President Charles de Gaulle called on citizens to approve a referendum proposal initiating the popular election of the president, which potentially gave to this office much greater influence in French government. Although voters approved this referendum, in 1969 de Gaulle failed to receive approval of a proposal to reform government administration, after which he resigned the presidency. A 2000 referendum, with just 25 percent of voters participating, resulted in the reduction of the presidential term from seven to five years.

In 1958 France became one of the six original members of the European Union, signing the Treaty of the European Economic Community (EEC) that established guidelines for a common market, as well as the Euratom Treaty that created common policies on atomic energy (Gallagher, Laver, and Mair 2006, 116–17). Since then, the European Union has expanded to 25 countries, and the European Parliament represents an electorate of more than 350 million. France has been granted 78 seats in the European Parliament (Gallagher, Laver, and Mair 2006, 125). In the 2004 election to select representatives to the EP, just 42.8 percent of French voters turned out to vote (Gallagher, Laver, and Mair 2006, 126), a rate similar to the turnout in other EU countries.

Germany

After Germany's defeat in World War I, the German Revolution in 1918 produced the Weimar Republic and a democratic constitution. Creating an electoral system based on pure proportional representation, the Weimar Republic proved highly unstable, producing 20 different governments between 1919 and 1933. With only four governments lasting more than a year and facing a series of domestic crises including high unemployment and heavy indebtedness, President Paul von Hindenburg turned over power to Adolph Hitler, marking the beginning of the infamous Third Reich (Roberts 2000).

With Hitler's defeat in World War II, democratic elections were reinstituted in 1949 under the Basic Law, West Germany's constitution. East Germany fell under the former Soviet Union's sphere of influence. The West Germans established a parliament consisting of a lower house (the Bundestag), elected directly by the people, and an upper house (the Bundesrat), representing the 16 federal states with its members appointed or removed by the states at any time. The Chancellor is elected by and accountable to the Bundestag and serves as the chief executive. In 1990 West Germany and East Germany were reunified, and East Germans were assimilated into the West German political structure (Roberts 2000).

After the use of a majority two-round system in the German Empire and the imposition of pure proportional representation in the Weimar Republic, the new system set up in 1949 established a combination of personal votes for candidates in single-member districts with proportional representation. Political parties are required to obtain a 5 percent vote threshold to win parliamentary seats (Germany: The Original Mixed Member Proportional System n.d.). The framers of the Basic Law sought a blend of proportional representation with a system of single-member districts, believing that this structure would ensure the accountability of legislators to their constituencies and also reduce the fragmentation experienced under the Weimar Republic ("Electoral System of Germany" n.d.).

Germany holds municipal, district, regional, and federal elections. Divided into 13,862 local authorities, voters elect municipal councils for each of these localities. With 306 regional districts, voters also elect district assemblies that perform local and regional functions. The individual regions (or Lander) determine how municipal and district elections will be held. Voters may cast a single vote for a party list. Seat allocation is determined by the d'Hondt method, with candidates being elected in the order in which their names appear on the ballot. The minimum voting age in some Lander is 16, and in others it remains at the national standard of 18. In municipal and district elections, party thresholds vary. Some use the 5 percent threshold, others use 3 percent, and still others use no threshold for excluding party representation.

Each of the 16 Lander has its own regional state parliament that is directly elected. Only parties that win 5 percent of the vote across the Lander may receive allocation of additional member seats. For regional elections and elections to the European Parliament, the Hare-Niemeyer method is used to allocate seats to parties. Party candidates are elected in the order in which their names appear on the ballot. In one region, Bremen, the Sainte-Laguë formula is used to allocate seats. Only a few Lander elect representatives without using a threshold. Voters directly elect the country's 99 members to the European Parliament from a single national multimember constituency, with the 5 percent threshold in place across the whole nation ("Voter Turnout in Western Europe Since 1945: A Regional Report" 2004).

For most municipal, district, and regional elections, as well as for elections to the Bundestag, the Hare-Niemeyer method, used only in Germany, awards seats to political parties by multiplying the number of seats by the number of votes a party wins and dividing the result by the total number of votes (Rose and Munro 2003). Direct election of the Bundestag requires political parties to win 5 percent of the party list votes across the whole country as a prerequisite for receiving allocation of additional seats. This threshold does not apply to parties that have already won three constituency seats or who represent a national minority.

Bundestag representatives who resign or die during their terms of office are automatically succeeded by the closest runner-up candidate on a party's list for the appropriate Land. German parties do not hold primary elections through which voters directly select party candidates. Instead, a small party elite nominates constituency candidates. Candidates who appear on party lists are selected at Land party conventions. Party officials at the federal level play no role in the nominating procedure. It is common for Bundestag candidates to run for a seat on both constituent and party lists to increase the likelihood of winning a seat ("Electoral System of Germany" n.d.).

German citizens aged 18 or over who have resided in the country for at least three months are eligible to vote. German nationals who have not resided in Germany for at least three months, who have left the country in the last 25 years, and who live abroad working as a German civil servant or soldier or reside in other EU member states may vote. Germans may be disqualified from voting by reason of civil commitment or mental illness ("Germany: Electoral System" n.d.).

Voters generally do not elect chief executives, although a few municipalities elect mayors through popular vote. Although elections are held every four years, the federal, Land, and local level contests are staggered so that government officials do not completely turn over at the same time. Therefore, elections are a continual part of German life, and each election becomes a test of the federal government's popularity versus the opposition's strength ("Electoral System of Germany" n.d.).

In contrast to the United States, where elections are held during the week, German elections occur on Sunday. If unable to vote in person, people may vote by mail. All citizens are automatically registered to vote and receive mailed notification from the appropriate municipality in which they are qualified to vote. Voters present their notification at the polling station and cast two votes: one for the personal candidate of choice and another for the political party. Germans make their choices on paper ballots, although some experimentation with electronic voting has occurred (von Brockel 2007). In the 2005 elections, approximately five million of Germany's 62 million eligible voters had access to electronic voting. More than 2000 electronic voting machines (EVMs) were used in 65 municipalities (Islam 2005; Niemoller n.d.).

Voter turnout in Germany has averaged approximately 90 percent in national elections but has decreased somewhat since the early 1980s. Voter turnout in West Germany declined from 89.1 percent in 1983 to 84.3 percent in 1987, then to 78.5 percent in 1990. The 1990 election—the first since the unification of West and East Germany—had the lowest voter turnout since the first West German elections in 1949 ("Electoral System of Germany" n.d.). Since 1945 turnout for national parliamentary elections has varied between a high of 91.1 percent and a low of 77.7 percent (in 2005). With an average of approximately 85 percent across 16 election cycles, Germany ranks tenth in Western Europe in voter turnout ("Electoral System: MMP Parliamentary Elections" 2007; "Voter Turnout in Western Europe Since 1945: A Regional Report" 2004).

The German electoral system was designed to reinstitute proportional representation as used during the Weimar Republic. At the same time, with the introduction of single-member districts, developers of the new system hoped to avoid the excessive fragmentation associated with the Weimar Republic and also promote greater accountability of representatives to their electoral districts or constituencies. This combination has produced a personalized form of proportional representation ("Electoral System of Germany" n.d.).

Under the system instituted following World War II and refined again in 1957, each voter has two votes: one for electing a candidate by majority vote in a single-member district and the other for a party list in the voter's Land. Voters may split their vote. In other words, they may select a single-member district candidate of one party but vote for a different party list in the Land. Party seats are allocated in proportion to the list votes received. Seat allocation is calculated according to the total vote received for all Land lists for each party (Roberts 2000, 14). To qualify for seats in the Bundestag, parties must obtain a minimum of 5 percent of the total votes cast for party lists to obtain any list seats (except for parties winning at least three constituency seats). If a party wins one or two constituency seats, it is ineligible for additional seats if it does not meet the 5 percent threshold. Thus, the threshold limits the success of minor political parties, making it harder for them to win seats. Smaller parties rarely win three constituency seats to gain exemption from the 5 percent rule. Although the success of smaller parties is limited by this requirement, the rule does not completely deny new entrants representation in the Bundestag. For example, in the 2002 elections 24 political parties competed nationally, and five of them met the threshold and obtained a proportional allocation of seats (Saalfeld 2005, 214).

Political campaigns in Germany have become lengthier, requiring more planning and more campaign staff. Locating campaign teams, securing a campaign budget, and establishing public opinion polling and public relations agencies require candidates to make decisions more than a year in advance of the election. Lengthier campaigns incur greater costs in time, money, and effort (Roberts 2000, 35).

The most complete press coverage is devoted to the well established political parties, and minor or small parties receive much less attention (Druck 2004, 63). In political campaigns, a candidate or party denied access to the only outlet in an electoral district may initiate a court challenge and obtain an injunction based on the abuse of a monopoly. Newspapers reserve the right to screen advertisements that editors conclude contain extremist or racist messages. Newspapers may publish a party's platform completely unedited, but editors have discretion regarding the publication of small parties' platforms. Rules do not specify how much space will be devoted to political advertisements and do not provide guidance on formatting. Public radio and television stations are required to provide airtime to eligible political parties during campaigns. If a political party is running in at least one Land and not just in a particularly electoral district, it is entitled to airtime. However, privately owned broadcast stations are not required to provide free airtime and are allowed to charge for their costs. Legal directives from the Conference of Directors of the State Media Board hold that public broadcasters can charge only for the costs of transmission, approximately 35 percent of normal advertising costs. Private broadcasters typically charge more than the public stations, with a rate of approximately 55 percent. Political parties that place false information on the air are held accountable if the content breaks the law (Druck 2004, 64–65). Each party receives at least two broadcasts at 2.5 and 1.5 minutes each and 1 minute in regional elections. Each party may also obtain more spots as determined by the percentage of parliamentary seats won in the previous election. The Law on Political Parties provides each party represented in the Bundestag "at least half as much time as any other party" (Druck 2004, 68).

In the early Federal Republic, political parties financed themselves. Although tax benefits were established in the 1950s to allow political parties to finance themselves through membership dues and donations, the federal Constitutional Court declared these tax benefits unconstitutional because they violated the equal opportunity of all political parties. Therefore, in 1959 the government began to fund political parties. However, the federal Constitutional Court ruled that this arrangement also was unconstitutional. Under guidance from the Court in 1967, funds for political education would no longer be provided; instead, a specific sum of tax money would be allocated for each eligible voter for the Bundestag and the European Parliament. The regulations led to large donations, some made to fictitious firms and others set up as dummy accounts with both being used as deductions from taxes as operating expenses (Von Alemann 2000)

In 1994 the federal Constitutional Court dispensed with the idea of total state financing of campaign costs and accepted the notion that the state would aid party activities in conjunction with party self-financing through donations. Parties now receive a grant based on votes received in Bundestag and European Parliament elections, as long as they received 0.05 percent of the vote. The first 5 million votes received by small parties result in a slightly higher remuneration rate. Donors and party members are allowed to deduct donations or membership fees from their tax payments, up to a specified limit. Membership fees are viewed as the most democratic form of party financing and now are much less controversial (Von Alemann 2000).

Germany's political parties are allowed to accept an unlimited amount of money in donations from individual as well as corporate donors. Donations that exceed 20,000 DM must be reported. Certain groups, including political foundations, parliamentary groups, nonprofit organizations, anonymous donations, and non-Germans who are not national minorities in countries adjacent to Germany, are forbidden from making donations to political parties. Donations made with the clear intent of obtaining a specific economic or political benefit are prohibited. Any German political party that accepts illegal funds loses its public funds (Von Alemann 2000).

Reformers call for greater use of investigative journalism, parliamentary committees of investigation, public prosecutor investigations, and academic analyses as a means of reducing the abuse of campaign finance procedures. Transparency International (2001) calls for additional measures to reduce corruption, such as a prohibiting corporate contributions, placing a monetary limit on donations, requiring disclosure of smaller donations, forbidding cash donations, and enacting stiffened sanctions or penalties for violation of the party finance laws.

Italy

Following Italy's defeat in World War II, the Italian monarchy was abolished by a popular referendum and a new constitution in 1948 established a republic with a president, a prime minister, and a popularly elected parliament. Italy's complex electoral structure has undergone many reforms. The proportional representation (PR) system used to allocate seats in the parliament from 1948 until 1993 was blamed for government instability. Electoral reform in 1993 established a single-member district system for three-fourths of seats in parliament and a proportional representation scheme for the remaining seats in 27 regions. In 2005 the electoral system was returned to a form of proportional representation.

Over 60 laws and decrees govern Italy's electoral process. Both houses of the bicameral parliament—the Chamber of Deputies and the Senate—elect Italy's head of state, the president, through a multiround system in which the successful candidate must receive two-thirds of the votes. The chief executive, the prime minister, is appointed by the president and confirmed by the parliament.

Citizens 18 years of age or older are eligible to vote. However, those voting for members of the Senate must be at least 25 years old. Voting in Italy is considered a civic duty and is compulsory. Although Italy imposes no sanctions on nonvoters, a large proportion of those who are eligible do vote. Some are disfranchised either temporarily or permanently through civil incapacitation (e.g., for being convicted of certain crimes) or for being found morally unfit (e.g., through bankruptcy adjudication).

Italy relies on paper ballots to record votes. Citizens are automatically registered where they reside. Voting occurs in polling stations organized at the local level, often in schools. Each polling station is divided into several polling rooms with approximately 500 voters allotted to cast their ballot in each room. Every eligible voter is issued an election card stating the place of enrollment for voting and the assigned polling room. The cards are valid for up to 18 elections (Electronic Voting and Democracy). Eligible voters housed in hospitals, prisons, detention centers, or other institutions, as well as the disabled and those unable to leave their home, have special voting procedures that allow them to vote. Italians living overseas may vote by mail or in person by returning to Italy.

Voting occurs on two consecutive days—usually Sunday and Monday—to accommodate those who work. Military personnel may vote in the cities where they serve. All vote operations are conducted openly, allowing any voter to monitor polling activities and to observe vote counting. Voters receive pencil-and-paper ballots, one ballot for each election. For instance, when the general election and town council election are held simultaneously, electors receive three paper ballots: one for the House, one for the Senate, and one for city council. Each polling room is staffed by a president who is nominated by the Court of Appeal, by a secretary who is selected by the president, and by four assistants (called scrutineers) who are appointed by local authorities. As individuals vote, a scrutineer records in the electoral register that they have voted (Electronic

Voting and Democracy). Each political party is entitled to have a representative in every polling room, and they too may play a monitoring role in the polling process (Electronic Voting and Democracy).

During the vote counting, only the six poll workers may handle the ballots. Official ballot results are signed and approved by the six poll workers, and two copies of an official record are generated. Local authorities calculate results on the local level, and the national government tallies the official results from all the polling room reports. Political parties also calculate results and may compare their tallies to those of the local and national governments. Results are often made available within six to eight hours after the polls close (Electronic Voting and Democracy). The government experimented with electronic voting in the April 2006 general elections. The experiment, held in four regions (Liguria, Lazio, Sardegna, and Puglia), accounted for 20 percent of voters nationwide. Manual vote counting still occurred, and manual results still became the official tally at each polling station (Electronic Voting and Democracy).

Voters participate in parliamentary elections, national referenda, regional elections, provincial elections, and municipal elections. Voter turnout in parliamentary elections averages nearly 90 percent, which is one of the highest rates in the world. Sixteen parliamentary elections have been held since 1946. The last two elections—2001 and 2006—exhibited lower voter turnout rates: 81.4 percent and 83.6 percent respectively (International Institute for Democracy and Electoral Assistance). Italian voters exhibit consistently high levels of partisan loyalty in different types of electoral contests. Their vote preferences are determined not so much by local bottom-up forms of mobilization, but by national politics, particularly voter concerns about Italy's place in the international community, European integration, and the role of religion in society (Cotta and Verzichelli 2007, 81).

Italy is divided into 8,101 municipalities, each having a municipal council elected for a term of five years. Municipal councils range from 12 to 80 members in a single municipality and elect members using a multimember system. Municipal elections are held in cities with a population more than 15,000. Voters cast two ballots—one for the mayor and one for the council. Split voting is allowed. Some smaller cities allow for only one vote, and the winning list receives two-thirds of the seats on a council and the mayoral seat. Party lists must attain at least 3 percent of the vote to receive representation on a council ("Voter Turnout in Western Europe Since 1945: A Regional Report" 2004, 25).

Under PR, the membership of parliament was fragmented among several parties and governing coalitions were unstable and short-lived. From 1945 to 1993, a total of 52 governments came to power and each lasted an average of less than one year. A triggering event for reform occurred in 1992 when the parliamentary election produced a situation in which no single party or coalition of parties could claim a majority of the seats in either the Chamber of Deputies or the Senate. A new government was formed, but the party alliance was shaky and lasted less than ten months (Alvarez-Rivera 2007). In response to the crisis, Mario Segni, a member of the former Christian Democratic Party (DC), led a movement for electoral reform and obtained enough petition signatures to force a referendum on the issue. The Italian electorate voted to repeal the 65 percent constituency threshold used in Senate elections. Although the referendum did not speak to the election of the Chamber of Deputies, the 82.7 percent vote in favor of the reform proposal was interpreted as a mandate to overhaul the electoral system in general (Alvarez-Rivera 2007).

In 1993 the parliament passed a law that required the Chamber of Deputies and the Senate to be elected by a combination of plurality and proportional representation methods. Consequently 75 percent of the seats in both chambers would be filled by plurality vote from single-member districts, and the remaining 25 percent of the seats would be allocated to candidates from party lists on a proportional basis. To make the allocation more proportional, the number of votes received by the victor in a single-member district was either fully (in the case of the Senate) or partially (for the Chamber of Deputies) subtracted before distributing the proportional seats ("Italy" 2007).

The 1993 reforms did not produce the desired political stability, with governments lasting slightly more than one year. Small parties such as the Lega Nord (Northern League), the Italian Democratic Socialists, the Federation of Greens, the Italian Communists, and the New Italian Socialist Party were able to obtain proportional representation even when they did not meet the 4 percent PR threshold. Significant policy disagreements among coalition partners proved too difficult to overcome and so no government under the Second Republic (1993 to the present) has been able to remain in office for a full five-year term (Alvarez-Rivera 2007).

In 2005 Silvio Berlusconi, at the end of his four-year term as prime minister, urged a return to proportional representation and pushed this reform through the parliament. Beginning in 2005, members of parliament were selected primarily through a proportional representation system and a closed party list with complex thresholds determining the allocation of seats. A closed list system allows each party or group to develop a list of candidates, and voters are required to choose one list. Seats are awarded to lists in proportion to votes cast. Italy is divided into 26 multimember constituencies plus the single-member constituency district in Aosta and one district representing all Italians living abroad. The average size of constituencies amounts to approximately 22.5 seats. Seat allocation is divided proportionally among party lists that have exceeded thresholds set by Law 270 passed in December 2005 (Cotta and Verzichelli 2007, 92).

Thresholds to obtain representation in the Chamber of Deputies vary, including 2 percent of the national vote for a single party in a coalition, 4 percent for a single party not in a coalition, and 10 percent for a coalition of political parties. Special provisions cover parties that represent linguistic minorities, allowing them to gain representation even if they do not reach the 2 percent threshold. Party coalitions that obtain a plurality of the vote are given a majority bonus or a minimum of 55 percent of all seats. Twelve seats are set aside for the Italian overseas constituency. For a coalition to gain control in the Chamber of Deputies, it must obtain 340 seats. The coalition that receives the highest number of votes receives a majority bonus to bring its allocation of seats to 340, if it has not already reached this number (Cotta and Verzichelli 2007, 92). The remaining seats from the multimember districts are allocated proportionately, based on which lists have the most votes.

The Senate has 315 members, with 302 senators elected from 20 regions under the proportional representation, closed party list system. The constituencies coincide with the 20 regions, thus basing election to the Senate on regional representation. The number of senators who can be elected from each region is set according to the size of the region's population, and the allocation of seats also follows the PR rule with the exceptions of Aosta Valley (with one seat automatically allocated) and Trentino-Alto Adige (with six single-member districts). A single party in a coalition receives 3 percent of seats, a single party not in a coalition receives 8 percent, and party coalitions win 20 percent. Six senators are elected under the first-past-the-post system in one region, and six are elected to represent Italians living overseas. Seven distinguished persons are appointed to serve as so-called senators for life. No threshold is allotted to ethnolinguistic minority parties in the regions. Like the Chamber of Deputies, the Senate employs a majority bonus rule for region-level votes (Cotta and Verzichelli 2007, 92). Many complain that the new system's rules are too complex (Cotta and Verzichelli 2007, 93).

In April 2006 Italy held parliamentary elections under the Berlusconi reforms of 2005. In an AP-Ipsos poll, only 20 percent of respondents said that they were very confident that their votes were counted accurately. Outgoing Premier Berlusconi claimed that voting irregularities affected the electoral outcome. Indeed, the 2006 election was the closest in the nation's history, and 80,000 contested votes were recounted to determine a winner (Fisher 2006). Berlusconi's reforms allowed a center-left coalition to secure majorities in both houses of parliament. Senator Giorgio Napolitano was chosen as president, and he appointed Romano Prodi as prime minister.

A series of corruption scandals in the early 1990s and into the 21st century led to changes in the funding of political parties. Law 195, passed in 1974, allowed political parties to receive state subsidies if they won 2 percent of the vote. In a 1993 national referendum, more than 90 percent of Italian voters expressed disapproval of state subsidies for political parties. In response, state financing of political parties was cut drastically, and candidates were forced to rely more on private financing. Campaign reimbursement replaced campaign subsidies, and political parties were held accountable for the disclosure of campaign spending and contributions. Law 515, passed in 1993, established a proportional distribution of monies to political parties based on the percentage of votes they received, and it required the media to provide equal access to broadcasting time for all candidates and parties. In addition, the 1993 law specified that the media must not publish poll results within 15 days prior to an election. (Feretti 2005).

In 1997 Law 2 established a means for taxpayers to designate a percentage of their income tax to publicly finance political parties and movements in order to supplement the state subsidies if parties did not solicit private contributions. The monies were deposited in a common pool and allocated on the basis of electoral results. All political parties or movements that elected at least one MP in one of the two parliamentary chambers received an allotment from the fund. The law also allowed legal entities a partial tax deduction from their income tax assessment based on their contributions to party funding. Under Law 2, parties must report all contributions and expenditures and provide campaign finance reports to the official gazette and two newspapers, one of which must have national circulation (Ferreti 2005).

In 1999 Law 157 abolished taxpayers' opportunity to permit a small portion of their income tax to be used for party funding, and it reinstituted public financing under what is called electoral reimbursement, allocating funds to parties proportionately to the votes received in an election. Parties receiving at least 1 percent of the vote are entitled to campaign reimbursement. If taxpayers contribute to a party, they receive a 19 percent deduction from their income tax assessments. State-owned companies are prohibited from making contributions (Ferreti 2005).

Expanding on Law 515, Law 28, passed in 2000, requires equal media space for all political subjects. National radio and television stations must provide free space for all campaign messages. However, political entities are limited to broadcasting only two messages per broadcasting unit. All political parties with members in parliament or who have a minimum of two representatives in the European Parliament are eligible for Law 28's benefits (Ferreti 2005). Unlike the regulations placed on the national media, local channels may broadcast paid political messages during election campaigns. If local channels broadcast free political messages, they may request government reimbursement. Newspapers and periodicals are less heavily regulated than radio and television media. They may distribute paid or free campaign advertisements or messages, but they must grant equal access to all candidates and political groups (Perrucci and Villa 2004).

Norway

From the 14th to the early 19th centuries, Denmark governed Norway. In 1814, in the Treaty of Kiel, Denmark, which had been on the losing side in the Napoleonic wars, ceded Norway to Sweden. Although the Norwegians quickly established their own constitution and parliament, the presence of the Swedish army forced Norway to accept the Swedish king as their head of state. Nonetheless, despite the union with Sweden, Norway maintained itself as an independent kingdom. Norway did not become a completely independent nation until 1905 when the Norwegian parliament declared that the union with Sweden was dissolved. When a plebiscite that same year resulted in nearly unanimous support for separation, Sweden agreed to Norway's independence. Norwegians voted in a subsequent plebiscite to establish a constitutional monarchy with a popularly elected parliament.

Bernt Aardal (2002) identifies five distinct eras in the history of Norwegian elections. The first period began in 1814 with the country's semi-independence from Sweden. The constitution adopted in that year granted the vote to three groups of citizens: civil servants, peasants who owned land or who had rented land for at least five years, and urban residents who owned property valued over a certain amount. Under these limitations, approximately 45 percent of the adult male population (10 to 11 percent of the overall population) possessed the franchise. This percentage at the time represented the most extensive right to vote among Western European nations (Aardal 2002, 174). Voters cast indirect ballots to select representatives in the national parliament (the Storting) by choosing electors from single- and multi-member districts by plurality vote. These electors then would elect the representatives to the Storting. The justification for this indirect system of election was that the interest of the nation rather than narrow self-interest would more likely influence the choice of representatives. This justification is roughly comparable to the original rationale for the system of electing the U.S. president by a relatively small group of electors. The development of political parties in the 1880s placed pressure on the system of indirect election, which could lead to highly disproportionate results, with one party gaining far more seats in the parliament than would be justified by the proportion of popular votes received (Aardal 2002, 180).

In 1905 the passage of a constitutional amendment introduced direct elections using single-member districts, thus establishing the second electoral era. The following year, additional legislation resulted in the formation of 41 urban districts and 82 rural districts, each of which elected one representative to the parliament (Aardal 2002, 183). The electoral system provided for a runoff election if no candidate received a majority on the first ballot. In 1917 the Storting established a new electoral commission to develop proposals for electoral reform. As a result, in 1919 the Storting approved a constitutional amendment establishing a proportional representation system with multimember districts. The final legislation was passed in 1920, thus preparing the way for the third electoral era. The new system benefited the Labor Party and achieved a level of representation for minority parties, at the same time guaranteeing the status of the older rural parties through overrepresentation of those regions of the country (Aardal 2002, 189).

Following World War II, during which Germany had occupied Norway, the Storting, led by the Labor Party, agreed to consider electoral reform once again. The resulting fourth electoral system, instituted in 1952, established new electoral districts, but maintained the electoral advantage of the rural areas. Therefore, not only political parties and population, but also territory (Norway's 19 counties), continued to gain representation in the parliament (Aardal 2002, 193). Although the electoral fortunes of small parties improved after 1952, they remained dissatisfied with the continuing disproportionality in election results compared to other European democracies. Reforms in 1988 established the fifth electoral system by introducing eight adjustment seats to the existing 157 seats in the Storting, which are allocated among 19 districts and distributed among the political parties receiving at least 4 percent of the national vote (Aardal 2002, 199). However, the small political parties remained dissatisfied with the number of adjustment seats. In 1997 the government established a new electoral reform commission that offered recommendations to streamline the electoral system. Commission proposals submitted to the Storting in 2002 would increase the number of adjustment seats, thus augmenting proportionality in the electoral system.

Electoral reform in Norway historically has balanced concerns with political party and group representation with geographical representation. Aardal (2002, 215) comments that the geographical distribution of seats in parliament advantages "the periphery" at the expense of "the central areas." Despite calls for reform, the cleavage has persisted in Norwegian politics and the overrepresentation of peripheral areas has continued to have popular support. In addition to territorial conflict, the history of Norwegian politics, including the development of electoral systems, has been influenced by sociocultural conflict, religious differences, and economic conflict between consumers and producers and between employers and employees (Aardal 2002, 170).

Norway holds elections every other year, with the selection of Storting members alternating with the filling of local offices. Therefore, each type of election is held every four years. The parliament, composed of 169 representatives, is unicameral. Norway is divided into 19 counties, each of which elects multiple representatives through a list system of proportional representation. A party must receive at least 4 percent of the popular vote nationwide to be eligible for gaining representation in the Storting. Nineteen seats—one for each county—are reserved for adjustments in representation. The number of representatives each county sends to the Storting is based on both the number of inhabitants as well as its geographical size. One result is that Norway's measure of disproportionality on Gallagher's index— 3.4—is slightly higher than two other Scandinavian countries— Denmark and Sweden—which have especially low measures of disproportionality (Gallagher, Laver, and Mair 2006, 364). The index is calculated by taking the difference between the percentage of the popular vote and the percentage of seats for each political party, dividing the sum of the differences by two, and finding the square root of the result. The index varies between 0 and 100, with higher values indicating greater, and lower values less, disproportionality in representation

Although Norwegian citizenship is one of the qualifications for voting, those who have lived in Norway for at least three years may vote in local elections. In 1898 universal manhood suffrage had been introduced and the voting age set at 25, which increased to approximately 20 percent the proportion of the population who had achieved the right to vote. Beginning in 1907, women who owned property and had a minimum income were granted the right to vote. The first woman member of the Storting gained election as an alternate in 1909 and won a seat in 1911 (Aardal 2002, 177). Women received the right to vote in 1913, seven years before passage of the Nineteenth Amendment to the U.S. Constitution granting woman suffrage. The voting age was lowered to 23 in 1921, to 21 in 1949, to 20 in 1969, and to 18 in 1979. The average turnout since 1945 is approximately 80 percent. Voter turnout since the 1950s has remained high, particularly relative to the United States. Average voter turnout reached a peak in the 1980s (83.1 percent). More recently (2000–2004), turnout averaged 75.5 percent (Gallagher, Laver, and Mair 2006, 291).

Of the eight countries considered in this chapter, Norway is the only one that is not a member of the European Union. Voters rejected membership in two national referenda: a 1972 referendum rejecting membership in the European Committee and a 1994 referendum rejecting membership in the European Union. Other referenda include two in 1905: one dissolving the union with Sweden and the second selecting Prince Charles of Denmark as the Norwegian king. Referenda in 1919 and 1926 were held on the issue of prohibition.

Poland

In many ways Poland is unique among the Eastern European countries. Prior to post–World War II Soviet domination, the country had a democratic tradition that can be traced back to the 16th century. Although its democratic practices applied only to nobility, Poland still was one of the more liberal governments in Europe. After World War I, Poland instigated another democratic experiment, allowing numerous small political parties to obtain representation in the parliament. This experiment failed when the parliament was so fragmented that a stalemate resulted. In 1926 Marsh Josef Pilsudski fostered a coup d'état, after which Pilsudski ruled despotically until his death in 1935 (Derleth 1999, 255).

After World War II, the Communist Party gained a monopoly on political power. Although Poland exhibited many of the classic characteristics of a communist-dominated system, it was different from the other Soviet-ruled countries. The Catholic Church to some extent remained a force independent of the Communist Party, small independent family businesses still thrived in gray or black markets, and periodic expressions of social discontent were relatively frequent. The Solidarity Movement in 1980 highlighted the weaknesses of communist rule. Thus, Poland was able to evolve from a repressive dictatorial political system into a softened but still corrupt form of authoritarianism (Millard 1999, 6–7).

Characterized as the most rebellious of the former Soviet-dominated countries, Poland formed an opposition strategy that contributed significantly to the downfall of communism (Dryzek and Holmes 2002, 225). Solidarity arose as a workers' rights movement that pressured government for the right to organize and strike. The failure of communists to respond to worker discontent ultimately led to democratic reform and free elections.

During the transition to a postcommunist democracy, Poland moved toward the West. After first holding open elections in 1991, Poland joined the North Atlantic Treaty Organization (NATO) in 1999 and became a member nation in the European Union in 2004, further indicating its Western leanings ("Nations in Transit—Poland" 2006).

Constitutional changes were delayed for eight years, between 1989 and 1997, because the idea of limited government was relatively new to Polish society, the political parties disagreed about what should be included in the new constitution, and the constitutional status of the Catholic Church and related issues remained unresolved. The 1997 constitution established a presidential-parliamentary democracy (Derleth 1999, 279), creating a president (head of state), a prime minister (head of government), a bicameral National Assembly (the Sejm and the Senate), a supreme court along with provincial and local courts, and a constitutional tribunal. The constitution also provided for checks and balances among the president, the prime minister, and the parliament ("Background Note: Poland" 2007).

Poland's semidemocratic elections of 1989 were heavily weighted to the advantage of the Communist Party; 35 percent of seats in the parliament were allotted to free voting and 65 percent were reserved for the communists. The first truly open elections since World War II occurred in 1991, beginning Poland's difficult journey into democracy (Kwiatkowska 2006).

Poland's constitutional reforms demonstrate that the framers identified with a number of Western traditions and fully intended to establish a parliamentary democracy. Parliamentary members in the lower house, the Sejm, are elected on the basis of proportional representation from closed lists. Members of the upper house, the Senate, are elected from two- or three-member winner-take-all districts. Since becoming a democracy, the Polish parliament has experienced a deep partisan divide and has had difficulties forming stable governing coalitions. With 29 parties gaining representation in 1991, coalition building was of utmost importance. In later elections, about six parties emerged to represent a broad spectrum of views. Because much of the competition occurs among parties who share the same ideological outlook, parties form around personalities, making coalition building and party agreements even more difficult (Kwiatkowska 2006).

In 1993 Poland established the universal right to vote for citizens at least 18 years of age. Voters cast ballots in referenda as well as for the president and representatives in the National Assembly. Voters choose their representatives directly (Kwiatkowska 2006, 3).

As in other countries, citizens who have been judged legally incapacitated due to mental illness or retardation may not vote. Disabled citizens may vote at polling places and request assistance from another individual, as long as the person offering assistance is not a poll observer. To maximize voting opportunities, hospitals and nursing homes with at least 50 residents are permitted to establish polling places. Unlike the United States and other nations, Poland allows voters in prison and detention centers to vote at polling stations set up for them ("Poland" n.d.).

Since Poland started holding democratic parliamentary elections in 1991, voter turnout reached a low level (40.6 percent) in the 2005 election after achieving a high of 52.1 percent in 1993. The decline in voter turnout in Poland is linked to lack of interest in civic affairs, voter alienation and mistrust of political parties that fail to fulfill their promises, and a misunderstanding of how to use the vote effectively under the current electoral system (Kwiatkowska 2006, 2).

The Polish electoral system has relied on two different methods for allocating parliamentary seats in the Sejm, which consists of 460 members. In 2005 Poland used the d'Hondt formula for allocating seats. The d'Hondt method divides the number of votes for each party by divisors equal to the number of seats allocated to the parties plus some constant. Prior to 2005 Poland used the Sainte-Laguë method, which results in more proportional representation and allows small parties to obtain more seats in parliament (Kwiatkowska 2006, 5). To gain representation in the Sejm, a political party must reach a 5 percent threshold of support, and those with preelection coalitions must obtain 8 percent. The threshold requirement often reduces the number of parties that gain representation. In 2005, for example, the two major parties received 34 percent and 29 percent of the seats, with 37 percent of the seats being divided among the six remaining parties that met the threshold requirement (Kwiatkowska 2006, 3). Of the 19 political parties contesting elections, six won seats in the Sejm.

The Senate, consisting of 100 members, oversees the work of the Sejm and may veto its bills. Unlike the Sejm, members of the Senate are selected from multimember districts using a winner-take-all, at-large system. Voters are allowed to vote for as many seats as there are seats to be filled (usually two or three) (Kwiatkowska 2006, 3). In 2005 83 percent of the seats in the Senate were allocated to two major parties, which supports the conventional wisdom that voters will back political parties with better chances of winning pluralities (Kwiatkowska 2006, 4).

Experiencing great increases in national election expenditures between 1990 and 2000, Poland instituted limits on the campaign expenditures of political parties and individual candidates in both parliamentary and presidential elections. The government also limits the amount of time candidates can devote to paid advertising, ruling that purchased time may not exceed 15 percent of the free airtime allocated to parties or candidates. The government does not permit individuals or groups not registered as candidates to spend more than a specified amount of money. Any campaigning that is done without election committee approval is deemed an independent expenditure (Walecki 2003, 73). Poland's efforts to limit the role of money in the political system do not appear to have been effective. The complex nature of the rules makes it difficult to ascertain how much money is actually spent. Although the government prohibits donations to political campaigns from corporations, foundations, and associations, it still has not been able to stop what has come to be called the political arms race (Walecki 2003, 77).

Charging membership fees is a common tool for party financing in Western Europe. However, in Central and Eastern European countries, especially those engaged in the postcommunist transition, party membership subscriptions were significantly lower than those raised in the West. Party taxes, a 1998 reform in Poland, require that elected or appointed party members pay a fixed percentage of their salaries to the party. These taxes apply to the 560 members of the parliament, hundreds of party members serving in government positions, members of supervisory boards, and thousands of local council members. The amount can range between 5 and 10 percent of one's salary. An estimated $4 million to $7 million are raised through the party taxes (Walecki 2003, 80). State subsidies to political parties were introduced in 1993. Public subsidies in 1997 constituted about 5 percent of party income. In 2001 more substantial public financing was introduced, increasing the amount that parties can receive through state subsidies (Walecki 2003, 84).

Parties also receive indirect government subsidies, including free airtime to broadcast their election programs. Election committees may purchase airtime on public and nonpublic radio and television stations up to a specified amount. Rates for political broadcasts cannot exceed 50 percent of those charged for commercial advertising. This free airtime aids small political parties that might otherwise be locked out of the opportunity to broadcast their political messages (Walecki 2003, 85).

Sweden

Democratic politics evolved in Sweden during the late 19th century with the establishment of popular movements that advocated specific causes, including groups supporting labor, temperance, consumer protection, and nonconformism (religious worship independent of the state church). By 1918 universal suffrage had been established for both men and women (Herz 1972, 26). The Social Democratic Party, founded in 1884, came to power in 1932 and, with few exceptions, governed the country for the remainder of the 20th century.

Bo Särlvik (2002) identifies six electoral eras in Swedish politics, beginning with the abolition of a four-estate parliament (Riksdag) in 1866. In the first (1866–1887) and second (1890–1908) electoral systems, the parliament was altered to include two houses, the First Chamber and the Second Chamber. Although those who at the time had gained the right to vote chose the Second Chamber members in general elections, county councils and cities elected the First Chamber members indirectly (Särlvik 2002, 232). An estimated 22 percent of males at least 21 years of age satisfied the property qualification for voting. As incomes gradually increased, a larger proportion of the male population became eligible to vote, reaching 35 percent by 1908 (Särlvik 2002, 232). The decision to alter electoral rules was made in 1909, thus leading to the third electoral era beginning in 1911, with Conservative Party leaders supporting a proportional representation system to preserve their representation in the Second Chamber and as a check on unrestricted majority rule with the introduction of more extensive suffrage rights. Särlvik (2002, 240) notes that a three-party system developed in Sweden before the introduction of proportional representation but that, by the 1917 election, five parties were competing for votes.

By 1921, with the passage of legislative measures to further democratize the political process, a fourth electoral era had emerged. Weighted voting based on income for county council and local government district elections was eliminated, and women gained the right to vote (Särlvik 2002, 241). However, as a concession to conservatives, the Left parties agreed to increase to 23 the voting age for Second Chamber elections, and the term of office for First Chamber representatives was increased from six to eight years. Not until 1945 was the voting age reduced to 21 for Second Chamber and for county and city council elections. To increase the level of proportionality among the parties, the number of constituencies was decreased from 56 to 28.

By 1952 changes had been made in the proportional representation system that constituted a shift to a fifth electoral system. Because the Sainte-Laguë formula, which replaced the d'Hondt system for the proportional allocation of legislative seats, tended to favor small parties, particularly the Communists, the system of seat allocation was modified to underrepresent small parties. The election of both chambers had become more democratic, even though representatives to the First Chamber continued to be elected indirectly (Särlvik 2002, 249). The sixth electoral era was ushered in by a constitutional change in 1969 that replaced the two-chamber parliament with one chamber of 350 members. Membership subsequently was reduced to 349 to avoid tie votes. The new electoral era brought a higher level of instability, with seven parties gaining parliamentary seats (Särlvik 2002, 259). Additional changes included lengthening terms of office from three to four years and allowing voters to express a candidate preference on the party lists. Särlvik (2002, 262) suggests that campaigning will continue to occur largely on public service television, that, in contrast to the United States, the main focus will continue to be on national party leaders, even with the introduction of preference voting allowing voters to cast a personal vote for a party candidate, and that no significant individual candidate fund-raising will occur.

Sweden holds four types of general election to select representatives to the national parliament (Riksdag), to municipal councils, to county councils, and to the European Parliament. Elections to the Riksdag and to the municipal and county councils are held every four years on the third Sunday in September ("Elections in Sweden: The Way It's Done!" 2006, 3). Sweden joined the European Union in 1995 and therefore takes part in elections to the European Parliament, which are held by all member states in June every five years.

Sweden employs the list system, a variation of the proportional representation system, to elect representatives. The Riksdag may call for an election at other times besides the four-year interval, which must occur within three months of the official decision. In addition to general elections, the Riksdag may hold two types of referenda: consultative and constitutional. Municipalities and county councils also may schedule referenda. During the 20th century, Sweden held just five national referenda, the most significant one occurring in 1994 when voters narrowly approved the country's entry into the European Union. In 2003 voters rejected a proposal to join the European Economic and Monetary Union (EMU) (Gallagher, Laver, and Mair 2006, 375). In the United States neither a national referendum nor an election to select representatives to an international body could occur under the present constitution. Sanford Levinson (2006), in his call for a hypothetical national referendum on the U.S. Constitution to correct what he considers fatal flaws in that document, suggests what in reality is a constitutional impossibility.

The right to vote in elections for representatives to the Riksdag is granted to Swedish citizens who are at least 18 years of age on election day and who are or have been registered residents in Sweden ("Elections in Sweden: The Way It's Done!" 2006, 4). To vote in a county council or municipal council election, individuals must be registered within the county council or municipal area in which they wish to cast their ballot. Unlike the United States, where voter registration is largely the responsibility of each citizen, government officials in Sweden establish a roll in each electoral district. Swedish citizens living outside Sweden for fewer than 10 years have the right to vote. Prior to an election, the national Election Authority prepares the rolls of voters and sends a voting card to each person who is eligible to vote. Advance (early) voting begins 18 days before the election, a practice similar to that in many U.S. states.

Each political party prepares a list of candidates for the Riksdag in the order in which they will be selected following the election. The election determines the number of seats awarded to each party based on the party's proportion of the vote. Reflecting a preference for local autonomy, county-level conventions, composed of delegates from the party's local organizations, select candidates to appear on the party list. Each party offers a list of candidates in each constituency, which normally contains as many candidates as there are seats to be filled in the district (constituency). Following the election, the seats are distributed among the parties according to an established formula. Nationally, a total of 349 seats are filled by a parliamentary election; 310 of these are categorized as permanent constituency seats that are distributed by county, and 39 are so-called adjustment seats, which are distributed based on a party's total proportion of the vote nationwide. The adjustment seats assure greater congruity between a party's proportion of the total vote and its proportion of legislative seats. A similar procedure is used in county elections, with 90 percent of the representation based on permanent constituency seats and 10 percent from adjustment seats ("Elections in Sweden: The Way It's Done!" 2006, 7). Elections for the municipal council involve only permanent seats. As for elections to the European Parliament, Swedish voters selected 19 representatives in 2004 and will select 18 in 2009.

Voting is done with paper ballots, which are prepared by the political parties. Parties that received at least 1 percent of the votes nationally in one of the two most recent Riksdag elections are eligible to have the ballot papers printed free of charge with the names of the candidates ("Elections in Sweden: The Way It's Done!" 2006, 8). Two alternative ballot papers are made available, one of which presents just the party's name; the second is blank and allows the voter to write in a party name. Election officials make the party ballot papers available at polling stations. At the polling place, each voter not personally known to election officials presents proof of identity. After casting their ballots, voters place a ballot paper for each election in an envelope, and then deposit each envelope in the appropriate ballot box. Individuals who are ill, have a physical disability, or are institutionalized may have their votes delivered by a messenger appointed by the local election committee. Those who are eligible to vote but who are living outside the country may vote by mail. Any persons who have voted in advance of election day may change their vote by appearing at the polling place on election day and casting a substitute ballot. In addition to voting for a party, voters may indicate a preference for one of the party candidates listed on the ballot, a process that can lead to the election of a candidate lower on the list of party candidates. This practice was introduced in 1998 and has had an effect on which candidates gain a seat in the Riksdag. In the 2002 election, nearly 26 percent of voters indicated a candidate preference, and approximately 10 candidates were elected based on personal votes.

The ballots are counted on election night. The Election Authority announces a provisional distribution of seats among the parties and presents a final count the Wednesday following the election. The permanent seats are allocated according to the number of votes each party receives in each constituency, and then seats are allocated to particular candidates according to preference votes and order of names on the party ballot. A party that receives at least 12 percent of the vote in a constituency can take part in the distribution of permanent constituency seats even though it fails the 4 percent nationwide threshold.

Election turnout in Sweden is high relative to the United States. Turnout for Riksdag elections was 88.1 percent in 1994, 81.4 percent in 1998, and 80.1 percent in 2002. The average voter turnout in Sweden over 18 parliamentary elections is 86 percent. This higher voter turnout pattern prevailed until the parliamentary elections in 1988 and 2002. The highest voter turnout in Sweden came in 1976 when almost 92 percent of registered voters went to the polls. Turnout in those years for county council and municipality seats were slightly lower, and turnout for representation in the European Parliament was significantly lower (41.6 percent in 1995, 38.8 percent in 1999, and 37.9 percent in 2004).

As Duverger's law (single-member district plurality systems of election tend to favor a two-party system) would lead us to expect, Sweden's use of proportional representation rather than the single-member district plurality system to elect representatives at the national, county, and municipal levels has led to the success of several political parties. The Social Democratic Party overall has had the greatest electoral success, but at least five other parties play significant roles in Swedish electoral politics: the Center Party, the Christian Democratic Party, the Ecology (Green) Party, the Left Party (formerly the Communist Party), and the Moderates (Conservatives). The Swedish electoral system results in highly proportional outcomes for the parties. In the 2006 Riksdag election, the Social Democrats won 33 percent of the vote and 37.2 percent of seats, the Moderates received 26.2 percent of the vote and 27.8 percent of seats, and five smaller parties correspondingly received percentages of Riksdag seats that closely mirrored their percentages of support in the electorate ("Riksdag Election Result 2006" 2006).

These results indicate a very close relationship between support in the general electorate and the proportion of seats that each party won. According to Gallagher, Laver, and Mair (2006,

364), Sweden's disproportionality score (measured on a scale from 0 to 100) is 1.8, one of the lower and hence more proportional scores of the 28 countries for which measures are provided. The proportion of women members of parliament (45 percent) is the highest of any of the 28 countries.

As in parliamentary systems in general, the electorate does not choose a chief executive directly. In Sweden, the speaker of the Riksdag, after consulting with the party leaders in the legislature, nominates a prime minister. If at least half of the membership approves of the nomination, the individual is elected. Once approved, the prime minister selects cabinet members, who are not subject to legislative confirmation (Gallagher, Laver, and Mair 2006, 39).

References

Aardal, Bernt. "Electoral Systems in Norway." In Bernard Grofman and Arend Lijphart, eds. *The Evolution of Electoral and Party Systems in the Nordic Countries.* New York: Agathon, 2002: 167–224

Alvarez-Rivera, Manuel. Election Resources on the Internet. 2007. electionresources.org

"Background Note: Poland." U.S. Department of State. 2007. www.state .gov/r/pa/ei/bgn/2875.htm

BritainUSA: Britain at Your Fingertips. No date. www.britainusa.com

Cotta, Maurizio, and Luca Verzichelli. *Political Institutions of Italy.* New York: Oxford University Press, 2007

Derleth, J. William. *The Transition in Central and Eastern European Politics.* Upper Saddle River, NJ: Prentice Hall, 1999

Druck, Helmut. "Germany." In Bernd-Peter Lange and David Ward, eds. *The Media and Elections: A Handbook and Comparative Study.* Mahwah, NJ: Lawrence Erlbaum Associates, 2004

Dryzek, John S., and Leslie T. Holmes. *Post-Communist Democratization: Political Discourses across Thirteen Countries.* New York: Cambridge University Press, 2002

"Elections and Referenda." France in Australia. 2002. www.ambafrance-au.org/article.php3?id_article=446

"Elections in Sweden: The Way It's Done!" Swedish Election Authority. 2006. www.val.se/pdf/electionsinsweden.pdf

"Electoral System: MMP Parliamentary Elections." International Institute for Democracy and Electoral Assistance. 2007. www.idea.int/vt/country_view.cfm?CountryCode=DE

"Electoral System of Germany." Welcome to germanculture.com. No date. www.germanculture.com/ua/library/facts/bl_electoral_system.htm

Electronic Voting and Democracy. No date. www.electronic-vote.org

Elklit, Jørgen. "The Politics of Electoral System Development and Change: The Danish Case." In Bernard Grofman and Arend Lijphart, eds. *The Evolution of Electoral and Party Systems in the Nordic Countries.* New York: Agathon, 2002

Elklit, Jørgen, and Anne Birte Pade. "Parliamentary Elections and Election Administration in Denmark." 1996. www.folketinget.dk/BAGGRUND/00000048/00232623.htm

Ferretti, Maria Paola. 2005. "Country Reports on Political Corruption and Party Financing: Italy." www.transparency.org/content/download/5460/31873/file/political_corruption_party_financing_italy.pdf

"First Past the Post." History Learning Site. No date. www.historylearningsite.co.uk/first_past_the_post.htm

Fisher, Ian. "Berlusconi Is Set Back But Won't Concede." *International Herald Tribune,* April 14, 2006. www.iht.com/articles/2006/04/14/news/italy.php

"France: Electoral System." International Parliamentary Union. 2007. www.ipu.org/praline-e/reports/2113_B.htm

Gallagher, Michael, Michael Laver, and Peter Mair. *Representative Government in Modern Europe.* New York: McGraw-Hill, 2006

"Germany: Electoral System." Inter-Parliamentary Union. No date. www.ipu.org/praline-e/reports/2121_B.htm

"Germany: The Original Mixed Member Proportional System." ACE Electoral Knowledge Network. No date. www/aceproject.org/ace-en/topics/es/esy/esy_de/

Herz, Ulrich. "Sweden Yesterday and Today." In Per-Axel Hildeman, ed. *Profile of Sweden.* Stockholm: Bonniers, 1972

Hill, Steven, and Guillaume Serina. Guerrilla News Network. 2007. "France's Presidential Election Method Is Flawed." gnn.tv/articles/3029/France_s_Presidential_Election_Method_is_Flawed.

"How British Elections Work." *Time,* November 5, 1951. www.time.com/time/magazine/printout/0,8816,856939,00.html

Islam, Ranty. "Voting Machines Still Rare in Germany." *Deutsche Welle,* June 9, 2005. www.dw-world.de/popups/popup_printcontent/0,169774 6,00.htm

"Italy." *Encyclopaedia Britannica.* Encyclopaedia Britannica Online. 2007. www.britannica.com/eb/article–258799.

Kwiatkowska, Inga. "International Snapshot: Poland—Parliamentary Elections, September 2005." 2006. www.fairvote.org.

Levinson, Sanford. *Our Undemocratic Constitution: Where the Constitution Goes Wrong (And How We the People Can Correct It).* New York: Oxford University Press, 2006

Millard, Francis. *Polish Politics and Society.* New York: Routledge, 1999

"Nations in Transit—Poland." Freedom House. 2006. www.freedom-house.org

Niemoller, Kees. "Appendix 2K: Experience with Voting Machines in the Netherlands and Germany." No date. www.cev.ie/htm/report/first _report/pdf/Appendix 2K.pdf

Norton, Bruce F. *Politics in Britain.* Washington, DC: CQ Press, 2007

Parigi, Paolo, and Peter Bearman. "Spaghetti Politics." Working Paper 06–05. New York: Columbia University Institute for Social and Economic Research and Policy, 2006

Perrucci, Teresa, and Marina Villa. "Italy." In Bernd-Peter Lange and David Ward, eds. *The Media and Elections: A Handbook and Comparative Study.* Mahwah, NJ: Lawrence Erlbaum Associates, 2004

"Poland." No date. www.electionaccess.org

"Riksdag Election Result 2006." Swedish Election Authority. 2006. www .val.se/in_english/index.html

Roberts, Geoffrey K. *German Politics Today.* Manchester, UK: Manchester University Press, 2000

Rose, Richard, and Neil Munro. *Elections and Parties in the New European Democracies.* Washington, DC: CQ Press, 2003

Saalfeld, Thomas. "Germany: Stability and Strategy in a Mixed-Member Proportional System." In Michael Gallagher and Paul Mitchell, eds. *The Politics of Electoral Systems.* New York: Oxford University Press, 2005: 209–27

Särlvik, Bo. "Party and Electoral System in Sweden." In Bernard Grofman and Arend Lijphart, eds. *The Evolution of Electoral and Party Systems in the Nordic Countries.* New York: Agathon, 2002

Transparency International. 2001. www.transparency.org

Von Alemann, Ulrich. "Party Finance, Party Donations, and Corruption." 2000. www.transparency.org/content/download/155131167317

Von Brockel, Jan. "Elections in Germany—One Year Earlier than Expected." Elections 2005 in Germany. 2007. www.janvonbroeckel.de /english/electoralsystem.html

"Voter Turnout in Western Europe Since 1945: A Regional Report." International Institute for Democracy and Electoral Assistance. 2004. Stockholm: International IDEA. www.idea.int/publications/voter_turnout _weurope/upload/Full-Report.pdf

Walecki, Marcin. 2003. *Money and Politics in Poland: A New Democracy in Comparative Perspective.* PhD thesis. New York: Oxford University Press.

4

Chronology

This chapter tracks the significant progress that has been made throughout American history to extend the right to vote to all adult citizens and to improve the electoral system and its representativeness. We have included events that decidedly represent steps backward for voting rights. For instance, during the last decades of the 19th century, while states outside the South were generally expanding voting rights, Southern states instituted provisions to restrict African Americans' access to the ballot box. We have also included periods in the history of campaigns and elections during which fraud and corruption played a notable role. The chronology of campaign and election reform is by no means complete, for measures continue to be urged, including further regulation of campaign contributions and spending, the enhancement of citizen representation through the establishment of alternative voting systems, and increased assurance of ballot integrity, especially with the introduction of new voting machine technologies.

1787   The delegates at the Constitutional Convention in Philadelphia decide to leave voting qualifications to the individual states because such qualifications vary considerably from state to state. Delegates do not agree on the method of electing the president until the closing days of the Convention. The president will be elected by states, with each state possessing as many electors as it has representatives and senators in Congress. Each elector will be granted two votes for president. The candidate who receives the most votes, assuming that this is a majority of the votes, will be

1787 *(cont.)*	elected president, and the candidate with the second-highest number of electoral votes will be elected vice president.
1796	Under the original provisions of the electoral college, in which the candidate with the highest number of electoral votes is elected president and the candidate with the second highest total is elected vice president, John Adams and Thomas Jefferson, leaders of rival political factions, become president and vice president respectively. These election results indicate that the electoral college requires revision.
1800	Thomas Jefferson and Aaron Burr receive the same number of electoral votes. The framers of the Constitution, when establishing the method of electing the president, did not foresee the development of political parties. The Democratic-Republican Party leadership designated Jefferson the party's presidential candidate and Burr the vice presidential candidate. However, electors who support this party cannot distinguish between a vote for president and a vote for vice president. Therefore the two candidates receive the same number of ballots for president.
1801	Due to the electoral college tie, the House of Representatives, after 35 ballots, elects Thomas Jefferson the next president. Aaron Burr becomes the vice president.
1804	Due to the dilemma raised by the outcome of the 1800 election, the Twelfth Amendment, which alters the method of electing the president, is ratified. Electors now will cast distinct ballots for president and vice president.
1812	The term "gerrymandering"—the redrawing of election district boundaries to advantage one party or group and disadvantage others—is coined. When the Massachusetts legislature creates an oddly shaped district with the grudging acquiescence of Gov. Elbridge Gerry, Elkanah Tinsdale draws a cartoon of the

district with the shape of a salamander superimposed over it, calling the district a gerrymander. The term soon becomes a part of the American political vocabulary.

1824 With five candidates running for the presidency, no presidential hopeful receives the necessary majority of the electoral vote in the November balloting. Choosing from among the top three candidates, the House of Representatives elects Adams president.

1825 After considerable deal making, the House of Representatives on February 9 elects John Quincy Adams president of the United States, even though Jackson led in both popular and electoral votes. With each state having one vote, Adams is elected by a majority of one state (13 votes for Adams, 7 for Jackson, and 4 for Crawford). The Jackson backers believe they have been cheated out of the presidency.

1828 Backers of John Quincy Adams and Andrew Jackson introduce questionable tactics into the presidential campaign. For instance, Adams, who used his own funds to acquire a billiard table for the White House, is accused of purchasing gaming tables with public money, and Jackson's opponents recount stories of his supposed premarital relations with Mrs. Jackson.

1831 The Anti-Masonic Party becomes the first political party to nominate a presidential candidate by the convention method. The minor party does not last, but the convention replaces the unpopular congressional caucus as the accepted method for nominating presidential candidates.

1832 The Democratic Party for the first time uses the convention method of nomination, selecting a vice presidential candidate to run with Jackson, who is the party's obvious presidential nominee.

1839 The Whig Party introduces into the Senate the first bill designed to regulate campaign finance. Under its

1839 *(cont.)*	provisions, no federal employees shall provide any funds for the election of national or state political officials. The measure fails.
1840	The Whigs win the presidency from incumbent Democratic president Martin Van Buren by nominating the war hero of Tippecanoe fame, William Henry Harrison, and John Tyler as his vice presidential running mate. The Whigs have no platform, avoid issues, and appeal to the emotions of the voters. The jingle "Tippecanoe and Tyler too" becomes part of American political folklore.
1845	Congress determines a uniform date on which all states will choose presidential electors: "on the Tuesday next after the first Monday in November, in every fourth year."
1848	Some of the women who attended the Anti-Slavery Convention in London in 1840 organize a meeting in Seneca Falls, New York, to call for woman suffrage.
1856	Religion becomes an issue in the dirty politics of the presidential campaign. The Know-Nothings, a political party movement opposed to the immigration of Roman Catholics, accuse Republican candidate John C. Frémont, an Episcopalian, of Catholic sympathies. Such pamphlets as *Frémont's Romanism Established* and *The Romanish Intrigue: Frémont a Catholic* are circulated among the electorate.
1867	On January 7 Congress passes a bill that grants blacks the right to vote in the District of Columbia. Congress subsequently overrides President Andrew Johnson's veto of the legislation. On January 10 Congress enacts legislation granting the right to vote to blacks in the territories. On March 2 Congress passes the Military Reconstruction Act, which provides for the governance of the

former Confederate states and their reentrance into the Union. Former slaves must be given the right to vote in elections to select delegates for constitutional conventions, and the new state constitutions must guarantee them suffrage rights.

On March 23 Congress enacts legislation that specifies the criteria for voter registration in the Southern states to determine who can vote in elections to select delegates to constitutional conventions. Blacks are enfranchised under this legislation.

Congress passes the Naval Appropriations Act, which includes a provision prohibiting any officer or government employee from asking a Navy yard worker to contribute funds for political purposes. A worker shall not be discharged for expressing political views.

1869   The National Woman Suffrage Association is established to further the fight for the right of women to vote. Elizabeth Cady Stanton becomes the president and Susan B. Anthony the vice president.

The American Woman Suffrage Association is formed later in the year, led by Lucy Stone. Unlike the National Woman Suffrage Association, whose leaders focus on a national policy, this more conservative organization prefers to follow a state-by-state strategy in winning the right to vote.

1870   The Fifteenth Amendment gains ratification, declaring that "the right of citizens of the United States to vote shall not be denied or abridged by the United States or by any State on account of race, color, or previous condition of servitude." Despite this amendment, black citizens find it increasingly difficult to exercise the right to vote.

Congress passes the Enforcement Act, which specifies criminal penalties for anyone who violates the constitutional right to vote.

1871   The Force Act establishes an enforcement mechanism to protect the right to vote that involves the appointment of federal officers to oversee elections.

A federal court in South Carolina (*United States v. Crosby*) refuses to punish those who employed intimidation to prevent a black man from going to the polls. Because the intimidation occurred on the black man's premises, the court rules the national Constitution and federal legislation do not apply.

1872   Susan B. Anthony, an avid supporter of woman suffrage, votes in the presidential election. She is arrested two weeks later and found guilty of violating a federal law against illegal voting. Anthony refuses to pay a modest fine, but the judge does not require her imprisonment, thus preventing her from appealing to the Supreme Court on a writ of habeas corpus. Nationally sanctioned woman suffrage is not achieved for nearly 50 years.

Congress enacts a provision requiring a secret ballot for electing members to the U.S. House of Representatives.

1874   A court in Kentucky (*United States v. Reese*) establishes a very narrow interpretation of the Fifteenth Amendment that makes it extremely difficult to demonstrate race as the motive for denying suffrage.

Congress establishes a uniform date for electing members of the U.S. House of Representatives, which in presidential election years coincides with the date for electing presidential electors: "the Tuesday next after the first Monday in November, in every even numbered year."

1876   Democratic presidential candidate Samuel Tilden receives more popular votes and is the apparent electoral vote winner over Rutherford B. Hayes, but Republican strategists take advantage of conflicting returns from three Southern states to challenge the results.

The U.S. Supreme Court, in *United States v. Reese* and *United States v. Cruikshank*, quashes indictments under the Enforcement Act of 1870 and the Force Act of 1871, claiming that the federal government has exceeded its authority. By its decisions, the Court has seriously weakened crucial sections of the legislation intended to protect the voting rights of blacks.

1877   Congress establishes an electoral commission in January to resolve the conflicting electoral vote returns in the 1876 presidential election. Composed of 15 persons, the commission decides the winner of the disputed 1876 presidential election along strict party lines. The eight Republicans overrule the seven Democrats and grant all contested electoral votes to Hayes, thus giving the Republican candidate a one-vote victory. Tempers run high, but violence is avoided. For a generation, resentful Democrats consider the election to have been stolen by the Republicans.

In the Compromise of 1877, Southern Democrats agree to accept the election commission decision in return for the withdrawal of federal troops from the South and a relaxation of the federal guarantee of voting rights. The compromise results in the increasing exclusion of Southern blacks from the electorate.

1881   A federal court in Indiana rules that no violation of national law has occurred in denying a citizen, white or black, the right to vote in a state election.

1882   South Carolina enacts the so-called Eight Box Law, which creates eight categories of election with eight separate ballot boxes. The measure is intended to disfranchise illiterate blacks.

1883   Congress passes the Pendleton (Civil Service Reform) Act. Among its provisions, the act states that no public employee may be obligated to contribute to a political fund and that no public employee may be removed from office for failing to do so.

1887   In response to the disputed 1876 presidential election, Congress passes the Electoral Count Act, establishing a means for dealing with the possible situation in which conflicting state authorities certify differing sets of electors.

Congress passes the Edmunds-Tucker Act, which outlaws the Mormon practice of plural marriage. The act also disfranchises women in the Utah Territory.

1888   Benjamin Harrison wins a majority of the electoral college votes and gains the presidency even though his Democratic opponent, incumbent President Grover Cleveland, received just over 110,000 more popular votes nationwide.

1890   The American and National Woman Suffrage Associations merge, creating the National American Woman Suffrage Association. Elizabeth Cady Stanton is elected president and Susan B. Anthony vice president.

The new Mississippi constitution includes provisions intended to disfranchise blacks. The constitution requires payment of a $2 poll tax and, after 1892, the ability to read or understand the constitution as criteria for granting suffrage.

1892   In *Sproule v. Fredericks*, the Mississippi constitution of 1890 survives the charge that by denying the franchise to blacks the state has violated the provisions for reentering the Union after the Civil War.

The first levered voting machine is used in Lockport, New York.

1893   The Arkansas constitution is amended to require payment of a poll tax as a qualification for voting.

1894   Congress repeals sections of the 1870 Enforcement Act and the 1871 Force Act.

1895   In addition to a literacy test, the South Carolina constitutional convention establishes a grandfather clause, which states that until 1898 all those who could vote in 1867 and their descendants, as well as naturalized citizens, are exempt from the literacy requirement. This provision is intended to disfranchise blacks while allowing illiterate whites to vote.

1896   Idaho amends its state constitution to grant the full franchise to women.

Utah enters the Union with a constitution that restores full suffrage rights to women, rights that were rescinded by the 1887 Edmunds-Tucker Act.

1898   A constitutional convention in Louisiana follows South Carolina's lead by establishing strict literacy tests that include a loophole for those who were qualified to vote in 1867, their descendants, and naturalized citizens—the so-called grandfather clause.

1899   Members of the National Municipal Reform League reach agreement on a model city charter that calls for the replacement of ward electoral systems by at-large electoral systems, the institution of nonpartisan elections, the holding of municipal elections at times different from those established for federal and state elections, and the elimination of larger bicameral city councils in favor of smaller unicameral councils.

1901   Alabama follows the lead of Mississippi, South Carolina, and Louisiana in denying suffrage to blacks. After providing exemptions to assure the franchise for whites, the new constitutional provisions dictate that after 1903 only those who can read and write any part of the constitution and who have been gainfully employed the preceding year may register to vote.

1902   Virginia adopts suffrage provisions similar to those enacted the previous year in Alabama, a major objective of which is to disfranchise blacks.

1903 The U.S. Supreme Court in *Giles v. Harris* upholds provisions of the Alabama constitution claimed to be discriminatory against blacks.

1904 In *Giles v. Teasley* the U.S. Supreme Court again denies the attempts of blacks to disallow disfranchisement methods established under Southern state constitutions.

1907 In response to allegations of heavy corporate funding for his 1904 presidential campaign, Theodore Roosevelt proposes that candidates for federal office disclose campaign finances and be prohibited from receiving corporate contributions.

    Congress passes the Tillman Act, which prohibits candidates for federal office from receiving corporate contributions.

1910 Congress passes the Federal Campaign Disclosure Law, which is the first federal legislation designed to require candidates for federal office to disclose sources of campaign financing.

1911 Congress sets the number of members of the U.S. House of Representatives at 435 and calls for the reapportionment of congressional districts every 10 years.

1912 Arizona enters the Union with a constitution that grants full suffrage rights to women.

1913 The Seventeenth Amendment to the U.S. Constitution is ratified, providing for the popular election of U.S. senators.

    The Illinois legislature grants women the right to vote for presidential electors.

1914 Congress establishes the time for electing senators, setting it to coincide with elections to the House of Representatives.

1915   In *Guinn v. United States*, a decision that ultimately does little to ensure minority voting rights, the U.S. Supreme Court declares Oklahoma's grandfather clause unconstitutional.

1917   The New York State constitution is amended to grant full suffrage rights to women.

1920   The Nineteenth Amendment to the U.S. Constitution is ratified, guaranteeing to women the right to vote in federal and state elections.

        After the final ratification of the Nineteenth Amendment, leaders of the National American Woman Suffrage Association organize the League of Women Voters.

1921   The United States Supreme Court in *Newberry v. United States* rules that congressional regulation of campaign financing does not extend to party primaries. Therefore, candidates in primaries cannot be required to disclose sources of campaign contributions and may engage in unlimited campaign spending.

        Lynn Frazier, governor of North Dakota since 1917, becomes the first state governor to be removed from office via a recall election.

1925   Due in part to such embarrassing incidents as the Teapot Dome scandal and corruption in Warren G. Harding's campaign of 1920, Congress passes the Federal Corrupt Practices Act, which requires congressional candidates to disclose campaign receipts and expenditures.

        Presidential candidates Herbert Hoover (Republican) and Al Smith (Democrat) introduce the first national radio commercials.

1935   In *Grovey v. Townsend*, the U.S. Supreme Court, ruling that the conduct of a political party's convention is

1935 *(cont.)*	not state action, finds the white primary constitutional. The court determines that the Democratic Party is a private organization and therefore is not subject to federal regulation when it excludes African Americans from participation in the primary election.
1937	In *Breedlove v. Suttles*, the U.S. Supreme Court upholds the constitutionality of the poll tax.
1939	The Hatch Act, or Political Activities Act, prohibits political parties from soliciting contributions and other support from federal employees. Federal employees are prohibited from taking part in such political activities as running for public office, campaigning for or against candidates, raising funds for candidates, circulating petitions, or organizing political rallies.
1940	Franklin Delano Roosevelt breaks the two-term tradition and is elected president for an unprecedented third term.
1941	The U.S. Supreme Court in *United States v. Classic* rejects its earlier position in *Newberry v United States* (1921) and asserts that Congress has the authority to regulate campaign finances in party primaries. Although Congress can now regulate the nomination process, it will not do so until 1971.
	Congress passes the Smith-Connally Act, which for the duration of World War II prohibits candidates for federal office from receiving financial contributions from labor unions.
1942	The Servicemen's Voting Act facilitates registration and voting by those actively engaged in the armed forces on military bases and overseas.
1943	The idea of term limits is raised in Congress but receives little support.
	The Congress of Industrial Organizations (CIO) creates the first political action committee.

1944   The U.S. Supreme Court in *Smith v. Allwright* declares the white primary unconstitutional. The Democratic Party in Southern states may no longer exclude African Americans from participation in the party nomination process. By striking down the white primary, the Supreme Court helps to ensure meaningful African American electoral involvement.

Delegates to the Democratic National Convention nominate President Franklin Delano Roosevelt for a fourth term. Although Roosevelt wins the election, the unprecedented nature of Roosevelt's four presidential election victories encourages a movement to ratify a constitutional amendment limiting a president to two terms.

1946   In *Colegrove v. Green* the U.S. Supreme Court holds that malapportionment of legislative districts is a political question to be decided through the political process, not by the courts.

1947   Congress passes the Taft-Hartley Act, which makes permanent the prohibition on the receipt of financial contributions from labor unions by candidates for federal office.

Senator W. Lee O'Daniel (D-TX) proposes term limitations for members of Congress, but the measure is soundly defeated.

1948   Election fraud is suspected when future president Lyndon B. Johnson wins a U.S. Senate seat from Texas. In the runoff Democratic primary election, a precinct worker in Duvall County who is friendly to Johnson suspiciously discovers 203 additional ballots, all but one of which has been cast for Johnson, giving the Democratic candidate an 87-vote victory.

1951   The Twenty-second Amendment to the U.S. Constitution is ratified, prohibiting anyone from holding the office of president for more than two full terms and

1951 *(cont.)*	limiting to a total of 10 years the time that office may be held by any one individual.
	North Dakota abolishes the requirement that voters register but allows cities to institute voter registration for local elections.
1952	Dwight D. Eisenhower, the Republican presidential candidate, introduces the first televised political ads.
1955	The Federal Voting Assistance Act provides assistance to members of the Armed Forces in registering and voting.
1957	Congress passes the first civil rights bill since the 1870s. Weak in its enforcement provisions, the law relies on litigation to protect citizens against discrimination in registration and voting procedures.
1959	In *Lassiter v. Northampton County Board of Elections*, the U.S. Supreme Court upholds the constitutionality of the literacy test as a criterion for voter registration.
1960	Congress passes a civil rights act that requires the retention of original registration and voting records for 22 months following an election so that they are available should questions or challenges arise.
	In *Gomillion v. Lightfoot,* the U.S. Supreme Court rules that racial gerrymandering in Tuskegee, Alabama, violates the Fifteenth Amendment guarantee of minority voting rights.
	Voter registration rates of African Americans in the South are still less than half that of whites.
1961	The Twenty-third Amendment to the U.S. Constitution is ratified, under which the District of Columbia is treated as a state for purposes of electing a president. The district shall have electoral votes equal to the number it would have if it were a state but no more than the least populous state.

President John F. Kennedy makes campaign financing a priority issue by establishing a bipartisan commission to study campaign costs.

1962 Overturning the 1946 *Colegrove v. Green* decision, the U.S. Supreme Court in *Baker v. Carr* rules that federal courts have jurisdiction over questions concerning apportionment for state legislative districts and declares that malapportionment can be so unfair as to deprive a person of equal protection under the law as provided by the Fourteenth Amendment to the U.S. Constitution.

1964 The Twenty-fourth Amendment to the U.S. Constitution is ratified, prohibiting the use of the poll tax as a condition for voting in any federal election, thereby outlawing a procedure long used by state legislatures to limit the right to vote.

The U.S. Supreme Court in *Reynolds v. Sims* rules that state legislative districts must be apportioned as equally as possible according to population, based on the principle of "one man, one vote."

The U.S. Supreme Court in *Wesberry v. Sanders* applies the principle of apportionment on the basis of "one man, one vote" to congressional districts.

Congress passes the Civil Rights Act, which, although not primarily aimed at protecting voting rights, does place limitations on the use of literacy tests as a criterion for voter registration.

1965 Congress passes the Voting Rights Act (VRA), which finally provides for effective enforcement of the Fourteenth and Fifteenth Amendments. This landmark legislation suspends the use of the literacy test as a prerequisite for voting. Under this act any form of discrimination that is meant to prevent African Americans from registering to vote and from voting is prohibited. Important results of this legislation are that African American voter registration substantially

1965
(cont.)
increases, especially in Southern states, and electoral arrangements that diminish African American voting strength, such as the at-large election, are challenged in federal court.

1966
The U.S. Supreme Court in *Harper v. Virginia State Board of Elections* declares unconstitutional the use of the poll tax as a condition for voting in state elections, thereby outlawing a procedure long used by state legislatures to limit the right to vote.

Congress passes the Long Act, which provides federal subsidies to political parties to be used in presidential elections. Although this act is signed into law by President Lyndon B. Johnson, it is never implemented; in 1967 Congress will vote to make the act inoperative.

1967
The Twenty-fifth Amendment to the U.S. Constitution is ratified, providing for the transition of power from president to vice president when a sitting president is unable to fulfill the duties of the office. The amendment includes detailed provisions for the suspension and resumption by the president of the duties of the office. In addition, it specifies that, on the resignation or death of a sitting president, the vice president immediately assumes the duties of the office and that, if the office of vice president becomes vacant, the president nominates a new vice president who is then approved by a majority vote in both houses of Congress.

The proportion of African Americans registered to vote in the Southern states covered by the special provisions of the 1965 Voting Rights Act now exceeds 50 percent.

Congress requires that the single-member district system be used by states in elections to the U.S. House of Representatives. Each state must create as many congressional districts as it has members in the House, with one member elected from each district.

1968   The Overseas Citizens Voting Rights Act expands the responsibilities of the Federal Voting Assistance Program.

1969   The U.S. House of Representatives approves an amendment to the U.S. Constitution establishing the direct election of president and vice president. A majority of the popular vote is required for election, and if no presidential ticket receives a popular vote majority, a runoff will be held between the top two vote getters. The United States Senate fails to act on this proposal.

Maine alters its method of selecting presidential electors. Two are to be chosen by statewide popular vote and the remainder by vote in each congressional district.

In *Allen v. State Board of Elections,* the U.S. Supreme Court rules that vote dilution methods such as gerrymandering can adversely affect the right to vote.

1970   Congress amends the Voting Rights Act to prohibit residency requirements for voting that exceed 30 days and to extend the right to vote to those 18, 19, and 20 years of age.

The Supreme Court rules in *Oregon v. Mitchell* that Congress does not possess the authority to set the voting age for state elections.

1971   The Twenty-sixth Amendment to the U.S. Constitution is ratified, granting to those 18, 19, and 20 years of age the right to vote in federal and state elections.

Congress passes the Federal Election Campaign Act, which replaces the Corrupt Practices Act of 1925. The new legislation sets limits on candidates' spending on communications media, establishes limits on financial contributions to candidates, and requires disclosure of financial contributions made by political committees and individuals greater than $10, as well

1971
(cont.)

as disclosure by candidates of contributors and expenditures greater than $100.

1973

The U.S. Supreme Court in *United States Civil Service Commission v. National Association of Letter Carriers* upholds provisions of the Hatch Act prohibiting federal employees from engaging in partisan political activity.

1974

As a result of investigations leading to and following Richard M. Nixon's resignation, substantial funding illegalities are discovered in the president's 1972 reelection campaign. The revelations provide the impetus for amendments to the Federal Election Campaign Act that establishes public funding of presidential campaigns. Congress establishes spending limits for presidential and congressional candidates and for national political parties that pertain to party primary, general, and runoff elections. The act also sets contribution limits on individuals, political action committees, and political parties and provides for voluntary public financing of presidential elections. The Federal Election Commission is established to implement these provisions by enforcing financial contribution and expenditure disclosure requirements.

The U.S. Supreme Court in *Richardson v. Ramirez* upholds the right of states to disfranchise convicted felons.

1975

Congress amends the Voting Rights Act to include language minorities, particularly Hispanic Americans, in addition to racial or ethnic minorities as groups that warrant special protection. Literacy tests are permanently eliminated as a condition for voter registration.

President Gerald Ford, Speaker of the House Carl Albert, and Senate President Pro Tempore James Eastland appoint the first two members to the Federal Election Commission.

Louisiana adopts the bipartisan primary, in which all candidates for the same office appear on the same ballot.

The Overseas Citizens Voting Rights Act, originally passed in 1968, is expanded.

The Office of Federal Elections, located in the General Accounting Office, signs an agreement with the National Bureau of Standards to develop guidelines ensuring the accuracy and security of computer-based voting systems.

1976   The U.S. Supreme Court in *Buckley v. Valeo* upholds limits on contributions to congressional office seekers but rules that candidate spending limits are an unjustified infringement on free expression. The Supreme Court declares unconstitutional the method by which Federal Election Commission members are appointed.

Congress amends the Federal Election Campaign Act to reflect the Supreme Court's decision in *Buckley v. Valeo* and to allow for expenditures by political committees on behalf of candidates. The act modifies contribution limits established in 1974, requires political action committees to keep accurate records, and changes the method by which members of the Federal Election Commission are chosen.

The Democratic Party moves away from the winner-take-all system of delegate selection in presidential primaries by adopting a system of proportional delegate selection. This change is meant to further democratize the nomination process.

The nation witnesses the first publicly funded presidential campaign.

1977   A Monterey, California, flood control district, with approximately 45,000 voters, conducts the first all-mail-ballot election.

1978   The Federal Election Commission allows the Kansas Republican State Committee to use donations from corporations and unions in federal as well as in state elections, thereby creating the opportunity to raise soft money contributions that circumvent Federal Election Campaign Act limitations on campaign contributions.

1979   Congress amends the Federal Election Campaign Act to ease contribution and expenditure disclosure requirements, establishing the distinction between hard and soft money. Voter registration efforts and get-out-the-vote campaigns for presidential candidates are made exempt from contribution and expenditure limits.

        Bypassing the governor and state legislature, California voters approve Proposition 13 in an initiative election. The measure places stringent limitations on the taxing authority of state and local government. Supporters of the proposition point to the initiative and referendum (procedures introduced during the Progressive era) as significant reforms in democratizing the U.S. electoral system, but opponents consider these election procedures misguided and detrimental to democracy.

        The U.S. Senate rejects a proposed constitutional amendment to elect the president and vice president by popular vote.

1980   In January Congress enacts additional amendments to the Federal Election Campaign Act, including measures that simplify reporting requirements, facilitate state and local political party activities, and expand public funding of the presidential nominating conventions.

1981   In the New Jersey gubernatorial election, the Republican Party reportedly hires armed off-duty police officers to serve as a National Ballot Security Task Force. Members of the group post signs at polling places in minority neighborhoods stating that the area is being patrolled by the Task Force and that "It is a Crime to Falsify a Ballot or to Violate Election Laws."

1982   Congress amends the Voting Rights Act, adding the so-called results test, which outlaws any electoral arrangement that has the effect of weakening minority group voting strength.

The Democratic National Committee (DNC) chair, concerned with the rising cost of the presidential nomination process, appoints a commission headed by Gov. James B. Hunt, Jr. of North Carolina to study the process. The Hunt Commission recommends shortening the presidential nomination process and setting aside a portion of delegate positions at the national nominating convention to be filled with elected officials and party leaders. The DNC accepts the commission's recommendations.

The number of political action committees (PACs) reaches 2,600, which represents a fourfold increase since passage of Federal Election Campaign Act amendments in 1974 that liberalized regulation of their creation.

1984   The Democratic Party introduces Super Tuesday into its presidential nomination process, whereby a series of mostly Southern states hold their presidential primaries on the same day. The purpose is to shorten the nomination process and to increase the nomination chances of moderate and conservative Democratic contenders.

The Democratic National Convention selects Geraldine Ferraro to be Walter Mondale's vice presidential running mate. Ferraro is the first woman to be nominated for the vice presidency by either major political party.

The Voting Accessibility for the Elderly and Handicapped Act requires states to provide polling places that are accessible to elderly and disabled voters.

1986   The U.S. Supreme Court in *Thornburg v. Gingles* rules that the "effects" provision of the 1982 Voting Rights Act amendment requires that state legislatures avoid discriminatory results in drawing legislative districts. Some observers interpret this decision to mean that states must act to maximize minority representation, although it is questionable just how far states can go in creating legislative districts that provide for the election of minority candidates.

       The Uniformed and Overseas Citizens Absentee Voting Act (UOCAVA) combines and replaces the 1955 Federal Voting Assistance Act and 1975 Overseas Citizens Voting Rights Act. The act is administered by the Federal Voting Assistance Program in the Pentagon. Members of the uniformed services and the merchant marine, along with spouses and dependents, and civilian U.S. citizens living abroad are guaranteed the right to register and vote in elections for federal office.

1988   In Wisconsin and Minnesota, which instituted election day registration in 1976, voter turnout nonetheless falls below the 1972 level. Turnout also declines in Texas, despite the introduction of a liberalized absentee voting program.

1990   Congress passes the Americans with Disabilities Act (ADA), which expands the responsibilities of state and local election officials in guaranteeing accessibility for all, regardless of physical disabilities, to voter registration offices and polling places.

1991   Senator Hank Brown (R-CO) fails to have an amendment included in the Senate campaign finance reform bill that would establish term limits.

       Texas becomes the first state to institute a system of early voting.

1992   Nearly 67 percent of voting-age African Americans in the South are now registered to vote, compared to 68 percent outside the South. These figures indicate the success of the Voting Rights Act.

It is estimated that in this year's election, two-thirds of the electorate will use a ballot that is electronically read and counted.

1993   The United States Supreme Court in *Shaw v. Reno* addresses the question of the extent to which states can proceed in creating legislative districts to ensure the election of minority candidates. The Court finds that any legislative districting done for obvious racial purposes that results in bizarrely shaped districts possibly violates the Fourteenth Amendment's equal protection clause, even when the purpose is to ensure the election of minority candidates.

The National Voter Registration Act requires states to offer citizens the opportunity to register or renew their registration when receiving or renewing driver's licenses; when applying for assistance from Aid to Families with Dependent Children (AFDC), for assistance from Special Supplemental Food Program for Women, Infants, and Children (WIC), or for disability benefits; and at armed forces recruiting offices.

Under amendments to the Hatch Act, federal government employees may run for office in a nonpartisan election, sign petitions for the ballot, assist in voter registration drives, serve as poll workers, and serve as poll watchers for a candidate or political party. Among the act's continued prohibitions are running for office in a partisan election and taking part in partisan political activities while working.

1994   Ballot measures in 20 states limit the congressional term of service. The constitutionality of such state provisions, however, is in question.

The Arkansas Supreme Court rules unconstitutional state-imposed congressional term limits.

1995   The National Voter Registration Act takes effect in
January.

The U.S. Supreme Court decides in *U.S. Term Limits
v. Thornton* that term limits imposed by states on
their representatives in the U.S. Congress are unconstitutional. The ruling is based on the qualifications clauses of the U.S. Constitution (Article I,
sections 2 and 3). The decision does not affect any
term limits that states have imposed on their own
state legislators.

The United States House of Representatives rejects a
proposed constitutional amendment to impose a 12-
year lifetime limit on congressional service in both the
House and the Senate. The House also rejects modifications to the amendment to allow states to place
term limits on congressional officeholders. The Senate
Judiciary Committee recommends that the full Senate
consider a 12-year congressional term limit.

President Bill Clinton and Speaker of the U.S. House
of Representatives Newt Gingrich agree to establish a
bipartisan commission to deal with the problems of
the electoral system.

1996   One year after President Bill Clinton and Speaker
Newt Gingrich pledged to work for election reform,
no action has been taken to form a commission.

Republican presidential candidate Robert Dole, at the
conclusion of a presidential debate with President
Clinton, becomes the first presidential candidate to
present his campaign Web site (although giving it inaccurately), thus opening a new era in presidential
election campaigning.

Oregon becomes the first state to hold a congressional
election by an all-mail ballot. The election is held in
January to fill the unexpired term of Sen. Robert Packwood (R-OR), who resigned in disgrace.

1997   In February, members of the U.S. House of Representatives vote on 11 different versions of term limit proposals, rejecting each one. Supporters of term limits disagree on whether the limit should be set at 6, 8, or 12 years.

                Revelations surface about campaign fund-raising for the 1996 election, including allegations that President Bill Clinton offered overnight stays in the White House to Democratic campaign contributors and that Vice President Albert Gore made phone solicitations from the White House for campaign funds. Additional claims, including charges that foreign governments contributed campaign money, lead to congressional hearings on campaign finance and allegations of wrongdoing.

2000   On the night of the presidential election, Democratic candidate Albert Gore initially concedes the election to Republican George W. Bush but withdraws the concession when the popular vote total in Florida appears extremely close and election irregularities in that state are reported. A bitter court battle ensues in which manual recounts of punch card ballots begin in key counties. Controversy centers around the interpretation of undervotes, punch cards on which chads have not been completely removed—the so-called hanging and dimpled, or pregnant, chads. In early December, in a 4-to-3 decision, the Florida supreme court orders that all undervotes that machines rejected as nonvotes must be manually counted. The Bush campaign appeals the decision to the U.S. Supreme Court, which issues a decision on December 12 permanently prohibiting the Florida supreme court from enforcing its mandated recount. The Florida secretary of state's certification of Bush as the state's popular vote winner by a 537-vote margin out of almost six million votes cast becomes effective and Bush is awarded Florida's electoral votes and a majority of the electoral college votes. Gore has received 544,000 more popular votes nationwide than has

2000 *(cont.)*	Bush, raising renewed questions about the operation of the electoral college. Questions also arise about electoral procedures in general, including the adequacy of current voting machine technology.
2001	Among the various studies of the 2000 presidential election in Florida, *The New York Times* reports that 10 days after the election Republicans filed lawsuits in 14 counties asking that rejected overseas absentee ballots be reevaluated. Ultimately, canvassing boards in 12 counties met and accepted ballots that previously were rejected.
	A federal government-funded group from the National Science Foundation concludes that the security risks related to Internet voting are widespread and cannot be solved with current technology.
2002	Congress enacts the Bipartisan Campaign Reform Act (BCRA), which bans soft money contributions to national political parties. The legislation regulates campaign advertisements financed by unions, corporations, and nonprofit groups that favor the election or defeat of specific candidates within 30 days of a primary or 60 days of a general election
	Due largely to the vote count difficulties in the 2000 presidential election, Congress passes the Help America Vote Act (HAVA). The act promises to provide funds to states for the purchase of voting machines to replace punch card systems and mechanical lever voting machines. It also requires that by the 2006 election every voting system inform voters if they vote for more than one candidate in the same race (i.e., overvote) and allow voters to review their ballot and allow them to correct any errors. The legislation mandates that each state institute a statewide voter registration system, offer the opportunity to individuals of questionable eligibility to cast a provisional ballot, and provide in each polling place at least one voting machine that is accessible to those with disabilities.

2003   In February antitax activist Ted Costa and radio talk show host Eric Hogue begin a recall campaign, called Rescue California, to remove Gov. Gray Davis. By July the movement has collected approximately 1.5 million petition signatures, far more than the 900,000 required to place the recall on the ballot. In an October special election, Gov. Davis is removed and voters select Arnold Schwarzenegger to complete Davis's term. This recall election is the first time that a governor has been removed from office since California adopted the recall option in 1911. Thirty-one previous efforts to remove a governor failed. Many react negatively to the recall, considering it a misguided democratic instrument that results in governing instability. The election costs California taxpayers $50 million.

The legislature of North Dakota, the only state that does not require voter registration, enacts legislation requiring voters to show identification in order to vote. The law will go into effect in 2004.

In August Walden O'Dell, the chief executive of Diebold Election Systems, an Ohio-based company that manufactures electronic voting machines, announces that he sent a fund-raising letter to Ohio Republicans in which he expressed the commitment to "helping Ohio deliver its electoral votes to the president [George W. Bush] next year." Critics raise the fear that Diebold voting machines will be biased in favor of Bush, but O'Dell states that he did not express himself well.

In December the U.S. Senate confirms the first four members of the U.S. Election Assistance Commission (EAC). The commission includes two Democrats (Gracia Hillman and Raymundo Martinez) and two Republicans (Paul DeGregorio and Deforest Soaries Jr.).

In December the U.S. Supreme Court in *McConnell v. Federal Election Commission* upholds most provisions of the Bipartisan Campaign Reform Act.

2004   In January, 3 of 10 technology experts employed by
        the Pentagon to evaluate the security of a $22 million
        pilot program for Internet voting intended to begin
        in November conclude that the voting plan cannot
        eliminate the possibility of lost, stolen, or hacked
        ballots. Their report results in the suspension of the
        program.

        In *Vieth et al. v. Jubelirer,* a divided U.S. Supreme
        Court refuses to invalidate a Pennsylvania redistrict-
        ing plan charged with excessively political gerry-
        mandering. Four justices conclude that the question
        of political gerrymandering is not justiciable. Justice
        Anthony Kennedy, although joining the majority
        that dismisses the complaint, contends that grounds
        still might be found for disallowing a political gerry-
        mander.

2005   The Connecticut legislature passes a clean money re-
        form bill that prohibits candidates' accepting campaign
        contributions from lobbyists and state contractors.

        The Arizona legislature enacts a voter identification
        law mandating that anyone without verification of
        identity cannot be issued a provisional ballot, in ap-
        parent conflict with the Help America Vote Act.

2006   In February the Overseas Vote Foundation (OVF)
        announces a new Internet-based Registration and
        Absentee Voter Application (RAVA) for military and
        overseas voters who are covered by the Uniformed
        and Overseas Citizens Absentee Voter Act. Voters
        are able to print a Federal Post Card Application
        that they can sign and mail to a state of previous
        residence.

        Although the Help America Voter Act requires only
        first-time voters who did not include identity verifi-
        cation when registering by mail to provide a form of
        identification when voting, 22 states have enacted
        measures requiring all individuals to provide iden-
        tification when registering and voting. Identifica-

tion requirements for voters are pending in additional states.

Hamilton Jordan and Jerry Rafshoon (former advisers to President Jimmy Carter), Angus King (former independent governor of Maine), and Douglas Bailey (a Republican political adviser) form Unity 08, a group dedicated to instituting a bipartisan third-party movement, hoping to nominate a presidential candidate via the Internet.

The Federal Election Commission, responding to a 2004 federal district court order, widens its definition of public communications subject to regulation to include Internet advertisements.

The U.S. Supreme Court in *League of United Latin American Citizens et al. v. Perry* upholds most of the controversial 2003 Texas congressional redistricting plan. Although the Court majority refuses to invalidate the plan as unacceptable political gerrymandering, the justices find one southwest Texas district in violation of the Voting Rights Act for diluting Hispanic vote strength.

Two Virginia jurisdictions (the city of Salem and the county of Botetourt) receive permission to bail out from the preclearance provisions of the Voting Rights Act, bringing to 12 the number of local jurisdictions in Virginia no longer required to submit voting procedure changes to the U.S. Justice Department.

U.S. Election Assistance Commission testimony in May before a Senate appropriations subcommittee indicates that more than $3 billion in Help America Vote Act funds have been distributed to the states to acquire updated voting systems and to make election administration improvements.

After filing suit against New York in March to require the state to comply with Help America Vote Act requirements for statewide voter registration and the

2006
(cont.)

introduction of updated voting systems, the Justice Department in May conditionally accepts New York's compliance plan.

In April, Sarah Evans Barker, judge for the U.S. District Court, Southern District of Indiana, dismisses a constitutional and legal challenge to an Indiana law requiring voters to present photo identification at the polls.

In May the U.S. Department of Justice files suit to require Alabama to comply with Help America Vote Act mandates, alleging that the state's current registration policies do not meet HAVA statewide voter registration system requirements.

In May the U.S. Court of Appeals for the Second Circuit rules that the Voting Rights Act cannot be interpreted as covering prisoner disfranchisement provisions in New York election law, stating that Congress did not indicate that the act should apply to such cases.

In June the U.S. Supreme Court in *Randall v. Sorell* finds that Vermont's contribution limits for political candidates are not adequately drawn to meet the state's interest. According to the majority decision, the restrictions limit the ability of challengers to campaign effectively, damage the right of association with a political party, impede individuals' ability to volunteer their services, fail to index contribution limits, and do not offer sufficient justification for the low contribution limits.

In June a federal judge rejects a U.S. Department of Justice request to impose a temporary restraining order prohibiting Arizona from enforcing a law, approved by voters in 2004, requiring proof of citizenship to vote. The law mandates documentation proving citizenship at the time of voter registration.

In September Georgia superior court judge T. Jackson Bedford rules that a state photo identification requirement deprives qualified voters of the right to vote because it adds an unconstitutional requirement.

In September the U.S. House Administration Committee, by a 4-to-3 vote, reports to the full House the Federal Election Integrity Act (H.R. 4844), amending the National Voter Registration Act. The bill contains a measure to require voters to present government-issued photo identification in federal elections beginning in November 2008. The House passes the bill, with Republicans largely in favor and Democrats opposed. Senate Democrats announce that they will block the bill if Republicans attempt to gain Senate passage.

In September a three-judge panel of the U.S. Court of Appeals for the Sixth Circuit finds unconstitutional Ohio statutes regulating ballot access for minor parties (*Libertarian Party of Ohio v. Blackwell*, No. 04–4251). The court majority rules that requiring all political parties to nominate candidates in a primary election and mandating that minor parties file a petition 120 days before the primary constitutes an undue burden without furthering a compelling public interest.

In October the U.S. Court of Appeals for the Ninth Circuit issues an order preventing Arizona from implementing a new voter identification statute in the coming November election.

In October the Missouri supreme court rules 6 to 1 that a state law requiring voters to present photo identification at the polls violates the Missouri constitution, which, the court argues, guarantees greater protection of voting rights than does the U.S. Constitution.

In October Princeton University professor Edward Felton, testifying before the Administration Committee of the U.S. House of Representatives, claims that, given the current state of technology, a voter-verified paper audit trail is necessary to ensure accurate and honest election results. Barbara Simons, former president of the Association for Computing Machinery, also testifies that paper trails are necessary.

Kimball Brace, president of Election Data Services, announces that in the November election, 56 percent of U.S. counties representing 48.9 percent of registered voters will use optical scan devices to cast ballots, and 36 percent of counties containing 38 percent of registered voters will use direct recording electronic voting machines. Most of the remaining voters will be using mechanical lever machines or punch cards.

Voters in four jurisdictions (Pierce County, Washington; Oakland and Davis, California; and Minneapolis, Minnesota) approve ballot measures to institute instant runoff voting in future elections.

In December four political scientists, who analyzed the controversial election results from Florida's thirteenth congressional district, conclude that the likely cause of 18,000 voters failing to cast a ballot in the race was due to the ballot format for Sarasota County's touch screen voting machines. Candidates for the congressional race were placed above and on the same screen as the candidates in the gubernatorial race. Democrat Christine Jennings, who lost to Republican Vern Buchanan by 369 votes, files suit in Leon County alleging that the large undervote is due to voting machine failures, not voter confusion caused by ballot design.

On December 20 Christine Jennings files a notice of contest in the U.S. House of Representatives challenging the outcome of the congressional election.

In December the Federal Voting Assistance Program (FVAP) announces its 2007 legislative agenda for simplifying voter registration and the absentee voting process followed by states for those individuals covered by the Uniformed and Overseas Citizens Absentee Voting Act. The FVAP requests that states permit a minimum of 45 days between the mailing of absentee ballots and the deadline for receiving voted ballots, and it recommends that states allow late registration for those who do not return from overseas assignments in time to meet the existing registration deadline.

In December the Federal Election Commission announces that in 2006 it collected $6.2 million in civil penalties, more than twice the amount assessed in any previous year in the commission's 31-year history. The commission levies fines totaling $629,000 on three fund-raising groups (Swiftboat Veterans and POWs for Truth, MoveOn.org's Voter Fund, and a fund of the League of Conservative Voters), charging that they violated election laws during the 2004 presidential election by receiving funds from large donors and corporations

2007   Based on a pilot study of one precinct in Cobb County, Georgia, Director of Elections Sharon Dunn announces in January that a manual recount of paper ballots from the November 2006 election demonstrates that the electronic voting machines accurately counted the votes.

In January a panel for the Seventh Circuit Court of Appeals issues a 2-to-1 decision upholding an Indiana law mandating that prospective voters present government-issued photo identification at the polls.

In February the 110-member Standards Board of the U.S. Election Assistance Commission (EAC) requests in formal resolutions that the EAC assist in delaying changes in the Help America Vote Act to move more slowly in implementing voting system guidelines. Board members indicate that Congress be informed that the HAVA should remain unchanged until July 2010 and that subsequent changes be made only with full funding and with the input of state and local government officials and election administrators.

2007
(cont.)

In February U.S. Rep. Rush Holt (D-NJ) introduces the Voter Confidence and Increased Accessibility Act (H.R. 811) in the House of Representatives. The proposed legislation calls for a voter-verifiable paper audit trail for each ballot cast, including alternative language capability and access for those with disabilities. The bill mandates that the paper audit trail would become the ballot of record for recounts and audits.

In March the Federal Election Commission, in a unanimous decision, requires Rep. Dennis Kucinich (D-OH) to pay $137,358 to the federal government for using federal matching funds in his 2004 presidential primary campaign after March 4 of that year, when poor showings in primaries disqualified him from using such funds for campaign purposes.

In March the U.S. Election Assistance Commission announces that it plans to initiate an extended study of state voter identification regulations and possible related influences on voter participation.

In March North Dakota governor John Hoeven signs into law an act passed by the state legislature that allows counties to conduct all elections, including primaries, by mail ballot, if a county's board of county commissioners decides to do so.

In April the first quarterly fund-raising reports of presidential hopefuls point to a furious competition to accumulate campaign resources. On the Democratic side, Sen. Hillary Rodham Clinton (D-NY) finishes first with $26 million and Sen. Barack Obama (D-IL) is a close second with $25 million. Among Republicans, former Massachusetts governor Mitt Romney raises the most money with $23 million, and Rudy Giuliani finishes second with $15 million.

In April Maryland becomes the first state to approve the interstate compact to elect the president according to the results of the national popular vote results.

Maryland governor Martin O'Malley signs a bill passed by the state legislature that contains the National Popular Vote Plan.

In April the U.S. Justice Department issues a report indicating that there is little evidence of organized activities to commit vote fraud. In recent years approximately 120 people have been charged with vote fraud and 85 were convicted. The report associates 24 convictions with local vote-buying schemes.

In April the U.S. House of Representatives passes a bill to grant to the District of Columbia one representative in the House. If it becomes law, the bill also would grant to Utah, which narrowly missed obtaining one more representative in the 2000 census, a temporary at-large seat in the House. However, if the bill gains Senate approval, the president is likely to veto the legislation, which many consider unconstitutional.

On April 11 Georgia secretary of state Karen Handel releases a report of a voter-verified paper audit trail (VVPAT) pilot test conducted during the November 2006 election in three Georgia precincts. The pilot study indicates that problems, including paper jams and confusing ballot tape layout, occurred; voting time increased; voter anonymity was not assured; and manual audits, while providing verification of the electronic vote count, are expensive, time-consuming, and subject to human error. However, voter confidence in the electronic voting system increased with the addition of the VVPAT.

In June the U.S. Supreme Court rules in *Federal Election Commission v. Wisconsin Right to Life, Inc.* that the limits on the funding of ads mentioning candidate names within 30 days before a primary or caucus or 60 days before a general election are unconstitutional if the ads can be reasonably interpreted as communications other than appeals to vote for or against a particular candidate.

2008   In February, the U.S. Government Accountability Office reports that, after testing the voting systems used in the 2006 congressional election in Florida's thirteenth district, it has "increased assurance" that the large number of undervotes in that contest, in which Republican Vern Buchanan defeated Democrat Christine Jennings by a narrow margin, were not caused by the electronic voting system.

The National Association of Secretaries of State issues a report, *The Case for Regional Presidential Primaries in 2012 and Beyond,* recommending the adoption of a system of rotating regional presidential primaries.

5

Biographical Sketches

The individuals selected for this chapter include both those presently active in some aspect of campaign and election reform and those from past generations who played a role in the attainment of voting rights and in the improvement of election procedures. Each has made significant contributions in such areas as regulations on campaign contributions and expenditures, alternative voting systems, woman suffrage, voter turnout, election procedures and administration, and limiting political corruption and vote fraud.

Herbert E. Alexander (b. 1927)

Herbert Alexander has been referred to as Mr. Campaign Finance in recognition of his expert knowledge of the use of money in politics and for his grasp of campaign reform issues. He studied patterns of campaign donations and spending for four decades in his position as executive director of the Citizens' Research Foundation, a position he assumed in 1958 and held until 1998. Alexander currently is professor emeritus of political science at the University of Southern California, and he chairs the Research Committee on Political Finance and Political Corruption of the International Political Science Association. When Alexander moved to the University of Southern California in 1978, the foundation moved with him. Every four years Alexander examined the financial records of political campaigns made available by the Federal Election Commission. He also interviewed many campaign workers to complete his analysis of money in local, state, and federal elections.

Alexander received his PhD from Yale University in 1958. In 1961 President John F. Kennedy appointed him the executive director of the President's Commission on Campaign Costs. In the 1970s and 1980s Alexander went on to serve in various capacities at the federal and state levels. In 1990 he served on the Senate Campaign Finance Reform Panel.

Alexander has written a number of studies dealing with campaign finance. He coauthored, with Anthony Corrado, *Financing the 1992 Election* (Armonk, NY: M. E. Sharpe, 1995). The book, the ninth in a series addressing campaign finance, examined funding of presidential and congressional elections, investigated the activities of political action committees, and analyzed the possibilities for electoral reform. Alexander's *Financing Politics: Money, Elections, and Political Reform* (Washington, DC: Congressional Quarterly Press, 1992) provided a historical overview of campaign finance, explored the various aspects of contemporary campaign finance on the national and state levels, and appraised reform efforts.

Douglas J. Amy (b. 1951)

Douglas Amy, an expert on electoral voting systems, is an advocate for election reform and the use of proportional representation in U.S. elections. In 1981 Amy received his PhD in political science from the University of Massachusetts at Amherst. He served as visiting assistant professor at Oberlin College before moving to the Department of Politics at Mount Holyoke College in 1981 where he presently serves as a full professor.

Since 1987 Amy's main research interest has been alternative electoral systems and the prospects for election reform in the United States. In 2002 he published an updated edition of *Real Choices, New Voices: How Proportional Representation Elections Revitalize American Democracy* (New York: Columbia University Press), originally published in 1993. Amy critiques the single-member district election system, which he sees as deeply flawed, and argues for replacing it with proportional representation (PR) elections. Amy argues that PR elections would ensure fair and accurate representation of all parties, help to eliminate gerrymandering, encourage the election of more women to office, increase voter turnout, encourage the creation of a multiparty system that would give Americans more choices at the polls, and help alleviate the growing discontent felt among many American voters. In *Behind the Ballot Box: A Citizen's Guide to Voting Systems* (Westport, CT: Greenwood Publishing Group, 2000), Amy examines the advantages and disadvantages associated with the voting systems used in Western democracies.

Since 1993 Amy has spent a good deal of time promoting PR election reform, writing numerous articles, papers, and op-ed pieces about the need for election reform. Amy has been active in several organizations that promote PR. In an effort to make information about proportional representation and election reform more readily available to the public, Amy created a Web site in 1996 containing information about proportional representation. Called the Proportional Representation Library (www.mtholyoke .edu/acad/polit/damy/prlib.htm), the site contains introductory readings on PR, in-depth articles, an extensive bibliography of readings, and a guide to other PR-related Web sites.

Susan Brownell Anthony (1820–1906)

Susan B. Anthony played a major role in the fight for woman suffrage during the second half of the 19th century. Anthony's involvement in the temperance movement led her to the realization that women could affect public policy only if they had full citizenship rights, including the right to vote. Beginning in 1865 she initiated an effort to have the rights of women protected under the Fourteenth and Fifteenth Amendments, along with those of former slaves. Anthony's fight for woman suffrage reached a critical stage in 1871 when she concluded that the Fourteenth Amendment could be used in the fight for the right to vote. She decided to test this interpretation by attempting to vote in the 1872 election. Anthony and a few other women in Rochester, New York, succeeded in registering and voting. Having attended the Republican National Convention earlier that year, where she received at least a glimmer of hope that the Republican Party favored rights for women, Anthony campaigned for the Republicans and voted a straight Republican ticket in that election. However, no flood of women followed her example. Within two weeks a deputy federal marshal arrested her for violating federal law originally intended to prevent former Southern rebels from voting. At the conclusion of the trial, the presiding judge stated that the right or privilege of voting originates in the state constitution, not in the national Constitution. Therefore, because state law forbade women to vote, the only course to take was to direct the jury to find the defendant guilty. Anthony was fined $100 and the costs of prosecution, an assessment she declared she would not pay. She was denied the opportunity of taking her case to the national arena when the judge stated that he would not require her imprisonment pending payment of the fine, thus blocking an appeal to the Supreme Court on a writ of habeas corpus.

Anthony spent the remaining 34 years of her life engaged in a campaign for suffrage that produced few clear victories. Her major objective was to see a woman suffrage amendment added to the federal Constitution, and in her pursuit of that goal she continued to lecture throughout the nation on behalf of the rights of women. Although Anthony favored a national rather than a state-by-state strategy, she campaigned in specific states and territories that showed promise of extending the franchise to women. Anthony served as president of the National American Woman Suffrage Association from 1892, when Elizabeth Cady Stanton retired from the office, until 1900, when she had reached the age of 80. In 1904 Anthony spoke for the last time before a U.S. Senate committee, advocating, with no perceptible results, a constitutional amendment guaranteeing woman suffrage. Anthony, frail and ill, attended her last convention in Baltimore in January 1906, less than two months before her death.

Kathleen L. Barber (b. 1924)

Kathleen Barber's distinguished career as a political scientist has been supplemented by active political involvement in the Cleveland, Ohio, area and by a deep concern for political reform. Her long experience culminated in the publication in 1995 of *Proportional Representation and Election Reform in Ohio* (Columbus: Ohio State University Press), the first book-length study to investigate the effects of proportional representation on municipal government.

Barber received a PhD in 1968 from Case Western Reserve University. She taught at John Carroll University in Cleveland from 1968 until her retirement in 1989, serving as chair of the Political Science Department from 1977 to 1985. A lifelong political activist, she has served in a number of political positions. In addition to holding various local Democratic Party positions, Barber twice served as a delegate to the Democratic National Convention. Among more recent community activities, Barber chaired the Citizens Committee for County Government Reform, appointed by the Cuyahoga County commissioners.

Barber has published articles in political science and law journals on various public policy questions, including Ohio judicial elections and reapportionment in Ohio and Michigan. Barber's book on proportional representation and election reform in Ohio presents case studies of five Ohio cities (Ashtabula, Cincinnati, Cleveland, Hamilton, and Toledo) that elected council members by proportional representation voting systems from 1915 to 1960. Barber discovered that, when proportional representation systems were used, independents, African Americans, and ethnic minorities succeeded in winning representation on city councils in areas where previously they had been excluded from holding seats. These results invoked controversial discussions about proportional representation, even though her findings indicate that the feared increase in political conflict and instability did not occur. In *A Right to Representation: Proportional Election Systems for the Twenty-First Century* (Columbus: Ohio State University Press, 2000), Barber examines alternative voting methods, including cumulative voting, limited voting, the instant runoff, and several types of proportional representation.

Kimball William Brace (b. 1951)

Kimball Brace is the founder and president of Election Data Services, Inc., a consulting firm specializing in redistricting, election administration, voting equipment usage, and census data analysis. Prior to founding Election Data Services, he was an associate editor of the biweekly newsletter, *Election Administration Reports*.

Brace attended American University in Washington, D.C., where he obtained a BA in political science in 1974. Brace founded Election Data Services in 1977 and has since become a nationally recognized expert on election administration issues. With 30 years of experience in consulting, he engages in the development of redistricting software and alternative redistricting plans, and provides on-site assistance with the redistricting operations of state legislatures and local governments.

Brace has provided expert testimony and litigation support in redistricting disputes. He has been involved in over 60 court cases, including *Albert Gore, Jr. et al. v. Katherine Harris as Secretary of State, State of Florida, et al.* (2000). In this, his most famous case, Brace testified on voting equipment design at the Leon County, Florida, Circuit Court hearing in December 2000. Brace testified about the punch card systems used in Miami-Dade, Nassau, Volusia, and Palm Beach counties in the 2000 presidential election, noting the problems associated with punch card chads. He stated that the accumulation of punched paper inside punch card voting machines could result in "chad build-up," possibly keeping voters from punching completely through a voting card.

In 1993 Brace edited *The Election Data Book: A Statistical Portrait of Voting America 1992* (Lanham, MD: Bernan Press), a detailed source of information on U.S. elections. In 2004 he analyzed the data of the Election Day Survey, the Military and Oversees Absentee Ballot Survey, and the National Voter Registration Survey on behalf of the U.S. Election Assistance Commission, and he testified before the commission in 2005, presenting the results. These studies lent support to statewide voter registration databases rather than locally administered registration rolls.

Richard A. Cloward (1926–2001)

Richard Cloward, in cooperation with Frances Fox Piven, his associate at the Human Service Employees Registration and Voter Education Campaign (Human SERVE), worked for over a decade to persuade government to institute programs to increase voter turnout. Cloward argued that government has not only the negative responsibility of not preventing people from registering to vote but also a positive duty to assure that eligible persons become voter registrants. Cofounder, treasurer, and executive director of Human SERVE, Cloward worked for the adoption of legislation that would allow people to register to vote when they apply for welfare, food stamps, Medicaid, unemployment benefits, and driver's licenses. Cloward's efforts proved successful in 1993 with the passage of the National Voter Registration Act, the so-called motor-voter bill. Cloward believed that motor-voter was an important step toward the complete enfranchisement of low-income and minority groups, and he hoped that, as a result of this legislation, 95 percent of Americans would become registered to vote.

Cloward received his PhD in sociology from Columbia University in 1958 and taught at the Columbia University School of Social Work from 1954 until 2001. In 1988 Cloward, with coauthor Frances Fox Piven, published *Why Americans Don't Vote* (New York: Pantheon), a book that attributed low voter turnout to a system that failed to encourage Americans sufficiently to register and vote. Twelve years later, Cloward and Pivens, in *Why Americans Still Don't Vote: And Why Politicians Like It That Way* (Boston: Beacon Press), argued that the major political parties are the culprits behind low voter turnout, each discouraging voter turnout from the opposite party rather than encouraging voters to participate in backing their candidates. In a eulogy delivered at the American Political Science Association meeting in 2001, Cloward's life was viewed as a testament to the combination of political activism and scholarship for the purpose of creating a more socially just world.

Chandler Davidson (b. 1936)

Chandler Davidson, well-known for his research on minority rights, taught at Rice University from 1966 to 2003 and still teaches part-time in his status as emeritus professor. He obtained his PhD from Princeton University in 1969. He was a founding member of the Department of Sociology at Rice and served as department chair for 14 years between 1979 and 2003.

In his first book, *Biracial Politics* (Baton Rouge: Louisiana State University Press, 1972), Davidson focused on the rise of black politics in the South beginning in the 1950s. His second, an edited collection of essays titled *Minority Vote Dilution* (Washington, DC: Howard University Press, 1984), was cited as an authoritative source in several legal opinions, including the 1986 U.S. Supreme Court opinion in *Thornburg v. Gingles*, a leading case on minority vote dilution. *Race and Class in Texas Politics* (Princeton, NJ: Princeton University Press) was published in 1990. Between 1987 and 1994, Davidson and Bernard Grofman, a political scientist at the University of California, Irvine, organized a research project focusing on the Voting Rights Act, funded by the National Science Foundation and the Rockefeller Foundation. This collaboration led to the publication of *Controversies in Minority Voting:*

The Voting Rights Act in Perspective (Washington, DC: Brookings Institution, 1992), an edited collection of papers on the Voting Rights Act. Davidson and Grofman published a second edited volume, *Quiet Revolution in the South: The Impact of the Voting Rights Act, 1965–1990* (Princeton, NJ: Princeton University Press, 1994), which contained the results of empirical studies by 27 scholars and voting rights lawyers that trace the impact of the Voting Rights Act. Both books have been cited by the U.S. Supreme Court in voting rights opinions.

Davidson has worked as a consultant or appeared as an expert witness in more than 30 lawsuits involving voting rights and other civil rights matters. In 1976 he was the plaintiffs' chief expert witness in the Houston area U.S. District Court case *Greater Houston Civic Council v. Mann* that eventually resulted in Houston's present method of electing council members. Davidson testified before the U.S. Senate Judiciary Committee in 1981 on a proposed amendment to section 2 of the Voting Rights Act that established a "totality of circumstances" test to determine violations of voting rights. Davidson has worked as a consultant to the U.S. Department of Justice in voting litigation in the South, including cases in Mobile and Selma, Alabama, and has conducted research for the state of Texas in *Vera v. Richards,* a congressional redistricting case growing out of the redistricting process in the 1990s.

David L. Dill (b. 1957)

David Dill is founder and member of the board of directors of the Verified Voting Foundation and VerfiedVoting.org. He opposes the use of paperless electronic voting machines, advocating instead voter-verified paper trails. The organization has been successful, particularly in Ohio, in dissuading election boards from purchasing paperless electronic voting machines.

Dill received his MS and PhD from Carnegie Mellon University and joined the Stanford University faculty in 1987. With more than 140 published works, Dill is an established scholar in his field. For his contributions to the verification of circuits and systems, he was named a fellow of the Institute of Electrical and Electronics Engineers (IEEE) in 2001. For his work in developing verifiable voting systems, he was named a fellow of the Association for Computing Machinery (ACM) in 2005.

Dill's interests in voting technology policy issues broadened in 2003 to include the role of election procedures as a means of securing trustworthy election results as well as the development of standards for voting systems. He authored the "Resolution on Electronic Voting" (www.verifiedvotingfoundation.org/article .php?id=5028), calling for a voter-verified paper trail. Many noted computer scientists endorsed this resolution.

As a distinguished authority on verifiable voting, Dill has served on the California Secretary of State's Ad Hoc Task Force on Touch-Screen Voting, the Citizens Direct Recording Electronic Voting System Oversight Board of the Santa Clara County Registrar of Voters, and the Institute of Electrical and Electronics Engineers Project 1583 Voting Equipment Standards Committee. He has testified about electronic voting before the U.S. Senate and the Commission on Federal Election Reform, cochaired by former president Jimmy Carter and former secretary of state James Baker III. For his work on verifiable voting and efforts to increase election transparency, Dill received the 2004 Electronic Frontier Foundation's Pioneer Award.

Richard L. Engstrom (b. 1946)

Richard Engstrom has conducted extensive research on electoral reform. He taught at the University of New Orleans from 1971 to 2006, where he was a research professor of political science. Engstrom moved to Chapel Hill, North Carolina, where he holds a position at the Center for Civil Rights at the University of North Carolina Law School. Engstrom received his PhD in 1971 from the University of Kentucky and joined the political science faculty at the University of New Orleans (UNO). He served as department chair at UNO from 1976 to 1979 and as the coordinator of graduate studies from 1990 to 1992 and from 1993 to 2006. His research has covered a wide array of topics, including the history of redistricting in Louisiana, cumulative voting elections in 15 Texas local government jurisdictions, racial gerrymandering, vote dilution, proportional representation, alternative judicial election systems, the single transferable vote, and the Voting Rights Act.

In *Fair and Effective Representation? Debating Electoral Reform and Minority Rights* (Lanham, MD: Rowman & Littlefield, 2001), coauthored with Mark E. Rush, Engstrom advocated limited, cumulative, and preference voting as mechanisms for reducing political conflict and redistricting litigation. Engstrom's published research has been cited in several rulings of the U.S. Supreme Court, including the landmark voting rights decision *Thornburgh v. Gingles* (1986). He has served as an expert witness in numerous court cases involving the voting rights of African Americans, Hispanic Americans, Native Americans, and Native Alaskans. He established himself as a leading authority on the use of modified multiseat electoral systems—such as limited, cumulative, and preference voting—as alternative remedies for dilutive electoral arrangements in the United States. In October 2005 he testified before the House Subcommittee on the Constitution regarding an oversight hearing on the "Voting Rights Act: The Continuing Need for Section 5."

Russ Feingold (b. 1953)

Russ Feingold, a U.S. senator (D-WI), led the effort along with Sen. John McCain (R-AZ) to gain passage of the Bipartisan Campaign Reform Act (BCRA) of 2002. They worked for nearly seven years to pass the legislation. The BCRA's main provision eliminates all soft money donations to the national political party committees but also doubles the contribution limit of hard money contributions from $1,000 to $2,000 per candidate per election cycle. It also prohibits issues ads on behalf of federal candidates funded by corporate or union money from running within 30 days of a primary or nominating convention or within 60 days of a general election.

Born in Wisconsin, Feingold graduated with a BA from the University of Wisconsin in 1975 and received a Rhodes Scholarship to attend Magdalen College at Oxford University, where he earned another BA in 1977. On his return to the United States, Feingold attended Harvard Law School and earned a JD in 1979. Feingold practiced law in Madison, Wisconsin, from 1979 to 1985. He was elected to the Wisconsin State Senate in 1982 and remained there until his bid for the U.S. Senate in 1992.

Since passage of the BCRA, Feingold has continued to support campaign finance and lobbying reform. He and McCain introduced a reform bill to control campaign donations from section 527 groups (named for the section of the Internal Revenue

Service code under which they are organized). The reform bill would require 527s to register as political committees, and, if they became involved in federal and state elections, they would be required to pay for those activities with at least 50 percent hard money from contributions limited by federal law. The bill also would limit the contributions to nonfederal accounts of all federal political committees to $25,000 per year.

In July 2005 Feingold and McCain introduced a lobbying reform bill that would ban all lobbyist gift giving to senators. In addition, lawmakers would be prohibited from accepting free travel on corporate jets. The bill would place a two-year moratorium on members of Congress, congressional staffers, and executive branch officials from becoming lobbyists after leaving government service, and it would require quarterly lobbying activity disclosure reports rather than the present semiannual reports. In the 108th Congress (2003–2005), McCain and Feingold, unhappy with the performance of the Federal Election Commission (FEC), introduced the Federal Election Administration Act, which would replace the FEC with a new agency, the Federal Election Administration, and grant the new agency broader regulatory powers and increased enforcement capabilities.

Bernard N. Grofman (b. 1944)

Bernard Grofman, a professor of political science and social psychology in the School of Social Sciences at the University of California, Irvine, has published extensively on such subjects as voting rights, voter turnout, and reapportionment. Born in Houston, Texas, he received a BS (1966), an MA (1968), and a PhD in political science (1972) from the University of Chicago.

In 1976 Grofman joined the political science faculty at the University of California at Irvine. In the 1980s his work in electoral systems began to blossom. He edited *Representation and Redistricting* (Lexington, MA: D. C. Heath, 1982), which investigated questions related to redistricting and minority representation. In 1984 and 1986 respectively, he edited *Choosing an Election System* (New Haven, CT: Yale University Press) and *Electoral Systems and Their Political Consequences* (New York: Agathon). In the 1990s Grofman served as an expert witness in several cases involving redistricting litigation or as a court-appointed expert on reapportionment.

Grofman, along with Chandler Davidson, initiated a research project funded by the National Science Foundation and the Rockefeller Foundation to investigate the consequences of the Voting Rights Act. Grofman and Davidson edited *Controversies in Minority Voting: The Voting Rights Act in Perspective* (Washington, DC: Brookings Institution Press, 1992), an examination of the 1965 Voting Rights Act and its amendments, and *Quiet Revolution in the South: The Impact of the Voting Rights Act, 1965–1990* (Princeton, NJ: Princeton University Press, 1994), which focuses on the effects of election reform on minority group representation. Grofman also edited *Legislative Term Limits: Public Choice Perspectives* (New York; Kluwer Academic Publishers, 1996), a balanced treatment of the probable effects of term limits on rates of legislative turnover and the operation of representation.

Minority Representation and the Quest for Voting Equality (New York: Cambridge University Press, 1992), which Grofman coauthored with Lisa Handley and Richard Niemi, provides an excellent overview of minority voting rights and an examination of congressional and court-established standards of vote dilution. In 1998 Grofman published another edited volume, *Race and Redistricting in the 1990s* (New York: Agathon), providing an overview of voting rights case law and the consequences of redistricting for racial representation.

Lani Guinier (b. 1950)

Lani Guinier, the first African American woman to become a tenured professor at Harvard Law School, is noted for her advocacy for civil rights, political equality, voting rights, and minority representation. Born in New York City, Guinier received a BA in 1971 from Radcliffe College and earned a JD in 1974 from Yale Law School. Guinier became assistant counsel for the NAACP Legal Defense Fund in New York City (1981–1988). She won major voting rights cases in Alabama and other Southern states. Her academic career began in 1988 with an associate professor appointment to the University of Pennsylvania Law School.

Guinier drew national attention in 1993 when President Bill Clinton, noting her accomplishments in the Civil Rights Division during the Carter administration, nominated her to be the first African American woman to head that office of the U.S. Justice Department. Due to her views on affirmative action, critics labeled her a "quota queen" and vehemently attacked her views on democracy and voting. Clinton withdrew the nomination and distanced himself from Guinier. This experience catapulted Guinier into the national limelight, and she spoke out publicly on issues of race, gender, and democracy.

The Tyranny of the Majority: Fundamental Fairness in Representative Democracy (New York: Free Press, 1994) is a collection of Guinier's already published law review articles, edited for a widened readership. Guinier examines the failure of majority rule at times to promote democratic principles in a heterogeneous society. To enhance minority representation in legislatures, she argues that legislators should be elected by a cumulative voting system from multimember districts rather than a plurality voting system with single-member districts. She also suggests that simple majority rule should be replaced by a procedure allowing for power sharing between minorities and the majority, giving the majority most of the victories but allowing minorities to achieve success on certain issues. In her view, Voting Rights Act case law, with its focus on electing minority office holders from single-member districts, has hindered the true achievement of political equality for minorities.

Stanley A. Halpin Jr. (b. 1940)

As part of his public interest law practice, Stanley Halpin has taken numerous cases dealing with voting rights. After receiving his BA in 1962 from the University of Southwestern Louisiana, Halpin went on to Tulane University Law School, where he earned his JD in 1965. From 1969 to 1972, he engaged in some 40 voting rights cases on behalf of African Americans, including East Carroll Parish School Board v. Marshall, argued before the U.S. Supreme Court in 1976. The Court decided that single-member districts must be used to elect school board members, barring any extenuating circumstances. In the meantime Halpin furthered his education, and in 1978 he received a PhD in political science from George Washington University.

From 1980 to 1983, Halpin served as a litigation training specialist for the New Mexico Legal Services Support Project in Albuquerque. In 1981 he took part in litigation invalidating New Mexico's redistricting efforts, which were determined to constitute racial gerrymandering against Native Americans and Hispanic

Americans. The case resulted in a federal court-drawn plan under which an additional number of Hispanic Americans and Native Americans were elected to the state legislature. From 1983 to 1988, Halpin directed the Farmworkers Legal Assistance Project of Louisiana, an organization that provided legal services with regard to employment questions for indigent seasonal and migrant farm workers. As part of his public interest law practice Halpin took part in ensuring fair electoral districting for Native Americans and Hispanic Americans in the 1990 redistricting of the New Mexico legislature. In Louisiana he challenged congressional districts on behalf of African American plaintiffs, which resulted in the election of William Jefferson, Louisiana's first black congressman since Reconstruction. In 2006, despite allegations of bribery and several electoral opponents, Jefferson retained his seat in the House in a runoff election.

Halpin joined the law faculty at Southern University Law Center in 1990 and served as coordinator of the Institute of Human Rights and Civil Rights. He conducts research on voting rights law and has published articles on voting rights and racial gerrymandering. He has made presentations on such topics as cumulative voting, limited voting and other remedies for minority vote dilution, the Voting Rights Act, and minority representation in Louisiana.

Bev Harris (b. 1951)

As founder and director of Black Box Voting Inc., Harris runs the antielectronic voting Web site, BlackBoxVoting.org, not to be confused with BlackBoxVoting.com. She has earned the moniker "godmother" of reforming electronic voting. Her nonpartisan elections watchdog group has filed the largest number of Freedom of Information Act requests in history to examine the internal audit logs of voting machines in 3,000 counties. As a journalist and an activist, Harris has written about electronic voting since 2002 and was the first to discover that U.S. Sen. Chuck Hagel (R.) of Nebraska had ownership interests in and had been CEO of the company that built the voting machines that counted his constituents' votes.

With an estimated 6,000 hours of research on the voting system industry, Harris wrote *Black Box Voting: Ballot Tampering in the 21st Century* (Renton, WA: Talion Publishing, 2004), widely considered an authoritative source on electronic voting. *Black Box Voting* provides details on the various conflicts of interest that accompany modern-day voting systems. In particular, many voting systems—run by private for-profit companies—do not have adequate oversight and certification standards, resulting in systems that are vulnerable to hackers and vote manipulation. Salon.com dubbed Harris the Erin Brockovich of elections as a result of her extensive investigative efforts.

In the course of her research, she discovered that a plan had been formulated to manipulate voting outcomes in a Georgia U.S. senatorial race. Her audit files were later used to uncover security flaws in Diebold voting machines. In 2003 Harris and a colleague sued Diebold Election Systems and won restitution from them for making fraudulent claims in selling a voting system to Alameda County, California. Her investigation of Sequoia Voting Systems found over 100,000 errors in the 2004 election logs in Palm County, Florida, including over 1,000 instances of tampering with voting machines during the middle of the election and 48 machines that had votes dated and time-stamped weeks before the election. Harris and a core of other electronic voting activists are responsible for a reexamination of the use and abuse of electronic voting machines.

Paul Jacob (b. 1960)

Paul Jacob is a prominent advocate of legislative term limits, initiative and referendum rights, and limited government. His radio commentary, "Common Sense," is heard on 272 radio stations in 49 states. Jacob also writes a weekly column accessible on the Web at Townhall.com. He serves as a senior fellow at Americans for Limited Government, from which he produces his radio and Internet commentary. Jacob first captured national attention in the 1980s as a draft registration resister. His principles were put to the test in 1985 when he was imprisoned for five months for violating the Selective Service Act.

Most recognized for his work in the term limits movement, Jacob was executive director of U.S. Term Limits, the premier advocacy organization lobbying for legislative term limits, from its creation in 1992 until 1999. He mobilized the passage of congressional term limit measures in several state legislatures only to have the U.S. Supreme Court in *U.S. Term Limits v. Thornton*

(1995) rule that state-imposed congressional term limits were unconstitutional. Due in part to Jacob's efforts, 15 state legislatures, 36 governorships, and thousands of local offices fall under term limits. Jacob continues to serve as a board member and senior fellow of U.S. Term Limits.

In 1998 Jacob testified before the Senate Judiciary Committee's Subcommittee on the Constitution, arguing that the 1970s campaign finance laws have been ineffective. He urged members of Congress to abide by term limits voluntarily to ensure fair and competitive elections. He has repeatedly attacked the Bipartisan Campaign Reform Act and other campaign finance reform laws as violations of the First Amendment guarantee of free speech. In 2001 Jacob founded Citizens in Charge, a group advocating expansion of initiative and referendum rights to additional states. As the president of Citizens in Charge, Jacob works to have more citizens gain access to the procedures of direct democracy.

David B. Magleby (b. 1949)

David Magleby has conducted research on such topics as initiatives and referenda as direct democracy devices and the role of money in politics and its influence on congressional and presidential elections. Magleby is Distinguished Professor of Political Science and Dean of the College of Family, Home, and Social Sciences at Brigham Young University (BYU) and Senior Research Fellow at the Center for the Study of Elections and Democracy at BYU. Born in Salt Lake City, Utah, he attended the University of Utah and received a BA in political science in 1973. He completed an MA (1974) and PhD (1980) in political science at the University of California, Berkeley.

With his colleagues at the Center for the Study of Elections and Democracy, Magleby has collected data on campaign spending and campaign communications in federal competitive elections since 1996. His more recent books include *The Battle for Congress: Iraq, Scandal and Campaign Finance* (edited with Kelly D. Patterson [Boulder, CO: Paradigm, 2008]), *Financing the 2004 Election* (Washington, DC: Brookings Institution Press, 2006, edited with Anthony Corrado and Kelly D. Patterson), and *The Last Hurrah? Soft Money and Issue Advocacy in the 2000 Congressional Elections* (Washington, DC: Brookings Institution Press, 2004, edited with J. Quin Monson). He is a longtime coauthor of the popular textbook *Government by the People* with James MacGregor Burns, J. W. Peltason, Thomas E. Cronin, David O'Brien, and Paul Light (Upper Saddle River, NJ: Prentice Hall). Magleby has served as an expert witness on numerous court cases at both the state and federal levels, most prominently during the litigation related to the Bipartisan Campaign Reform Act (BCRA) of 2002.

Michael J. Malbin (b. 1943)

Michael Malbin is founder of the Campaign Finance Institute (CFI), serving as the organization's director since 1999. Writing extensively about the role of money in politics for more than 30 years, Malbin has become a leading scholar in the field. Through numerous books and journal articles, he has influenced the debate on campaign finance reform. Born in Brooklyn, New York, Malbin received a PhD in political science from Cornell University in 1973. Before taking a faculty position at the State University of New York at Albany, Malbin worked for the Iran-Contra Committee and the House Republican Conference, served as a speech writer for then Secretary of Defense Dick Cheney (1989–1990), was a presidential appointee to the National Humanities Council (1990–1994), and served as a visiting professor at Yale University (spring 1996) and at George Washington University (fall 1999).

From 1990 to 1999, Malbin directed the Center for Legislative and Political Studies in the Rockefeller Institute. From 1997 to 1998, Malbin was a guest scholar at the Brookings Institution where he coauthored *The Day after Reform: Sobering Campaign Finance Lessons from the American States* (Albany, NY: Rockefeller Institute Press, 1998) with Thomas L. Gais. The authors survey the agencies in the 50 states responsible for administering campaign finance laws. This survey of revisions in state campaign finance laws and their operation was one of the first of its kind. Shortly after his Brookings Institution appointment, Malbin founded the Campaign Finance Institute. Affiliated with George Washington University, the CFI conducts research, recruits task forces, and makes recommendations for campaign finance reform.

Since founding the CFI, Malbin has edited two books on campaign finance reform, *Life after Reform: When the Bipartisan Campaign Reform Act Meets Politics* (Lanham, MD: Rowman & Littlefield, 2003) and *The Election after Reform: Money, Politics and the*

Bipartisan Campaign Reform Act (Lanham, MD: Rowman & Little-field, 2006). In *The Election after Reform,* he and other contributors debunk the claim that the soft money ban provision in the Bipartisan Campaign Reform Act simply caused contributors to shift donations to 527 groups.

Thomas E. Mann (b. 1944)

Thomas Mann is a senior fellow and W. Averell Harriman Chair at the Brookings Institution. He has published extensively on the subjects of campaign finance, redistricting, and election reform. Mann received a BA in political science from the University of Florida in 1966 and went on to obtain his MA (1968) and PhD (1977) at the University of Michigan. He has taught at or been named distinguished lecturer at numerous universities, including American University, Baylor University, Bowdoin College, Georgetown University, Johns Hopkins University, Loyola University, Princeton University, and University of Virginia.

From 1981 until 1987, Mann served as executive director of the American Political Science Association. He went to the Brookings Institution in 1987 to direct the Governmental Studies Program and remained in that position until 1999. Among Mann's publications are the coauthored works *The New Campaign Finance Sourcebook* (Washington, DC: Brookings Institution Press, 2005) and *Inside the Campaign Finance Battle: Court Testimony on the New Reforms* (Washington, DC: Brookings Institution Press, 2003). Mann has testified as an expert witness for the U.S. Department of Justice, the Federal Election Commission, and Defendant Intervenors in *McConnell v. Federal Election Commission* (2003) concerning the Bipartisan Campaign Finance Act of 2002. His current focus is on redistricting, election reform, and party polarization. His latest book, published with Norman Ornstein, is *The Broken Branch: How Congress Is Failing America and How to Get It Back on Track* (New York: Oxford University Press, 2006).

John S. McCain III (b. 1936)

John McCain, a war hero and longtime elected official, has sponsored campaign finance reform bills since 1992 and finally succeeded with the passage of the Bipartisan Campaign Reform Act

(BCRA) in 2002. The BCRA's main provision eliminates soft money donations to the national political party committees and at the same time doubles the individual contribution limit of hard money from $1,000 to $2,000 per candidate per election cycle. The legislation also restricts issues ads, created on behalf of federal candidates and paid for by corporate or union money, from running within 30 days of a primary or nominating convention or within 60 days of a general election.

With Russell Feingold, McCain has sponsored several reform measures, including a requirement that 527 groups, named for the section of the U.S. tax code under which they are established, to register as political committees; lobbying reforms that curb lobbyist gifts to members of Congress; revisions to the public funding of presidential primaries and elections that eliminate state-by-state spending limits and increase overall spending restrictions; restructuring of the Federal Election Commission; and broadcast advertising reform requiring broadcast stations to devote a reasonable amount of airtime to election programming.

Following a family tradition, McCain attended the U.S. Naval Academy and graduated in 1958. As a Navy pilot, his aircraft was shot down over North Vietnam in 1967, and he was captured and imprisoned in the notorious Hanoi Hilton, a brutal prisoner of war camp. He returned to the United States in 1973 and continued to serve in the Navy until 1981. In 1982 McCain was elected as a Republican to the U.S. House of Representatives from Arizona's first congressional district, and in 1986 he gained election to the U.S. Senate. Often cast as a maverick due to his willingness to cross party lines, McCain is conservative on many issues.

Heralded for his crusade against pork barrel spending and his involvement in campaign finance reform, in 1997 *Time* magazine named McCain one of the "25 Most Influential People in America." Nine years later *Time* ranked him among "America's 10 Best Senators." McCain's career evidences a devotion to campaign finance reform, due in part to his involvement in the Keating Five, a group of U.S. senators in the late 1980s who allegedly aided Charles Keating, the banker charged with mismanaging savings and loan company assets. McCain later cited his association with the Keating Five scandal as one of the reasons he undertook campaign finance reform. Although defeated in the Republican primaries for the presidential nomination in 2000, McCain used his continued popularity to negotiate successfully with President George W. Bush for campaign finance reform legislation.

Laughlin McDonald (b. 1938)

Laughlin McDonald has been the director of the Voting Rights Project of the American Civil Liberties Union (ACLU) in Atlanta, Georgia, since 1972. He has supported the voting rights of minorities, including African Americans and Native Americans, in numerous discrimination cases. McDonald has argued cases before the U.S. Supreme Court, one of which defined and significantly expanded the scope of the preclearance of state and local alterations in voting rules under section 5 of the Voting Rights Act.

Born in South Carolina, McDonald received his JD degree from the University of Virginia Law School in 1965. McDonald has published several articles on voting rights, including treatments of the disfranchisement of African Americans in South Carolina, the need for preclearance, universal voter registration as a means of reducing nonparticipation, and vote dilution. He has coauthored a number of books including *Racial Equality* (Lincolnwood, IL: National Textbook Co., 1977); *The Rights of Racial Minorities* (New York: Harper Collins, the 1980, 1993, and 1998 editions of the ACLU's handbook on racial minority rights); *Litigation under the Voting Rights Act* (1986), a publication of the Center for Constitutional Rights; *Voting Rights in the South: Ten Years of Litigation Challenging Continuing Discrimination against Minorities* (New York: American Civil Liberties Union, 1982); and *A Voting Rights Odyssey: Black Enfranchisement in Georgia* (New York: Cambridge University Press, 2003). In *A Voting Rights Odyssey,* McDonald examines Georgia political leaders' efforts to maintain the status quo of white supremacy after the white primary was declared unconstitutional, and he offers insights into the many challenges that the Civil Rights Movement faced.

Louise Overacker (1891–1982)

Louise Overacker, a noted political scientist, focused much of her research efforts on campaign and electoral reform, making significant contributions to a clearer understanding of the process and potential difficulties of campaign finance. She lent her impressive record as a political scientist to the question of campaign finance reform. After receiving her PhD from the University of Chicago in 1925, Overacker taught at Wellesley College for 22 years.

In the 1920s Overacker conducted pioneering research on the primary election process and in 1932 completed *Money in Elections* (New York: Macmillan), a landmark treatise on campaign financing. She examined efforts to bring about finance regulation, identified the results of each effort, and suggested potentially more effective controls on campaign funding procedures.

In the 1930s Overacker investigated such topics as the effects of the Depression on the level and sources of campaign donations. After passage of the Hatch Act in 1939, legislation that among other things prohibited political parties from soliciting political contributions and other assistance from federal employees, Overacker investigated the effects of the new legislation on the 1940 presidential election. During this period she also examined the political activities of labor unions, including the consequences of legislation forbidding unions from making campaign contributions. In 1946 Overacker published *Presidential Campaign Funds* (Boston: Boston University Press). Though noting the rising cost of campaigns, she concluded that such costs themselves were not related directly to corruption. Of greater concern was the source of contributions. Without direct regulation of campaign funding, she advocated publicity as a means of controlling donations.

Mark P. Petracca (b. 1955)

Since 1991 Mark Petracca has focused much of his scholarly activity on term limits for public officials, becoming a noted advocate of the claimed advantages of such limits. A native of Quincy, Massachusetts, Petracca received his AB in government from Cornell University (1977) and AM (1979) and PhD (1986) in political science from the University of Chicago. He joined the political science department at the University of California at Irvine. Petracca chaired the political science department at UC Irvine from 1996 to 2002 and resumed chair duties in 2004.

Petracca has lectured extensively in defense of term limits and has contributed commentary to newspapers around the nation, including the *Christian Science Monitor, Houston Chronicle,*

Los Angeles Times, and *Chicago Tribune.* He has testified before the House Judiciary Committee's Subcommittee on Civil and Constitutional Rights (1993) and the Senate Judiciary Committee's Subcommittee on the Constitution (1995). Petracca supports term limits as a means of restoring the idea of rotation in office as a fundamental principle of representative government and combating the professionalization of legislative politics.

Petracca prefers a limit of fewer than 12 years for members of the House because he believes a 12-year, or 6-term, limit would do little to introduce the principle of rotation in office and to eliminate professionalism. He recommends the gradual introduction of limits so that the House will not experience a massive replacement of members in the same year, which would leave the legislative chamber devoid of experienced legislators. Having reconsidered whether a one-size-fits-all term limit proposal is workable, Petracca argues that, if elected officials were committed to the voluntary principle of rotation in office, term limits would not be necessary.

Richard H. Pildes (b. 1957)

The Sudler Family Professor of Constitutional Law at the New York University School of Law, Richard Pildes for many years has advocated election reform. He received his BA from Princeton University in 1979, majoring in theoretical physical chemistry, and he received his JD from Harvard Law School (1983) and served as a judicial clerk to U.S. Supreme Court Justice Thurgood Marshall (1984–1985). After entering private practice in Boston for a brief period, he joined the faculty at the University of Michigan Law School in 1988 and remained there until 2000.

Pildes has published extensively on subjects relevant to electoral reform, including articles dealing with cumulative voting, the Voting Rights Act, the controversy over the 2000 presidential election, and the Supreme Court decision in *Shaw v. Reno* (1993) on racial redistricting. He contributed a chapter on cumulative voting to a volume dealing with representation and reapportionment and coauthored *The Law of Democracy: Legal Structure of the Political Process* (New York: Foundation Press, 1998, 2001, 2005 supplement) and *When Elections Go Bad: The Law of Democracy and the 2000 Presidential Election* (New York: Foundation Press, 2001) with Pamela Karlan and Samuel

Issacharoff. In 2006 Pildes coedited *The Future of the Voting Rights Act* for the Russell Sage Foundation (New York). His writings have appeared in popular publications on such topics as political gerrymandering, racial redistricting, and alternative voting systems.

In addition to his academic work, Pildes is an active public law litigator. He has served as a federal court-appointed independent expert on voting rights litigation and has worked with North Carolina in redistricting litigation before the U.S. Supreme Court. He has assisted Ohio's legislature with court-ordered redistricting and prepared a brief for the U.S. Supreme Court in a case challenging the redistricting of the St. Louis City Council. He currently serves as codirector of the New York University Center for Law and Security and is a member of the National Commission on Elections and Voting.

Frances Fox Piven (b. 1932)

In cooperation with Richard Cloward, Frances Fox Piven has worked toward government reform of voter registration laws. Believing that the 1965 Voting Rights Act, which contained provisions restricting possible attempts of state and local governments to deny the right to vote, was insufficient to guarantee suffrage rights, Piven has advocated a more positive role for government in encouraging voter registration. She has focused her attention on enfranchising low-income and minority Americans. As a cofounder of the Human Service Employees Registration and Voter Education Campaign (Human SERVE) in 1983, Piven for over a decade advocated registering people to vote when they apply for welfare, food stamps, Medicaid, unemployment benefits, and drivers' licenses. The efforts of Human SERVE came to partial fruition in May 1993 when President Bill Clinton signed into law the National Voter Registration Act (the so-called motor-voter bill).

Born in Calgary, Alberta, Canada, Piven came to the United States in 1933 and became a naturalized citizen in 1953, the same year she received her BA in city planning from the University of Chicago. She obtained a master of arts degree in city planning (1956) and a PhD in social science (1962), also from the University of Chicago. She became a research associate for the city's antipoverty agency, Mobilization for Youth, a community-based service organization on New York's Lower East Side. Before moving to the Graduate Center at the City University of New York (CUNY) as a distinguished professor of political science and sociology, Piven taught at several other universities.

At the School of Social Work at Columbia University, she collaborated with Richard Cloward, publishing books on various social welfare topics. In 1988 Piven and Cloward published *Why Americans Don't Vote* (New York: Pantheon), arguing that commonly accepted explanations for low voter turnout in the United States that focus on apathy and alienation are inadequate. Instead they stressed electoral laws that discouraged people from registering and exercising their right to vote. Twelve years later, in *Why Americans Still Don't Vote: And Why Politicians Like It That Way* (Boston: Beacon Press), they argued that the major political parties discourage voter turnout among supporters of the opposing party rather than encouraging voters to participate in backing their candidates. In *The War at Home: The Domestic Costs of Bush's Militarism* (New York: New Press, 2004), Piven argues that the war on terror has helped President George W. Bush shore up his political base and furthers what she considers a regressive social and economic agenda. Piven is currently developing a historical and theoretical explanation of how protest movements affect American political development.

Trevor Potter (b. 1955)

Trevor Potter is president and general counsel of the Campaign Legal Center. He joined the Caplin & Drysdale law firm based in Washington, D.C., in 2001 and heads its political activities practice. He is chair of the American Bar Association's Election Law Committee of the Administrative Law Section. Potter also serves as a legal adviser to the Committee on Economic Development's task force on campaign finance reform. He served as counsel for congressional sponsors of the Bipartisan Campaign Reform Act (BCRA) in *McConnell v. the Federal Election Commission* (2003), helping to defend the BCRA against its challengers. Potter served as a commissioner on the Federal Election Commission (FEC) from 1991 to 1995 and was chairman of the FEC in 1994. In 1988 Potter was deputy general counsel for George H. W. Bush's 1988 campaign, and in 2000 he served as general counsel for John McCain's primary campaign for the Republican presidential nomination.

Potter received an AB from Harvard College (1978) and a JD from the University of Virginia's School of Law (1982). As a nonresident Fellow at the Brookings Institution, he has published, edited, or contributed to several books in the field of campaign finance, including *The Campaign Finance Sourcebook* (Washington, DC: Brookings Institution Press, 1997), *Political Activity, Lobbying Laws and Gift Rules* (Little Falls, NJ: Glasser Legal Works, 1999, 2004), and *The New Campaign Finance Sourcebook* (Washington, DC: Brookings Institution Press, 2005). Potter serves as an editor of the "Campaign Finance Law" Web site at the Brookings Institution. He has testified before the Federal Election Commission on Internet issues and has appeared as an election law expert on several television and radio news programs.

Under Potter's leadership since 2002, the Campaign Legal Center has focused on campaign finance, campaign communications, and governmental ethics. The organization monitors the enforcement of campaign finance laws and participates in the Federal Election Commission advisory opinion and rule-making proceedings. In November 2006 Potter ceased participating in Campaign Legal Center activities directly related to the campaigns of potential 2008 presidential candidates because he represented Sen. John McCain's (R-AZ) presidential exploratory committee in his private legal practice.

Robert "Rob" Richie (b. 1962)

Rob Richie is executive director of FairVote—the Center for Voting and Democracy, a nonprofit organization that conducts research and distributes information on electoral reforms to promote voter participation and fair representation. Richie, an expert on both international and domestic electoral systems, has directed the Center since its founding in 1992. He graduated from Haverford with a BA in philosophy in 1987.

Richie was working for a nonprofit law and policy center in Washington, D.C., when he met his future wife, Cynthia Terrell, a political consultant. Together they worked for Jolene Unsoeld (D-WA), congresswoman from Washington, in her 1990 reelection campaign. After winning the closest congressional race in the nation in 1988, Unsoeld was the target of the best funded challenge to a House incumbent in 1990. Richie prepared and packaged research on her opponent. Although the research was factual, the process demonstrated the pressures facing candidates in winner-take-all elections to oversimplify issues. Unsoeld ultimately won by a comfortable margin, but in the process she downplayed some of the issues of particular interest to her core supporters in order to appeal to swing voters. Richie's new belief in the significance of electoral politics was tempered by an increased understanding of serious flaws in the current electoral process.

Richie and Terrell volunteered to work on a campaign for proportional representation (PR) in the Cincinnati, Ohio, city council elections. Although the campaign fell short of victory, Richie's article about the campaign that appeared in the national publication *In These Times* helped identify other national allies. Richie met Matthew Cossolotto, a former congressional aide who had formed an organization also called Citizens for Proportional Representation. With Cincinnati activist Bill Collins, they scheduled a founding meeting for June 1992 to establish a national organization. The meeting attracted PR supporters from 17 states. Richie moved to Washington, D.C., to work full-time as the organization's director. In 1993 Citizens for Proportional Representation changed its name to the Center for Voting and Democracy.

Richie worked with Cynthia McKinney's congressional staff to develop the States' Choice of Voting Systems Act, a bill designed to allow states to use multimember districts and proportional representation voting systems. He worked with congressional staff again in 2000 to draft the Bipartisan Federal Elections Review Act, a bill to study the feasibility of PR voting systems, the instant runoff, cumulative voting, and other voting reforms. Richie coauthored *Reflecting All of Us: The Case for Proportional Representation* (Boston: Beacon Press, 1999) and *Whose Vote Counts?* (Boston: Beacon Press, 2001) with Steven Hill, Joshua Cohen, and Joel Rogers.

Richie is a frequent source for print, radio, and television journalists, and his commentary has appeared in such publications as *The New York Times, The Wall Street Journal, The Washington Post, The New Republic,* and *The Nation.* He edits the Center's newsletter and other publications, such as the organization's Voting and Democracy reports, which contain biennial analyses of congressional elections.

Elizabeth Cady Stanton (1815–1902)

Elizabeth Cady Stanton, the daughter of a judge, became one of the foremost advocates of women's rights. In her youth she learned about the second-class status of women, overhearing stories in her father's law office of women forced to endure maltreatment with no relief available under existing laws. In 1840 she accompanied her husband, an abolitionist, to the world anti-slavery convention in London, England. At the convention she met other American women who shared a desire to further their rights. Eventually they would form the core of a woman suffrage movement in the United States.

In July 1848 Stanton succeeded in organizing a women's rights convention in Seneca Falls, New York, where she was then residing with her husband. At this convention Stanton introduced a woman suffrage resolution and succeeded in obtaining its adoption over objections that the women would be ridiculed for it. She met Susan B. Anthony in 1851, and the two women began a lifelong collaboration in support of woman suffrage. In 1869 the National Woman Suffrage Association was established, and the members chose Stanton as the organization's president, a position she held until the formation of the National American Woman Suffrage Association in 1890. In 1887, while Stanton was in Europe, the U.S. Senate for the first time voted on a constitutional amendment proposing woman suffrage. The amendment was defeated, with only 16 senators supporting the measure. While the National American Woman Suffrage Association met in Washington in February 1890, Stanton testified before a Senate committee that once again was exploring the possibility of woman suffrage. From 1881 to 1886, Stanton collaborated with Susan B. Anthony and Matilda Joslyn Gage in preparing the three-volume work, *History of Woman Suffrage* (New York: Arno Press, 1969).

Stanton's concerns went far beyond gaining the right to vote. She insisted on the right of women to act for themselves, not only in the voting booth but in all aspects of life, insisting on physical, intellectual, financial, and legal autonomy. In 1902, shortly before her death, Stanton wrote her last letters to President and Mrs. Theodore Roosevelt, appealing for their support for woman suffrage at the national level. Although final victory for woman suffrage was not achieved until 18 years after her death, with the ratification of the Nineteenth Amendment, Stanton was able to live her life, especially in her later years, much as she chose. Her life stood as a model for those women seeking greater recognition of women's rights after the victory of suffrage had been achieved.

Edward Still (b. 1946)

A lawyer in Birmingham, Alabama, Edward Still has played a prominent role in many reapportionment and voting rights cases. Born in Augusta, Georgia, Still received a BA degree from the University of Alabama (1968) and a JD degree from the university's law school (1971). While in law school, he joined the board of directors of the Legal Aid Program at Tuscaloosa. After practicing in a private partnership for four years in Tuscaloosa, he set up his own law office in Birmingham in 1975 and made the city his home until 1997. In the late 1970s, Still contracted with the Birmingham Area Legal Services Corporation to provide legal services to the poor. From 1997 to 2001, he was director of the Voting Rights Project of the Lawyers' Committee for Civil Rights Under Law, a nonprofit public interest law firm in Washington, D.C. He served as special counsel for the law firm of Dickstein, Shapiro, Morin, and Oshinksky (2001–2002) and reopened his Birmingham law practice in mid-2002.

Still's career includes service as counsel for numerous Alabama cities in redistricting matters and for minority groups in over 200 Voting Rights Act cases. Still has been a guest lecturer on the history of voting rights litigation and on election methods at several universities. During the 1984, 1988, and 1992 presidential elections, Still organized a statewide network of lawyers in Alabama for election-day ballot security and polling place irregularities.

Among the subjects of Still's publications are the impact of the Voting Rights Act of 1965 on Alabama; alternatives to the single-member district system; cumulative and limited voting in Chilton County, Alabama; the gerrymander; *Shaw v. Reno* (1993); and minority vote dilution. Still has played an active role in the Center for Voting and Democracy, an organization that provides information on, and analysis of, alternative electoral systems. A charter member of the organization, he was on the board from 1993 to 2003, serving a term as chair.

The many voting rights cases in which Still has been engaged involve such subjects as a local law restricting campaign-

ing on election day, an Alabama constitutional provision disfran-
chising "wife beaters," and limitations placed on the availability
of absentee ballots. Still's tenaciousness as a lawyer has been hon-
ored by author Isaac Asimov, who wrote a limerick that begins:

> Don't mess around with Lawyer Ed Still,
> For he puts those opposed through the mill.

Fred Wertheimer (b. 1939)

President of Common Cause from 1981 to 1995, Fred Wertheimer
is one of the nation's leading advocates of campaign finance reform. Wertheimer has for over 30 years worked on issues of electoral reform and government accountability. During his tenure at
Common Cause, he pushed for campaign finance reform and
higher ethical standards for public officials. In 1997 Wertheimer
founded Democracy 21, an organization dedicated to closing
loopholes in campaign finance laws, reforming the Federal Election Commission, improving the public financing system for
presidential elections, and promoting effective congressional
ethics rules.

Wertheimer is a graduate of the University of Michigan and
Harvard Law School. During his career Wertheimer has worked
as an attorney for the Securities and Exchange Commission,
served as counsel to the House Small Business Committee, and
worked for the late Massachusetts congressman Silvio Conte (R)
as his legislative counsel. Not until 1976 did Wertheimer begin
his work on campaign finance reform by serving as legal counsel
to Common Cause in the *Buckley v. Valeo* case (1976).

Called the "people's advocate" by *U.S. News and World Report,* Wertheimer has strongly supported campaign reform. He is
author of "Campaign Finance Reform: The Unfinished Agenda"
[*Annals of the American Academy of Political Science and Social Science,* 486 (July 1986)] and argued for reducing the costs of television advertisements in political campaigns in "TV Ad Wars:
How to Cut Advertising Costs in Political Campaigns" [*Harvard
International Journal of Press/Politics,* 2, 3 (1997)]. Frequently
sought as a commentator, Wertheimer has written articles for several newspapers and served as a political analyst and consultant
for television news programs.

6

Data and Documents

This chapter provides public opinion survey data, current information on campaign and election reform, and a summary of campaign finance regulations at the state level. Also included are survey data of attitudes toward campaign finance laws, regulation of special interest groups, public confidence in accurate vote counts, public financing of congressional campaigns, and the influence of money in elections. Major U.S. Supreme Court cases on campaign finance, political participation, and redistricting are identified and summarized. Given that many reformers have expressed deep concern about the increased influence of political action committees (PACs) on candidate success and election outcomes, we investigate the link between PAC expenditures in federal elections and the influence of money on American politics. In addition, the most expensive races for the U.S. House of Representatives and the U.S. Senate are identified. The data highlight the concrete linkage between money and success in politics, which to many indicates the need for further campaign finance reforms.

National voter turnout from 1960 through 2006 is taken as an indicator of political participation. Although voting is one of several ways to participate in politics, scholars often look to voter turnout as an indicator either of system legitimacy or of the level of citizen apathy. Those who supported the National Voter Registration Act of 1993 (NVRA) contended that, if voter registration was easier and less time-consuming, more Americans would vote. This proposition may be tested by determining whether the voter turnout rate rose since the enactment of the NVRA.

189

Campaign Finance Law

Since the early 1970s, Americans have been concerned periodically about the effects of campaign spending on the political process. In response, Congress passed major legislation in 1974 and 2002 to address the role of money in U.S. elections. Campaign finance laws mainly require public disclosure of the amount and source of donations and place contribution limits on individuals and groups.

The Federal Election Campaign Act (FECA) of 1974 limited campaign spending; required public disclosure of donor names; limited campaign contributions for national office from individuals, political parties and political action committees; instituted public financing of presidential elections; and prohibited cash contributions of more than $100. In addition, the FECA created the Federal Election Commission to enforce the law. Because the Supreme Court found some provisions unconstitutional, primarily the campaign spending limits, the 1974 law did not meet its primary objective except for the public disclosure requirements.

Senators John McCain (R-AZ) and Russ Feingold (D-WI) led the charge for the Bipartisan Campaign Reform Act (BCRA), which gained congressional approval amid the Enron scandal. The BCRA banned the raising or spending of soft money by national political parties, as well as by state and local party organizations engaged in federal election activities. It also placed time limits on when nonpartisan issues ads could be aired. Under the BCRA, hard money contribution limits were raised. The U.S. Supreme Court has struck down a few of its provisions, including the prohibition on minors under the age of 18, from making political contributions; the requirement that political parties in a general election must choose between making independent or coordinated expenditures on a candidate's behalf; and the prohibition on the broadcast of issues ads 30 days before a primary or caucus or 60 days before a general election if the ads can be interpreted as communications other than appeals to vote for or against a particular candidate (Sherman 2007).

In the post-FECA and -BCRA eras, state governments also have approved campaign finance initiatives. Trying to reduce the role of money in politics, a number of these initiatives sharply limit the amount of campaign contributions, and some states and localities have adopted public financing of campaign measures. Numerous states have launched and won approval of campaign finance reform initiatives. Interest groups, such as Common Cause, Clean Elections, and the Center for New Democracy, are leading advocates of campaign finance reform at the federal and state levels.

All states have reporting requirements, with two states mandating reports from political committees only and the rest requiring candidate and committee reports. The majority of states place candidate contribution limits on individuals (37 states), PACs (36 states), candidates themselves (41 states), candidate families (25 states), political parties (29 states), corporations (44 states), and labor unions (42 states). Half of the states completely prohibit anonymous contributions, 16 others place some restrictions, and 9 states have no limits. Twenty-eight states restrict the giving or solicitation of contributions during a legislative session. Cash contributions in campaigns are unlimited in 19 states, and other states allow varying amounts of cash donations or prohibit them completely.

From 1972 until 1996, 45 referenda and initiatives dealing with campaign and election reform were placed on state ballots, with 75 percent of these efforts occurring since 1985. During this period the voters supported the enactment of 36 reforms. These reforms included contribution limits, spending limits, and public financing measures (Hoover Institution n.d.). Twelve of the 16 public financing measures were approved. From 1998 until 2006, 30 referenda and initiatives dealing with campaign and election reform were placed on state ballots, with 15 securing passage. These reforms included new measures on public financing, campaign contribution limits, redistricting, voting ballot security, and voting rights (Initiative and Referendum Institute n.d.).

In the wake of the U.S. Supreme Court's rejection in *Buckley v. Valeo* (1976) of expenditure limits as a means of reducing the influence of money and moneyed interests in campaigns, many states have enacted public financing mechanisms for state elections. Overall, 15 states publicly finance candidates for various offices. The source of public funds for elective office varies, and some states, including Maine, Minnesota, Kentucky, and Rhode Island, rely on more than one source. Fifteen states use a voluntary tax checkoff, similar to the federal government's checkoff system, varying from $1 to $5. Ten states rely on a tax add-on, allowing taxpayers either to reduce their tax refund or increase their tax payment to finance campaigns. Seven states furnish direct legislative appropriations to fund public financing provisions. Minnesota provides a tax refund to taxpayers who make political contributions. Eleven states allocate their monies to the taxpayer's designated political party, and three states use a distribution formula to divide the money equitably between the major political parties. The other states either allocate money directly to statewide candidates or specify particular types of offices that qualify for public financing.

Public Attitudes toward Campaign Finance Laws

Americans typically have not viewed campaign finance reform as a top priority for the federal government to address. Yet when asked in 1997 whether the way federal campaigns are financed required a complete overhaul, a major change, minor changes, or no change, 70 percent of those interviewed agreed it was time for major changes (Saad 1997). However, in 1999 just 39 percent of those surveyed saw campaign finance reform as a high- or top-priority agenda item (Moore 2001).

Although Americans usually have not viewed campaign finance reform as a top priority, they generally support new laws regulating the role of money in campaigns. Table 6.1 indicates that since 1999 a majority of Americans have favored passage of new federal campaign finance laws (Moore 2001). After the Enron scandal, a February 2002 Gallup poll revealed that 7 in 10 Americans supported new campaign finance legislation and that 50 percent were dissatisfied with existing pre-BCRA campaign finance laws. A significant relationship was found between knowledge of the Enron scandal and support for new campaign finance regulations (Jones 2002).

Public opinion polls taken between 1972 and 1996 consistently indicate that a majority of Americans support the idea that the federal government should provide a fixed amount of money for election campaigns for Congress and that all private contributions from other sources should be prohibited. However, in other polls, Americans are not as supportive of public financing of political campaigns in general, especially when asked whether "government funds" or "taxpayer money" should be used. These varying results suggest that respondents may be sensitive to the wording of survey questions and may not necessarily be strongly opposed to public financing.

TABLE 6.1
Public Support for Passage of New Campaign Finance Laws.

Good people being discouraged from running for office by the high cost of campaigns? Is this a major problem for the country's political system today, somewhat of a problem, or is it not much of a problem?

Date	Percent major problem	Percent somewhat of a problem	Percent not much of a problem	Percent don't know
1999 (October)	63	24	9	4

Political contributions having too much influence on elections and government policy? Is this a major problem for this country's political system today, somewhat of a problem, or is it not much of a problem?

Date	Percent major problem	Percent somewhat of a problem	Percent not much of a problem	Percent don't know
1999 (October)	59	31	7	3

Do you support or oppose stricter laws controlling the way political campaigns can raise or spend money?

Date	Percent support	Percent oppose	Percent no opinion
2001 (March)	74	23	3

Source: ABC News/*Washington Post* Poll. March 22–25, 2001. *N* = 903 adults nationwide. Fieldwork by TNS Intersearch.

Last year Congress passed and President Bush signed into law a bill which restricted the way candidates and political parties raise and spend money. Based on what you have read or heard about this bill, do you think it is a good thing for the country or a bad thing for the country?

Date	Percent good thing	Percent bad thing	Percent not sure
2003 (September)	58	18	24

The first amendment to the Constitution gives all Americans the right to free speech. Do you think the first amendment also gives Americans the right to contribute as much money as they want to political parties and candidates, or don't you think so?

Date	Percent does give the right	Percent don't think so	Percent not sure
2003 (September)	40	52	8

Source: Time/CNN Poll conducted by Harris Interactive. September 3–4, 2003. *N* = 1,003 adults nationwide.

continues

TABLE 6.1 Continued
Public Support for Passage of New Campaign Finance Laws.

Which of the following three statements comes closest to expressing your overall view of the way political campaigns are funding in the United States? (1) On the whole, the system for funding political campaigns works pretty well and only minor changes are necessary to make it work better. OR, (2) There are some good things in the system for funding political campaigns but fundamental changes are needed. OR, (3) The system for funding political campaigns has so much wrong with it that we need to completely rebuild it.

Date	Percent minor changes	Percent fundamental changes	Percent completely rebuild	Percent don't know/no answer
2000 (March)	11	43	42	4

Source: CBS NewsPoll. March 19–20, 2000. N = 909 registered voters nationwide.

Source: Compiled with permission from PollingReport.com, www.pollingreport.com/politics2.htm

In polls, Americans waver in their support for public financing of federal election campaigns. A 2007 poll asking whether presidential candidates should accept public funds to run their campaigns seemingly indicates a lack of public support for public financing. More than 50 percent of those polled expressed the view that presidential candidates should decide not to take public financing for their campaigns. Only about 1 out of 10 Americans participate in the voluntary $3 checkoff tax payment program that supports public funding of presidential campaigns. The steady decline over time in the number of those participating in the checkoff program is yet another sign of low public support for public financing. Table 6.2 presents public opinion data on public financing of political campaigns.

Despite general supportive attitudes toward the increased use of campaign finance regulations, Americans still are not satisfied with the state of the nation's campaign finance regulations. Recent polls show that at least 50 percent of Americans are somewhat dissatisfied or very dissatisfied with federal campaign finance laws. At the same time, most Americans remain skeptical that new campaign finance laws will actually curb the power of special interest groups in the nation's capital. Roughly two-thirds of Americans believe that, even with new laws, special interest groups will find a way to maintain their influence in the nation's capital. Americans generally are pessimistic about Congress's ability to uphold high ethical standards and pass legislation that will control corrupt influences (Moore 2001; Saad

TABLE 6.2
Public Attitudes toward Public Financing of Political Campaigns.

Do you strongly favor or oppose limiting the influence of special interests by using public funding to help pay for campaigns?

Date	Percent favor	Percent oppose	Percent don't know
1995 (September)	50	43	7

Source: Mellman/Public Opinion Strategies for Campaign for America. 2005. www.cfinst.org/president/pdf PublicFunding_Surveys.pdf

Under this proposal, candidates would no longer raise money from private sources. Instead each candidate would receive a set amount of money from a publicly financed election fund. Spending by candidates would be limited to the amount they receive from the fund. Do you favor or oppose this proposal?

Date	Percent favor	Percent oppose	Percent don't know
1996 (August)	68	23	9

Source: Mellman for Center for Responsive Politics. 2007. www.opensecrets.org

Would you personally be willing to pay more in taxes to help fund the election campaigns of candidates for the presidency and Congress—if those candidates agreed to federal restrictions on the amount of money they could spend on their campaigns?

Date	Percent yes	Percent no	Percent depends	Percent don't know
1997 (March)	30	67	2	2

Source: Gallup for CNN and USA Today. 1997. www.cnn.com

Some people have proposed public financing of political campaigns—that is using only tax money to pay for political campaigns. Would you favor or oppose public financing to pay for political campaigns?

Date	Percent favor	Percent oppose	Percent don't know
1997 (April)	18	78	4

Source: CBS/New York Times. 1997. www.nytimes.com

Some people have proposed public financing of political campaigns—that is using only tax money to pay for political campaigns. Would you favor or oppose public financing to pay for political campaigns?

Date	Percent favor	Percent oppose	Percent don't know
2000 (February 14)	20	75	5

Source: CBS/New York Times. 2000. www.nytimes.com

continues

TABLE 6.2 Continued
Public Attitudes toward Public Financing of Political Campaigns.

Next, I'm going to read a few proposals for changing the way political campaigns are financed. For each one, please say whether you think that change would make campaign financing better or not … Establishing federal financing of presidential and congressional campaigns—in which ALL AMERICANS would be required to pay some additional taxes, and candidates would agree to federal restrictions on the amount of money they could spend?

Date	Percent better	Percent not better	Percent don't know/refused
1997 (March 26)	35	60	5

Public financing of political campaigns—that is, using tax money to pay for campaigns and prohibiting large donations from individuals and special interest groups—do you favor or oppose that?

Date	Percent favor	Percent oppose	Percent don't know
1999 (July 14)	37	58	5

Source: CBS. 1999. www.cbsnews.com

Source: Compiled with permission from PollingReport.com, www.pollingreport.com/politics.htm

2006). Americans also have doubts about the efficacy of campaign finance legislation. According to a Gallup poll (February 8–10, 2002), two-thirds of Americans believe that campaign finance laws will not deter special interests from maintaining their power in Washington (Jones 2002). Despite their doubts about the ability of regulations to rein in special interests, almost two-thirds of Americans still believe stricter campaign finance laws will reduce the influence of money in politics.

Electoral and Voting Controversies

As one of the closest electoral contests in U.S. history, the 2000 presidential election raised the specter of a constitutional crisis. George W. Bush's narrow victory over Albert Gore in the electoral college placed the media spotlight not only on the college but also on election administration and voting procedures. The unusual role played by the U.S. Supreme Court, which in effect declared Bush the winner of the presidential election by halting the ballot recount in Florida, threatened to undermine the public's confidence in the electoral process.

The 2000 elections brought other electoral disputes and voting controversies to light. Civil rights advocates claimed that the vote-counting scandal in Florida in the 2000 presidential election was just the tip of the iceberg. A study conducted by the California and Massachusetts Institutes of Technology found that the voting problems extended well beyond Florida, and they estimated that up to six million of the 100 million votes cast in 2000 were never counted. The study concluded that flaws in registration data and faulty voting equipment and procedures led to inaccurate vote counts (Cooper 2004).

The Help America Vote Act (HAVA) of 2002 required states to maintain centralized databases of all registered voters, leaving the method of doing so up to individual states. Seven states, including Washington, used the no-match purge method. The Washington legislature required the secretary of state to purge registered voters from the rolls if their identifying information—first and last name on the roll—did not match identifying information in state records, such as the name on a driver's license. This method of voter purging is controversial because it can remove from the rolls legitimate registrants, such as those whose names have changed due to marriage or divorce. Before the 2000 election, Florida officials removed thousands of registered voters from the rolls because state records identified them as convicted felons, but a large number of them were mistakenly identified as such. In 2002 Florida, in a court settlement, agreed to restore eligible voters to the registration rolls and to enact measures to improve election procedures (Katel 2006).

In addition to centralized database requirements, the HAVA requires first-time voters who register by mail to submit identification when they go to a polling place to vote. Twenty-three states enacted voter identification requirements for all voters who appear at the polls. Aimed at preventing fraudulent voting, these measures have been challenged in the courts. Critics argue that toughened identification requirements disproportionately affect minorities because fewer minority group members possess such valid pieces of photo identification as driver's licenses. Critics also contend that frequent failure to apply voter identification requirements to absentee voters is discriminatory because whites are twice as likely to vote by absentee ballot than are African Americans (Katel 2006).

Although the Voting Rights Act of 1965 sought to remedy a history of voter intimidation, monitoring groups such as the

National Association for the Advancement of Colored Peoples (NAACP) and the People for the American Way continue to document alleged voter intimidation and suppression. In a Philadelphia mayoral contest, for instance, official-looking people appeared outside polling stations in minority precincts asking voters for identification. Almost 10 percent of African Americans in Philadelphia reported encounters of this nature (Cooper 2004). Evidence of these types of practices has led to calls for nonpartisan, well trained poll watchers.

Also under close examination is the use of electronic voting equipment. Some direct recording electronic (DRE) voting devices, mostly touch screen, do not leave paper trails. Without a paper printout of votes, an accurate recount cannot be conducted. Computer scientists allege that DRE machines are not tamperproof. Given the suspicions generated after the 2000 elections, critics argue that electronic voting equipment is dangerous to democracy and the election process. The DREs open the door to speculation that election results were manipulated or that machines were improperly programmed, resulting in vote miscounts (Katel 2006).

After the 2000 presidential election, many state legislatures enacted major election system reforms. Passage of the Help America Vote Act in 2002 has also spurred reform of election administration. Many states have purchased new voting equipment, spending over $200 million for new optical scan and touch screen voting systems. In addition, about a half dozen states passed new voting system standards and testing, and six states have banned the use of punch card machines. In response to the inaccurate vote counting debacle in Florida, approximately 14 states passed measures specifying the procedure for counting ballots with hanging chads and interpreting stray marks or dimples on ballots. At least 16 states specified more clearly the procedures for recounting votes. Another controversial issue—the counting of provisional ballots—was also taken up by several states after November 2000. These states established improved procedures for issuing these ballots and verifying voter eligibility. By 2002 half of the states had passed laws requiring training for poll workers. To attract better poll workers, the states increased salaries, recruited high school and college students to work at the polls, and removed partisanship requirements. To address accessibility concerns, 16 states enacted legislation requiring that new voting systems be accessible to the disabled and provide some means for the visually impaired to cast a secret ballot (National Conference of State Legislatures 2003).

Public Attitudes toward the Electoral and Voting Processes

Attitude surveys since 1944 have indicated that Americans are dissatisfied with the operation of the electoral college. When asked whether they support a constitutional amendment that would eliminate the college and replace it with the popular election of the president, approximately two-thirds of Americans consistently agree with the proposed change. The 2000 presidential election triggered a new round of public opinion surveys on the electoral college, which indicated that the public still supports its abolition. Two advantages that defenders of the electoral college see in the present system is that it disadvantages third parties and forces presidential candidates to build national coalitions. Opponents, however, believe the system is outmoded and antidemocratic. Table 6.3 offers insights into public opinion on the Electoral College. On average, less than a third of Americans prefer to keep the Electoral College (Carlson 2004; Newport 2001).

The 2000 election forced Americans to examine vote recording and counting procedures. Although surveys indicate that a majority of Americans have "some confidence" in the electoral system, only one in four say that they were "very confident" that votes would be counted accurately in the 2006 elections. When that trust erodes, and suspicions about accurate vote counts arise, election outcomes may come under challenge, and the legitimacy of elected officials is questioned.

Table 6.4 reports the level of confidence the general public has in the voting process, reflecting in part reaction to the 2000 elections. In December 2000, only 27 percent of respondents expressed a great deal of confidence or quite a lot of confidence in how votes are cast and counted in the United States. In a November 8, 2000 poll taken by *NBC News*, 23 percent said that the 2000 election outcome had raised doubts in their minds about the importance of their vote. In December, 70 percent of those surveyed believed that the system by which votes are cast and counted in the United States needed major reforms. By 2001 the percentage

TABLE 6.3
Public Opinion on the Electoral College.

Would you approve or disapprove of an amendment to the Constitution which would do away with the Electoral College and base the election of a President on the total vote cast throughout the nation?

Date	Percent approve	Percent disapprove	Percent no opinion
2000 (November 10)	63	29	8

Source: CNN/Time Poll. November 10, 2000. Conducted by Yankelovich Partners. *N* = 1,154.

For future presidential elections, would you support or oppose changing to a system in which the president is elected by direct popular vote, instead of the electoral college?

Date	Percent support	Percent oppose	Percent no opinion
2000 (November 12)	63	31	6

Source: ABC News/*Washington Post* Poll. November 12, 2000. *N* = 762 adults nationwide. Fieldwork by TNS Intersearch.

Presidents are elected by the Electoral College, in which each state gets as many votes as it has members of Congress and can cast all of them for whoever wins in that state. Do you think we should keep the Electoral College, or should we amend the Constitution and elect as president whoever gets the most votes in the whole country?

Date	Percent keep Electoral College	Percent amend the Constitution	Percent don't know
1987	33	61	6
2000	31	60	9

Source: CBS News/*New York Times* Poll. November 10–12, 2000. *N* = 1,720 adults nationwide.

Some people have proposed public financing of political campaigns—that is using only tax money to pay for political campaigns. Would you favor or oppose public financing to pay for political campaigns?

Date	Percent favor	Percent oppose	Percent don't know
1997 (April)	18	78	4

Source: CBS/*New York Times.* 1997. www.nytimes.com

continues

TABLE 6.3 Continued
Public Opinion on the Electoral College.

It is possible in our election system for one presidential candidate to receive the most state ELECTORAL votes, while another candidate receives the most POPULAR votes nationwide. In this case, who do you think has a MORE legitimate claim to the presidency: the electoral vote winner or the popular vote winner, or does neither have a legitimate claim?

Date	Percent popular-vote winner	Percent electoral-vote winner	Percent neither	Percent don't know
2000 (November 12)	45	39	10	6
2000 (November 28)	43	40	10	7

Source: CBS News/*New York Times* Poll. November 10–12, 2000 and November 26–28, 2000. *N* = 1,720 adults nationwide.

Source: Compiled with permission from PollingReport.com, www.pollingreport.com/wh2post3.htm and www.pollingreport.com/wh04misc.htm

of respondents expressing a great deal or quite a lot of confidence in how votes are cast or counted had risen to 41 percent, with 57 percent having only some confidence or very little confidence. Those who believed the system needed major reform declined from 70 percent to 43 percent. In subsequent polls, taken in 2004 and 2006, approximately one-fourth of Americans said they lacked confidence in how votes are cast or counted—almost a complete reversal from the opinion expressed after the 2000 presidential election (Carroll 2004, 2006).

Polls reveal that American confidence in how votes are cast and counted has improved dramatically since 2000. However, when asked in a 2006 *CNN Poll* whether technical problems with voting machinery (created, for instance, by computer hackers or people working for candidates) could cause a significant number of machines to produce inaccurate results, 66 percent of those surveyed believed it was very likely or somewhat likely. Similarly, when respondents were asked whether technical problems accidentally caused by election workers or the companies that make the machines could cause a significant number of voting machines to produce inaccurate results, 61 percent believed this scenario was very likely or somewhat likely. Clearly, confidence in voting systems, if not in the process itself, has been shaken.

TABLE 6.4
Public Confidence in Accurate Vote Counts.

How much confidence do you have in the system in which votes are cast, and counted, in this country—a great deal, quite a lot, some, or very little?

Date	Percent a great deal	Percent quite a lot	Percent some	Percent very little	Percent unsure
2004 (July 18–20)	30	28	26	14	2

Source: National Public Radio Poll. July 18–20, 2004. Conducted by Public Opinion Strategies and Greenberg Quinian Rosner Research (D). *N* = 800 likely voters nationwide.

How confident are you that, across the country, the votes will be accurately cast and counted in this year's election?

Date	Percent very confident	Percent somewhat confident	Percent not too confident	Percent not at all confident	Percent no opinion/ unsure
2006 (October 13–15)	31	47	14	8	N/A

Source: CNN Poll. October 13–15, 2006. Conducted by Opinion Research Corporation. *N* = 1,012 adults nationwide.

2006 (November 1–4)	49	34	9	6	2

Source: ABC News/*Washington Post* Poll. November 1–4, 2006. *N* = 1,205 registered voters nationwide. Fieldwork by TNS.

Sources: Compiled with permission from PollingReport.com, www.pollingreport.com/wh04misc.htm and www.pollingreport.com/politics2.htm

Major U.S. Supreme Court Decisions on Campaign Finance

Table 6.5 provides the evolution of case law on campaign finance, summarizing decisions since the 1976 U.S. Supreme Court ruling in *Buckley v. Valeo* that struck down expenditure limits in political campaigns as a violation of the First Amendment. The Court has continued to uphold *Buckley* and to expand on its reasoning in such cases. While upholding contribution limits, the Court has rejected attempts to limit independent expenditures, as noted in the 1996 case *Colorado Republican Federal Campaign Committee v. FEC*, in which the Federal Election Commission (FEC) sought to limit

TABLE 6.5
Major U.S. Supreme Court Decisions on Campaign Finance.

Date	Case	Holding
1976	*Buckley v. Valeo* (424 U.S. 1)	Upheld the constitutionality of the Federal Election Campaign Act except for the provisions limiting campaign expenditures, including independent expenditures and what individuals could spend on their own campaigns.
1981	*California Medical Association v. FEC* (453 U.S. 182)	Upheld the constitutionality of limits on contributions to a PAC to $5,000 per year per contributor.
1986	*FEC v. Massachusetts Citizens for Life (MCFL)* (479 U.S. 238)	Held that a Massachusetts law's banning of corporate expenditures was unconstitutional as applied to independent expenditures made by narrowly defined types of nonprofit corporations that take positions on abortion, busing, gun control, and other issues.
1990	*Austin v. Michigan State Chamber of Commerce* (494 U.S. 652)	Ruled that Michigan state law prohibiting independent expenditures by corporations was constitutional.
1991	*U.S. v. McCormick* (500 U.S. 257)	Overturned the Hobbs Act conviction of a West Virginia state legislator who introduced legislation after accepting $2,900 from a lobbyist, claiming that such conduct is unavoidable in privately financed election campaigns.
1996	*Colorado Republican Federal Campaign Committee v. FEC* (64 U.S.L.W. 4663)	Held that federal campaign finance limits on the amount of money political parties spend independently of a candidate's campaign are unconstitutional.
1998	*FEC v. Akins* (524 U.S. 11)	Held that private citizens have standing to sue the FEC if FECA's disclosure provisions are not enforced because voters suffer an injury when denied access to campaign disclosure information.
2000	*Nixon v. Shrink Missouri Government PAC* (528 U.S. 377)	Upheld a Missouri law limiting campaign contributions to $1,000, stating that such limits "prevent corruption and appearance of corruption."
2001	*FEC v. Colorado Republican Federal* (533 U.S. 431)	Colorado II upheld limits on coordinated political party expenditures on behalf of *Campaign Committee* their candidates, stating that these types of expenditures are not "truly independent."
2003	*McConnell v. FEC* (540 U.S. 93)	Upheld core provisions of the Bipartisan Campaign Reform Act, including the ban on raising and spending soft money by national political parties, federal office holders, and federal candidates and the electioneering communication provisions, which require the use of hard money to finance certain advertisements aired within 30 days of a primary or 60 days of a general election.
2003	*FEC v. Beaumont* (539 U.S. 146)	Upheld ban on contributions of incorporated nonprofit advocacy groups to federal candidates.

continues

TABLE 6.5 Continued
Major U.S. Supreme Court Decisions on Campaign Finance.

Date	Case	Holding
2006	*Randall v. Sorrell* (126 S.Ct. 2479)	Struck down a Vermont law that placed strict caps on campaign contributions and expenditures as violating the First Amendment's free speech guarantees.
2007	*FEC v. Wisconsin Right to Life; McCain et al. v. Wisconsin Right to Life* (551 U.S. _____)	Held that part of the BCRA had been unconstitutionally applied by the FEC to an advertisement that the Wisconsin Right to Life group sought to air before the 2004 election, stating that it was not an electioneering ad.

the amount of money political parties could spend independently of a candidate's campaign. The Supreme Court declared campaign finance limits of this sort unconstitutional. However, the Supreme Court in 2001 upheld limits on party-coordinated expenditures on behalf of federal election candidates, arguing that, unlike truly independent expenditures, coordinated expenditures could be limited so that contribution limits would not be circumvented. Furthermore, in 2003 the Court in *McConnell v. Federal Election Commission* upheld most provisions of the Bipartisan Campaign Finance Reform Act (BCRA).

U.S. Supreme Court Decisions on Political Participation

Since 1944 the U.S. Supreme Court has expanded political participation for minorities and the poor by striking down mechanisms designed to limit their opportunity to vote. Table 6.6 presents several major cases that have provided access to the voting booth to millions of Americans. By 1966 white primaries, poll taxes, and literacy tests, used primarily in the South to deny the vote to African Americans and the poor, had been declared unconstitutional. Lengthy residency requirements, which disproportionately disadvantaged students and other mobile individuals, were struck down in 1972.

TABLE 6.6
Major U.S. Supreme Court Cases on Political Participation.

Date	Case	Holding
1944	Smith v. Allwright (213 U.S. 649)	Held that white primaries violated the Fifteenth Amendment and Texas could not prevent blacks from participating by holding white-only state conventions.
1966	Harper v. Virginia State Board of Education (383 U.S. 663)	Held poll taxes unconstitutional under the equal protection clause of the Fourteenth Amendment.
1966	South Carolina v. Katzenbach (383 U.S. 301)	Upheld suspension of literacy tests under the Voting Rights Act of 1965.
1970	Oregon v. Mitchell (400 U.S. 112)	Upheld the voting rights extension that lowered the voting age to 18 for national elections but declared that state and local elections were not governed by this provision.
1972	Dunn v. Blumstein (405 U.S. 330)	Struck down residency requirements in excess of 30 days as a prerequisite to register to vote.
1983	United States v. Grace (461 U.S. 171)	Upheld distribution of leaflets and picketing on public sidewalks as constitutional under the First Amendment.
1995	U.S. Term Limits, Inc. v. Thornton (514 U.S. 779)	Struck down the state of Arkansas's attempt to impose congressional term limits, stating that state-imposed qualifications would undermine the right of the people to vote for whomever they wish.
1996	Morse v. Republican Party of Virginia (64 U.S.L.W. 4207)	Held that political parties in states covered by the federal Voting Rights Act must get federal preclearance to charge fees to delegates attending nomination conventions.
2000	Rice v. Cayetano (528 U.S. 495)	Overturned a provision in Hawaii's constitution that allowed only descendants of original Hawaiians to vote for the Office of Hawaiian Affairs, a state agency that administers public money, as violating the equal protection clause.
2000	California Democratic Party v. Jones (530 U.S. 567)	Declared California's blanket primary unconstitutional, stating that political parties have First Amendment freedom of association rights that must be respected.
2000	Bush v. Gore (531 U.S. 98)	Held that the Florida Supreme Court's failure to create uniform vote counting standards violated the equal protection clause, effectively ending the partial manual vote count underway in Florida to find out whether Bush or Gore won the majority of Florida's electoral votes.

U.S. Supreme Court Decisions on Redistricting

Although the Supreme Court initially declared that redistricting and apportionment issues were political questions best resolved by state legislatures, the process of redrawing state legislative and congressional district lines ultimately came under court scrutiny. The Supreme Court and lower federal courts are often the final arbiters of redistricting plans proposed by state legislatures. Various forms of gerrymandering—for partisan purposes, for protecting incumbents, and for racial equality—have been upheld.

In *Baker v. Carr* (1962), the Supreme Court held that the courts should hear reapportionment disputes because voters in more populous districts were denied equal protection under the law when their votes often counted less than those in more rural districts. In *Reynolds v. Sims* (1964) and *Wesberry v. Sanders* (1964), the Court held that the principle of one person, one vote applied to state legislative and congressional districts (Rush 1993, 13). Since 1964 the Supreme Court has dealt primarily with technical matters associated with implementing the one person, one vote principle.

In 1986, in *Thornburg v. Gingles*, the Supreme Court issued a three-pronged test for deciding whether the Voting Rights Act requires states to create majority–minority districts when they reapportion. Majority black districts were drawn in Alabama, Florida, North Carolina, South Carolina, Louisiana, Texas, and Virginia, some of which have been challenged as unconstitutional racial gerrymandering. Since 1993 the Supreme Court has demonstrated a willingness to impose limits on how states comply with the Voting Rights Act of 1982, stating that, if race is the sole factor in the redistricting process, the state redistricting plan could be challenged and struck down as unconstitutional (Scarrow 2000).

The Supreme Court has consistently allowed partisan-based redistricting. Although the Court has held that political parties could be given relief if they were egregiously mistreated by an opponent during redistricting, it has rarely intervened on behalf of an aggrieved party. In the 2004 case *Vieth v. Jubelirer*, for example, the Supreme Court upheld the redistricting plan drawn by Pennsylvania's Republican-controlled legislature, stating that it was impossible to objectively discern whether the redrawing of congressional districts that eliminated seats held by Democratic incumbents was in violation of the equal treatment provision in the state's constitution (Bullock 2005, 164–66).

The census itself became an issue in 2000 when the state of Utah complained that it had lost one representative in Congress to the state of North Carolina based on a data-gathering process known as imputation. Under imputation, a census taker who is unable to reach certain residents estimates the number of individuals living in a dwelling based on past demographic data. Utah officials sought to force the Census Bureau to revise its results based on imputation. However, the Supreme Court rejected their arguments. As a result, North Carolina retained its additional congressional seat.

The Costs of Elections

Money obviously plays in important role in campaigns and elections, but it is not the only determinant of a candidate's success. For example, many wealthy candidates for the U.S. House of Representatives and Senate have failed to gain election by outspending their opponent. In 2002, 29 candidates spent over $500,000 of their own money but only three of them were elected. Of these, only one who spent more than $1 million of his own money—Sen. Frank R. Lautenberg (D-NJ)—won. Of the 30 candidates who spent over $500,000 in 2004, only Rep. Michael McCaul (R-TX) was elected. The failure of so many wealthy candidates to win election suggests that the availability of large amounts of personal funds does not guarantee success.

Although the availability of personal wealth may not be the deciding factor in winning congressional elections, the ability to raise money and build a war chest is crucial for candidate viability. To receive the "serious contender" label, candidates must raise enough money to run a credible campaign and to attract endorsements from organized interests. In primary elections, having available sufficient campaign funds is extremely important. If potential supporters do not see candidates as viable, they may desert them in the primary, fearing their votes could be wasted. Primary election candidates often are not well-known, making adequate campaign funds essential to increasing name recognition. When candidates attract media attention and attract greater popular support, they appear successful and gain momentum, attracting even more money (Mutz 1995). If all other factors are equal, studies suggest that fund-raising abilities influence election outcomes. In 2002, 90 percent of congressional candidates who raised the most money won the primary election. This percentage was 91 percent in 2004 and 2006 (U.S. Pirg Education Fund 2006).

In 2000 candidates who raised the most money won 93 percent of all congressional seats. This trend continued in 2002 and in 2006, with 92 percent of House and Senate candidates who raised the most money also winning their seats (U.S. Pirg Education Fund 2006). To win a House seat, candidates spend increasing amounts of money in each election cycle. Table 6.7 describes the average cost of winning a House and a Senate seat in nominal and in 2004 dollars from 1986 through 2004.

Although political action committees provide a large amount of funding, individual donors—both small and large—still provide the largest proportion of campaign funding. Party funding, candidate-to-candidate funding, and other sources make up the smallest sources of campaign funding. Congressional incumbents enjoy a huge fund-raising advantage, as illustrated by the amount of PAC money they receive compared to challengers. Table 6.8 presents U.S. House and Senate total campaign spending and funding sources.

Not only are incumbents usually reelected, they often win by landslide margins (Abramowitz 1991). The incumbency advantage, based in part on name recognition and experience in office, helps them raise money early. PACs traditionally have favored incumbents over challengers (Herrnson 2000). In 2004, 98 percent of House incumbents were reelected, along with 96 percent of incumbent Senators. Table 6.9 provides the U.S. House and Senate reelection rates from 1964 until 2006. Challengers, trying to unseat incumbents, face long odds.

Even when challengers outspend incumbents, the chance of victory is slim. For example, in 2004 a challenger in a House race who spent under $1 million had no chance of winning, whereas a challenger who spent $1.0 million to $1.5 million had odds of 16 to 1 of being successful. Challengers spending over $1.5 million raised their odds to 5 to 2. Table 6.10 describes the costs of defeating a House incumbent and the number of challengers who have won seats.

TABLE 6.7
U.S. House and Senate Average Winner Expenditures, 1986–2006 (in nominal and
2006 dollars).

House of Representatives		
Year	Nominal dollars	2006 dollars
2006	1,259,791	1,259,791
2004	1,038,391	1,115,883
2002	911,644	1,027,319
2000	845,907	998,448
1998	677,807	838,318
1996	686,198	887,917
1994	541,121	741,101
1992	556,475	805,929
1990	423,245	662,985
1988	400,386	674,334
1986	359,577	658,408
Senate		
Year	Nominal dollars	2006 dollars
2006	8,835,416	8,835,416
2004	7,183,825	7,719,931
2002	3,728,644	4,201,759
2000	7,198,644	8,496,499
1998	4,655,806	5,758,347
1996	3,291,653	5,074,488
1994	4,488,195	6,146,876
1992	3,353,115	4,856,236
1990	3,298,324	5,166,605
1988	3,746,225	6,309,432
1986	3,067,559	5,616,893

Source: The Campaign Finance Institute. www.cfinst.org/data/pdf/VitalStats_t1.pdf

TABLE 6.8
U.S. House and Senate Campaign Funding Sources and Expenditures, 1984–2006 (net dollars in millions and percentages).

House	1984	1986	1988	1990	1992	1994	1996	1998	2000	2002	2004	2006
Number of candidates	816	810	782	807	851	824	873	792	820	807	812	815
Total dollar contributions*	209	234	249	258	332	371	461	436	550	557	610	778
Percentage individual	47	48	46	44	47	49	53	51	51	49	57	54
Percentage PAC	36	36	40	40	36	64	33	35	34	36	36	35
Percentage PAC to incumbent	58	51	55	58	53	55	55	66	63	61	65	43
Percentage party	7	4	4	3	3	5	4	3	2	2	2	1
Percentage candidate to candidate	6	6	5	6	6	8	6	6	7	9	4	5
Percentage other	5	6	5	7	7	4	4	4	5	4	0	5
Total dollar expenditures	177	218	225	235	330	346	423	397	515	526	581	752

continues

TABLE 6.8 Continued
U.S. House and Senate Campaign Funding Sources and Expenditures, 1984–2006 (net dollars in millions and percentages).

Senate	1984	1986	1988	1990	1992	1994	1996	1998	2000	2002	2004	2006
Number of candidates	68	68	66	67	71	70	68	70	70	69	69	65
Total dollar contributions*	158	209	199	191	214	292	242	266	387	301	367	531
Percentage individual	61	60	59	61	58	54	58	58	53	63	73	67
Percentage PAC	18	21	22	21	21	15	17	18	13	19	17	13
Percentage PAC to incumbent	17	18	19	20	14	14	10	19	14	14	14	15
Percentage party	6	9	9	7	13	8	9	7	4	5	6	2
Percentage candidate to candidate	10	6	5	5	5	19	12	11	24	8	4	13
Percentage other	4	4	5	8	3	4	4	7	6	6	0	5
Total dollar expenditures	142	183	185	173	194	279	230	249	385	282	368	515

*Total campaign contributions and expenditures were rounded up to the nearest million. For example, if total contributions were 141.7 million, the number was rounded to 142.

Source: Campaign Finance Institute (2006); Cantor (1997).

TABLE 6.9
Congressional Reelection Rates, 1964–2006.

Year	House percentage	Senate percentage
1964	87	85
1966	88	88
1968	97	71
1970	85	77
1972	94	74
1974	88	85
1976	96	64
1978	94	60
1980	91	55
1982	90	83
1984	95	90
1986	98	75
1988	98	85
1990	96	96
1992	88	83
1994	90	92
1996	94	91
1998	98	90
2000	98	79
2002	96	86
2004	98	86
2006	94	77

Source: The Center for Responsive Politics. 2007. opensecrets.org

Voter Turnout and Voter Registration

Voter registration rates have risen somewhat, from 72 percent in 1992 to almost 81 percent in 2004, indicating the possible influence of the 1993 National Voter Registration Act in expanding the voter rolls. The effects of the NVRA on voter turnout, however, have been mixed. Reducing the costs associated with voter regis-

TABLE 6.10
Average Challenger Costs versus Average Incumbents Costs to Win
U.S. House Elections, 1974–2004.

Year	Actual dollars spent by average challenger	Actual dollars spent by average incumbent	Number of winning challengers
1974	100,435	101,102	40
1976	144,720	154,774	12
1978	217,083	200,607	19
1980	343,093	286,559	31
1982	296,273	453,458	23
1984	518,781	463,070	17
1986	523,308	562,139	6
1988	703,740	876,678	7
1990	462,546	631,025	16
1992	433,482	840,922	19
1994	644,640	945,608	34
1996	1,070,162	1,040,878	21
1998	1,123,783	1,281,633	6
2000	2,024,725	2,511,366	6
2002	1,595,805	846,250	4
2004	1,611,835	2,003,504	5

Source: The Center for Responsive Politics. 2006. www.opensecrets.org

tration does not necessarily guarantee high voter turnout. Voter turnout in 1996, 1998, and 2002 was not substantially higher than pre-NVRA turnout levels. In 2004, 32 million people reported that they were not registered to vote. Forty-seven percent of those not registered stated that they were not interested in the 2004 election or were not involved in politics, and 17 percent reported that they failed to meet the registration deadline. Others failed to register for reasons such as illness or disability or believing their vote would not make a difference (U.S. Census Bureau 2006, 13).

Table 6.11 provides a summary of voter turnout in federal elections. Voter turnout has been relatively low, falling below 50 percent in all midterm elections since 1960 and in one general election. Making voting easier still does not address such factors

TABLE 6.11
Voter Turnout in United States, 1960–2006.

Presidential election years		Nonpresidential election years	
Year	Percentage turnout	Year	Percentage turnout
1960	63.8	1962	47.4
1964	62.8	1966	48.7
1968	62.5	1970	47.3
1972	56.2	1974	39.1
1976	54.8	1978	39.0*
1980	54.2	1982	42.1*
1984	55.2	1986	38.1
1988	52.8	1990	38.4
1992	58.1	1994	41.1
1996	51.7	1998	38.1
2000	54.2	2002	39.5
2004	60.3	2006	40.4

*The asterisk beside 1978 and 1982 percentage turnout denotes that Louisiana's second ballot system resulted in excluding the state from the numerator and denominator for these two election cycles.

Source: McDonald (n.d.).

as political apathy, the failures of the political parties to mobilize voters, and voter disillusionment with negative campaigning.

Some states, such as Oregon, have responded to perceived structural barriers to voting by sponsoring vote by mail, allowing voters to mail in their ballots at their convenience rather than vote at a polling place. Twenty-three states provide for early voting, allowing voters to cast their ballots at satellite polling places 10 to 14 days prior to the election. In addition, while all states offer absentee ballot voting, 26 of them permit registered voters to vote by absentee ballot without having to offer an excuse or reason for voting absentee. Several states, including Idaho, Maine, Minnesota, Montana, New Hampshire, Wisconsin, Wyoming, and Iowa (beginning in the 2008 elections) make it convenient to register by allowing election day registration (EDR). EDR states have 10 to 12 percent higher voter turnout than non-EDR states; in 2006 the average voter turnout in EDR

TABLE 6.12
Convenient Voting Mechanisms State by State.

No excuse absentee voting	Early voting	Election day registration
Alaska	Alaska	Idaho
Arizona	Arizona	Iowa (beginning in 2008)
California	Arkansas	Maine
Colorado	California	Minnesota
Florida	Colorado	Montana
Hawaii	Florida	New Hampshire
Idaho	Georgia	Wisconsin
Indiana	Hawaii	Wyoming
Iowa	Indiana	
Kansas	Iowa	
Maine	Kansas	
Montana	Maine	
Nebraska	Nebraska	
Nevada	Nevada	
New Mexico	New Mexico	
North Carolina	North Carolina	
North Dakota	North Dakota**	
Oklahoma	Oklahoma	
Oregon*	Tennessee	
South Dakota	Texas	
Utah	Utah	
Vermont	Vermont	
Washington	West Virginia	
West Virginia		
Wisconsin		
Wyoming		

*Oregon conducts its elections solely by mail-in ballot.

**North Dakota does not offer early voting in all counties. County election officers decide whether to provide for early voting.

Sources: "Absentee and Early Voting" (2004); "Voters Win with Election Day Registration" (2007).

states was 48.7 percent but only 38.2 percent in the non-EDR states. States can increase voter registration and turnout through a variety of innovations. Table 6.12 provides a summary of state voting mechanisms intended to make voting more convenient.

Quotations

The following quotations present the attitudes of a wide range of individuals—including elected and appointed officials, interest group representatives, and students of political reform—toward campaign finance reform, electoral reform, balloting, redistricting, term limits, and gerrymandering.

Alternate Electoral Systems

In a five-seat race, the voter's calculation with preference voting is a simple one: which candidate do I like best, which do I like next best and so on, knowing that a lower choice will never help defeat a higher choice and also knowing that ranking a lower choice might help that candidate defeat a candidate you dislike. With cumulative voting, it's not so easy. You like one candidate best and yes, you could put all your votes on that candidate. . . . [T]he possibility of "too many" candidates points to a serious problem with cumulative voting: wasted votes. If voters make a "wrong" calculation . . . then one candidate could end up with far too many votes and others with too few.

> Rob Richie, executive director of the Center for Voting and Democracy, "Preference Voting vs. Cumulative Voting: Preference Voting Is the Better System for Local Government." In *Voting and Democracy Report 1995*. Washington, DC: The Center for Voting and Democracy, 1995: 73–76

Under proportional representation, interests tend to coagulate into a handful of substantial parties. And we can eliminate the problem of tiny fanatical parties, which has bedeviled Israel, by insisting that no party can get seats in the legislature unless it wins a certain threshold—say, 5 percent—of the national vote. Thus, even if neo-Nazis win a district in Louisiana, they won't be seated in Congress unless they pass the national threshold. . . . Far from being alien to American society, proportional representation is arguably the only appropriate electoral system for a society as diverse as ours. It encourages social peace by giving every major segment of the population a piece of the action.

Michael Lind, "Alice Doesn't Vote Here Anymore," *Mother Jones Magazine*, March–April 1998

Interest representation . . . fulfills the dual vision of the Voting Rights Act that minority groups should enjoy equal voting weight and equal voting power. Instead of emphasizing arbitrary territorial boundaries, which waste the votes of both minority and majority groups, interest representation favors allowing voters of the same interests to join in voting for candidates of choice, regardless of where the voters live in the jurisdiction. This at-large system, however, would be modified in one critical respect. The winner-take-all feature of majority rule would be discarded in favor of cumulative voting, which allows voters to cumulate their votes in order to express the intensity of their preferences. In this fashion, interest representation strives to ensure that groups that are politically cohesive, sufficiently numerous, and strategically mobilized will be able to elect a representative to the legislative body.

Lani Guinier, *The Tyranny of the Majority: Fundamental Fairness in Representative Democracy* (New York: Free Press, 1994)

Balloting and Voting

Democracy's dirty little secret: Vote counting is a messy business. In nearly every election, votes that shouldn't be counted are, and votes that should be counted aren't. In the 2004 election, at least 850,000 ballots cast somewhere in the nation were never counted. . . . Some voters inadvertently invalidated their absentee ballots by failing to sign them. Other absentee ballots were signed but weren't counted because scanners failed to detect a signature.

Brian Friel, "Let the Recounts Begin," *National Journal* 38, 44 (November 7, 2006): 14–21

To determine what it would take to hack a U.S. election, a team of cybersecurity experts turned to a fictional battleground state called Pennasota and a fictional gubernatorial race between Tom Jefferson and Johnny Adams. It's the year 2007, and the state uses electronic voting machines. Jefferson was forecast to win the race by about 80,000 votes, or 2.3 percent of the vote. Adams's conspirators thought, "How easily can we manipulate the election results?" The experts thought about all the ways to do it. And they concluded in a report . . . that it would take only one person, with a sophisticated technical knowledge and timely access to the software that runs the voting machines, to change the outcome.

> Zachary A. Goldfarb, "A Single Person Could Swing an Election," *Washington Post,* June 28, 2006: A7

Voting experts say it is impossible to say how many votes [in the 2000 elections] were not counted that should have been. But in Florida alone, the discrepancies reported across Sarasota County and three others amount to more than 60,000 votes. In Colorado, as many as 20,000 people gave up trying to vote, election officials say, as new online systems for verifying voter registrations crashed repeatedly. And in Arkansas, election officials tallied votes three times in one county, and each time the number of ballots cast changed by more than 30,000.

> Ian Urbina and Christopher Drew, "Experts Concerned as Ballot Problems Persist," *New York Times,* November 26, 2006

The "voter fraud" bogeyman is used to justify solutions that don't really work for a problem that doesn't really exist. Restrictive rules—like identification requirements—then sprout like weeds, becoming unnecessary and unlawful impediments to the exercise of a fundamental constitutional right. Meanwhile, the list of real problems grows: flyers spread misinformation, voting machines register inaccurate tallies; election officials misunderstand [voter] eligibility rules; actual voters are mistakenly purged. Americans deserve policies grounded in facts, not hysteria. . . . Voter fraud is nowhere near the top of that list.

> Justin Levitt, Associate Counsel at the Brennan Center for Justice, *CQ Researcher,* September 15, 2006: 761

Across the nation eight out of every ten voters will be casting their ballots . . . on electronic voting machines. And these machines time and again have demonstrated to be extremely vulnerable to tampering and error, and many of them have no voter-verified paper trail. . . . The problems with electronic voting aren't necessarily new, yet we're still not ready for the midterm [2006 elections]. During the 2004 presidential election, one voting machine reportedly added nearly 3,900 additional votes to Bush's total. Officials caught the machine's error because only 638 voters cast presidential ballots, but in a heavily populated district, can we really be sure the votes will be counted correctly?

> Lou Dobbs, CNN commentator, "Voting Machines Put U.S. Democracy at Risk," CNN.com, September 21, 2006

The ballot is perhaps the single greatest privilege we have. Protecting it must be considered a matter of public interest as important as a threat of outbreak of disease or any other impending national disaster. . . . America deserves a foolproof voting system. It must be dependable and easy to use. Whoever designs the system must be able to prove that the system cannot be cheated and be able to explain why to the average eighth-grader. No American should have to trust someone else, someone with obscure expertise regarding the integrity of the system; it must be simple enough that every citizen can evaluate it for himself or herself.

> Aviel D. Rubin, professor of computer science, Johns Hopkins University, and director of ACCURATE (the Center for Correct, Usable, Reliable, Auditable, and Transparent Elections), *Brave New Ballot: The Battle to Safeguard Democracy in the Age of Electronic Voting* (New York: Broadway, 2006): 267–68

If I was a programmer at one of these [electronic voting machine] companies and I wanted to steal an election, it would be very easy. I could put something in the software that would be impossible to detect, and it would change the votes from one party to another. And you could do it so it's not going to show up statistically as an anomaly.

> David L. Dill, professor of computer science at Stanford University, quoted in "Machine Politics in the Digital Age," *New York Times*, November 9, 2003

Buckley v. Valeo

I think *Buckley v. Valeo* was wrongly decided. And we should reconsider it. . . . I'd want to put some restrictions on individuals loaning money to themselves; the [Rep. Michael] Huffington example [the Republican who set a record in 1994 by spending more than $28 million of his own money on his unsuccessful Senate campaign] presents a really serious problem, because it more and more allows people of great wealth to move away from any restrictions. And the public *likes* that. All the arguments that it will produce a gilded Congress of rich people doesn't affect people very much. They sort of like it when [Ross] Perot says, "I'm buying this election for you."

> Former House Speaker Tom Foley, quoted in Martin Schram, *Speaking Freely: Former Members of Congress Talk about Money in Politics* (Washington, DC: Center for Responsive Politics, 1995)

I continue to believe that *Buckley* provides insufficient protection to political speech, the core of the First Amendment. The illegitimacy of *Buckley* is further underscored by the continuing inability of the Court . . . to apply *Buckley* in a coherent fashion. As a result, *stare decisis* should pose no bar to overruling *Buckley*, and replacing it with a standard faithful to the First Amendment.

> Justice Clarence Thomas in his concurring opinion in *Randall v. Sorrell* (2006)

[C]ritically, the *Buckley* Court did not conclude that the Constitution would always prohibit expenditure limits, regardless of the reasons asserted and the record supporting the limitations. It simply held that based on the record before it, "[n]o governmental interest that had been suggested is sufficient to justify" the federal expenditure limits. Accordingly, after *Buckley*, there remains the possibility that a legislature could identify a sufficiently strong interest, and develop a supporting record, such that some expenditure limits could survive constitutional reviews.

> *Landell v. Sorrell*, 382 F. 2d 91, 107–108 (2d Cir. 2004), quoting *Buckley v. Valeo*

Buckley v. Valeo seems to be almost universally reviled: People either say the Court went too far in allowing restrictions on political contributions and expenditures, or not far enough. I want to do something radical, which is to say that the Court got it pretty much right. . . . The question is not whether the money is speech, but whether the First Amendment *protects your right to speak using your money.* After all, money isn't lawyering, but the Sixth Amendment secures criminal defendants' right to hire a lawyer. Money isn't contraception or abortions, but people have a right to buy condoms or pay doctors to perform abortions. Money isn't speech, but people have a right to spend money to publish in *The New York Times.* . . . Money isn't speech. But restricting speech that uses money is a speech restriction.

> Eugene Volokh, professor of law at UCLA School of Law, "Why *Buckley v. Valeo* Is Basically Right," *Arizona State Law Journal* 34 (2002): 1102

Under a system of private financing of elections, a candidate lacking immense personal or family wealth must depend on financial contributions from others to provide the resources necessary to conduct a successful campaign. . . . To the extent that large contributions are given to secure a political quid pro quo from current and potential office holders, the integrity of our system of representative democracy is undermined. . . . We find that . . . the weighty interests served by restricting the size of financial contributions to political candidates are sufficient to justify the limited effect upon First Amendment freedoms caused by the $1,000 contribution ceiling [imposed on individuals]. . . . The Act's [FECA of 1974] expenditure ceilings [however] impose direct and substantial restraints on the quantity of speech. . . . We conclude that the independent expenditure limitation is unconstitutional under the First Amendment.

> Per curiam opinion of the U.S. Supreme Court in *Buckley v. Valeo*, 424 U.S. 1 (1976)

Campaign Finance and Ethics

I would argue that the way big money has come to dominate politics has become the ethical issue of our time. I say to all of my colleagues . . . that all of us in office should hate this system. On the one hand, it is a bit like the play *Fiddler on the Roof*—you can argue that, well, no, people should not hate the system because in a way the current system is wired for incumbents. . . . But I really think all of us should hate this system, because even if you believe in your heart of hearts, even if you are absolutely convinced that the compelling need to raise money has never affected any position you have taken on any issue, even if you believe that . . . it sure does not look that way to the people. If we want people to believe in this political process . . . then we better get this big money out of politics and we better turn this system upside down—it is upside down right now—we better turn this system right side up.

Sen. Paul Wellstone (D-MN), *Congressional Record,* January 23, 1997

When [George W.] Bush ran for President, Ken Lay was right there with him. Lay helped to raise $112,000 for Bush's White House bid, sending a letter to 200 executives at the company encouraging them "voluntarily" to give money to Bush in order to make Lay a leading "Pioneer." He also arranged for Bush campaign aides and family members to use Enron jets, and even helped to underwrite the 2000 GOP convention, the Republican Florida recount campaign and the inauguration. Enron's generosity was rewarded. Company executives enjoyed at least 40 meetings with White House officials in 2001 and met a total of 72 times with officials from various federal departments and agencies. . . . Lay and other Enron officials privately advised Vice President Cheney in six closed-door energy policy meetings, exerting influence on an energy policy that read like an Enron wishlist with its commitments to further deregulation of the electricity industry.

Lee Drutman, "White House for Sale," *Multinational Monitor* 25 (May–June 2004): 32

When you go through the list [of Bush/Cheney 2004 donors], what hits you again and again is that the average Bush Pioneer or Ranger is somebody who either wants something from government in terms of appointments or contacts or who wants to have federal regulators taken off the beat. . . . The most damaging stuff is policy. . . . That's what comes at the expense of average Americans. If a big donor sleeps in the White House, that doesn't directly come at the expense of the average American. And if some bozo cowboy is ambassador to England, that may not be the best representation. But when the administration supports deregulatory policies, and say, lets its guard down on meat safety rules, people are affected.

Andrew Wheat, research director of Texans for Public Justice, quoted in Lee Drutman, "White House for Sale," in *Multinational-Monitor* (May–June 2004): 33

I never thought I would live to see a major drug dealer give 20,000 bucks in Florida and then be invited to a big Democratic reception by the vice president of the United States, Al Gore, and then be invited to the White House for a reception. Now keep in mind that you can't get into the White House unless the Secret Service clears you. This guy had been convicted, arrested twice in the '80s. It's in the computer.

> Ross Perot, PBS, *The NewsHour with Jim Lehrer*, November 28, 1996

Most people assume—I certainly do—that someone making an extraordinarily large [campaign] contribution is going to get something extraordinary in return.

> Justice David H. Souter at oral arguments of *Nixon v. Shrink Missouri Government PAC 528 US 377* (2000)

Campaign Finance Reform

Five years ago . . . President Bush signed into law the Bipartisan Campaign Reform Act of 2002. Today, American politics is so clean you could eat off of it—except for the mud-slinging, back-scratching, favor-trading, influence-peddling, bald-faced lying, indictments, and convictions.

> Ryan Sager, online editor, "Reformers' Victory Is Empty," *New York Sun*, March 27, 2007

[W]hile a car cannot run without fuel, a candidate can speak without spending money. And while a car can only travel so many miles per gallon, there is no limit on the number of speeches or interviews a candidate may give on a limited budget. . . . Just as a driver need not use a Hummer to reach her destination, so a candidate need not flood the airways with ceaseless sound-bites of trivial information in order to provide voters with a reason to support her.

> Justice John Paul Stevens in his dissenting opinion in *Randall v. Sorrell 136 S.Ct. 35* (2005)

It [BCRA] improves the system because it enables an individual to give more money, and what I want to do is have a system that encourages more individual participation as well as more disclosure. I've always been concerned about a system where money is given to entities and the stakeholders have no say, so I was concerned about the shareholders of corporate

America not having a say, as well as labor union members not having a say about how their money is being spent. This bill improves the system.

President George W. Bush, PBS *News Hour with Jim Lehrer,* March 27, 2002

Campaign finance reform doesn't keep money out of politics. . . . It merely skews the market, making it harder for rookies and amateurs to get in and easier for the pros and incumbents to game the system.

Jonah Goldberg, online editor at large, "Campaign Reform? Try Campaign Inflation," *National Review,* March 28, 2007

I favor transparency. Let people make contributions and report it on the Web site, so you know who's contributed to whom, but McCain-Feingold has not worked. It's hurt my party, it hurts First Amendment rights. I think it was a bad bill. . . . The American people should be able to exercise their First Amendment rights without having to think about hiring a lawyer.

Mitt Romney, former governor of Massachusetts, quoted in "Romney Assails McCain-Feingold Law," MSNBC.com, May 1, 2007

For 2 years . . . the Senator from Arizona and I have been stymied by opponents of reform who desperately cling to the absurd notion that the more money you pour into the political system that our democracy somehow gets better. Sometimes the comparison is made that we spend as much money on elections as we spend on potato chips. I don't know what this has to do with the question of political reform but it is an argument we are treated to anyway. Of course, no one outside the Washington Beltway believes in this argument. No one outside of this town thinks we need more money spent on the political process.

Sen. Russ Feingold (D-WI), PBS *News Hour with Jim Lehrer,* September 29, 1997

I'm no free speech purist. But since no one else is either, maybe we can borrow from the public-health sector. Let's treat politicians like Twinkies. They have to disclose their ingredients—i.e., where their money comes from—beyond that, let the buyer beware.

Jonah Goldberg, online editor at large, "The Twinkie Approach," *National Review,* March 1, 2007

I think you'll have a much better government [because of BCRA]. There's very few benefits of growing old, but I ran for the first time in 1982. We had much cleaner campaigns; we had grass-roots campaigns; we had stronger parties than we have today, and we had a much greater approval from the American people. The '74 reforms were pretty effective up into the '90s and then the system broke apart, as you know, and this—this fix won't last for-ever. If we pass it—If we pass this reform, twenty, twenty-five years from now, there will be two crazy guys like me and Russ Feingold saying we've got to fix the system again.

Sen. John McCain (R-AZ), PBS *News Hour with Jim Lehrer,* April 2, 2001

During the last decade, campaign finance orthodoxies without a crumb of support have addled the nation: that too much is expended to inform voters; that public cynicism is fueled by substantial contributions or expenditures; that officeholders ignore the public interest in favor of special interests; that laws are skewed to benefit the rich and famous; and, that campaign finance reform is necessary to cure American's corrupted democracy by driving money from politics like Jesus and the moneychangers. . . . But no election campaign expense is superfluous or excessive. Each dollar devoted to informing and persuading voters is praiseworthy. . . . By any enlightened yardstick, election campaign spending is too little, not too expensive.

Bruce Fein, attorney, quoted on Center for Individual Freedom (CFIF), CFIF.org, October 7, 2005

Like a virus, the campaign finance "reform" passed by Congress in McCain-Feingold and approved by the Supreme Court in *McConnell v. FEC* is mutating and spreading in the states. The law raised contribution limits to federal candidates but imposed substantial restrictions on political parties and citizens' groups. State politicians are taking McCain-Feingold and *McConnell* as a license to enact much broader restrictions on core political speech. . . . All these state provisions share an unappealing element: They benefit incumbents. The guise of "reform" offers incumbents semi-respectable cover for their assault on free elections. Unless stopped, the virus will kill the First Amendment and democratic self-government.

James Bopp Jr., general counsel for the James Madison Center for Free Speech, "Reformzilla," *The Wall Street Journal*, January 12, 2006: A12

Banning money from campaigns means banning speech. How so? Most of us are either unable or unwilling to run for office. Consequently, we want to communicate our support for certain candidates—and opposition to others—through the money we give to campaigns. If we give money to a campaign, we help it thrive. If we refuse to give money to a campaign—or if we give money to its opponent—we harm it. This is how we communicate in a representative democracy. The extent to which we ban money from campaigns is the extent to which we ban our own ability to express ourselves.

Michael J. Hurd, "Finance Reform Bill Jeopardizes Free Speech," DrHurd.com, April 2, 2001

As the comprehensive and sustained attack on Americans' freedom of political speech intensifies, the city [of Seattle, WA] has become a battleground. Campaign finance "reformers," who advocate ever-increasing government regulation of the quantity, timing and content of political speech, always argue that they want to regulate "only" money which, they say, leaves speech unaffected. But here they argue that political speech is money, and hence must be regulated. By demanding that the speech of two talk-radio hosts be monetized and strictly limited, reformers reveal the next stage in their stealthy repeal of the First Amendment.

George F. Will, "Speechless in Seattle," *Newsweek*, October 9, 2006

Candidates for federal office do face great obstacles in raising money to make their voices heard and to respond to the charges of their opponents. . . . When I ran for president in 1996, contribution and spending limits forced me to spend 70 percent of my time raising money in amounts no greater than $1,000. To raise $10 million during 1995 I had to travel to 250 fundraising events—about one for every campaign day. One million of that $10 million was spent on the costs of complying with federal rules; another $2.5 million went to pay for the cost of raising the

money; much of the rest was eaten up by the long campaign necessary to raise so much money! So, I understand what these of-
fice-holders are complaining about. It's as if they are engaged in a
spirited game of paint ball, only instead of paint balls the independent groups have real bullets.

> Lamar Alexander, former Republican presidential candidate,
> "Should Tom Paine Have Filed with the FEC?: The Loss of Com-
> mon Sense in Campaign Finance Reform," *Vital Speeches of the Day,*
> 64, 12 (April 1, 1998): 381–385

Campaign finance regulation has been packaged as a
means of returning power to "ordinary people." In truth, however, such regulation has had the effect of excluding ordinary
people from the political process in a variety of ways: It has insu-
lated incumbents from the voting public, in both the electoral
and legislative spheres; it has increased the incentives for legislative "shirking;" it has increased the ability of certain elites to
dominate the debate by eliminating competing voices; it has
placed a renewed premium on personal wealth in political candidates, and it has hampered grassroots political activity. These
problems are not the result of a poorly designed regulatory
structure but rather the inevitable result of a regulatory structure
built on faulty assumptions.

> Bradley A. Smith, *Unfree Speech: The Folly of Campaign Finance Re-
> form* (Princeton, NJ: Princeton University Press, 2001): 86

Electoral College

For those who want to defend the current electoral college system, I want to ask, What are the philosophical underpinnings
that lie at its foundation? I submit there are none. Instead, the
electoral college was a contrived institution, created to appeal to
a majority of the delegates at the Constitutional Convention of
1787, who were divided by the issue of Federal versus State powers, big State versus small State rivalries, the balance of power between the branches of Government, and slavery.... [T]he
electoral college is undemocratic and unfair. It distorts the election process, with some votes by design having more weight than
others. Imagine for a moment if you were told as follows "We
want you to vote for President. We are going to give you one vote
in the selection of the President, but a neighbor of yours is going

to have three votes in selecting the President." You would say that is not American, that is fundamentally unfair. We live in a nation that is one person—one citizen, one vote.

> Sen. Richard Durbin (D-IL), *Congressional Record,* December 6, 2000

The current attack on the Electoral College is off-point to begin with. The Electoral College was not the reason for the ballot problems in Florida in November [of 2000]. It did not cause the purging of the voter rolls, nor did it cause a single hanging chad. Abolish the Electoral College and every antiquated voting machine in this country will remain exactly where it is. We need to upgrade the nation's voting system, and we can. That doesn't mean scrapping the Electoral College, though. Minorities and rural areas should have a voice in our presidential politics, and the Electoral College helps ensure that they do.

> Sen. Byron Dorgan (D-ND), "Electoral College Works Quietly, Just as the Founders Intended," *Roll Call,* January 15, 2001: B35

I support the electoral vote system because it produces the right winner, and the right winner is the candidate who can govern this vast country because he has built a broad cross-national federal coalition, because he can win the popular vote in enough states. . . . The right winner of the World Series is the team that wins the most games, not the team that scored the most runs over all. The win-games principle is the best test of the two teams' abilities. In presidential elections, the win-states principle is the best test of the candidates' abilities to govern. It penalizes sectional and regional candidates, single-issue and ideological candidates. It rewards candidates whose votes are properly distributed; it is designed to achieve majority rule with minority consent.

> Judith A. Best, distinguished teaching professor, State University of New York at Cortland, *CQ Researcher,* 42, 42 (December 8, 2000): 1001

At its best, the electoral college operates in an inherently distorted manner in transforming popular votes into electoral votes. In addition, it has enormous potential to be a dangerous institution threatening the certainty of our elections and the legitimacy of our presidents. The defects of the contemporary electoral college cannot be dealt with by patchwork reforms such as abolishing the office of presidential elector. This distorted and unwieldy counting device must be abolished entirely, and the votes of the American people—wherever cast—must be counted directly and equally in determining who shall be the president of the United States. It is all too likely that the election of 2000, or one in the future, will finally provide the American public with indisputable evidence of the failings of the electoral college as a means of electing the people's president.

> Lawrence D. Longley and Neal R. Pierce, *The Electoral College Primer 2000* (New Haven, CT: Yale University Press, 1999): 175

We cannot justify the electoral college as a result of the framers' coherent design based on clear political principles. The founders did not articulate a theory to justify political inequality. . . . We have . . . seen that the electoral college does not protect important interests that would be overlooked or harmed under a system of direct election of the president. States—including states with small populations—do not embody coherent, unified, interests and communities, and they have little need for protection. Even if they did, the electoral college does not provide it. Contrary to the claim of its supporters, candidates do not pay attention to small states. The electoral college actually distorts the campaign so that candidates ignore many large and most small states and devote most of their attention to competitive states.

> George Edwards III, *Why the Electoral College Is Bad for America* (New Haven, CT: Yale University Press, 2004): 151

Money and Elections

Washington [DC] is now a corporate-occupied territory. There's a "For Sale" sign on almost every door of agencies and departments where these corporations dominate and they put their appointments in high office. The Congress is what Will Rogers once called "the best money can buy." Money is flowing in like never before that sells our elections. What does that mean to the American people? It means that corporations are saying no to the necessities of the American people.

> Ralph Nader, *Meet the Press*, February 22, 2004

As we voters prepare to make our final choices on Election Day, it is worth remembering that wealthy interests have already winnowed the field of candidates through a money-based primary that plagues America's electoral system. Not only are voters left with fewer and less representative choices, but candidates are trapped by the rules of the money game. . . . When a candidate's primary task is to endlessly make calls to wealthy contributors instead of communicating with voters on the issues, our electoral system is clearly in crisis. This is what the wealth primary—the effective elimination of political candidates who don't have access to wealthy donors—has bought us.

> Chris Fick, "Commentary: May the Richest Candidate Win?" *The Daily Record* (Baltimore, MD), October 29, 2004: 1

[W]e now have a colossal irony. Politicians sell access to something we own: the government. Broadcasters sell access to something we own: the public airwaves. Both do so, they tell us, in our name. By creating this system of selling and buying access, we have a campaign system that makes good people do bad things and bad people do worse things, a system that we do not want, that corrupts and trivializes public discourse, and that we have the power and the duty, a last chance, to change.

> Newton Minow, former chairman of the FEC, "Campaign Finance Reform: We Have Failed to Solve the Problem," *Vital Speeches of the Day*, 63, 18 (July 1, 1997): 555–559

How much money matters is not exactly clear. Money gives some sense of strength of a candidate's support. It also provides the wherewithal to employ the best brains in the political business. . . . Money is not a guarantee of success nor is lack of it a guarantee of failure. Phil Gramm and Steven Forbes have both proved that truckloads of money do not necessarily translate into political momentum. And Bill Clinton proved that you can win the presidency without being the big money candidate.

> Anonymous, "United States: The Money Primary; Campaign Funding," *The Economist*, April 7, 2007: 49

Politicians are forced to spend as much time begging as they do campaigning.

> David Wilson, lobbyist and former Vermont secretary of administration, quoted in "Vermont Legislature Needs Campaign Finance Reform," *Burlington Free Press*, January 30, 1997

Spending frugally in campaigns has almost become a sign of weakness. It used to be that you ran the campaign like you would want to govern, watching every penny. . . . Now that seems not to be a plus but a minus.

> Bill Gardner, New Hampshire secretary of state, quoted in Kevin Landrigan, "The Cost of Getting Elected in the Granite State," *Business NH Magazine*, September 1, 1998: 49

With its ruling in *Randall*, the Court is supporting the segregation of Americans into two distinct classes. . . . Today, one political class is the overwhelming majority—we express our preferences with our votes or volunteer efforts. The other class consists of those wielding real power—the ability to finance the bulk of candidates' campaigns and effectively "set the menu" of candidates from which the rest of us choose. The justices' motivation for treating money as speech may not be racist, but the impact is. Major political donors are fully unrepresentative of Americans. According to a 1996 study by the Joyce Foundation, eighty percent of people investing $200 or more in political candidates are males from households with annual income[s] exceeding $100,000, and about 95 percent are white.

> Jeff Milchen, director of ReclaimDemocracy.org, "It's Time to Overrule the Supreme Court: Overturning *Buckley v. Valeo* Is an Essential Step toward Enabling a Democratic Republic," July 18, 2006

[S]everal New York bankers and lawyers privately say that they . . . are spreading largess among multiple presidential candidates. Some say they are doing this so to promote debate, giving multiple candidates an opportunity to state their views. . . . People are also giving to multiple candidates as favors to friends and business associates—and to hedge their bets to make sure they have done something for whoever becomes the general campaign's candidate.

> Laurie P. Cohen, "Lawmakers Join Hunt to Bag Big Donors Early; Presidential Herd Spurs Rush for Limited Funds; 'I Get a Lot of Invites,'" *The Wall Street Journal*, March 28, 2007: A1

If I walked into [Sen. Christopher] Dodd's office with $250,000, I've hung the moon. For Barrack [Sen. Obama], I'm the greatest thing since sliced bread. Hillary's office? Get in line.

Democratic fund-raiser, quoted in Ana Marie Cox, "How Big Money Picks a Winner," *Time*, February 26, 2007: 42

Racial Gerrymandering

A reapportionment plan that includes one district of individuals who belong to the same race, but who are otherwise widely separated by geographical and political boundaries, and who may have little in common with one another but the color of their skin bears an uncomfortable resemblance to political apartheid. For these reasons we conclude that a plaintiff challenging a reapportionment statute under the Equal Protection Clause may state a claim by alleging that the legislation, though race-neutral on its face, rationally cannot be understood as anything other than an effort to separate voters into different districts on the basis of race, and that the separation lacks sufficient justification. . . . Racial gerrymandering, even for remedial purposes, may balkanize us into competing racial factions; it threatens to carry us further from the goal of a political system in which face no longer matters.

Justice Sandra Day O'Connor, majority opinion in *Shaw v. Reno*, 509 U.S. 630, 1993

Until today the court has analyzed equal protection claims involving race in electoral districting differently from equal protection claims involving other forms of governmental conduct. . . . As long as members of racial groups have the commonality of interest implicit in our ability to talk about concepts like "minority voting strength" and "dilution of minority votes," and as long as racial bloc voting takes place, legislators will have to take race into account in order to avoid dilution of minority voting strength in districting plans they adopt. A second distinction between districting and most other governmental decisions in which race has figured is that those other decisions using racial criteria characteristically occur in circumstances in which the use of race to the advantage of one person is necessarily at the obvious expense of a member of a different race. . . . In districting, by contrast, the mere placement of an individual in one district instead of another denies no one a right or benefit provided to others.

Justice David H. Souter, dissenting opinion in *Shaw v. Reno*, 509 U.S. 630, 1993

[S]o long as they do not subordinate traditional districting criteria to the use of race for its own sake or as a proxy, States may intentionally create majority minority districts, and may otherwise take race into consideration, without coming under strict scrutiny. . . . [H]owever, districts that are bizarrely shaped and non-compact, and that otherwise neglect traditional districting principles and deviate substantially from the hypothetical court drawn district, for predominantly racial reasons, are unconstitutional.

Justice Sandra Day O'Connor, concurring opinion in *Bush v. Vera*, 517 U.S. 952, 1996

Not every redistricting experience is especially divisive, but redesigning districts is always potentially conflictive. While stimulated by the need to bring districts into compliance with the one person, one vote rule, the battles themselves have little to do anymore with the concerns that districts be equipopulous. The conflictive potential relates to who is grouped with whom, rather than how many people are grouped together. Numerous districting plans can be drawn to satisfy the basic one person, one vote requirement but have vastly different electoral consequences. . . . It is these potential consequences that make the process so contentious.

Richard S. Engstrom, "The Political Thicket, Electoral Reform, and Minority Voting Rights." In Mark E. Rush and Richard L. Engstrom, eds., *Fair and Effective Representation? Debating Electoral Reform and Minority Rights* (Lanham, MD: Rowman & Littlefield, 2001)

The dabbling in political theory that [vote] dilution cases have prompted . . . is hardly the worst aspect of our vote dilution jurisprudence. Far more pernicious has been the Court's willingness to accept the one underlying premise that must inform every minority vote dilution claim: the assumption that the group asserting dilution is not merely a racial or ethnic group, but a group having distinct political interests as well. . . . We have acted on the implicit assumption that members of racial and ethnic groups must all think alike on important matters of public policy and must have their own "minority preferred" representatives holding seats in elected bodies if they are to be considered represented at all.

Justice Clarence Thomas, joined by Justice Antonin Scalia, concurring opinion in *Holder v. Hall*, 512 U.S. 874, 1994

In the long run, proportional representation [PR] may be the only politically and constitutionally viable solution to the problem of minority representation in the U.S. PR would allow minorities a fair chance to elect their own candidates without resorting to the kind of race-based districting that has provoked the recent legal backlash. White voters would have nothing to complain about with PR since it would allow them to elect their fair share of representatives, and it wouldn't involve the drawing of special or "funny shaped" districts to benefit minorities. In this sense, proportional representation is truly a "race neutral" approach to districting, and one that would finally resolve once and for all this festering political problem.

Douglas J. Amy, "Fair Representation for Racial Minorities: Is Proportional Representation the Answer?" *PR Library*, April 8, 2005

Redistricting and Reapportionment

In gerrymandered election districts, the voters don't choose their politicians—the politicians choose their voters!

Anonymous, quoted by Michael D. Robbins, *Fraud Factor* Web page, December 5, 2000, rev. January 2, 2007

At the risk of destroying yet another cherished illusion from your high school civics class, I regretfully inform you that, contrary to what you have been told, you do not elect your member of Congress. . . . The reason for this is that members of Congress are, in fact, selected, not elected, by a process called redistricting that takes place every 10 years following the national census. Voters have no say in redistricting. The lines for congressional districts are drawn in almost all states by governors and state legislators, who have two main concerns: 1) ensuring that their party, Republican or Democratic, depending on who's in charge, controls as many districts as possible, and 2) carving out districts that they themselves might be able to run in to move up the political ladder to federal office. By creating districts heavily weighted toward one party or the other, the state politicians who draw the lines determine the outcome of all but a small percentage of congressional races for the next 10 years, until it's time to redraw the lines again.

Tom Brazaitis, "Our Unduly Selected Representatives," *Cleveland Plain Dealer,* January 13, 2002

Legislators represent people, not trees or acres. Legislators are elected by voters, not farms or cities or economic interests. As long as ours is a representative form of government, and our legislatures are those instruments of government elected directly by and directly representative of the people, the right to elect legislators in a free and unimpaired fashion is a bedrock of our political system. . . . And, if a State should provide that the votes of citizens in one part of the State should be given two times, or five times, or 10 times the weight of votes of citizens in another part of the State, it could hardly be contended that the right to vote of those residing in the disfavored areas had not been effectively diluted.

Chief Justice Earl Warren, majority opinion in *Reynolds v. Sims,* 377 U.S. 533, 1964

[Referring to mid decade redistricting in Texas] It's never been done. I mean, it's an unprecedented action to take up redistricting when you weren't under a court order to do so, and when it wasn't immediately following a census, we don't do it every time there's a change in power. Think of the instability of our country. If every time, every two years we redistrict Congress just because we could or we didn't . . . or the people in power didn't like who the people were electing, what kind of instability would that create in our federal government?

Rep. Jim Dunnam (D-TX), PBS *News Hour with Jim Lehrer,* "Tussle in Texas," July 13, 2003

Anytime the state starts to redistrict, the language used in its decisions is whether this is a Polish district, a black district, this is a Democratic district, this is a Republican district, and the trick is to get it right in terms of the mix. This means if you want to create a Polish district, you want about 60 percent Polish. 100 percent is packing, and that means that you have to throw people in there that the state has said, "You get in that district because we need you to fill out the numbers, but we don't really want you to affect the outcome. This is not your district."

Samuel Issacharoff, professor of law, Texas School of Law, "Has the Supreme Court Destabilized Single-Member Districts?" A report at www.FairVote.org

Term Limits

Asking an incumbent member of Congress to vote on term limits is a bit like asking a chicken to vote for Colonel Sanders.

Rep. Bob Inglis (R-SC), *Reader's Digest*, October 1995

Term limits are anti-democratic. The right to choose our representatives is a cornerstone of democracy. It would be an arrogant power grab for politician . . . to tell you whom you can and cannot elect. It's none of our business whom you choose. The example set by our founders is instructive. Thomas Jefferson was in politics for almost 60 years. Benjamin Franklin, John Adams, James Madison, were all "career politicians" who spent decades learning and honing their craft. It would have been tragic to lose these giants to a gimmick like term limits.

Daylin Leach (D), Pennsylvania state representative, "Don't Dumb Down the Legislature," *Philadelphia Daily News*, April 24, 2007

Things have changed due to term limits [in Colorado], and much more. The old lions are gone, there is a lack of statesmanship, more ideology, more local power over members by local political hacks in the county parties, there is more campaign shrillness and this follows what is happening nationally and it carries over into governing.

Colorado state legislator, quoted in Johan A Straayer and Jennie Drage Bowser, "Colorado Legislative Term Limits: A Joint Project on Term Limits 2004." In Powell Richard, *Legislating without Experience: Case Studies in State Legislative Term Limits* (Lanham, MD: Rowman & Littlefield, 2005)

Voting Rights

The right to vote freely for the candidate of one's choice is the essence of a democratic society, and any restrictions on that right strike at the heart of representative government. And the right of suffrage can be denied by debasement or dilution of the weight of a citizen's vote just as effectively as by wholly prohibiting the free exercise of the franchise.

Chief Justice Earl Warren, majority opinion, *Reynolds v. Sims*, 377 U.S. 533, 1964

I think it was Wendell Phillips who said something like this, "if women are like men, then they certainly possess the same brain and that should entitle them to the ballot; if they are not like men, then they certainly need the ballot, for no man can understand what they want." And we ask you upon those lines to give the ballot to women.

Carrie Chapman Catt at the Delaware Constitutional Convention, 1897

It was we, the people; now we, the white male citizens; nor yet we, the male citizens; but we, the whole people, who formed the Union. And we formed it, not to give the blessings of liberty, but to secure them; not to the half of ourselves and the half of our posterity, but to the whole people—women as well as men. And it is downright mockery to talk to women of their enjoyment of the blessings of liberty while they are denied the use of the only means of securing them provided by this democratic-republican government—the ballot. . . . Are women persons? And I hardly believe any of our opponents will have the hardihood to say they are not. Being persons, then, women are citizens; and no State has a right to make any law, or to enforce any old law, that shall abridge their privileges and immunities. Hence, every discrimination against women in the constitutions and laws of the several States is today null and void, precisely as in every one against negroes.

Susan B. Anthony, speech in New York, 1873

References

Abramowitz, Alan I. "Incumbency, Campaign Spending, and the Decline of Competition in U.S. House Elections." *Journal of Politics* 53 (February 1991): 34–56

"Absentee and Early Voting." National Conference of State Legislatures. October 27, 2004. www.ncsl.org/programs/legismgt/elect/absentearly .htm

Alexander, Lamar. "Should Tom Paine Have Filed with the FEC?: The Loss of Common Sense in Campaign Finance Reform." *Vital Speeches of the Day* 64 (April 1): 381ff. 0-proquest.umi.com.wncln.wncln:80/pqdweb ?d=28581324=2&Fmt=3&clientld=15105&RQT=309&VName=PQD

"Ballotwatch." Initiative and Referendum Institute. No date. www .iandrinstitute.org

Bullock, Charles S. III. 2005. "Redistricting: Racial and Partisan Considerations." In Matthew J. Streb, ed., *Law and Election Politics: The Rules of the Game*. Boulder, CO: Lynne Rienner Publishers: 151–69

Campaign Finance Institute. 2006. Table 3-8, "Campaign Funding Sources for House and Senate Candidates, 1984–2006 at www.cfinst.org /data/pdf/VitalStats_t8.pdf; various tables, including "Campaign Funding Sources for House and Senate Candidates, 1984–2006," "House Campaign Expenditure, 1980–2006," and "Senate Campaign Expenditures, 1990–2006," www.cfinst.org/data/VitalStats.aspx

"Campaign Finance: State and Local Overview." Hoover Institution. No date. www.campaignfinancesite.org/structure/states1.html

Cantor, Joseph E. "Congressional Campaign Spending: 1976–1996." Washington, DC: Congressional Research Service. 97-793 GOV, August 19, 1997

Carlson, Darren K. "Public Flunks Electoral College System." *Gallup Brain*. November 2, 2004. 0-institution.gallup.com.wncln.wncln.org/ content/default. aspx?ci=13918

Carroll, Joseph. "Are Americans Worried about Voter Fraud?" *Gallup Brain*. October 26, 2004. 0-institution.gallup.com.wncln.wncln.org /content/default. aspx?ci=13780

Carroll, Joseph. "Is Public Confident That Votes Will Be Accurately Counted on Nov. 7?: Americans Trust Electronic, Paper Ballots Equally." *Gallup Brain*. October 27, 2006. 0-institution.gallup.com.wncln.wncln.org /content/default. aspx?ci=25189

Common Cause. "Public Financing in the States." April 2005. www .commoncause.org/site/pp.asp?c=dkLNK1MQIwG&b=507399

"Contribution Limits." National Conference of State Legislatures. 2005. www.ncsl.org/programs/legismgt/about/ContribLimits.htm

Cooper, Mary H. 2004 (October 29). "Voting Rights." *CQ Researcher* 14 (October 29, 2004): 901–24. CQ Researcher Online. 0-library .cqpress.com. wncln.wncln.org:80/cqresearcher/cqresrre2004102900

Edwards, George III. *Why the Electoral College Is Bad for America*. New Haven, CT, and London: Yale University Press, 2004

Engstrom, Richard L. "The Political Thicket, Electoral Reform, and Minority Voting Rights." In Mark E. Rush and Richard L. Engstrom, eds., *Fair and Effective Representation? Debating Electoral Reform and Minority Rights*. Lanham, MD: Rowman & Littlefield, 2005: 3–67

Fieganbaum, Edward D., and James A. Palmer. "Campaign Finance Law." Washington, DC: Federal Election Commission, 2002. www.fec .gov/pubrec/cfl/ cfl02/cfl02.shtml

Guinier, Lani. *The Tyranny of the Majority: Fundamental Fairness in Representative Democracy.* New York: Free Press, 1994

Herrnson, Paul S. *Congressional Elections: Campaigning at Home and in Washington,* 3rd ed. Washington, DC: CQ Press, 2000

Hoover Institution. 2004. "Public Policy Inquiry: Campaign Finance." www.campaignfinancesite.org/

Initiative and Referendum Institute. 2007. www.iandrinstitute.org

Jones, Jeffrey M. "Seven in 10 Support New Campaign Finance Legislation: But Few Doubt It Will Limit the Powers of Special Interests."*Gallup Brain.* February 13, 2002. 0-institution.gallup.com.wncln.wncln.org /content/default aspx?ci=5329

Katel, Peter. "Voting Controversies." *CQ Researcher* 16 (September 15, 2006): 745–768. CQ Researcher Online. 0-library.cqpress.com. wncln .wncln.org:80/cqresearcher/cqresrre2006091500

"Limits on Contributions during the Legislative Session." National Conference of State Legislatures. April 2006. www.ncsl.org/programs /legismgt/about/duringsessionchart.htm

Longley, Lawrence D., and Neal R. Pierce. *The Electoral College Primer 2000.* New Haven, CT, and London: Yale University Press, 1999

McDonald, Michael P. United States Election Project. No date. elections .gmu.edu/voter_turnout.htm

Minow, Newton. "Campaign Finance Reform: We Have Failed to Solve the Problem." *Vital Speeches of the Day* 63 (July 1, 1997): 555ff. 0-proquest.umi.com.wncln.wncln:80/pqdweb?d=12919630&sid=2&Fmt=3& clientld=15105&RQT=309&VName=PQD

Moore, David W. "Public Dissatisfied with Campaign Finance Laws, Supports Limits on Contributions: But Opposes Government Financing of Elections; Rates Issue of Low Importance." *Gallup Brain.* August 3, 2001. 0-institution.gallup.com.wncln.wncln.org/content/default.aspx?ci=4765

Mutz, Diana C. "Effects of Horse-Race Coverage on Campaign Coffers: Strategic Contributing to Presidential Primaries." *Journal of Politics* 57 (November 1995): 1015–42

National Conference of State Legislatures. "The States Tackle Election Reform." 2003. www.ncsl.org/programs/legismgt/03BillSum.htm

Newport, Frank. "Americans Support Proposal to Eliminate Electoral College System." *Gallup Brain.* January 5, 2001. 0-institution.gallup.com .wncln.wncln.org/ content/default.aspx?ci=2140

Nice, David C. "Campaign Spending and Presidential Election Results." *Polity* 19 (Spring 1987): 464–76

Rubin, Aviel D. *Brave New Ballot: The Battle to Safeguard Democracy in the Age of Electronic Voting.* New York: Morgan Road Books, 2006

Rush, Mark E. *Does Redistricting Make a Difference? Partisan and Electoral Behavior.* Baltimore, MD: Johns Hopkins University Press, 1993

Saad, Lydia. "No Public Outcry for Campaign Finance Reform: Americans Unphased by Democratic Fundraising Charges." *Gallup Brain.* February 22, 1997. 0-institution.gallup.com.wncln.wncln.org/content/default.aspx?ci=4474

Saad, Lydia. "Americans Dubious Congress Can Curb Corruption: But Less Than Half Think It's a Very Serious Problem." *Gallup Brain.* May 8, 2006. 0-institution.gallup.com.wncln.wncln.org/content/default.aspx?ci=22699.

Scarrow, Howard A. "Vote Dilution, Party Dilution, and the Voting Rights Act: The Search for 'Fair and Effective Representation.'" In David K. Ryden, ed., *The U.S. Supreme Court and the Electoral Process.* Washington, DC: Georgetown University Press, 2000: 40–57

Sherman, Mark. "Justices' Scales May Be Tipping to the Right." *Houston Chronicle,* June 26, 2007: A1

Smith, Bradley A. *Unfree Speech: The Folly of Campaign Finance Reform.* Princeton, NJ and Oxford: Princeton University Press, 2001

Strayer, John A., and Jennie Drage Bowser. "Colorado's Legislative Term Limits: Joint Project on Term Limits." Denver, CO, and Washington, DC: National Conference of State Legislatures, 2005

U.S. Census Bureau. "Voting and Registration in the Election of November 2004." Washington, DC: U.S. Department of Commerce, Economics and Statistics Administration, 2006

U.S. Pirg Education Fund. "The Wealthy Primary: The Role of Big Money in the 2006 Congress Primaries." November 2006. www.uspirg.org

Volokh, Eugene. "Why *Buckley v. Valeo* Is Basically Right." *Arizona State Law Journal* 34 (Winter 2002): 1095–1103.

"Voters Win with Election Day Registration." Demos: A Network of Ideas and Action. January 31, 2007. www.demos.org/pubs/voters_win_web.pdf

7

Directory of Organizations

The organizations listed in this chapter vary widely in political ideology and intent. Included are for-profit and nonprofit organizations, government agencies, and intergovernmental associations. The common denominator is that all are working for improved campaign and election processes. Among the concerns of these organizations are increased political participation, campaign finance reform, term limits, voter education, alternative election systems, more efficient election administration, vote fraud and election crime, voter intimidation, voter registration, and voting rights.

ACCURATE: Center for Correct, Usable, Reliable, Auditable, and Transparent Elections
Johns Hopkins University
Department of Computer Science
accurate-voting.org

This organization presents research on voting systems and provides access to conference proceedings on electronic voting, voting machines, and paper ballots. Members give testimony at public hearings at the local, state, and national levels on voting security.

American Association of Political Consultants (AAPC)
www.theaapc.org

Established in 1969, this organization includes individual and corporate members who engage in political counseling and other activities related to electoral politics. Student, academic, and business memberships are available with different benefits packages. The AAPC conducts meetings every two years to provide information on innovative campaign tactics and other political developments.

Publications: The *AAPC Update* is a biweekly newsletter available online, and *PollingReport.com* offers national survey results to subscribers.

American Enterprise Institute (AEI) for Public Policy Research/ Brookings Institution: Election Reform Project
www.aei.org/research/projectID.25,filter.all/project.asp

The AEI/Brookings Election Reform Project, a collaboration between the American Enterprise Institute and the Brookings Institution, two Washington-based think tanks, presents research on a host of election reforms, including voter registration, the use of provisional ballots, and the integrity of the electoral process. This organization seeks to promote the effective implementation of the Help America Vote Act.

Publications: The *AEI Newsletter* provides timely information and reports on the activities of the American Enterprise Institute, including developments in electoral reform.

Americans to Limit Congressional Terms
See U.S. Term Limits

Ballot Initiative Strategy Center (BISC)
Launched in 2002 to reinvigorate a progressive ballot initiative process, the BISC provides research, training, and consultation to managers of ballot initiatives across the country. The organization shares articles and ballot initiative election results at its Web page.

Black Box Voting
www.blackboxvoting.org

Calling themselves the official consumer protection group for elections, Black Box Voting members monitor the voting irregularities associated with voting machines. Their Web site reports problems, such as the lack of security, inaccuracies, and ethical breaches associated with computerized voting. The organization provides a Citizen Tool Kit on monitoring vote counting and elections, encouraging citizens to regain control of elections.

Publications: The book, *Black Box Voting: Ballot Tampering in the 21st Century,* discusses vote rigging, electronic vote tampering, and problems associated with proprietary voting software.

Brennan Center for Justice
www.brennancenter.org

The Brennan Center seeks to safeguard fundamental freedoms, such as voting rights. The organization promotes democratic processes, advocating secure voting systems, campaign finance reform for more competitive elections, and a wide array of electoral reforms such as the full implementation of the Help America Vote Act, the removal of barriers to voter registration, and the restoration of voting rights to those convicted of a felony. The Brennan Center provides educational materials through its op-ed pieces and news releases.

Caltech/MIT Voting Technology Project
California Institute of Technology
www.vote.caltech.edu

Established in 2000, this organization evaluates the reliability of U.S. voting systems, establishes criteria for assessing the reliability of voting systems, and proposes guidelines for implementing the criteria. Through workshops and conferences, the organization seeks to promote more accurate and dependable voting systems. The group's Web site offers the results of research on the implementation of more convenient voting options.

Campaign Finance Institute (CFI)
www.cfinst.org

Affiliated with George Washington University, the CFI conducts research, recruits task forces, and makes recommendations for campaign finance reform. Its task force recommendations and much of its research are available at the CFI Web site.
Publications: The *Campaign Finance eGuide* is an interactive, user-friendly guide to campaign finance reform laws.

Campaign Legal Center (CLC)
www.camlc.org

The CLC is a clearinghouse of information on campaign finance and media laws and their enforcement. The organization took part in a successful defense of the Bipartisan Campaign Reform Act of 2002 when the U.S. Supreme Court upheld major provisions of the legislation in *McConnell v. Federal Election Commission* (2004). The CLC offers analyses on political advertising, disclosure, contribution limits, and enforcement issues associated with other campaign finance and media-related matters. The group regularly comments on Federal Election Commission proceedings and offers advisory opinions.

Publications: The *Legal Center Weekly Report* provides updates on the latest developments in campaign finance and media law; *The Campaign Finance Guide* offers a comprehensive overview of federal campaign finance laws; *The Campaign Media Guide* explains in detail the obligations of broadcasters in an election year, as well as candidate and citizen rights during an election.

Center for Democracy and Citizenship (CDCC)
Humphrey Institute of Public Affairs
publicwork.org

Established in 1989 as part of the Hubert H. Humphrey Institute of Public Affairs, the CDCC espouses the principle that citizenship requires effort and that public action needs ordinary citizen involvement. The organization conducts research, offers workshops, and makes presentations on citizen involvement in public affairs. The CDCC fosters a variety of projects aimed at youth civic education, community involvement, and immigrant mobilization.

Center for Democracy and Election Management (CDEM)
American University
www.american.edu/ia/cdem

Established in 2002, the CDEM trains undergraduate and graduate students as well as in-service professionals in the best methods to manage elections. The Center sponsors policy discussions among U.S. and international scholars about the transition to democracy and the promotion of free and fair elections. The CDEM organized the Commission on Federal Election Reform, cochaired by former president Jimmy Carter and former U.S. secretary of state James A. Baker III. This 21-member commission conducted public hearings in Washington and Houston, Texas, and in 2005 it offered 87 recommendations to strengthen the U.S.

electoral system and reconstitute public confidence in the political process. Their recommendations included requiring an identification card at polling places, instituting voter-verifiable paper audit trails on all electronic voting machines, and strengthening the U.S. Election Assistance Commission and state election management agencies.

Publications: CDEM issues working papers, journal articles, and books on electoral issues in the United States and abroad.

Center for Individual Freedom Foundation (CFIF)
www.centerforindividualfreedom.org

Founded in 1998, the CFIF lobbies, participates in lawsuits, and issues papers and briefings on policy questions dealing with individual liberty. The organization challenges campaign finance reform in court as infringing on free speech and vigorously opposes the Bipartisan Campaign Reform Act in court cases.

Center for Public Integrity (CPI)
www.publicintegrity.org

Founded in 1990, the CPI provides investigative reports on public policy issues, including campaign finance, lobbying activities, and state referenda and initiatives. The organization seeks to educate citizens so that they may hold government and other institutions accountable.

Publications: E-mail newsletters highlight a number of the organization's investigative reports; the CPI also provides online access to campaign finance databases on 527 organizations, the top 100 lobbies and their expenditures, and state party donations to political campaigns.

Center for Representative Government (CRG)
Cato Institute
www.cato.org/research/crg

Established in 1977 by Edward Crane, Cato is a libertarian organization dedicated to promoting limited government. As part of the Cato Institute, the CRG seeks to promote a limited, representative government. Viewing career politicians and government expansion as the source of many problems, it advocates repeal of most campaign finance reforms, including campaign contribution limits, and the institution of congressional term limits as a means of promoting competitive elections. The CRG hopes to bring citizen legislators back to the forefront of American politics.

Publications: CRG has published *The Fallacy of Campaign Finance Reform* (Chicago: University of Chicago Press, 2006) by John Samples and *The Marketplace of Democracy: Electoral Competition and American Politics* (Washington, DC: Brookings Institution Press, 2006), edited by Michael P. McDonald and John Samples; the *CATO Journal* and *Policy Studies* is devoted to addressing current public policy issues; *Policy Report* is a free bimonthly newsletter that provides book reviews and summaries of the organization's research.

Center for Responsive Politics (CRP)
www.opensecrets.org

Founded in 1983, the CRP works for a more efficient and productive Congress and political process. The organization compiles data, conducts surveys, and holds educational seminars to disseminate information about U.S. politics. The CRP tracks the influence of money on elections and public policy outcomes. Among the Center's objectives are campaign finance reform, improved ethics in government, and more effective public policy. The CRP provides computer services with databases on campaign finance, financial disclosure, lobbyists, and soft money.

Publications: CRP has published *Speaking Freely: Washington Insiders Talk about Money in Politics* (Washington, DC: Center for Responsive Politics, 2002), by Larry Makinson; *CapitalEye.org* is a money-in-politics online newsletter.

Center for the Study of the American Electorate (CSAE)
www.american.edu/ia/cdem/csae

Founded in 1976, the CSAE investigates the decline of political participation in the United States. The organization organizes conferences and encourages authorities in the field of American political participation to attend.

Publications: Five or six reports are issued every two years on voter registration and turnout.

Center for Voting and Democracy
See Fair Vote

Century Foundation (CF)
www.tcf.org

Founded in 1919, The CF conducts research and conferences to examine the strengths and weaknesses of different public policy approaches and to promote a more effective government and an open democracy. The organization offers results of its research on electoral reform, including instituting best practices to combat voter fraud, procedures for counting provisional ballots, and effective means for voter registration verification. The CF provides educational materials on the advantages and disadvantages of early voting, voter identification requirements, and felon re-enfranchisement.

Publications: A variety of works are available in PDF format on voting fraud and intimidation, improving voter participation, implementation of the Help America Vote Act, electronic voting, and ballot access for minor parties.

Cincinnatus Political Action Commmittee
See Citizens for a Fair Vote Count

Citizen Advocacy Center (CAC)
www.citizenadvocacycenter.org

Through public education, community organizing, issue advocacy, and litigation, the Center works to remove obstacles to citizen engagement. The organization provides information about obtaining government-held information, having a petition placed on the ballot, and speaking out at public hearings. The CAC hosts open forums at community gatherings and offers a Citizen Training Corps seminar encouragement engagement in community action.

Publications: A quarterly e-mail newsletter offers information on the organization's activities and accomplishments.

Citizens' Debate Commission (CDC)
www.citizensdebate.org

Expressing grave concerns about the Commission on Presidential Debates (CPD), the Citizens' Debate Commission seeks to sponsor future presidential debates. Its primary concern is the CPD's exclusion of most minor political party candidates. The group proposes to sponsor five 90-minute presidential debates and one 90-minute vice presidential debate with more representation from a spectrum of political parties.

Citizens for a Fair Vote Count
www.votefraud.org

Originally established by James J. Condit Jr. as Cincinnatus Polit-ical Action Committee in 1972, the Fair Vote Count Web site pro-vides news stories and reports on vote fraud and advocates maintaining printed ballots. The organization offers a documen-tary titled *The Right to Vote,* which examines the control that pri-vate companies exert over voting systems, provides accounts of alleged vote fraud, and assesses the problems associated with electronic and computerized voting.

Citizens for Term Limits (CTL)
www.termlimits.org

Believing that term limits will improve the quality of congres-sional leadership and promote citizen legislators who act as public servants, CTL supports an amendment to the U.S. Constitution limiting the number of years a person may hold office in each chamber of the U.S. Congress. Senators would be limited to one six-year term in the U.S. Senate, and members of the House of Representatives could serve three two-year terms.

Citizens in Charge Foundation
www.citizensincharge.org

Citizens in Charge, supported by the Citizens in Charge Founda-tion, works to educate the public on the benefits of initiative, ref-erendum, and recall elections, using litigation to preserve and expand these processes. The organization provides access to a blog for commentary on reports related to the initiative, referen-dum, and recall.

Publications: E-mail updates are available on the latest ef-forts to protect and expand the use of direct democracy proce-dures in American politics.

Citizens' Research Foundation
University of California
Institute of Government Studies
www.igs.berkeley.edu/research_programs/CRF

Established in 1958 as the Political Research Foundation, this or-ganization conducts research on the role of money in politics and campaign finance reform.

Publications: The foundation issues studies on money in politics that focus on methods of raising, allocating, and spending funds in campaigns.

Coalition for Free and Open Elections (COFOE)

www.cofoe.org

Founded in 1985, the COFOE opposes restrictive state regulations that govern the establishment of minor political parties. The organization claims that these regulations protect the two major parties from competition and therefore act as limitations on open electoral democracy. The organization holds that, with more liberal voter registration procedures and the introduction of proportional representation, minor parties would have a greater chance of winning public offices.

Publications: The *Ballot Access News,* published monthly, contains legislative action information and describes judicial decisions that affect the conduct of elections.

Commission on Presidential Debates (CPD)

www.debates.org

Founded in 1987, the nonpartisan commission conducts voter education programs and sponsors and produces U.S. presidential and vice presidential candidate debates. It provides guidelines to those who would like to sponsor debates in other forums by including information on budgeting, handling the media, debate formats, staging, and postdebate activities. The commission offers technical assistance to emerging democracies on the conduct of candidate debates.

Committee for the Study of the American Electorate

See Center for the Study of the American Electorate

Common Cause (CC)

www.commoncause.org

With nearly 300,000 members and supporters and 38 state organizations, Common Cause organizes lobbying activities to support campaign spending limits, public financing of elections, and the direct election of the president. Founded in 1970 as the Urban Coalition Action Council, the organization successfully lobbied for the National Voter Registration Act, the Help America Vote Act, and the Bipartisan Campaign Reform Act. CC's education fund is used to promote increased voter participation and improved voter education.

Publications: Common Cause, published from 1980 to 1996, was the organization's magazine; reports on election reform, media and democracy, redistricting, holding public official accountable, and money in politics are available on CC's Web site.

Computer Professionals for Social Responsibility (CPSR)
www.cpsr.org

Founded in 1981, this organization, comprised of computer scientists, educates policy makers on the role of the Internet in society, including its effects on governance and civil liberties. The organization conducts research on voting technologies and election systems and offers advice on voting systems standards.

Publications: The CPSR Compiler, an electronic monthly newsletter for members, offers commentary on the latest projects sponsored by the organization; *CPSR Working Papers* is an online series of research papers on computer-related issues.

Congressional Quarterly (CQ)
www.cq.com

Founded in 1945, Congressional Quarterly provides information about the American political process. Its sponsored research on American politics ranges from campaigns and elections to the operation of governing institutions.

Publications: Much of CQ's research is now available online, including *CQ Researcher,* a monthly publication providing in-depth coverage of public policy issues; *CQ weekly,* a periodical focusing on the personalities and events in national politics; *Governing,* a daily online magazine with a monthly hard copy version covering state and local government issues; and *Vital Statistics on American Politics,* an annual publication providing useful data for all subfields in American government. CQ issues the *Guide to U.S. Elections,* a historical summary of presidential, congressional, and state gubernatorial elections.

Council of State Governments (CSG)
www.csg.org

Founded in 1933, the CSG has Eastern, Midwestern, Western, and Southern regional offices as well as a national office based in

Washington, D.C. The organization provides educational materials on the executive, judicial, and legislative branches of state governments. Because state governments are still the major source of policy making regarding election administration, the CSG's facilitation of communication and cooperation among states can be an important factor in the coordination of election procedures.

Publications: Book of the States, issued yearly since 1935, contains a wealth of information on state election results and on the institutions of state governments; *State News* is a magazine that covers policy issues of relevance to state officials; *State Directories* contains the names and contact information for key government officials.

Democracy Matters (DM)
www.democracymatters.org

Formed to encourage student activism, DM promotes student involvement in a wide array of areas, including campaign finance reform, civil rights, and social justice. The organization offers workshops and downloadable materials for teachers and students on promoting student involvement in political campaigns.

Democracy 21
www.democracy21.org

Founded in 1997, Democracy 21 works to reduce the role of big money in American politics. The organization monitors the enforcement of campaign finance reform legislation and frequently files court briefs with the Federal Election Commission (FEC). Democracy 21 seeks the reform of the FEC and an overhaul of the public financing system for presidential elections. The organization issues letters and reports to Congress calling for ethics, lobbying, and campaign finance reforms.

Election Administration Research Center (EARC)
earc.berkeley.edu

Established in 2005 within the Institute of Governmental Studies at the University of California at Berkeley, the EARC seeks to improve election administration through research, education, and public outreach. The Center issues studies on state and local elections to election officials, academic researchers, and the general public and provides a variety of services, including a summary of election laws, information about voter registration procedures, and poll worker training.

Election Assistance Commission (EAC)
www.eac.gov

Established in 2002 by the Help America Vote Act (HAVA), the commission's central role is to serve as a national clearinghouse and resource for information about the administration of federal elections. The EAC provides election administration guidance, voluntary voting guidelines, research on federal election administration, testing and certification of voting systems, a national voter registration form, distribution of grants to help states meet HAVA requirements, and annual reports to Congress describing its activities.

Publications: EAC has published *Best Practices in Election Administration; Best Practices Report on Voting by Uniformed and Overseas Citizens.*

Election Center (EC)
www.electioncenter.org

The EC offers services for registration and election administration officials at the state, county, and municipal levels, providing updates to members regarding legislation, regulations, court decisions, and Justice Department rulings that affect voter registration and election administration. Through annual national conferences and periodic regional workshops and seminars, the EC promotes an exchange of information about election administration procedures among officials. The organization trains and certifies from 600 to 1,000 voter registration and election administration officials annually.

Publications: The EC issues election center task force reports and professional practice papers on policy developments in election administration.

Election Crimes Branch (ECB)
Public Integrity Section
U.S. Department of Justice
www.usdoj.gov/criminal/pin

Created in 1980 to supervise the enforcement of federal laws against criminal misconduct in the electoral process, the ECB is part of the Public Integrity Section of the Criminal Division at the U.S. Department of Justice. The agency conducts investigations of such election law violations as election fraud, intimidation and coercion of voters, violation of federal campaign financing and reporting regulations, solicitation of illegal contributions or activities from public employees, and violations of restrictions on the use of public funds for lobbying. Agency personnel conduct training sessions for federal law enforcement officials who will investigate possible election crimes and recommend antifraud techniques to state and local election officials. The ECB cooperates with the Federal Election Commission in efforts to maintain ballot security.

Publications: The ECB has published *Federal Prosecution of Election Offenses* by Craig Donsanto and Nancy L. Simmons (Washington, DC: 7th ed. in 2007).

Election Data Services (EDS)
www.electiondataservices.com

Founded in 1977, EDS is an independent political consulting firm specializing in election administration, redistricting, and the use of Geological Information Systems (GIS) to analyze census and election data. Among its services, the EDS helps local officials select voting equipment and customize their computer software for tallying ballots and presenting election results. The organization sponsors forums for election officials on such topics as new voting equipment, redistricting methodology, and the maintenance of county-level data on voter registration, turnout, and election results.

Election Reform Information Project
www.electiononline.org

The Election Reform Information Project provides up-to-date news on election reform. The organization's Web page offers access to statewide voter registration databases and other reform links.

Publications: Electionline Weekly, an online e-mail newsletter, summarizes the latest election reform developments. The organization also offers briefings on electoral reforms, including alternative voting systems, provisional balloting, electronic voting, and implementation of the Help America Vote Act.

Election Science Institute (ESI)
www.electionscience.org

The Election Science Institute, formerly Votewatch, was established in 2002 following the voting irregularities in the 2000 presidential election. By asking voters to register with them at their Web site to become volunteer vote watchers on election day, the organization receives reports on voter experiences, including any problems encountered. The ESI provides an Internet-based repository of election day voter comments and identifies voting anomalies prior to the certification of election results. The organization offers to assist election officials and state secretaries of state in complying with voting laws, recruitment of poll workers, and certification of voting machinery.

Electronic Frontier Foundation (EFF)
www.eff.org

Founded in 1990, the EFF seeks local election reform requiring verified voting, random audits of electronic voting machines, and public access to all codes used in elections. The Foundation participates in litigation regarding potentially flawed electronic voting systems. The organization issues press releases and offers archived articles at its Web site.

E-Voter Institute
evoterinstitute.com

Founded in 1999, this trade organization promotes Web publisher interests and sponsors research about the Internet and politics. The institute developed from a project examining the impact of online advertising on political candidates. The Institute advocates increasing the use of the Internet in political and advocacy campaigns, arguing that this will foster a better democratic process.

Publications: Crossing the River: The Coming of Age in Politics and Advocacy (Philadelphia, PA: Xlibris Corporation, 2005), by Karen A. B. Jagoda, examines the impact of the Internet on political campaigns.

Fair Vote: The Center for Voting and Democracy
www.fairvote.org

Fair Vote seeks to promote increased voter turnout and a more responsive and accountable government. The group sponsors the Right to Vote Initiative, Instant Runoff Voting America, the Presidential Elections Reform Program, Democracy USA, the Voting and Democracy Research Center, and the Electoral Services Group. The Center supports such election reforms as an instant runoff voting process, proportional representation, direct election of the president, and better ballot access for minor political parties.

Publications: Public policy reports, snapshots of elections in various countries, and issue-related reports are available online.

Federal Election Commission (FEC)
www.fec.gov

Established by Congress in 1975 to enforce the Federal Election Campaign Act of 1974, the FEC is an independent regulatory agency that administers all federal campaign finance laws, including public funding of presidential elections, contributions and spending in federal elections, bans on soft money in federal elections, and the disclosure of campaign finance information submitted by political action committees. Consisting of six voting commissioners appointed by the president and confirmed by the Senate for six-year overlapping terms, the FEC meets approximately twice a week. The clerk of the House of Representatives and the secretary of the Senate serve as ex officio nonvoting members of the commission.

Publications: The FEC issues *The Record*, a monthly newsletter on agency regulations and decisions; *Federal/State Disclosure and Election Directory;* and numerous brochures and campaign guides for federal election candidates. Since 1996 the FEC has published annual reports informing the president and Congress of commission activities during the year, summarizing advisory opinions and litigation, and explaining new developments in the administration of election law.

Federal Voting Assistance Program (FVAP)
Department of Defense
www.fvap.gov

Created in 1955 under the Federal Voting Assistance Act and expanded in 1968 and 1975 under the Overseas Citizens Voting Rights Act and in 1986 under the Uniformed and Overseas Voting Rights Act, the FVAP helps members of the armed forces, their spouses and dependents, and any qualified U.S. citizen residing overseas to register and vote. The program recommends an official postcard form to states for use in absentee registration and voting. FVAP acts as an ombudsman for local election officials and for those wishing to vote absentee under provisions of federal law, and it works with states to improve absentee registration and voting programs.

Publications: Voting Assistance Guide describes each state's absentee voting regulations, lists the mailing addresses of local election officials, and includes the Uniform and Overseas Citizens Absentee Voting Rights Act; FVAP also issues *Voter Information News,* a newsletter providing information on upcoming elections, including primary election calendars sorted by state and month, and general election deadlines for the uniformed services.

Funders' Committee for Civic Participation (FCCP)
www.discoverthenetwork.org/groupProfile.asp?grpid=6492

The FCCP represents numerous corporate, community, and private foundations, including the Rockefeller Family Fund and the Arca Foundation. Established in 1983, the Funders' Committee solicits foundations to fund voter registration, civic education, voting rights, and campaign finance reform initiatives. The group's most recent concern is the erosion of economic and political rights of immigrants and of those seeking asylum in the United States.

Publications: Voter Engagement Evaluation Project Report provides information about the effectiveness of voter engagement projects; *New American Vote! An Action Brief for Funding* is issued with Grantmakers Concerned with Immigrants and Refugees.

Global Exchange (GE)
VOTEJUSTICE.org
www.globalexchange.org

Global Exchange, a San Francisco–based human rights organization founded in 1988, created the Fair Election International project, a group that observes elections in the United States and abroad. The organization advocates electoral reforms, including streamlining voter registration, ensuring equal access for minor political party candidates to the ballot and to public debates, reforming voting systems and balloting, and abolishing the electoral college.

Publications: GE issues fact sheets on various reform initiatives.

Harvard Institute of Politics (HIP)
www.iop.harvard.edu

In 2003 the HIP launched the National Campaign for Political and Civic Engagement with a focus on engaging young people in politics. Through H-Vote (Harvard Voter Outreach and Turnout Effort), the Institute provides information about voter registration, absentee voting, and becoming politically active beyond voting. The Institute also offers opportunities for practical political experience through paid internships.

Publications: IOP Newsletter publicizes surveys and other Institute-related activities.

Honest Ballot Association (HBA)
www.honestballot.com

The HBA, founded in 1909, focuses on ensuring that elections are free from dishonest practices. Its goals include the prevention of fraudulent voter registration, repetitive voting, and voter intimidation and coercion. The organization trains individuals to serve as poll watchers, who assume responsibility for monitoring election procedures to assure honesty and efficiency. The HBA conducts elections for labor unions, credit unions, tenant groups, housing cooperatives, and school boards.

Publications: The HBA distributes pamphlets and provides basic facts about election laws.

Immigrant Voting Project (IVP)
City University of New York
www.immigrantvoting.org

The IVP supports resident voting, that is, allowing immigrants to vote in local elections as a means of promoting civic participation and responsibility. The organization analyzes past and current resident voting initiatives and disseminates research through its Web site.

Publications: Democracy for All: Restoring Immigrant Voting Rights in the United States, by Ron Hayduk (New York: Routledge, 2006); *Why America Keeps Getting Immigration Wrong When Our Prosperity Depends on Getting It Right* (New York: Public Affairs Books), by Michele Wucker.

Institute for the Study of Civic Values (ISCV)
www.iscv.org

Established in 1973, the ISCV seeks to strengthen democracy by mobilizing urban voters, community organizations, and youth into a "politics of community." The Institute takes part in get-out-the-vote campaigns.

Institute on Money in State Politics (IMSP)
www.followthemoney.org

Launched as a national organization in 1999, the Institute on Money in State Politics places searchable databases online and provides analyses of the information to illustrate the effects of campaign contributions on public policy debates. The Institute conducts campaign finance research in all 50 states.

Publications: The Institute issues a series of reports on the role of money in politics.

International Association of Clerks, Recorders, Election Officials, and Treasurers (IACREOT)
www.iacreot.com

This organization, founded in 1971, facilitates information and idea sharing among county, municipal, and state government officials about the conduct of elections. The IACREOT represents its membership in Washington, D.C., and in the state capitals. It conducts annual meetings to discuss new administrative procedures and to organize workshops and conferences in various areas of administration, including elections.

Publications: IACREOT News, a quarterly newsletter, promotes the exchange of information among members, presents reports on organizational committee activities, and advertises upcoming educational forums.

International Foundation for Electoral Systems (IFES)
www.ifes.org

Established in 1987, the IFES observes elections in countries that request its assistance and strives to improve electoral procedures to help guarantee free and fair elections. The foundation has operated in over 100 countries and currently works in over 20 new and developing democracies. With 150 professionals from 25 countries, the organization offers advice to election officers about regularized electoral procedures, including appropriate statutes, training for poll workers, efficient and honest vote-counting methods, security procedures, and voter education programs. The IFES hosts two organizations, the Center for Transitional and Post-Conflict Governance and the F. Clifton White Applied Research Center for Democracy and Elections.

Publications: Democracy at Large, a quarterly magazine, offers news, analysis, and debate on building democratic societies; *The Resolution of Election Disputes: Legal Principles That Control Election Challenges* (Washington, DC: IFES, 2006), by Barry Weinberg, former deputy chief of the civil rights division of the U.S. Department of Justice, explains the legal principles in resolving election disputes; *IFES Buyer's Guide to Election Suppliers* provides an online directory of companies selling election supplies and equipment.

International Institute for Democracy and Electoral Assistance (IDEA)
www.idea.int

Established in 1995, the IDEA, an intergovernmental organization, includes countries from around the world. It supports sustainable democracies and works with long established and new democracies to build democratic institutions, strengthen electoral processes, develop political parties, and sponsor political equality through the participation of traditionally underrepresented groups.

Publications: A newsletter highlights democratic developments around the world; annual reports delineate the organization's objectives and activities.

Justice at Stake (JS)
www.justiceatstake.org

Justice at Stake consists of over 30 judicial, legal, and citizen organizations that seek to reduce the role of money in state judicial campaigns and maintain judicial independence.

Publications: Eyes on Justice, a periodic newsletter, communicates the latest threats to judicial independence; also available are Web-based videos from forums and media commentaries on the importance of reducing the role of special interests in judicial elections and defending judicial independence.

Kids Voting USA (KVUSA)
www.kidsvotingusa.org

KVUSA seeks to strengthen democracy in the United States by engaging young people in politics. The organization cooperates with a national network of community-based affiliates to offer civic learning opportunities to students from kindergarten through high school. After involvement in classroom learning activities, students may take part in a voting experience using ballots that mirror the adults versions and that offer the same candidates and issues. The organization conducts research on deliberative democracy and the foundations of civic involvement

Publications: A quarterly newsletter provides members with the latest organizational developments.

Lawyers' Committee for Civil Rights under Law
www.lawyerscomm.org

Formed in 1963 at the request of President John F. Kennedy, the Lawyer's Committee provides legal services to victims of racial discrimination in educational, business, and employment settings. One of the committee's major undertakings is the Voting Rights Project. Working with other civil rights organizations, the group created the National Commission on the Voting Rights Act to support the 1965 act's reauthorization and to prepare a report detailing discrimination in voting since 1982. The committee also fosters the National Campaign for Fair Elections, which calls for the removal of voter registration barriers.

Leadership Conference on Civil Rights (LCCR)
www.civilrights.org

Founded in 1950, the LCCR is a coalition of more than 190 national organizations representing people of color, women, children, labor unions, senior citizens, gays and lesbians, and major religious organizations. It has a broad array of policy interests, including ensuring equal opportunity, promoting civic engagement and awareness, reforming the criminal justice system, maintaining judicial independence, and building stronger communities. The organization lobbies for election reforms and for better access to voting rights.

Publications: Civil Rights Monitor, a quarterly publication, examines civil rights legislation on the federal government's agenda. The LCCR also issues a series of reports on race relations and diversity.

League of Women Voters (LWV)

www.lwv.org

Founded in 1920 as an outgrowth of the National American Woman Suffrage Association, the League of Women Voters promotes responsible citizen participation in government through sponsored political candidate debates and educational forums on policy issues. Formerly the National League of Women Voters, the League's regional, state, and local groups distribute informational voter guides on political candidates and their issue positions. The organization supports such reforms as free airtime for political candidates, elected representation in Congress for the District of Columbia, and improved voting systems and election administration.

Publications: LeaguE-Voice, a monthly electronic newsletter, provides news reports on issues of concern to the League's membership.

National Association for the Advancement of Colored People (NAACP)

www.naacp.org

Created in 1909, the NAACP is an interracial American organization working toward the elimination of racial discrimination in housing, education, transportation, and voting. The group's activities have helped to secure the passage of civil rights laws, including the Civil Rights Act of 1964 and the Voting Rights Act of 1965 and the Civil Rights Act of 1964, and it has frequently argued cases before the U.S. Supreme Court dealing with discrimination in all its forms. The NAACP developed a voter empowerment project to raise African American awareness of and participation in the electoral process.

Publications: The Crisis, a bimonthly magazine recounts the organization's continuing struggle for civil rights, including the right to vote.

National Association of Counties (NACo)

www.naco.org

Founded in 1935, NACo has members from 2,000 of the 3,066 counties in the United States representing 80 percent of the nation's population. The organization provides legislative, research, technical, and public affairs assistance to counties, which are the primary level of election administration, to improve their overall operations. The organization meets each summer, holds a legislative conference each winter, and sponsors numerous seminars and workshops for county officials.

Publications: County News, a biweekly newspaper with a circulation of 29,000, keeps members informed about national policy changes and trends in county administration; *American County Platform,* a compilation of policies from the NACo's 11 policy steering committees, provides the basis for the organization's lobbying activities.

National Association of County Recorders, Election Officials, and Clerks (NACRC)
www.nacrc.org

This organization, representing elected and appointed county officials, advocates more effective operation of county government offices, including voter registration and election administration. As an affiliate of the National Association of Counties, the NACRC conducts workshops on a number of topics, including elections, and provides information on new computer and voting technologies. Founded in 1949, the organization meets three times a year at regional and national locales to share information about forthcoming legislation and rule changes. It provides information on archiving and storing public records and the issues associated with recording electronic data.

Publications: Bulletin is a quarterly newsletter available to members that reports on legislative actions and organizational activities.

National Association of Secretaries of State (NASS)
www.nass.org

The NASS, an affiliate of the Council of State Governments, was established in 1904 to facilitate communication among the secretaries of state of the several states. Because secretaries of state are often the chief election officer of a state, the organization is involved in election reform, get-out-the-vote programs, cooperative reporting of election results, and observation of election procedures in other countries. The NASS holds two conferences each year.

Publications: NASS e-Gov Primer provides an overview of Web development by several states; *Pillars of Public Service* examines the history of the NASS and provides descriptions of secretary of state positions and statistical information on secretaries of state; *NASS New Millennium State Practices Survey* offers data on state voter registration procedures and recruiting poll workers.

National Association of State Election Directors (NASED)
www.nased.org

NASED was established in 1989 out of concern that national networks were releasing presidential election results before polls officially closed. Its purpose has broadened, especially since the passage of the Help America Vote Act. The organization seeks to serve as a clearinghouse for the exchange of best practices and ideas among state election directors. At its Web site, the NASED provides a list of state election officials and voting systems that are NASED-certified.

Publications: News provides an online presentation to electronic voting system studies.

National Coalition on Black Civic Participation (NCBCP)
www.ncbcp.org

This coalition of labor and religious organizations, black caucuses, fraternities and sororities, and political groups was established in 1976. Seeking to engage African Americans in politics, the Coalition sponsors a variety of programs, including encouraging the black youth vote and engaging in civic education and grassroots voter registration activities. The NCBCP hosts Operation Big Vote, a get-out-the-vote campaign, and the Black Women's Roundtable, which was initiated in 1983 to encourage involvement in the political process among African American women

Publications: Building Partnerships for the Future is a report on the organization's activities during the 2004 election cycle.

National Committee for an Effective Congress (NCEC)
www.ncec.org

Formed in 1948 by Eleanor Roosevelt and her associates, the NCEC promotes the pooling of resources from small campaign contributors across the nation to elect progressive candidates to the U.S. Senate and House. The organization provides services to candidates, including electoral and demographic precinct targeting, get-out-the-vote plans, media market analyses, candidate scheduling procedures, and polling sample selection.

Publications: Election Insider, a weekly newsletter, informs members about the latest election news and developments.

National Committee for Voting Integrity (NCVI)
www.votingintegrity.org

The NCVI advocates more secure and accurate election systems that preserve the secret ballot. The organization makes recommendations to state and local election officials on secure procedures for electronic voting and provides appraisals of voting technology.

Publications: Electronic Voting Research Tool is an online guide for researchers, activists, and others interested in recent developments in electronic voting.

National Conference of State Legislatures (NCSL)
www.ncsl.org

Founded in 1975, the NCSL serves state legislators and their staff, offering research, consulting, and technical assistance. The organization also represents state interests before the federal government. The NCSL works with legislators on legislative questions, including election policy and redistricting, and provides professional staff and research resources through workshops and training sessions.

Publications: State Legislatures, a magazine issued 10 times per year, reports on state policy developments; *Directory of State Legislators,* an online database, offers profiles of individual members and their leadership roles; NCSL also offers an online database on election reform legislation.

National Initiative for Democracy (NI4D)
Democracy Foundation
www.nationalinitiative.us

Developed by the Democracy Foundation, the NI4D supports a proposed national constitutional amendment granting citizens the authority to enact laws using ballot initiatives, as well as a proposed federal statute creating an administrative agency, the Electoral Trust, to facilitate a so-called Legislature of the People, allowing national votes on initiatives. The NI4D raises voter awareness about its national initiative proposals and solicits donations to finance an election to validate support for the organization's proposals.

Publications: National Initiative News is an occasional newsletter.

National Organization on Disability (NOD)
www.nod.org

The NOD was established in 1983 to continue the gains made during the 1981 International Year of Disabled Persons. Fostering full participation rights for the disabled, the organization educates the public and political actors about the needs of disabled citizens. The group sponsors get-out-the-vote campaigns to mobilize disabled voters and seeks to remove barriers, such as inaccessible polling places and inadequate voter registration options, that restrict the voting rights of those with physical disabilities.

Publications: N.O.D. E-Newsletter provides access to disability-related news articles.

National Voting Rights Institute (NVRI)
www.nvri.org

Holding that the principles of fairness, equality, and justice demand a change in the rules governing U.S. politics, the NVRI advocates campaign finance reform, including the public funding of political campaigns and placing limits on campaign expenditures. The NVRI engages in public information campaigns, advises legislators on the drafting of reform legislation, and initiates litigation to obtain adequate enforcement of voting rights legislation by such agencies as the Federal Election Commission.

Publications: NVRI Update informs members of the organization's activities and new public policy developments.

Open Debates
www.opendebates.org

Through sponsorship of the Citizens' Debate Commission as an alternative to the Commission on Presidential Debates, Open Debates seeks to reform the presidential and vice presidential debate process. The organization calls for more inclusive presidential and vice presidential debate forums that include minor political party candidates.

Open Voting Consortium (OVC)
openvotingconsortium.org

Comprised of computer scientists, voting experts, and voting rights activists, the OVC seeks development of reliable, user-friendly voting systems for public elections. Having participated in the verifiable voting movement in California, the group developed a prototype version of software for electronic voting machines that permits the printing and scanning of paper ballots so that voters can verify vote choices.

Publications: E-mail updates of OVC activities are sent to those requesting such information online.

Philadelphia II
votep2.us

Serving as the election arm of the National Initiative for Democracy (NI4D), Philadelphia II promotes a national election in which Americans can vote to validate the NI4D initiatives. The NI4D proposes a federal constitutional amendment giving the people of the United States the power to approve laws using ballot initiatives and a federal statute creating an administrative agency, the Electoral Trust, to facilitate a Legislature of the People allowing national votes on initiatives.

Political Research Foundation
See Citizens' Research Foundation

Project Vote
www.projectvote.org

Since its creation in 1982, Project Vote has encouraged active participation in politics from all sectors of society, including low-income and minority communities. The organization provides training and technical services on key issues related to voter participation. Project Vote has developed model voter registration and education programs. Through its Election Administration Program, the group seeks to improve election processes from the design of voter registration applications to vote counting procedures.

Publications: Policy briefings and reports on improving election administration and maximizing voter registration are issued; model bills are posted on the group's Web page.

Project Vote Smart
www.vote-smart.org

Incorporated in 1988, Project Vote Smart provides biographical and contact information on local, state, and federal elected officials; public statements of the president, governors, and congressional representatives; voting records of Congress members; and the campaign finance records of elected officials. The organization questions thousands of political candidates at the state and national levels on their political knowledge and their willingness to state positions on issues of interest to voters. In addition, Vote Smart provides over 150 interest group ratings of representatives in Congress. The organization encourages voter registration and provides voter registration forms, absentee ballots, and election schedules for each state.

Publications: Voter's Defense Manual is an 80-page report on each state congressional delegation; *Reporter's Resource Source Book* is available to working journalists; *Vote Smart Web Yellow Pages* is an online directory of special interests, advocacy groups, think tanks, and experts on a variety of issues.

Public Campaign Action Fund
www.campaignmoney.org

Established in 1997, Public Campaign, with more than 70,000 online members and state organizations based in over 36 states, supports public financing of political campaigns at the state level. Through its education campaigns, the group informs the public about the effects of big money influence in political campaigns and its effects on public policy.

Publications: Paid For By . . . is a Web log containing news stories relevant to campaign finance reform.

Public Citizen
www.citizen.org

Ralph Nader founded Public Citizen in 1971 to advocate consumer interests and consumer protection. Substantially involved in health, safety, environment, energy, and trade issues, Public Citizen also devotes substantial attention to campaign finance, election, and government ethics reform. The organization tracks the activities of lobby organizations and special interests, nonprofit groups that are active in elections, and the influence of private money in presidential campaigns.

ReclaimDemocracy.org (Restoring Citizen Authority over Corporations)
www.reclaimdemocracy.org

ReclaimDemocracy.org states that it promotes a better vision for representative democracy by revoking corporate "free speech" and reserving this freedom to individuals as they believe the Constitution intended and by overturning the U.S. Supreme Court decision in *Buckley v. Valeo* (1976), thus enabling the establishment of political campaign spending limits. Believing that political democracy is inseparable from economic democracy, this organization advocates establishing a grassroots democracy movement.

Publications: The Liberator and *The Insurgent* serve as newsletters for those interested in the democracy movement; online primers provide guidance for citizens to enhance the democratic process.

Reform Institute
www.reforminstitute.org

Founded in 2001 by Senator John McCain (R.) of Arizona, the Reform Institute consists of bipartisan academics, legal experts, election administrators, and public officials who champion reforms in a variety of public policy areas, including campaigns and elections, homeland security, immigration, and energy. In the area of campaign and election reform, the members advocate the enforcement of the major provisions in the Bipartisan Campaign Finance Reform Act, the reform of section 527 political organizations, the improvement of the voter registration process, the use of open primaries, and the updating of voting hardware and software.

S.A.V.E. Democracy (Secure, Accurate, and Verifiable Elections)
www.wesavedemocracy.org

Concerned with vote fraud and unaccountable private voting machine vendors, this organization advocates the use of paper ballots rather than reliance on electronic voting machines. The group supports supplementing paper ballots with a voting process that can be videotaped at any party's request.

Southwest Voter Registration Education Project (SVREP)
www.svrep.org

Founded in San Antonio, Texas in 1974, the SVREP's chief goal is to increase Latino participation in the electoral system. The group educates Latino communities about voter registration and participation. The SVREP has conducted over 2,200 voter registration campaigns in 14 states and has successfully undertaken the litigation of more than 100 voting rights cases.

Publications: The *Latino Vote Reporter,* published twice a year, reports on the SVREP's get-out-the-vote initiatives and fund-raising efforts.

Students for Clean Elections
www.yale.edu/cleanelections

Based at Yale University, Students for Clean Elections informs college students about the role of money in politics. This organization encourages students to support clean election reforms.

2020 Vision
www.2020vision.org

Active since 2000, 20/20 Vision engages in voter education and registration drives and seeks to increase citizen participation in public policy making. The organization focuses particularly on peace, environment, and democracy issues and urges the adoption of the public financing of elections.

Publications: Viewpoint, a newsletter on public policy issues of interest to members, is distributed three times a year.

U.S. Term Limits (USTL)
www.ustl.org

U.S. Term Limits, formerly Americans to Limit Congressional Terms, was established in 1992. The organization seeks to limit the terms of politicians at the local, state, and federal level and has enjoyed some successes with state legislatures. It offers a database on existing term limits for state legislative and gubernatorial seats.

Publications: No Uncertain Terms, a bimonthly newsletter, reports on the latest developments in the term limits movement.

Vanishing Voter Project
Joan Shorenstein Center on the Press, Politics and Public Policy
John F. Kennedy School of Government
Harvard University
www.vanishingvoter.org

Seeking to raise the awareness of and participation in the electoral process, the Vanishing Voter Project, based at the Joan Shorenstein Center on the Press, Politics, and Public Policy in the John F. Kennedy School of Government, Harvard University, concentrates on young voter mobilization. The Project provides information on issues, candidates, and the electoral process to promote civic engagement. The organization issues regular press releases on the status of voter involvement in elections.

Publications: The results of a two-year study (1999–2001) based on surveys of citizen involvement in an election campaign culminated in Thomas Patterson's *The Vanishing Voter: Public Involvement in an Age of Uncertainty* (New York: Knopf, 2002).

Verified Voting Foundation (VVF)
www.verifiedvoting.org

The VVF publicizes the need for voter-verified paper ballots when electronic voting machines are in use. The organization supports a legislative agenda to ensure confidence and accountability in voting procedures and engages in litigation to ensure accessibility to voting machines for the disabled and to challenge uncertified voting systems. In 2004 the VVF began an election incident reporting system.

Publications: Verified Voting Foundation Newsletter provides information on the organization's projects and presents updates on new developments.

VoteTrustUSA
www.votetrustusa.org

VoteTrustUSA is a national network of state-based organizations that lobbies for verifiable paper ballots when electronic voting machines are used. The group conducts research on electronic voting and evaluates election administration proposals.

Publications: Various articles on electronic voting are available on the organization's Web site.

Votewatch
See Election Science Institute

Voting Section, Civil Rights Division
Department of Justice
www.usdoj.gov/crt/voting

The Voting Section of the U.S. Justice Department's Civil Rights Division is responsible for enforcing federal civil rights voting laws. The Civil Rights Division was established in 1957 to enforce statutes prohibiting discrimination in employment, housing, educational opportunity, and voting. The Voting Section enforces the Voting Rights Act of 1965, including its reauthorization legislation, and the National Voter Registration Act of 1993. The Voting Section staff members initiate lawsuits dealing with violations of these statutes.

White House Project (WHP)
www.thewhitehouseproject.org

The White House Project promotes the advancement of women's leadership in all communities and sectors and supports awareness of women's issues and concerns. The group sponsors programs, such as Vote, Run, Lead, that recruit and train women to run for public office. Through a special program, Elect a President, the WHP tries to bring women's leadership to the highest of levels of politics. The organization also conducts research on media coverage of female candidates and the significance of women in the political process, and it sponsors conferences that bring women together from all fields to discuss their role in the public realm.

Publications: Several reports of the organization's research and analyses of women's involvement in politics are available online.

Young Voter Strategies (YVS)
www.youngvoterstrategies.org

This organization through its Web site provides the tools needed to find and mobilize young voters.

Publications: YVS has published *Young Voter Mobilization Tactics I and II; Top Ten Tips to Mobilize Young Voters,* a handbook.

Youth Leadership Initiative (YLI)
University of Virginia Center for Politics
www.youthleadership.net

The Youth Leadership Initiative develops civic education programs for the public schools designed to encourage student interest and participation in politics. Through the organization's Web site, students may participate in campaign simulations, mock elections, and a mock Congress. The organization offers services to educators free of charge, providing downloadable civics and government lessons.

Publications: Newsroom, an online newsletter, presents information about YLI activities and upcoming events.

8

Resources

Print Resources

Books

The works listed in this section are divided into six groups. The first includes sources that examine the role of money and political action committees in campaigns, fund-raising strategies, and attempts to introduce finance reform. The second presents sources on campaign strategy, corrupt practices, and suggestions for campaign reform, and the third includes more general works that deal with the relationship between the electoral system and the operation of democracy and representation. The fourth contains sources on election administration and the electoral procedures used to select public officials and election administration. The fifth section, on the mass media and politics, presents works that investigate the influence of the media on the electoral process. The final section includes sources that investigate various attempts to expand the right to vote, particularly the struggle for woman suffrage and voting rights for minorities. We include older volumes that represent significant landmarks in campaign and election research or that offer significant historical treatments of the topic.

Campaign Finance

Ackerman, Bruce, and Ian Ayres. *Voting with Dollars: A New Paradigm for Campaign Finance.* New Haven, CT: Yale University Press, 2002

Writing before the passage of the Bipartisan Campaign Reform Act, Ackerman and Ayres criticize the then current trend in campaign reform and offer an alternative they claim would avoid past policy mistakes.

Biersack, Bob, ed. *PAC Activity Increases for 2004 Elections: A Report by the Federal Election Commission.* **Collingdale, PA: Diane Pub. Co., 2006**

This report notes the increased fund-raising and spending activities of political action committees in the 2004 election cycle compared to the 2002 cycle. PAC fund-raising increased 28 percent from the 2002 to the 2004 election cycle. Incumbents continued to be the major recipients of PAC contributions.

Biersack, Bob, ed. *The 2004 Presidential Campaign Financial Activity Summarized: A Report by the Federal Election Commission.* **Collingdale, PA: Diane Pub. Co., 2006**

This report provides information about presidential candidate and political party financial activity during the 2004 election cycle. For instance, the report notes that the two major political parties raised nearly $1.5 billion and spent more than $1.4 billion.

Corrado, Anthony, Thomas E. Mann, and Trevor Potter, eds. *Inside the Campaign Finance Battle: Court Testimony on the New Reforms.* **Washington, DC: Brookings Institution Press, 2003**

Contributors present competing arguments about campaign finance law following passage of the Bipartisan Campaign Finance Reform Act and the initiation of legal challenges to the new legislation.

Corrado, Anthony, Thomas E. Mann, Daniel Ortiz, and Trevor Potter, eds. *The New Campaign Finance Sourcebook.* **Washington, DC: Brookings Institution Press, 2005**

This volume presents an analysis of campaign finance law, including the history of campaign finance regulation, the initial implementation of the Bipartisan Campaign Reform Act, public financing of presidential elections, and regulation of Internet campaigning.

Francia, Peter L., Paul S. Herrnson, John C. Green, Lynda W. Powell, and Clyde Wilcox. *The Financiers of Congressional Elec-*

tions: Investors, Ideologues, and Intimates. New York: Columbia University Press, 2003

The authors explore the role of individual donors to congressional campaigns, focusing on the influence on U.S. politics of those who contribute more than $200.

Gross, Donald A., and Robert K. Goidel. *The States of Campaign Finance Reform.* Columbus: Ohio State University Press, 2003

Gross and Goidel identify and analyze the intended and unintended consequences of campaign finance reform, especially in state gubernatorial elections.

Magleby, David B., ed. *The Other Campaign: Soft Money and Issue Advocacy in the 2000 Congressional Campaigns.* Lanham, MD: Rowman & Littlefield, 2002

Published before passage of the Bipartisan Campaign Reform Act, this volume provides information about the role of soft money in the 2000 congressional elections.

Magleby, David B., and J. Quin Monson, eds. *The Last Hurrah? Soft Money and Issue Advocacy in the 2002 Congressional Elections.* Washington, DC: Brookings Institution Press, 2004

Contributors to this volume examine the role of money in the 2002 midterm election, which was the last national election before the Bipartisan Campaign Reform Act took effect.

Makinson, Larry. *Speaking Freely: Washington Insiders Talk about Money in Politics,* 2nd ed. Washington, DC: Center for Responsive Politics, 2003

Makinson presents conversations with 24 current and former members of Congress, lobbyists, political action committee directors, and campaign contributors about the role of money in politics.

Malbin, Michael J., ed. *The Election after Reform: Money, Politics, and the Bipartisan Campaign Reform Act.* Lanham, MD: Rowman & Littlefield, 2006

Malbin investigates the influence of the Bipartisan Campaign Reform Act on the 2004 campaign, focusing on such topics as the presidential and congressional campaigns, television advertisements, section 527 groups, political parties, and interest groups.

Samples, John Curtis. *The Fallacy of Campaign Finance Reform.* **Chicago: University of Chicago Press, 2006**

Questioning the value of such legislation as the Bipartisan Campaign Reform Act, Samples claims that there is little evidence that campaign contributions actually influence the votes of members of Congress, and he argues that contribution limits protect incumbent representatives.

Campaigns, Corruption, and Reform

Boller Jr., Paul F. *Presidential Campaigns: From George Washington to George W. Bush,* **rev. ed. New York: Oxford University Press, 2004**

Boller offers entertaining accounts of presidential campaigns from 1789 to 2000, demonstrating how the presidential selection process has evolved through time.

Brady, Henry E., and Richard Johnston, eds. *Capturing Campaign Effects.* **Ann Arbor: University of Michigan Press, 2006**

The essays in this volume examine various aspects of campaigns in the United States as well as other countries, focusing on news coverage, debates, advertising, and polling.

Campbell, Tracy. *Deliver the Vote: A History of Election Fraud, An American Political Tradition—1742–2004.* **New York: Carroll and Graf Publishers, 2006**

Campbell describes the corrupt nature of U.S. elections from the colonial era to the 2004 election, presenting examples of electoral outcomes that overruled the popular will. The author provides recommendations to voters about assuring that elections are fair and honest.

Gumbel, Andrew. *Steal This Vote: Dirty Elections and the Rotten History of Democracy in America.* **Murfreesboro, TN: Avalon Press, 2005**

Gumbel presents the history of dishonest election practices in the United States from the 18th century to the present and argues that violations of the principle of free and fair elections have been frequent occurrences.

Hayduk, Ronald, and Kevin Mattson, eds. *Democracy's Moment: Reforming the American Political System for the 21st Century.* **Lanham, MD: Rowman & Littlefield, 2002**

The 15 essays in this volume propose reforms intended to increase government responsiveness, including campaign finance reform, deliberative democracy, community organizing, proportional representation, instant runoff voting, and greater access for minor political party candidates to campaign debates.

Herrnson, Paul, ed. *Guide to Political Campaigns in America.* **Washington, DC: CQ Press, 2005**

This volume examines the evolution of political campaigns, focusing on such topics as the right to vote, access to the ballot, campaign fund-raising, campaign strategy—including polling and opposition research—legal regulation of campaigns, and efforts to institute additional campaign and election reform measures.

Lathrop, Douglas A. *The Campaign Continues: How Political Consultants and Campaign Tactics Affect Public Policy.* **Westport, CT: Praeger, 2003**

Lathrop investigates the role that political consultants play in establishing campaign tactics and examines their ultimate influence on the formation of public policy.

Magleby, David B., J. Quin Monson, and Kelly D. Patterson, eds. *Dancing without Partners: How Candidates, Parties, and Interest Groups Interact in the Presidential Campaign.* **Lanham, MD: Rowman & Littlefield, 2006**

The essays in this volume concentrate on five competitive states in the 2004 presidential campaign, examining the interaction of candidates, political parties, and interest groups.

Mark, David. *Going Dirty: The Art of Negative Campaigning.* **Lanham, MD: Rowman & Littlefield, 2006**

Using case studies of particular races, Mark presents a history of negative campaigning in the United States and current trends in the use of the strategy.

Nelson, Candice J., David A. Dulio, and Stephen K. Medvic, eds. *Shades of Gray: Perspectives on Campaign Ethics.* Washington, DC: Brookings Institution Press, 2002

Contributors deal with the ethical questions that face political candidates, campaign consultants, political parties, interest groups, the mass media, and voters.

Roberts, Robert North, and Scott John Hammond. *Encyclopedia of Presidential Campaigns, Slogans, Issues, and Platforms.* Westport, CT: Praeger, 2004

Roberts and Hammond investigate the various methods—including speeches, campaign buttons, slogans, and television advertisements—that presidential candidates have used since the beginning of the republic to convey their platform message to the voting public.

Semiatim, Richard. *Campaigns in the 21st Century.* New York: McGraw-Hill, 2004

Semiatim examines the actual operation of national campaigns, noting that candidates must continuously adjust strategy to political, social, and cultural fluctuations to succeed.

Shade, William G., Ballard C. Campbell, and Craig R. Coenen, eds. *American Presidential Campaigns and Elections.* Armonk, NY: M. E. Sharpe, 2003

This three-volume reference work presents information on every U.S. campaign and election from 1788 to the controversial election of 2000. The work includes campaign documents and state popular and electoral votes for each election.

Shaw, Catherine. *The Campaign Manager: Running and Winning Local Elections,* 3rd ed. Boulder, CO: Perseus, 2004

Shaw explores the use of new campaign technology in each area of campaign management. The author discusses direct mail techniques, the use of television advertising, and the most effective use of campaign funds.

Shea, Daniel M., and Michael John Burton. *Campaign Craft: The Strategies, Tactics, and Art of Political Campaign Management.* Westport, CT: Greenwood Press, 2006

Shea and Burton examine various facets of political campaigns, including use of the mass media, conducting demographic research, deciding on a campaign strategy, and developing techniques for contacting prospective voters.

Sidlow, Edward I. *Challenging the Incumbent: An Underdog's Undertaking.* **Washington, DC: CQ Press, 2004**

Sidlow presents an account of the 2000 Illinois congressional race between Lance Pressl and eighth district incumbent Phil Crane, focusing on the significant difficulties a challenger faces.

Swint, Kerwin C. *Mudslingers: The Top 25 Negative Political Campaigns of All Time, Countdown from No. 25 to No. 1.* **Westport, CT: Greenwood Press, 2005**

Swint notes that, even though many criticize the practice, negative campaigning often has assumed a major role in election campaigns. He examines the history of negative campaigning, focusing primarily but not exclusively on two eras—1863 to 1892 and 1988 to the present—in which such tactics tended to prevail.

Thurber, James A., and Candice J. Nelson. *Campaigns and Elections American Style,* **2nd ed. Boulder, CO: Westview Press, 2004**

Thurber and Nelson discuss the current nature of U.S. campaigns and elections, exploring campaign strategy and the role of fund-raising and the mass media in the 2000 and 2002 election cycles.

Elections and the Political Process

Abramowitz, Alan. *Voice of the People: Elections and Voting in the United States.* **New York: McGraw-Hill, 2004**

Abramowitz introduces readers to the electoral process, discussing the theoretical approaches used to investigate elections.

Abramson, Paul R., John H. Aldrich, and David W. Rohde. *Change and Continuity in the 2004 and 2006 Elections.* **Washington, DC: CQ Press, 2007**

The authors analyze election data from the 2004 presidential election and the 2006 midterm election. They examine the influences on election outcomes, focusing on the factors that affect voter choices.

Bensel, Richard Franklin. *The American Ballot Box in the Mid-Nineteenth Century.* **New York: Cambridge University Press, 2004**

Bensel portrays the voting experience during the Civil War era, emphasizing the symbolic meaning of the vote for individuals who otherwise might not have had great interest in the political process.

Birch, Anthony H. *The Concepts and Theories of Modern Democracy,* **3rd ed. New York: Routledge, 2007**

Birch's helpful discussion of democracy provides a theoretical context in which to evaluate proposed election reforms and introduces comparisons among democratic nations. In a discussion of political participation, Birch examines suggestions that the United States adopt policies such as compulsory voting and create political parties with mass memberships.

Buchanan, Bruce. *The Policy Partnership: Presidential Elections and American Democracy.* **New York: Taylor & Francis, 2004**

Buchanan explores trends during the last 50 years in the significance of presidential elections to subsequent presidential policy initiatives. The author claims that the public seldom responds critically to the failure of presidents to address voter concerns.

Buell, Emmett H., and William G. Mayer, eds. *Enduring Controversies in Presidential Nominating Politics.* **Pittsburgh, PA: University of Pittsburgh Press, 2004**

These essays explore the history and evolution of the presidential nominating process in the United States, from the early years of caucuses to the present system of primaries and nominating conventions.

Ceaser, James, and Andrew Busch. *The Perfect Tie: The True Story of the 2000 Presidential Election.* **Lanham, MD: Rowman & Littlefield, 2001**

Ceaser and Busch analyze significant elements in the 2000 presidential election, including the electoral college, the campaign strategies of the George W. Bush and Albert Gore camps, the role of independent candidates, and the party platforms.

Congressional Quarterly. *Guide to U.S. Elections,* **5th ed., 2 vols. Washington, DC: CQ Press, 2005**

This volume offers an overview of U.S. elections, including historical depictions of presidential, congressional, and gubernatorial elections; the influence of computerized voting and Internet fund-raising; redistricting controversies such as the mid-decade Texas case; court decisions; trends in voter turnout; and continuing efforts to institute reforms.

Cook, Rhodes. *United States Presidential Primary Elections 2000–2004.* **Washington, DC: CQ Press, 2006**

This volume presents Democratic and Republican presidential primary election returns by county for the 2000 and 2004 election cycles. Included are state maps indicating county boundaries and major cities.

Craig, Stephen, ed. *The Electoral Challenge: Theory Meets Practice.* **Washington, DC: CQ Press, 2006**

Contributors attempt to bridge the gap between academic studies of elections and the understandings of political consultants in dealing with the factors that determine the outcome of elections.

Dinkin, Robert J. *Election Day: A Documentary History.* **Westport, CT: Greenwood Press, 2002**

Dinkin explores the history of election day, providing accounts from candidates, election officials, voters, reporters, and historians.

Dionne, E. J., and William Kristol, eds. *Bush v. Gore: The Court Cases and the Commentary.* **Washington, DC: Brookings Institution Press, 2001**

This volume presents the legal arguments from the Florida Supreme Court and the U.S. Supreme Court regarding the conflict over the Florida popular vote results in the 2000 presidential election.

Doron, Gideon, and Michael Harris. *Term Limits.* **Lanham, MD: Rowman & Littlefield, 2001**

Doron and Harris investigate the origins and consequences of the term limits movement, analyze the theoretical understanding of the concept, and explore the implementation of term limits at the state level.

Dover, E. D. *The Disputed Presidential Election of 2000: A History and Reference Guide.* **Westport, CT: Greenwood Press, 2003**

Dover presents an overview of the 2000 presidential campaign and election, focusing on specific issues crucial to the election outcome.

Dworkin, Ronald M., ed. *A Badly Flawed Election: Debating Bush v. Gore, the Supreme Court, and American Democracy.* **New York: New Press, 2002**

In this examination of the U.S. Supreme Court decision ending the vote count in the 2000 presidential election, some contributors defend the *Bush v. Gore* decision and others argue that basic reforms such as abolishing the electoral college should be introduced.

Evans, Jocelyn A. J. *Voters and Voting.* **Thousand Oaks, CA: Sage, 2004**

In this guide to theories of elections and voting behavior, Evans summarizes various approaches, including social and psychological, rational choice, spatial, and economic theories as well as more recent models.

Frantzich, Stephen E. *Citizen Democracy: Political Activists in a Cynical Age.* **Lanham, MD: Rowman & Littlefield, 2004**

Frantzich reports on 19 cases of citizen involvement in various public actions, such as changing public opinion, establishing new interest groups, engaging in political campaigns, and supporting ballot measures.

Gaddie, Ronald Keith. *Born to Run: Origins of the Political Career.* **Lanham, MD: Rowman & Littlefield, 2003**

To understand what motivates individuals to enter politics, Gaddie examines the experiences of nine young politicians in Wisconsin, Oklahoma, Georgia, Nebraska, and Maine who became political candidates.

Ginsberg, Benjamin, and Martin Shefter. *Politics by Other Means: Politicians, Prosecutors and the Press in the Post-Electoral Era,* **3rd ed. New York: W. W. Norton, 2003**

According to Ginsberg and Shefter, the United States is entering a period of postelectoral politics in which the mass media, congressional investigations, and judicial decision making are displacing elections as the principal instrument of political competition.

Green, Donald P., and Alan S. Gerber. *Get Out the Vote! How to Increase Voter Turnout.* **Washington, DC: Brookings Institution Press, 2004**

Basing the recommendations on the empirical examination of such tactics as door-to-door canvassing, phone contacts, and direct mail campaigns, Green and Gerber offer a practical guide for voter mobilization campaigns.

Grofman, Bernard N., and Arend Lijphart, eds. *Electoral Laws and Their Political Consequences.* **New York: Algora Publishing, 2003**

Contributors focus on the relationship between racial identity and the redrawing of legislative districts. Authors discuss the specific features of race-conscious redistricting.

Harrup, Martin, and William L. Miller, eds. *Elections and Voters: A Comparative Introduction.* **Chicago: Ivan R. Dee, 2005**

The contributors to this volume offer comparative analyses of the purpose of elections in different countries, contrasting competitive with noncompetitive systems.

Harvard Institute of Politics. *Campaign for President: The Managers Look at 2004.* **Lanham, MD: Rowman & Littlefield, 2005**

The contributors to this volume deal with various topics relevant to the 2004 election, including Internet fund-raising, the strategies of campaign managers, the presidential debates, negative campaigning, and the influence of section 527 groups.

Herrnson, Paul. *Congressional Elections: Campaigning at Home and in Washington,* 4th ed. **Washington, DC: CQ Press, 2004**

Employing survey research results and interviews with more than 400 congressional candidates and political workers, Herrnson analyzes the campaign strategies of candidates, political parties, and political action committees.

Hill, David Lee. *American Voter Turnout: An Institutional Approach.* **Boulder, CO: Westview Press, 2006**

In explaining low voter turnout in the United States, Hill focuses on the institutional structure that establishes the rules of participation, procedures for representation, and the processes of governance, all of which the author claims discourage higher rates of participation.

Hudson, William E. *American Democracy in Peril: Eight Challenges to America's Future,* 5th ed. **Washington, DC: CQ Press, 2006**

Hudson discusses eight challenges to contemporary American democracy, one of which is the trivial nature of elections. Related challenges include the privileged position of business, the separation of powers system, continuing racial inequality, and the threat to civil liberties posed by the national security state.

Jamieson, Kathleen Hall, ed. 2005. *Electing the President 2004: The Insiders' View.* **Philadelphia, PA: University of Pennsylvania Press.**

Political consultants on the 2004 George W. Bush and John Kerry campaigns explain the strategies used in such areas as campaign advertising and the candidate debates and explore the significance of such influences as 527 groups.

Klein, Joe. *Politics Lost: How American Democracy Was Trivialized by People Who Think You're Stupid.* **New York: Doubleday, 2006**

Klein, reporter for *Time* magazine, reveals the deprecating attitudes that political professionals—consultants and pollsters—have toward the voting public. The author argues that these professionals tend to trivialize the political process.

Leduc, Lawrence. *The Politics of Direct Democracy: Referendums in Global Perspective.* **Orchard Park, NY: Broadview, 2003**

Leduc provides a survey of direct democracy procedures. Among the cases presented are the California referendum model, the two Quebec sovereignty referendums, the 1999 Australian referendum on the British monarchy, the 2000 Danish referendum on the Euro currency, and the Irish referenda on divorce and abortion.

Mattson, Kevin. *Engaging Youth: Combating the Apathy of Young Americans toward Politics.* **Washington, DC: Brookings Institution Press, 2003**

Unimpressed with current strategies to engage youth in politics and voting, Mattson recommends more thorough education programs, public service internships, and the use of the Internet to attract younger participants to the political process.

McGillivray, Alice V., Richard Scammon, and Rhodes Cook. *America at the Polls 1960–2004: John F. Kennedy to George W. Bush—A Handbook of American Presidential Election Statistics.* **Washington, DC: CQ Press, 2005**

This volume provides state-by-state data on the presidential election popular vote and the electoral college vote in each election for the two major political parties as well as for third-party candidates.

Miller, Mark Crispin. *Fooled Again: On the 2004 Election.* **New York: Basic Books, 2005**

Crispin presents a partisan argument that the outcome of the 2004 presidential election was determined not by moral values but by the illegal manipulation of the voting process. Although Ohio is the major focus for charges of election irregularities, the author claims that election officials in other states, including Arizona, Florida, Oregon, Pennsylvania, and New Mexico, engaged in illegal practices that tended to favor George W. Bush's election.

Nelson, Michael, ed. *The Elections of 2004.* **Washington, DC: CQ Press, 2005**

The nine essays in this volume analyze the 2004 campaigns and elections, focusing on such topics as campaign finance, the use of the Internet for fund-raising and campaigning, and the increased polarization of the U.S. electorate.

Nicholson, Stephen P. *Voting the Agenda: Candidates, Elections, and Ballot Propositions.* **Princeton, NJ: Princeton University Press, 2005**

Nicholson explores the influence that such statewide ballot initiatives and referenda issues as abortion, taxation, environmental regulation, illegal immigration, and affirmative action have on voters' preferences for political candidates.

Parenti, Michael. *Democracy for the Few.* **Boston: Wadsworth, 2007**

Parenti argues that major economic interests, including corporations, have violated democratic institutions in the United States, including the electoral process. The author investigates such topics as alleged conspiracies, vote fraud, government secrecy, and propaganda.

Pleasants, Julian M. *Hanging Chads: The Inside Story of the 2000 Presidential Recount in Florida.* **New York: Palgrave Macmillan, 2004**

Focusing on the crucial presidential election contest between Albert Gore and George W. Bush in Florida, Pleasants presents interviews with 11 major public figures involved in the ballot recount following the election.

Rose, Richard, and Neil Munro. *Elections and Parties in New European Democracies.* **Washington, DC: CQ Press, 2003**

Rose and Munro present a comparative analysis of the electoral systems of European democracies formed since the fall of communism in 1989. The authors explain the electoral systems of Bulgaria, the Czech Republic, Estonia, Hungary, Latvia, Lithuania, Poland, Romania, Russia, Slovakia, and Slovenia.

Sabato, Larry J., ed. *Get in the Booth: A Citizen's Guide to the 2006 Midterm Elections.* **Upper Saddle River, NJ: Pearson, 2006**

Sabato, along with other journalists and scholars, analyze the major issues in the 2006 congressional elections, which ultimately resulted in the Democratic Party retaking control of both the U.S.

House of Representatives and Senate.

Scammon, Richard M., Rhodes Cook, and Alice V. McGillivary. *American Votes 26: Election Returns by State,* **26th ed. Washington, DC: CQ Press, 2005**

This volume contains vote results for the 2004 election cycle for each state by county and by district for U.S. House and Senate races and for gubernatorial elections.

Schier, Steven E. *You Call This an Election? America's Peculiar Democracy.* **Washington, DC: Georgetown University Press, 2004**

Starting from the difficulties experienced in the 2000 presidential election, Schier explores four aspects of a well-run democratic system: the promotion of stability, the accountability of elected officials, improvement in the voter turnout rate, and the effective surveillance of government policy.

Wayne, Stephen J. *Is This Any Way to Run a Democratic Election?* **3rd ed. Washington, DC: CQ Press, 2007**

Addressing the claim that U.S. elections are dominated by special interests and large financial contributions, Wayne discusses such topics as low voter turnout, alleged voting fraud, campaign finance legislation, the front-loading of the presidential nomination process, the use of the Internet in campaigns, and the role of the mass media in campaigns and elections.

Electoral Rules, Mechanics, and Administration
Ackerman, Bruce, and James Fishkin. *Deliberation Day.* **New Haven, CT: Yale University Press, 2005**

Based on past experiments with deliberative polling, Ackerman and Fishkin propose a national holiday, to be known as Deliberation Day, which would be held each presidential election year. On that day, people around the country would meet to take part in debates about issues in the presidential campaign so that they could make a better informed vote choice.

Alvarez, R. Michael, and Thad E. Hall. *Point, Click, and Vote: The Future of Internet Voting.* Washington, DC: Brookings Institution Press, 2004

Alvarez and Hall examine strategies for instituting pilot Internet voting programs around the nation, thus allowing voters in selected regions to cast ballots through their preferred Internet connection.

Balinski, Michel L., and H. Peyton Young. *Fair Representation: Meeting the Ideal of One Man, One Vote.* Washington, DC: Brookings Institution Press, 2001

While the authors admit that the reapportionment process demands decisions that are ultimately political, they indicate that sophisticated mathematical principles should be employed. Balinski and Young examine the history of apportionment methods and offer a theory of fair representation.

Barber, Kathleen L. *Right to Representation: Proportional Election Systems for the Twenty-First Century.* Columbus: Ohio State University Press, 2000

Barber discusses the historical development of proportional representation systems and their current applicability. The author explains the use of proportional representation voting systems in five Ohio cities during the 20th century.

Bositis, David A. *Voting Rights and Minority Representation: Redistricting, 1992–2002.* Lanham, MD: University Press of America, 2006

The six papers included in this volume were originally presented at a 2002 conference organized by the Joint Center for Political and Economic Studies. The contributions deal with the redistricting process following the 2000 census.

Bowler, Shaun, and Bruce E. Cain, eds. *Clicker Politics: Essays on the California Recall.* Upper Saddle River, NJ: Prentice Hall, 2006

Contributors to this volume discuss the causes and consequences of the 2003 California recall election in which voters removed Gov. Gray Davis from office and installed Arnold Schwarzenegger as the state's new governor.

Cain, Bruce E., and Elisabeth R. Gerber, eds. *Voting at the Political Fault Line: California's Experiment with the Blanket Primary.* **Berkeley: University of California Press, 2002**

Articles include a discussion of the legal challenge to the California blanket primary measure leading to the U.S. Supreme Court decision in *California Democratic Party v. Jones* (2000), which held that the blanket primary violated a political party's freedom of association as protected in the First Amendment.

Colomer, Josep M., ed. *Handbook of Electoral System Choice.* **New York: Palgrave Macmillan, 2004**

This volume focuses on various electoral reform issues related to the success of different electoral systems, democratization, and the operation of established democracies.

Congressional Quarterly. *National Party Conventions 1831–2004.* **Washington, DC: CQ Press, 2005**

This volume presents the history and evolution of national political party nominating conventions from the first convention in 1831 to 2004. Topics include relevant portions of party platforms, descriptions of convention operations, convention decisions on disputes over the admission of delegates, and the development of presidential primaries.

Crigler, Ann N., Marion R. Just, and Edward J. McCaffery, eds. *Rethinking the Vote: The Politics and Prospects of American Election Reform.* **New York: Oxford University Press, 2003**

In the context of the problems confronted in the 2000 presidential election, including ballot design, voting procedures, overseas and military absentee ballots, judicial oversight of the electoral process, and the operation of the electoral college, contributors explore the legal, political, and institutional difficulties faced in conducting elections.

Dudley, Robert L., and Alan R. Gitelson. *American Elections: The Rules Matter.* **Upper Saddle River, NJ: Pearson, 2001**

Dudley and Gitelson detail the rules that govern the conduct of elections in the United States and influence voting behavior. The authors emphasize the significance of federalism in understanding the U.S. electoral system.

Edwards III, George C. *Why the Electoral College Is Bad for America*. New Haven, CT: Yale University Press, 2004

Edwards analyzes and rejects arguments supporting the electoral college and offers reasons for establishing the direct popular vote election of the president.

Fortier, John C., ed. *After the People Vote: A Guide to the Electoral College*, 3rd ed. Washington, DC: American Enterprise Institute, 2004

This volume provides detailed information about the process of electing the president, including a brief history of contested presidential elections, essays arguing in favor of and against the electoral college, and an explanation of the period between the November election and the official casting of electoral ballots in December.

Fortier, John C. *Absentee and Early Voting: Trends, Promises, and Perils*. Washington, DC: American Enterprise Institute, 2006

Fortier examines the increased use of absentee and early voting. The author details the different procedures that states have instituted, explains their effects on the electoral process, and suggests further changes that could be instituted.

Grant, George. *The Importance of the Electoral College*. San Antonio, TX: Vision Forum, 2004

Grant argues for the virtues of the electoral college in response to those who advocate its elimination. The author considers the presidential election system to have resulted from the genius of the constitutional framers.

Gregg II, Gary L., ed. *Securing Democracy: Why We Have an Electoral College*. Wilmington, DE: ISI Books, 2001

Responding to those who call for the abolition of the electoral college, the contributors to this volume argue that the present procedure for electing the president, considered a crucial aspect of the U.S. constitutional system, contributes to political stability and actually enhances the operation of democracy.

Karunaratne, Garvin. *The Administrative Bungling That Hijacked the 2000 U.S. Presidential Election*. Lanham, MD: University Press of America, 2004

Karunaratne explores electoral management in Florida during the 2000 election, contending that administrative bungling allowed George W. Bush to win Florida's electoral votes and ultimately the presidency.

Kurtz, Karl T., Richard G. Niemi, and Bruce E. Cain, eds. *Institutional Change in American Politics: The Case of Term Limits.* **Ann Arbor: University of Michigan Press, 2007**

Contributors discuss the introduction of term limits and their influence on the governmental process at the state level.

Maisel, Sandy Louis, Darrell M. West, and Brett M. Clifton. *Evaluating Campaign Quality: Can the Electoral Process Be Improved?* **New York: Cambridge University Press, 2007**

Given widespread criticism of the U.S. electoral process, including negative and superficial campaigning, the authors have evaluated attempts, including voluntary codes of conduct and more stringent ethics regulations for consultants, to raise the level of campaign discourse in U.S. House and Senate races.

Mayer, William G., and Andrew E. Busch. *The Front-Loading Problem in Presidential Nominations.* **Washington, DC: Brookings Institution Press, 2003**

The authors discuss the so-called frontloading problem in the presidential nomination process: States are moving their primary dates earlier in the primary season.

Moen, Matthew C. *Changing Members: The Maine Legislature in the Era of Term Limits.* **Lanham, MD: Rowman & Littlefield, 2004**

Moen uses surveys of Maine's state legislators, in-depth interviews with legislative members and other political activists, and direct observation of legislative proceedings to evaluate the effects of legislative terms limits, which were instituted in 1996.

National Commission on Federal Election Reform. *To Assure Pride and Confidence in the Electoral Process.* **Washington, DC: Brookings Institution Press, 2002**

The report of the National Commission on Federal Election Reform, chaired by Jimmy Carter, Gerald R. Ford, Lloyd N. Cutler, and Robert H. Michel, provides an analysis of the difficulties experienced in the 2000 national election and makes recommendations for improving the electoral process, many of which were incorporated in the Help America Vote Act.

O'Leary, Kevin. *Saving Democracy: A Plan for Real Representation in America.* **Stanford, CA: Stanford University Press, 2006**

Asserting that the U.S. democratic system has been corrupted and fails to represent citizens, O'Leary recommends strategies to return power to the people and thus save democracy. The author urges the merger of the Internet with such traditional democratic principles as the town hall meeting.

Palazzolo, Daniel J., and James W. Ceaser, eds. *Election Reform: Politics and Policy.* **Lanham, MD: Rowman & Littlefield, 2004**

Contributors examine actions taken at the state level following the problems experienced with voting procedures during the 2000 election. The essays present analyses of election law and the process of electoral reform.

Rush, Mark E., and Richard L. Engstrom. *Fair and Effective Representation? Debating Electoral Reform and Minority Rights.* **Lanham, MD: Rowman & Littlefield, 2001**

Rush and Engstrom discuss the possible benefits and disadvantages of electoral reform, particularly the shift from the current single-member district plurality system to some variation of proportional representation.

Saltman, Roy G. *The History and Politics of Voting Technology: In Quest of Integrity and Public Confidence.* **New York: Palgrave Macmillan, 2006**

In the context of the problems encountered in the 2000 Florida presidential vote count, Saltman provides a detailed history of the evolution of voting technology, claiming that the outdated voting systems used in 2000 were a result of the Industrial Revolution and early computer developments.

Sarbaugh-Thompson, Marjorie, Lyke Thompson, Charles D. Elder, John State, and Richard C. Elling. *The Political and Institutional Effects of Term Limits.* **New York: Palgrave Macmillan, 2004**

The authors examine the effects of term limits on electoral competition and campaign contributions. Using in-depth interviews with legislators, they evaluate the effects of term limits on the performance of the Michigan state legislature.

Shugart, Matthew Soberg, and Martin P. Wattenberg, eds. *Mixed-Member Electoral Systems: The Best of Both Worlds?* **New York: Oxford University Press, 2003**

This volume investigates the introduction in various democratic systems of mixed-member proportional representation systems, which allow for the election of legislative members from geographic areas as well as members from political parties based on proportional electoral support.

Schumaker, Paul D, and Burdett A. Loomis, eds. *Choosing a President: The Electoral College and Beyond.* **Washington, DC: CQ Press, 2002**

Each contributor to this volume examines an aspect of the electoral college, including the 2000 presidential election, the history of presidential elections, the role of federalism in electing the president, the college's influence on campaign strategy, and possible reforms of the presidential election system.

Streb, Matthew J., ed. *Law and Election Politics: The Rules of the Game.* **Boulder, CO: Lynne Rienner, 2005**

The contributors to this volume present the basic legal regulations and court decisions regarding elections, including those involving fund-raising, campaign advertising, the redistricting process, issue advocacy, voting rights, and campaign finance.

Media and Elections

Adams, William C. *Election Night News and Voter Turnout: Solving the Projection Puzzle.* **Boulder, CO: Lynne Rienner, 2005**

Adams employs such methods as content analysis, focus groups, surveys, and time-series analysis to determine the effects on voter turnout of projecting the outcome of the presidential election.

Baker, C. Edwin. *Media Concentration and Democracy: Why Ownership Matters.* **New York: Cambridge University Press, 2006**

The author, who opposes the deregulation of the mass media, argues that, to maintain democracy, ownership of the mass media should be dispersed. According to Baker, wider ownership would lead to more socially responsible journalism.

Bimber, Bruce, and Richard Davis. *Campaigning Online: The Internet in U.S. Elections.* **New York: Oxford University Press, 2003**

Basing their analysis on statewide surveys and interviews with campaign workers, Bimber and Davis present a description of the role that campaign Web sites play in U.S. elections, and they offer their view of the future prospects for online campaigning.

Brader, Ted. *Campaigning for Hearts and Minds: How Emotional Appeals in Political Ads Work.* **Chicago: University of Chicago Press, 2006**

Brader surveyed the influences of televised political advertisements in campaigns, concluding that nonverbal changes in an ad such as music and images elicit different responses from viewers and that emotional appeals prevail over more rational persuasion in approximately 75 percent of ads.

Bystrom, Dianne G., Lynda L. Kaid, Mary C. Banwart, and Terry A. Robertson, eds. *The Gendering of Candidate Communication: Videostyle, Webstyle, Newstyle.* **New York: Taylor & Francis, 2004**

This volume presents investigations into media advertisements, campaign Web sites, and newspaper coverage to discover and analyze the methods that successful candidates have used to respond to gender stereotypes.

Davies, John Phillip, and Bruce I. Newman, eds. *Winning Elections with Political Marketing.* **Binghamton, NY: Haworth Press, 2006**

This volume explores the use of political communication and marketing techniques in U.S. and British elections. The topics covered include advertising, image management, the combination of business methods and social science theory, and the effect of political marketing on democracy.

Denton, Robert E., ed. *The 2004 Presidential Campaign: A Communication Perspective.* **Lanham, MD: Rowman & Littlefield, 2005**

The 13 essays in this volume investigate the communication strategies of the 2004 presidential candidates, focusing on such topics as the nominating conventions, section 527 groups, the candidate debates, political advertising, and use of the Internet.

Farnsworth, Stephen J., and S. Robert Lichter. *Television's Coverage of U.S. Presidential Elections, 1988–2004.* **Lanham, MD: Rowman & Littlefield, 2006**

Farnsworth and Lichter discuss television coverage of presidential elections, arguing that the quality of such reporting has declined.

Foot, Kirsten A., and Steven M. Schneider. *Web Campaigning.* **Cambridge, MA: Massachusetts Institute of Technology Press, 2006**

Foot and Schneider examine the development of Web use in campaigns in recent elections. Focusing on candidate Web sites in the 2000, 2002, and 2004 elections, the authors analyze the special characteristics of Internet communication and the strategies that candidate organizations use to inform, involve, and mobilize supporters.

Geer, John G. *In Defense of Negativity: Attack Ads in Presidential Campaigns.* **Chicago: University of Chicago Press, 2006**

Having investigated negative advertising in presidential campaigns from 1960 to 2004, Geer concludes that attack ads are more likely than positive ads to emphasize significant issues rather than simply the candidates' personal characteristics.

Pfau, Michael, J. Brian Houston, and Shane Semmler, eds. *Mediating the Vote: The Changing Media Landscape in U.S. Presidential Elections.* **Lanham, MD: Rowman & Littlefield, 2006**

This volume examines the effects of various types of communication—including newspapers, television new programs, the Internet, and films—on the 2004 presidential election.

Powell, Larry, and Joseph Cowart. *Political Campaign Communication: Inside and Out.* **Boston, MA: Allyn and Bacon, 2002**

Powell and Cowart discuss the principles and practices of political campaigning, including such topics as campaign finance and the ethics of campaigning. The authors present case studies and interviews with campaign consultants.

Schultz, David A., ed. *Lights, Camera, Campaign! Media, Politics, and Political Advertising.* **New York: Peter Lang, 2004**

This volume explores various topics related to the role of the mass media in election campaigns, including the influence of negative advertising, the effects of network news projections on election results, advertising for ballot initiatives, and a comparison of U.S. and Canadian campaign advertising.

West, Darrell M. *Air Wars: Television Advertising in Election Campaigns, 1952–2004,* **4th ed. Washington, DC: CQ Press, 2005**

West examines the use of television advertisements in campaigns from 1952 through 2004. The author explores candidate strategies, advertisements in congressional elections, the content of ad messages, issue advocacy advertising, the use of the Internet to reach voters, and the success of ads in appealing to voters.

Woodward, Gary C. *Center Stage: Media and the Performance of American Politics.* **Lanham, MD: Rowman & Littlefield, 2006**

Woodward explores such media topics as the war on terror, the development of new technology, the economic influences on the political media, foreign news reporting, and media coverage of the presidency, Congress, and the courts.

Voting Rights

Baker, Jean H. *Sisters: The Lives of America's Suffragists.* **New York: Farrar, Straus and Giroux, 2006**

Baker provides a portrait of the private lives and public activities of Lucy Stone, Susan B. Anthony, Elizabeth Cady Stanton,

Frances Willard, and Alice Paul, five women who played crucial roles in the struggle for woman suffrage.

Bowler, Shaun, Todd Donovan, and David Brockington. *Electoral Reform and Minority Representation.* **Columbus: Ohio State University Press, 2003**

The authors argue that cumulative voting systems result in more competitive campaigns, higher voter turnout, and greater minority representation than do majoritarian elections.

Burrell, Barbara C. *Women and Political Participation: A Reference Handbook.* **Santa Barbara, CA: ABC-CLIO, 2004**

Burrell examines protest politics beginning with the early suffrage movement through the passage of the Nineteenth Amendment, which granted to women the right to vote. The author discusses women's participation in public office, providing historical documents from 1848 to 2000.

Carroll, Susan, and Richard L. Fox. *Gender and Elections: Shaping the Future of American Politics.* **New York: Cambridge University Press, 2005**

Carroll and Fox explore the role of gender in U.S. elections, including such topics as voter participation, vote choices, congressional elections, women's organizations, the participation rates of African American women, campaign strategies, and state elections.

Clift, Eleanor. *Founding Sisters and the Nineteenth Amendment.* **New York: John Wiley & Sons, 2003**

Clift describes the difficult road that women traveled in the struggle to achieve suffrage rights. Although early supporters of woman suffrage also advocated the abolition of slavery, resentment developed over granting the right to vote to former male slaves while women still were denied suffrage rights.

Mead, Rebecca J. *How the Vote Was Won: Woman Suffrage in the Western United States, 1868–1914.* **New York: New York University Press, 2004**

Mead examines the women's struggle between the end of the Civil War and the beginning of World War I over attaining the franchise. What victories were achieved during this time period occurred almost exclusively in Western states.

Palmer, Barbara, and Dennis Simon. *Breaking the Political Glass Ceiling: Women and Congressional Elections.* **London: Routledge, 2006**

Employing data on women candidates for the U.S. Congress from 1956 to 2002, the authors explore how such factors as incumbency and general social attitudes influence the decision of women to seek elective office.

Piven, Frances Fox, and Richard A. Cloward. *Why Americans Still Don't Vote and Why Politicians Want It That Way.* **Boston: Beacon Press, 2000**

Piven and Cloward, major supporters of the National Voter Registration Act of 1993—legislation that was intended to increase voter registration and subsequently voter turnout—attempt to explain why voter turnout did not increase as much as they predicted it would.

Stanton, Elizabeth Cady, Susan B. Anthony, and Matilda Joslyn Gage, eds. *History of Woman Suffrage.* **Six vols. New York: Arno and the New York Times, 1969**

This multivolume history of woman suffrage was edited by the most noted 19th century advocates of the cause. The first volume recounts the beginning of the suffrage movement at a meeting held in Seneca Falls, New York, in July 1848, and traces its development to the Civil War. Succeeding volumes continue the movement's progress to final victory with ratification of the Nineteenth Amendment in 1920.

Swain, Carol M. *Black Faces, Black Interests: The Representation of African Americans in Congress,* **enlarged ed. Lanham, MD: University Press of America, 2006**

Swain examines representatives in Congress who were elected from differing districts—historically black, newly black, mixed white and black, and majority white—and concludes that black representation is complex, with white members of Congress capable of representing black interests.

Thomas, Sue, and Clyde Wilcox, eds. *Women and Elective Office: Past, Present, and Future,* 2nd ed. New York: Oxford University Press, 2005

Contributors to this volume analyze the recruitment of women candidates and media depictions of and voter responses to women candidates. Topics include women in Congress, minority female candidates and officeholders, and a comparison of women in representative assemblies around the world.

Valelly, Richard, ed. *The Voting Rights Act: Securing the Ballot.* Washington, DC: CQ Press, 2005

This volume presents an account of the events leading to passage of the 1965 Voting Rights Act and evaluates the significance, the consequences, and the continuing importance of the act for U.S. public policy.

Wattenberg, Martin P. *Is Voting for Young People?* New York: Pearson Longman, 2007

Wattenberg attempts to explain why young people are less likely to vote and to engage in politics than older citizens and offers possible strategies for increasing political participation among younger citizens.

Zelden, Charles L. *Voting Rights on Trial.* Indianapolis, IN: Hackett, 2004

Zelden presents the history of restrictions on voting rights and the practice of vote dilution from colonial times to the 2000 presidential election. The author relates the major court cases that restored voting rights and discusses the prospects for voting rights in the 21st century.

Periodicals

Some of the following periodicals and journals are devoted almost exclusively to issues related to campaign and election reform, while others are more general publications that regularly include topics on election reform. Many of these publications are available electronically and on the Internet.

American Association of Political Consultants Update
www.theaapc.org

The biweekly e-newsletter provides information for professional political consultants regarding employment, member activities, and client contacts.

American Journal of Political Science
www.ajps.org

This quarterly journal regularly contains articles on subjects relevant to campaign and election reform, such as electoral dynamics, the mass media and voters' attitudes, the single transferable vote, the relationship between electoral institutions and the number of political parties, and the legislative effects of single-member versus multimember districts.

American Politics Quarterly
www.uwm.edu/Org/APQ

This journal contains articles dealing with the various aspects of American politics, including such topics as legislative redistricting, majority–minority districts and the influence of racial composition on legislators' behavior, the impact of electronic voting machines, and registration reform and its effects on voter turnout.

American Prospect
www.prospect.org

This quarterly journal includes articles by renowned journalists and social scientists that focus on major political issues, including campaign and election reform.

America Votes
cqpress.com/product/America-Votes–27.html

Published every two years following the general election, *America Votes* contains a wealth of information about elections. Included are vote breakdowns in the presidential, congressional, and gubernatorial elections, and maps of the most recent reapportionment plans in each state.

Ballot Access News
Coalition for Free and Open Elections

www.ballot-access.org

This monthly periodical supplies information about state legislative actions and judicial decisions regarding the conduct of elections.

Campaign Finance Law: A Summary of State Campaign Finance Laws
Federal Election Commission
www.fec.gov/pubrec/cfl/cfl02/cfl02.shtml

This publication offers current information about state campaign finance laws. It includes useful charts and references to the legal regulations of each state.

Congressional Digest
www.congressionaldigest.org

This monthly publication provides summaries of proposed legislation currently before Congress, commentary on testimony presented before congressional committees, and selected debates in congressional committees.

County News Magazine
National Association of Counties
www.naco.org/CountyNewsTemplate.cfm?Section=County
_News

This publication for county officials contains articles dealing with various aspects of county management, including election regulations. Innovations and model programs are often discussed.

Election Center FaxCast
www.electioncenter.org

This service for members provides information about developments in registration and election practices and reports on Congress's consideration of legislation concerned with elections.

Electoral Studies
www.elsevier.com

This quarterly international journal, published in Great Britain, includes scholarly articles on election administration around the world. Among the topics covered in recent issues are campaign spending, proportional representation systems, the effects of mandatory voting, and measurement of electoral inequality.

Governing
Congressional Quarterly
www.governing.com

This monthly magazine reports on current public policy initiatives and government operations at the state and national levels, including issues related to campaigns and elections.

Journal of Democracy
www.journalofdemocracy.org

This quarterly journal includes articles that cover various topics relevant to the nature of democracy and strategies for improving the democratic process.

Legislative Studies Quarterly
www.uiowa.edu/~lsq

This journal frequently contains articles that deal with the election of representatives to Congress and state legislatures. Among the topics covered are the influence of PACs, advantages of incumbency, the role of money in congressional campaigns, and the effects of term limits.

National Civic Review
National Civic League
www3.interscience.wiley.com

Published four times each year for civic leaders and students of politics, this periodical contains general information about public affairs, including issues related to elections and electoral reform.

National Journal
www.nationaljournal.com

This weekly periodical on politics offers coverage and analysis of important issues facing the nation, including campaign and election reform.

National Voter
www.lwv.org

This publication of the League of Women Voters provides articles on a number of topics, including social policy, the environment, international relations, the governing structure, and the electoral process.

Political Moneyline
Congressional Quarterly
www.moneyline.cq.com

This newsletter includes presentations on campaign finance and proposed political reforms. Also included are reports on campaign spending in specific elections and reviews of recent publications on campaign finance reform.

Politics (Campaigns & Elections)
www.campaignsandelections.com

Although this magazine focuses primarily on providing political activists and prospective candidates with inside information about the political process and advice for running campaigns, such reform topics as the limitations of the electoral college, the consequences of term limits, the ethics of negative campaigning, and the prospects for vote by mail and Web-based voting are treated.

PS: Political Science and Politics
www.apsanet.org

This quarterly publication of the American Political Science Association offers articles by professional political scientists that often treat contemporary issues, including election reform. Among the subjects of recent articles are the National Voter Registration Act, congressional term limits, alternative voting systems, and U.S. Supreme Court decisions regarding majority–minority districts.

Public Opinion Quarterly
www.poq.oxfordjournals.org

This journal contains articles dealing with the measurement and analysis of public opinion. Among the topics relevant to campaign and election reform are the effects of campaign ads and presidential debates on opinion, the level of support for legislative term limits, and the influence that polling has on political attitudes.

Voting and Democracy Review
www.fairvote.org

Issued by The Center for Voting and Democracy, this quarterly publication provides information about the organization's activities in support of election reform, particularly the introduction of proportional representation.

Nonprint Resources

This section presents a variety of nonprint resources on campaign finance and election reform, including videotapes, DVDs, films, computer software, CD-ROMs, databases, and Internet sites. These resources focus on many issues relevant to campaign and election reform at the state and national levels, including the importance of elections to representative democracy, extensions of the right to vote, prevention of vote fraud, voting hardware and software security, redistricting and gerrymandering, the encouragement of voter turnout, the use of technology in campaigning, and the involvement of young Americans in politics.

Videotapes, DVDs, and Films

Absentee Ballots
Type: DVD
Date: 2000
Source: Nightline
www.abcnewsstore.com

This *Nightline* program discusses the controversy over balloting in the 2000 presidential election, including the counting of absentee ballots, court rulings, and the George W. Bush and Albert Gore press conferences following the election.

Absentee Ballot Voting
Type: VHS, DVD
Date: 2004
Source: C-SPAN
www.c-spanarchives.org

In a Washington, D.C., forum, Curtis Gans of the Committee for the Study of the American Electorate, Rebecca Vigil-Giron of the

National Association of Secretaries of State, and John Fortier of the American Enterprise Institute examine absentee voting practices, differences in state election laws, and the possibility for close and possibly contested elections in 2004.

African American Presidential Campaigns
Type: VHS, DVD
Date: 2003
Source: C-SPAN
www.c-spanarchives.org

In Philadelphia, Pennsylvania, at a forum sponsored by the American Political Science Association, academicians discuss the role that African Americans and African American candidates such as Jesse Jackson, Al Sharpton, Shirley Chisholm, and Carol Moseley Braun have played in presidential politics.

African American Voter Participation
Type: VHS, DVD
Date: 2002
Source: C-SPAN
www.c-spanarchives.org

Ten panel participants discuss African American voter turnout in the 2002 midterm elections and the impact of the African American vote on election results.

American Blackout
Type: VHS, DVD
Date: 2005
Source: Guerrilla News Network
www.gnn.tv

Featuring the career of Rep. Cynthia McKinney (D-GA), this documentary examines the possible subversion of democratic processes, including the claimed attempts to discourage African Americans from voting in Florida and Ohio.

American Voting Practices
Type: VHS, DVD
Date: 2004
Source: C-SPAN
www.c-spanarchives.org

Curtis Gans, director of the Committee for the Study of the American Electorate, discusses voter turnout in U.S. elections compared to other democratic nations.

Campaign Finance Law Decision
Cost: $60
Date: 2003
Source: C-SPAN
www.c-spanarchives.org

At a forum held in Washington, D.C., attorneys and analysts examine the effects of the U.S. Supreme Court case *McConnell v. FEC*, which involved challenges to the 2002 Bipartisan Campaign Reform Act.

Campaign Finance Laws
Type: VHS, DVD
Date: 2005
Source: C-SPAN
www.c-spanarchihves.org

On C-SPAN's *Washington Journal,* Federal Election Commission representatives discuss campaign finance laws, the role of money in politics, and the challenges facing the Bipartisan Campaign Reform Act.

Campaign Finance Reform
Type: VHS, DVD
Date: 2006
Source: C-SPAN
www.c-spanarchives.org

Moderator Michael Malbin of the Campaign Finance Institute and panelists discuss recent lobbying scandals, political campaign spending, and methods used for campaign fund-raising.

Campaign Finance Reform Town Hall Meeting
Type: VHS, DVD
Date: 2001
Source: C-SPAN
www.c-spanarchives.org

At a town hall meeting held in New Orleans, Louisiana, Sens. Russell Feingold (D-WI) and John McCain (R-AZ) discuss the need for campaign finance reform.

Campaign Finance Rules
Type: VHS, DVD
Date: 2004
Source: C-SPAN
www.c-spanarchives.org

Federal Election Commission members discuss the regulations placed on section 527 groups and the effects of such regulations on their activities.

The Choice 2004
Type: VHS, DVD
Date: 2004
Source: PBS Video
www.pbs.org/wgbh/pages/frontline/view

This *Frontline* special examines the sound bites and campaign styles of the 2004 presidential candidates and includes a discussion of the factors that contribute to victory or defeat in presidential campaigns.

Classic Presidential Campaigns: Volume 1
Type: VHS, DVD
Date: 2000
Source: Educational Video Group
        291 Southwind Way
        Greenwood, IN 46142
www.evgonline.com

Volume I of the classic presidential campaigns collection examines the presidential campaigns of 1800 (Thomas Jefferson versus John Adams), 1860 (Abraham Lincoln versus Stephen Douglas), 1876 (Rutherford B. Hayes versus Samuel Tilden), and 1912 (Theodore Roosevelt versus William Howard Taft and Woodrow Wilson).

Classic Presidential Campaigns: Volume 2
Type: VHS, DVD
Date: 2000
Source: Educational Video Group
        291 Southwind Way
        Greenwood, IN 46142
www.evgonline.com

Volume II of the classic presidential campaigns collection examines the presidential campaigns of 1828 (Andrew Jackson versus John

Quincy Adams), 1840 (William Henry Harrison versus Martin Van Buren), 1856 (James Buchanan versus John C. Frémont and Millard Fillmore), and 1896 (William McKinley versus William Jennings Bryan).

Clean Elections
Type: DVD
Date: 2006
Source: PBS Video
www.shoppbs.org/

This video examines the movement to bring about fair elections and campaign finance reform.

Congressional Forum on Vote Fraud
Type: Streaming video
Date: 2004
Source: Showshoe Documentaries
www.snowshoefilms.com/elections.html

This streaming video examines congressional testimony on vote fraud and vote suppression in Ohio. Speakers include Rev. Jesse Jackson, Susan Truan, Joan Quinn, and Rev. William Moss.

Congressional Redistricting
Type: VHS, DVD
Date: 2001
Source: C-SPAN
www.c-spanarchives.org

In a forum discussion in Washington, D.C., panelists, including Charles Cook of *Cook Political Report* and Bob Benenson of *Congressional Quarterly*, discuss the 2000 Census, the subsequent reapportionment process, and its impact on the composition of the U.S. House of Representatives.

Crashing the Parties: 2004
Type: DVD
Date: 2004
Source: Award Productions
www.awardproductions.com

Part of the PBS "By the People" series, this documentary follows the 2004 minor party presidential candidates on the campaign trial and chronicles their efforts to have their names placed on the ballot.

D.C. Voting Rights
Type: VHS, DVD
Date: 2005
Source: C-SPAN
www.c-spanarchives.org

In speeches given in Washington, D.C., Rep. Thomas Davis (R-VA) and congressional delegate Eleanor Holmes discuss voting rights in the District of Columbia and possible congressional representation and statehood for the District.

Democracy in Action
Type: DVD
Date: 2007
Source: Films for the Humanities and Sciences
www.films.com

This video examines the right to vote and its importance to U.S. citizens by recounting suffrage expansion through the Fifteenth, Eighteenth, Twenty-third, Twenty-fourth, and Twenty-sixth Amendments and discusses other constitutional amendments that aided the implementation of democracy in the United States.

Discrimination in Voting: Historical Overview
Type: VHS, DVD
Date: 2005
Source: C-SPAN
www.c-spanarchives.org

The National Commission on the Voting Rights Act, at its first hearing, examines the pending reauthorization of the Voting Rights Act and the record of racial discrimination in voting since its last reauthorization in 1982.

Disrupting the Election
Type: DVD
Date: 2004
Source: Nightline
www.abcnewsstore.com

This *Nightline* program examines the possibility that Al Qaeda might strike to disrupt the 2004 elections. Noting that the government has no emergency measures in place, this program asks what should be done if polling places are attacked on election day.

Electing the President: Six Steps to the Summit (Revised)
Type: VHS, DVD
Date: Not available
Source: Educational Video Group, Inc.
www.evgonline.com

Revised for the 2008 presidential election, this film provides an overview of the presidential selection process, including the significance of the primaries, the purpose of national conventions, the changing nature of presidential campaign strategies, the impact of presidential debates, voting procedures, and the election process.

The Election Process in America
Type: VHS
Date: 2002
Source: VHS Goldhil Educational Edition
www.amazon.com

This video describes the electoral college and how officials are elected in the United States.

Election Reform
Type: DVD
Date: 2000
Source: Nightline
www.abcnewsstore.com

Guests on *Nightline* examine the U.S. electoral process and possible reforms to improve it. Commentators include Rep. Peter DeFazio (D-OR), Prof. Pamela Karlan of Stanford University Law School, and Edwin Meese, Ronald Reagan Fellow in Public Policy at the Heritage Foundation.

Electronic Voting Machines
Type: VHS, DVD
Date: 2006
Source: C-SPAN
www.c-spanarchives.org

Witnesses testify before the House Administration Committee on electronic voting devices, security problems, successes in electronic voting, and changes in voting procedures following the passage of the Help America Vote Act.

Electronic Voting Security
Type: VHS, DVD
Date: 2004
Source: C-SPAN
www.c-spanarchives.org

Witnesses testify before a U.S. House of Representatives committee regarding the security, accuracy, and verifiability of electronic voting systems. They address the Help America Vote Act, voter registration issues, and whether it is necessary to keep paper records of votes.

Florida Voting Irregularities
Type: VHS, DVD
Date: 2001
Source: C-SPAN
www.c-spanarchives.org

Mary Frances Berry, chair of the U.S. Commission on Civil Rights, discusses the commission's preliminary findings and reports its investigation into voting irregularities in Florida.

Getting the Vote
Type: VHS, DVD
Date: 2004
Source: Kids on the Hill
www.kidsonthehill.org

This film provides a history of voting rights and depicts the views of young people, ages 12 to 16, regarding voting inequality.

Give Me a Break—Campaign Finance Reform
Type: DVD
Date: 2000
Source: 20/20
www.abcnewsstore.com

John Stossel presents a segment on campaign finance reform. He examines the views of Sen. John McCain (R-AZ) and others who advocate banning soft money in presidential campaigns.

Hanging Chads and Butterfly Ballots
Type: VHS, DVD

Date: 2001
Source: C-SPAN
www.c-spanarchives.org

In a forum in Los Angeles, California, Ronald Brownstein, a *Los Angeles Times* correspondent, moderates a panel discussion on the 2000 election controversy in Florida, including such topics as hanging chads and butterfly ballots.

I'm on the Ballot
Type: VHS
Date: 2000
Source: Award Productions
www.awardproductions.com

Produced for the PBS Democracy Project, this documentary features the minor party nominees of the Reform, Green, Constitution, Libertarian, Socialist, and Natural Law parties, and explores whether voting for a minor party candidate results in a wasted vote or, alternatively, whether third parties strengthen democracy.

Internet and Political Campaigns
Type: VHS, DVD
Date: 2004
Source: C-SPAN
www.c-spanarchives.org

Campaign managers for President George W. Bush and presidential candidate Howard Dean, along with a political consultant, discuss the historical use of technology in political campaigns, focusing specifically on the use of the Internet in the 2004 presidential campaign.

Internet Use in Campaigns
Type: VHS, DVD
Date: 2004
Source: C-SPAN
www.c-spanarchives.org

Michael Panetta speaks to students at American University about the use of the Internet in political campaigns, examining topics such as online fund-raising, tracking and gathering information about supporters, and using Web logs.

Is This Democracy?
Type: VHS, DVD
Date: 2006
Source: Films for the Humanities and Sciences
www.films.com

Shedding light on the dark side of American politics, this Bill Moyers program investigates the fall of Jack Abramoff, a prominent lobbyist, and asks the question, "Who really owns the U.S. government?"

The Last Campaign
Type: VHS, DVD, streaming video
Date: 2005
Source: Wayne Ewing
www.thelastcampaign.com

This film covers the 2004 judicial campaign of Justice Warren Mc-Graw as he sought reelection to the West Virginia Supreme Court. Focusing on what has been called one of the nastiest judicial campaigns in history and one of the most expensive, the program provides an inside view into the rising stakes in judicial campaigns.

Minorities and Redistricting
Type: VHS, DVD
Date: 2003
Source: C-SPAN
www.c-spanarchives.org

Laughlin McDonald, director of the American Civil Liberties Union in the Southern Region, and Carol Swain, professor at Vanderbilt University School of Law, examine the possible benefits and disadvantages of creating minority voting districts.

Nationwide Election Reform
Type: VHS, DVD
Date: 2002
Source: C-SPAN
www.c-spanarchives.org

At a news conference held in Washington, D.C., participants discuss proposed election law reforms. Topics include current election procedures, new voting machine technology, voter registration procedures, and the advisability of national standards for the conduct of elections.

New Hampshire Presidential Campaigns
Type: VHS, DVD
Date: 2003
Source: C-SPAN
www.c-spanarchives.org

In Concord, New Hampshire, state librarian Michael York discusses presidential primary election campaigns in New Hampshire, the history of primary elections, the unique nature of the New Hampshire electorate, and the significance of the New Hampshire primary to the outcome of the presidential election.

News Coverage of Election Campaigns
Type: VHS, DVD
Date: 2004
Source: C-SPAN
www.c-spanarchives.org

Media representatives discuss the campaigns of President George W. Bush and Sen. John Kerry (D-MA), the battleground states, election administration changes since 2000, and claims of voter fraud and intimidation.

Not Again
Type: DVD
Date: 2004
Source: Nightline
www.abcnewsstore.com

With a focus on Ohio and Florida, this program investigates the electoral college and ballot issues that at the time were thought to endanger the credibility of the 2004 presidential election.

Political Campaigns Past and Present
Type: VHS, DVD
Date: 2004
Source: C-SPAN
www.c-spanarchives.org

On C-SPAN's *Washington Journal,* veteran political reporters discuss the 2004 presidential campaign, comparing it to previous campaigns.

Primaries: Defining the Battle in New Hampshire
Type: VHS, DVD
Date: 2004
Source: Films for the Humanities and Sciences
www.films.com

Providing an overview of the presidential primary process, this film explains how presidential candidates are winnowed through the primaries and illustrates the significant impact of primaries on presidential selection.

The Right to Count
Type: VHS, DVD
Date: 2002
Source: Roaming Video
Re: The Right to Count
www.therighttocount.com

This documentary on electronic voting discusses the claimed failings of computerized voting and its impact on election outcomes. Witnesses of vote fraud share their stories.

Road to the White House
Type: DVD
Date: 2004
Source: Nightline
www.abcnewsstore.com

Ted Koppel describes each presidential candidate's continued campaigning up to the last moments before the November 2004 election. The video claims that exit poll results were misleading, giving false hope to the Kerry campaign.

State Judicial Campaigns
Type: VHS, DVD
Date: 2004
Source: C-SPAN
www.c-spanarchives.org

At a Washington, D.C., forum, panelists examine the effects of election spending on the administration of justice and the relationships among elected judges, campaign contributors, and special interest groups.

Total Recall
Type: DVD
Date: 2003
Source: Nightline
www.abcnewsstore.com

This *Nightline* program examines Arnold Schwarzenegger's announcement to run for governor in California and the 400 other Californians requesting a place on the ballot as a result of the impending recall election of Gov. Gray Davis.

Trouble in Paradise
Type: VHS, DVD
Date: 2004
Source: Laurel Greenberg
www.troubleinparadise.org

This documentary follows five Floridians, from the 2000 election to 2002, who sought to address the problems surrounding voting irregularities. Becoming political activists, they search for answers to questions about election procedures.

2004 Campaign Finance Practices
Type: VHS, DVD
Date: November 17, 2004
Source: C-SPAN
www.c-spanarchives.org

The Campaign Legal Center hosts this forum of more than a dozen panelists who discuss the influence of campaign finance laws on the 2004 elections, examining the strategy of President George W. Bush and Sen. John Kerry (D-MA) to opt out of the federal system that provides matching funds for presidential primary candidates who abide by spending limits.

Unprecedented: The 2000 Presidential Election
Type: VHS, DVD, 16mm, 35mm, streaming video
Date: 2004

Source: Richard Perez and Joan Sekler
www.unprecedented.org

This documentary examines the Florida voting controversies in the 2000 presidential election, focusing on the flaws of the so-called Butterfly Ballot and alleged civil rights abuses.

Voices in Democracy Series
Type: VHS
Date: 2001
Source: GPN Educational Media
www.gpn.unl.edu

This 20-segment series describes how people can bring about meaningful change in a representative democracy. It provides lessons on the U.S. Constitution, encourages citizen participation, and examines the struggle for equal rights.

Vote or Fraud
Type: DVD
Date: 2005
Source: Nightline
www.abcnewsstore.com

In this broadcast, *Nightline* correspondents Ted Koppel and Chris Bury examine voting irregularities in Ohio on election day in the 2004 presidential race. The program speculates that the outcome of the election might have been different with more voting machines in place and nonpartisan oversight of the voting process.

Votergate
Type: Streaming video
Date: 2004
Source: Votergate
Worldwide Plaza
www.prisonplanet.tv/articles/december2004/161204votergate
.htm

This documentary follows investigators as they examine the problems with U.S. voting systems and election procedures. For example, the video illustrates the susceptibility of touch screen voting systems to hacking, highlighting the need for proper oversight.

Voter Participation
Type: VHS, DVD
Date: 2002
Source: C-SPAN
www.c-spanarchives.org

Thomas Patterson, a professor at Harvard University's Kennedy School of Government, discusses low voter turnout, its causes, and its consequences.

Voting and Election Reform
Type: VHS, DVD
Date: 2004
Source: C-SPAN
www.c-spanarchives.org

Witnesses before the U.S. Commission on Civil Rights testify about the need for electoral reform. They discuss such issues as absentee ballots, implementation of new voter identification requirements, and possible voter intimidation.

Voting Irregularities in Ohio
Type: VHS, DVD
Date: 2004
Source: C-SPAN
www.c-spanarchives.org

Representatives and witnesses testify before a committee of the U.S. House of Representatives about voting irregularities in the 2004 Ohio election. They examine civil rights issues, local variations in election procedures, and proposed electoral reforms.

Voting Machines
Type: VHS, DVD
Date: 2004
Source: C-SPAN
www.c-spanarchives.org

At a forum in Washington, D.C., panelists sponsored by Common Cause discuss the use and reliability of new voting technologies in the 2004 presidential election.

Voting Rights Amendment Series
Amendments 15 and 24: Prohibiting Discrimination in Voting on the Basis of Race and Rights of Citizens to Vote/Poll Tax

Amendment 17: Direct Election of U.S. Senators
Amendment 19: Women's Right to Vote
Amendment 23: D.C. Voting
Amendment 26: Voting for 18-Year-Olds
Type: VHS, DVD
Date: 1998
Source: Films for the Humanities and Sciences
www.films.com

This five-part series examines each amendment relevant to voting rights, its historical interpretation, and implications for the extension of voting rights.

Voting Technology
Type: VHS, DVD
Date: 2005
Source: C-SPAN
www.c-spanarchives.org

At the first meeting of the Carter-Baker Commission on Federal Election Reform, panelists examine the use of electronic voting systems in the 2004 elections, allegations of machine malfunctions, the maintenance of voting records, and issues related to voter access to new election technologies.

When Campaigns Were Fun: The Insiders
Type: VHS, DVD
Date: 2000
Source: C-SPAN
www.c-spanarchives.org

In a Grand Rapids, Michigan, forum, former presidential aides discuss changes in political campaigns over the past few decades, offering personal insights into television influences on candidates and campaigns.

When Campaigns Were Fun: The Reporters
Type: VHS, DVD
Date: 2000
Source: C-SPAN
www.c-spanarchives.org

Correspondents and mass media representatives discuss changes in political campaigns over the past decades and provide personal insights about the different personalities, the changing nature of conventions, and the impact of television.

Who's Behind Local Ballot Initiatives?
Type: DVD
Date: 2006
Source: PBS Video
www.shoppbs.org

This video examines the organized interests that sponsor ballot initiatives and use the media to gain electoral support.

Women Running Campaigns
Type: VHS, DVD
Date: 2005
Source: C-SPAN
www.c-spanarchives.org

Panelists discuss women candidates and women's roles in political campaigns. They examine launching successful campaigns and suggest lessons to be learned from the 2004 campaign season.

Youth Voting and Participation
Type: VHS, DVD
Date: 2004
Source: C-SPAN
www.c-spanarchives.org

John Zogby of Zogby International and participants from the Center for the Study of the Presidency examine youth voting patterns and political participation levels. They discuss issues that affect young voters and communication between politicians and youth.

Youth Voting Practices
Type: VHS, DVD
Date: 2003
Source: C-SPAN
www.c-spanarchives.org

In an American University forum, participants discuss the low voting rate of young Americans and examine programs that might motivate them to participate in the electoral process.

Databases

These databases can yield considerable information relevant to campaign finance and electoral reform.

C-SPAN
www.c-span.org

C-SPAN has created a searchable campaign finance database that originates with the Federal Election Commission. The database contains financial data for each two-year congressional campaign cycle from 1994 through 2004. It can be searched using donor name, candidate name, or zip code.

Federal Election Commission
www.fec.gov

The Federal Election Commission furnishes online computer access to federal campaign finance records, a combined federal and state disclosure directory, a summary of campaign finance law at the state and federal levels, and many other resources.

Internet Resources

Balloting and Voting

Ballot Access News
www.ballot-access.org

Edited by Richard Winger, this Web site offers up-to-date and archival news on ballot access issues. It also provides access to *Ballot Access News* magazine.

Brennan Center Democracy Program
www.brennancenter.org

Promoting electoral access, the Brennan Center Web page discusses restoring the voting rights of convicted felons, eliminating barriers to voter registration, and making efforts to ensure equal voting opportunities.

Civilrights.org
www.civilrights.org

This Web site examines a number of political issues and focuses on securing voting rights for all Americans.

Consumer Protection for Elections
blackboxvoting.org

Black Box Voting provides coverage of voting irregularities and vote fraud. It investigates citizen complaints and furnishes a tool kit for citizens who wish to monitor elections.

Easy to Vote: A Voter Registration Guide
www.easytovote.com

This Web site provides voter registration information by state with printable voter registration application forms.

Election Law Journal
www.liebertpub.com/publication.aspx?pub_id=101

This Web page provides access to a peer-reviewed online journal examining legislation and litigation related to changes in election law and election systems.

Electronic Voting
www.notablesoftware.com/evote.html

Produced and copyrighted by Rebecca Mercuri, Electronic Voting provides information on electronic voting and the security problems associated with it.

E-Voting: Introduction
aceproject.org/ace-en/focus/e-voting

This Web page, the Administration and Costs of Elections (ACE) Project, presents the appropriate standards for e-voting. It examines the risks and challenges as well as the opportunities of e-voting.

Federal Voting Assistance Program
www.fvap.gov

The Federal Voting Assistance Program web page offers state-by-state instructions on voting, state voter registration procedures, and on-line voting and absentee ballots.

Fraud Factor
www.fraudfactor.com

Fraud Factor provides data, articles, and reports on alleged vote fraud.

Insure Democracy
www.insuredemocracy.com

This Web page explains the importance of voting and provides voter registration information.

Reform Elections.org
www.reformelections.org

In support of a variety of voting and ballot reforms, this Web page includes information about election day registration, government-issued photo identification for voting, stiffened enforcement of vote fraud laws, better funding of the Help America Vote Act, a voter-verified paper trail, and early voting.

VotersUnite.Org
www.votersunite.org

Votersunite.org hosts a collection of articles from local and national media outlets on voting issues and addresses the alleged problems associated with electronic voting.

Campaign Finance Reform
Campaign Disclosure Project
www.campaigndisclosure.org

With a database on state disclosure laws, this Web site grades states on the quality of campaign finance disclosure and provides a model law for publicly reporting campaign finances.

Campaign Finance Reform
archive.newsmax.com/hottopics/Campaign_Finance_Reform.shtml

This Web page provides daily news stories on campaign finance reform and the challenges of implementing existing laws.

Campaign Finance Reform News: Free Speech Election Law Reform
www.campaignfinancereformnews.org

This Web page examines campaign finance reform news, court cases, the use of soft money in campaigns, issue advocacy and free speech issues, and election law.

Democracy 21
www.democracy21.org

Democracy21 advocates closing campaign finance loopholes and proposes reforms of the public financing system for presidential elections, as well as lobbying and ethics reforms for Congress.

Freedom Keys: About Campaign Finance Reform
freedomkeys.com/finance.htm

This Web page provides numerous quotes from politicians, news correspondents, and reformers on campaign finance reform.

National Institute for Money in Campaigns
www.followthemoney.org

The Institute's Web site provides research data on the role of contributions in state political campaigns and examines the effect of campaign finances on public policy outcomes.

Opensecrets.org: Your Guide to the Money in U.S. Elections
www.opensecrets.org

This Web site of the Center for Responsive Politics provides campaign contribution data on congressional and presidential candidates and political parties. It identifies the source of campaign contributions, especially the top donors, and what type of money is given (soft versus hard).

Political Money Line
www.tray.com

Included in the databases of money in politics at this site are ones for U.S. House, Senate, and presidential campaigns. It furnishes access to disbursements, donors, PAC contributions, independent expenditures, and other campaign finance data.

Public Campaign: Clean Money, Clean Elections
www.publiccampaign.org

Public Campaign advocates public financing of political campaigns at the state and national levels. Numerous states have clean election Web pages, including Arizona, California, Connecticut, Iowa, Maine, Massachusetts, New Jersey, New Mexico, New York, Pennsylvania, and Rhode Island.

The Rest of Us
therestofus.org

This website discusses the role of money in politics and advocates campaign finance reform.

Electoral Reform
Accurate Democracy
accuratedemocracy.com

This Web page provides information on proportional representation and advocates its use.

Campaign Institute
www.campaigninstitute.org/

By recruiting and training electoral activists, the Campaign Institute encourages the development of grassroots campaign strategies and fund-raising for grassroots reform.

Dennis Kucinich on Campaign Reform and IRV
www.kucinich.us/issues/campaignreform-irv.php

Representative Dennis Kucinich (D-OH) expresses support for various electoral reforms, including instant runoff voting (IRV), public financing of elections, free television time for political candidates, election day registration, an election day holiday, proportional representation, and reenfranchisement of convicted felons.

Direct Democracy League
www.ddleague-usa.net

The Direct Democracy League presents various electoral reforms, including creating a unicameral Congress, establishing regional-to-national nonpartisan presidential primaries, setting up nonpartisan election administration, and abolishing the electoral college.

EC: The U.S. Electoral College Web Zine
www.avagara.com/e_c/index.htm

This Web site provides resources, references, and news articles on the electoral college and defends the continued use of the present procedure for electing the president.

Election Reform Information Network
erin.home.4t.com

Examining a variety of election issues, this Web site outlines the claimed benefits and disadvantages of early voting, the electoral college, and various election systems, including Internet voting and voting by mail. The site advocates a national voter registration system.

Electoral College.Org
www.electoralcollege.org

With a focus on the electoral college, its history and operation, this Web site also provides up-to-date political news.

Electoral College Primer
www.ksg.harvard.edu/case/3pt/electoral.html

This Web site examines the operation of the electoral college, the system's benefits and disadvantages, and proposals for reform.

Electoral College Reform
www.fakeisthenewreal.org/reform

This Web page advocates reforming the electoral college by redividing the territory of the United States into 50 equally populated regions to ensure that large states do not carry more influence than small states.

National Popular Vote!
www.nationalpopularvote.com

This Web page critiques the electoral college and proposes an interstate compact to implement a national popular election of the president by having states within the compact agree in advance to award all their electoral votes to the presidential candidate receiving the most popular votes.

PR Library: Readings in Proportional Representation
www.mtholyoke.edu/acad/polit/damy/prlib.htm

Maintained by Douglas Amy at Mount Holyoke College, the PR Library provides articles, books, and other readings on proportional representation.

The State PIRG's Democracy Program
pirg.org/democracy/democracy.asp

The democracy program of the state Public Interest Research Groups (PIRGs) advocates numerous reforms, including establishing a campaign finance system that relies on small donors, nonpartisan election administration, verifiable paper trails for voting machines, the use of cumulative voting, equal access to ballots for all political parties, congressional representation for the District of Columbia, instant runoff voting, and nonpartisan redistricting commissions.

VOTEJUSTICE.org
www.votejustice.org

This Web site examines a host of electoral reforms, including a constitutional amendment guaranteeing the right to vote, reenfranchisement of convicted felons, election day registration, instituting an election day holiday, instant runoff voting, verifiable paper records of election results, proportional representation, uniform national voting standards, public campaign finance, electoral college reform, and nonpartisan officials as poll watchers.

Vote Pair
votepair.org

Vote Pair advocates alternative voting systems, such as instant runoff voting and approval voting. It also seeks a greater role for third parties by providing them equal ballot access.

Political Participation
Citizens' Debate Commission
citizensdebate.org

This Web site advocates allowing minor party participation in presidential debates, eschewing the current practice of focusing almost exclusively on Republican and Democratic candidates.

Declare Yourself
www.declareyourself.org

Declare Yourself seeks to energize a new wave of young voters to participate in the electoral process. The site promotes get-out-the-vote campaigns, registration drives, and nationwide voter education initiatives aimed at high school seniors.

International IDEA: Women in Politics
www.idea.int/gender

The International Institute for Democracy and Electoral Assistance advocates removing barriers to female participation in politics worldwide. This Web page highlights research projects and activities geared toward advancing gender equality and democracy.

National Organization on Disability—Political Participation
www.nod.org

This Web page discusses the barriers to voting that disabled persons experience and educates the disabled community on their voting rights.

New Voters Project
www.newvotersproject.org

The New Voters Project seeks to mobilize voter registration and participation of the young population.

Political Grassroots: Change through Involvement
www.politicalgrassroots.org/participation.html

Political Grassroots provides advice about becoming an informed voter and getting involved in the political process.

Political Participation: Voting
users.dickinson.edu/~cliftonb/voting.htm

This Web site examines the importance of voting in a democracy. It provides voter turnout data from 1960 to 2000 and analyzes the demographic characteristics of those who vote in contrast to those who do not.

President Elect
www.presidentelect.org

This Web site provides information on presidential elections from 1972 to 2004, election law, the electoral college, and relevant constitutional issues.

Project Vote Smart
www.votesmart.org/index.htm

Project Vote Smart seeks to increase political participation by providing access to information about candidates, including biographical profiles, issue positions, voting records, interest group ratings, and campaign finances.

P2008—The 2008 Presidential Campaign
www.gwu.edu/~action/2008/P2008.html

P2008 provides information on possible Republican and Democratic candidates for the 2008 presidential election campaign. It examines the presidential nomination process, current party activities, campaign financing issues, and criticisms of the electoral college.

Rock the Vote
www.rockthevote.org

Rock the Vote encourages young people to register to vote and provides a Web log for readers.

Smackdown Your Vote!
vote.wwe.com

Smackdown Your Vote!, sponsored by World Wide Wrestling and nonpartisan partners, describes itself as an "apartisan" Web page encouraging young people to get involved in politics and to vote.

Su Voto Es Su Voz (Your Vote Is Your Voice)
www.svrep.org

This Web page reaches out to Latino communities to educate them about the importance of voter registration and participation.

United States Presidential Elections
www.multied.com/elections

This site provides information about presidential elections from 1789 to the present. It discusses disputed elections, the operation of presidential nominating conventions, and the original intent of the electoral college.

Reapportionment, Redistricting, and Gerrymandering
Fair Plan—Community-Based Redistricting Solutions
members.tripod.com/fairplan2000/index.html

The Fair Plan page discusses redistricting in 19 states and provides get-out-the-vote maps for 30 states, encouraging canvassers to target low voter turnout by precinct.

Fraud Factor—Redistricting and the Gerrymander
www.fraudfactor.com/ffgerrymander.html

This Web page contains a comprehensive article by Michael D. Robbins on the gerrymander and the need for redistricting reform.

Gerrymandering—Source Watch
www.sourcewatch.org/index.php?title-Gerrymandering

This page provides background information about, and examples of, gerrymandering.

Referendums and Initiatives
Citizens for U.S. Direct Initiatives
www.cusdi.org

This Web site advocates direct democracy initiatives and proposes an amendment to the U.S. Constitution establishing the direct initiative at the national level.

Citizens in Charge
www.citizensincharge.org

The Web site of Citizens in Charge provides information on the availability of initiative and referendum procedures at the state level as a means of enhancing citizen control over government.

Initiative and Referendum Institute
http:www.iandrinstitute.org

The Institute provides information on trends in statewide ballot propositions and the use of referendum and initiative procedures. It critically analyzes the use of referenda and initiatives on the ballot.

National Conference of State Legislatures: Initiative, Referendum and Recall
www.ncsl.org/programs/legman/elect/initiat.htm

This Web page provides background information on the initiative, referendum, and recall, as well as a database of ballot measures and initiative and referendum election results.

New Rules Project—The Governance Sector: Devolving Authority and Democratizing Decisionmaking
www.newrules.org/gov/iandr.html

The New Rules Project advocates greater use of direct democracy procedures and discusses such issues as campaign finance reform and proportional representation.

On Political Participation: The Effects of New Technologies— Referendums and Increased Political Participation
www.reed.edu/~gronkep/webofpolitics/projects/techandpartic ipation/referendum.html

This Web site provides information about the effects of political participation with a focus on referenda, online voting, and electronic town hall meetings.

Worldwide Direct Democracy Movement
world-wide-democracy.net

This site promotes the use of direct democracy methods as the only genuine version of democracy.

Term Limits
Citizens for Term Limits
www.termlimits.com

This Web site offers research results on, and arguments for, congressional term limits.

Glossary

absentee ballot   *See* absentee voting.

absentee voting   A form of voting in which qualified voters are allowed to cast their votes without going to the polls on election day. If voters anticipate that they will be unable to cast their ballots at the polls on election day, they may obtain a ballot within a specified time period leading up to the election, mark it, have it notarized or witnessed, and then return the sealed ballot to the proper authority. State laws or provisions in state constitutions enable this practice. First used during the Civil War to allow union troops to vote, such provisions also allow American citizens residing overseas to vote.

add-on voting   *See* cumulative voting.

advisory primary   A primary that is nonbinding and merely registers voter preferences.

affirmative gerrymandering   A variation of gerrymandering in which district lines are redrawn to help a minority group candidate consolidate minority votes to win representation. *See also* gerrymandering.

alienation   A sense of helplessness that individuals experience when confronted with the political process, believing that their votes do not count or that their government is not responsive to their needs. Distrust, cynicism, or outright rejection of the political system are associated with alienation.

all-mail-ballot election   A type of election in which registered voters in a voting jurisdiction receive a ballot through the mail instead of going to a polling place on election day. Voters then return the completed ballot by mail or drop it off at a designated site before a specified date. Most often used in nonpartisan and referendum voting, some states, most notably Oregon, use mailed ballots to elect public officials in partisan elections.

apportionment The allocation of seats in state legislatures, Congress, and other representative bodies. District lines are drawn to provide roughly equal representation to all citizens.

approval voting An electoral process in which voters can vote for (approve of) as many of the candidates as they desire but cannot cast more than one vote for each candidate. Voters do not rank candidates, and the candidate with the greatest number of votes wins. This system has been rarely used.

at-large election A type of election in which all of the voters in a large geographic area, rather than smaller subdivisions or districts, choose delegates to a representative body. Voters select several of the candidates to represent them rather than only one. While proponents of this system claim that representatives elected tend to serve the interests of the whole community, some argue that at-large elections disadvantage minority candidates and hence fail to represent minority interests adequately.

Australian ballot A secret ballot that is printed, distributed, and tabulated by government officials. This reform, which originated in Australia as a replacement for party ballots and oral voting, was instituted in the United States to protect voters from coercion at the polls and to discourage vote buying.

ballot box stuffing A form of vote fraud that occurs when corrupt election officials mark ballots illegally and place them in ballot boxes to assist a favored candidate or political party.

ballot propositions Issues placed on the ballot for a vote during a primary or general election.

ballot rolloff *See* voter rolloff.

beauty contest primary A type of primary that occurs in the presidential primary election season. Voters register their preference for a favored candidate in party primaries, caucuses, or state conventions without selecting delegates to the national nominating convention.

Bipartisan Campaign Reform Act (BCRA) A law passed in 2002 that amended the Federal Election Campaign Act, placing limitations on the use of soft money and the broadcast of election advertisements supported by corporations, unions, or other groups 30 days before a primary and 60 days before a general election. The law has been challenged in the courts, most notably in *McConnell v. Federal Election Commission* (2003), in which the U.S. Supreme Court upheld most of the legislation, and *Federal Election Commission v. Wisconsin Right to Life, Inc.* (2007), in which the Court found the restrictions on advertising too limiting.

blanket primary Sometimes called a wide-open primary, this system of nomination allows voters, regardless of their party label, to participate in nominating candidates from more than one party. Participants are limited only in that they may not vote for more than one candidate for the same office.

Buckley v. Valeo, **424 U.S. 1, 1976**   A case in which the U.S. Supreme Court upheld the constitutionality of the Federal Election Campaign Act but disallowed provisions that would have limited campaign spending and the resources that a candidate could devote to a campaign. The Court held that such provisions violated the First Amendment, stating that government cannot have ultimate power over campaign spending because an individual's financial resources can be an important ingredient in promoting political views. People must retain ultimate control over the quantity and scope of political debate.

bullet voting   A voting strategy that is likely to occur when several seats are open for the same office, such as city council or board of education, and voters have multiple votes. A group of people engage in bullet voting when they cast all or most of their votes for a favored candidate, thus increasing the probability that this person will be elected. A minority party or group has a greater chance of winning representation under a system that allows bullet voting.

bundling   The combining of several small donations into one large contribution. To circumvent federal limits on individual donations to candidates, fund-raisers use bundling. Several maximum contributions are solicited from, for instance, a corporation's executives and their families, and the checks are sent together to a candidate. While no one has given more than the law allows, a significant amount of money has in fact come from one source.

canvassing board   A state or local government unit that receives vote counts from election precincts, tabulates the votes, and certifies winners.

cemetery vote   A vote by someone who resides in the local cemetery and who appears to rise from the dead at least long enough to vote. This form of vote fraud is possible because voter registration lists are not adequately monitored and therefore the names of individuals who have died are not purged from the voting rolls.

checkoff   *See* IRS checkoff.

civic duty   The responsibility of citizens to take part in such public activities as voting. Those with high socioeconomic status tend to have a greater sense of civic duty, thus helping to explain their higher voter turnout rates relative to the less well-to-do.

closed primary   A primary in which voters must declare their party affiliation and vote on the party's primary ballot only.

compulsory union dues   Contributions that union members are required to make to the organization. Among the uses of such funds has been supporting political activities. Some have sought to prohibit unions from spending workers' required dues for such activities, arguing that union leaders may contribute workers' resources to causes that the rank-and-file members do not support.

compulsory voting   An electoral process in which voters are compelled by law to vote. In the United States, there is no legal requirement that eligible voters cast a ballot on election day. This practice was held unconstitutional in a 1939 U.S. Supreme Court decision, *Lane v. Wilson,* which stated that penalties for not voting are invalid and in violation of the Fifteenth Amendment. However, other countries have instituted systems of compulsory voting.

concentration gerrymandering   The grouping of identifiable populations in one or a few "safe" districts so that the seats are won by huge margins. This tactic can be a way of limiting the influence of a particular political or racial group and is also used to protect incumbents. Also known as packing.

conflict of interest   A situation that occurs when the personal or financial interests of officeholders influence or are likely to affect their public policy decisions. A suggested campaign reform proposal would require candidates to reveal any conflict between personal interests and the performance of public duties.

congressional and senatorial campaign committees   Committees established by members of the two major political parties in Congress to raise money for congressional and senatorial campaigns. They may also establish linkages with efforts sponsored by the state and local committees of their respective parties. However, the Bipartisan Campaign Reform Act of 2002 requires that national party organizations adhere to federal limits on donations in national as well as state and local campaigns.

constitutional initiative   A type of initiative that involves proposals aimed at amending a state constitution. In states that have adopted this procedure, citizens rather than state legislators propose by petition and ratify by election any amendments to the state constitution.

contested election   An election that is disputed when more than one candidate for the office claims to have won. This may lead to a recount, or, if left unresolved, the controversy could be decided in court. With the adoption in recent years of electronic voting in many jurisdictions, questions have been raised about the resolution of a contested election when no paper trail of votes has been maintained.

contribution limits   At the federal level, limits on contributions to candidates for federal office, as set by the Federal Election Campaign Act as amended in 1974 and revised in the Bipartisan Campaign Reform Act of 2002. For example, during the 2007–2008 campaign season, an individual could give a maximum of $2,300 to a candidate or a candidate committee per election, and $28,500 to a national party committee in a calendar year. Political action committees could give no more than $5,000 to a candidate in each election. Corporations, labor unions, and foreign nationals may not contribute at all. A number of loopholes, however, make it possible to give far more than these prescribed limits.

corruption Broadly, any unlawful or unethical behavior in campaigning, in the conduct of elections, or in governing once in office. It may also refer to the unauthorized use of public office for private benefit.

Corrupt Practices Acts Federal legislation, beginning with the Federal Corrupt Practices Act of 1925, that seeks to regulate sources of campaign contributions and expenditures in federal elections. These measures include the Political Activities Act of 1939, the Federal Election Campaign Acts of 1972 and 1974, and the 1971 Revenue Act.

cracking *See* dispersal gerrymandering.

critical election An election that indicates a long-term shift in partisan identification among the electorate and results in the ascendancy of a new political majority at the state and national levels. V. O. Key in "A Theory of Critical Elections" [*The Journal of Politics* 17, 1 (February 1955): 3–18] proposed this concept.

cross filing A practice, allowed in some states, that permits a candidate to file for elective office in the primary elections of more than one political party.

crossover vote A vote, in open primaries, that is cast for a candidate of the opposition party with which the voter is not normally affiliated in order to help that party's weakest candidate gain the nomination or to support the least objectionable candidate. Some crossover voters sincerely support a favored candidate who happens to belong to another party.

cumulative voting A voting system in which voters cast more than one vote in the simultaneous election of several candidates for political office. Each individual can give two or more votes to a single candidate or distribute them among several. This voting procedure may be used to obtain greater representation for third parties or for minority groups.

direct initiative A type of initiative in which legislative proposals must be submitted directly to voters in a special or general election for approval or rejection and that requires no action by the legislature.

direct primary A primary that allows voters to select the political party nominees by ballot without any intervening decision by the party organization, as in a convention.

disfranchise The loss of voting rights, under certain circumstances. Convicted felons, those who fail to register during specified time periods, and those who lose their citizenship are examples of people who may be disfranchised. Citizens may be illegally disfranchised as when African Americans were denied the right to vote in the South following Reconstruction.

dispersal gerrymandering   A form of gerrymandering that disperses members of an identifiable group into two or more districts so that their votes can no longer determine the outcome of an election. *See* also vote dilution.

donor fatigue   The reaction of many campaign contributors who feel coerced into giving ever larger sums of money to political campaigns in order to be assured of access to government officials, concluding that the system is in need of reform to protect them from such pressures.

Dunn v. Blumstein, **405 U.S. 330, 1972**   A U.S. Supreme Court case in which durational (or unusually long) residency requirements for purposes of voting were declared constitutional. However, the Court recognized that closing voter registration rolls 30 to 60 days prior to an election could be considered a practical necessity.

Duverger's law   A so-called law, drawn from the writings of Maurice Duverger, holding that the single-member district plurality electoral system favors a strong two-party system such as that in the United States. A more general conclusion is that electoral rules are not necessarily neutral but rather may favor a particular outcome.

early money   Contributions made early in a political contest that are valued because they allow candidates to build their campaign organizations and gain early media exposure.

early voting   Voting prior to election day. In some states, voters may cast their ballots at designated sites, such as supermarkets, shopping malls, and government buildings during a period of time prior to election day. Any qualified voter has the option of early voting.

electoral college   The U.S. body that consists of 538 electors who gather in their respective state capitals to cast their vote for president on the first Monday after the second Wednesday in December of a presidential election year. They officially elect the president and vice president. Every state but Maine and Nebraska follow the unit rule, whereby the candidate who receives the most popular votes in a state wins all that state's electoral votes. Each state has a number of electors equal to the total number of senators and representatives it has in Congress. Each political party nominates a prospective slate of electors, and the slate pledged to the candidate who wins the most popular votes is selected to vote for president and vice president.

electoral vote   *See* electoral college.

endless chain   *See* Tasmanian dodge.

equal time rule   A requirement, established and enforced by the Federal Communications Commission (FCC), stipulating that candidates for public office should be given equal access to free or paid use of television. If a radio or television broadcast sells time to one political candidate, the broadcaster must also be willing to sell equal time to opposing candidates.

ethanol tax break   One of several famous (or infamous) tax loopholes that was extended by Congress in 1996. It is a subsidy that costs consumers approximately $770 million a year and is particularly beneficial to the Archer-Daniels-Midland agribusiness giant. This company alone contributed almost $750,000 in PAC and soft money contributions in 1996. The Energy Policy Act of 2005 maintained tax credits for biodiesel and ethanol producers.

Ethics in Government Act of 1978   An act that requires financial disclosure by senior federal government officials and their families and that restricts their outside earned income to 15 percent of their salaries. The act also limits the activities of public officials as representatives before government agencies.

Ethics Reform Act of 1989   An act that requires personal financial disclosures from federal candidates.

exit polls   Interviews conducted by pollsters and news organizations immediately after voters have finished voting and are leaving the polling place. The so-called exit polls are used to make projections about who will win an election. Sometimes winners of presidential contests have been projected before all the polls close on the West Coast, creating controversy about the practice of exit polling. To avoid this problem, some have recommended uniform poll hours across the nation.

fail-safe voting   A voting system in which election officials at polling places allow individuals to cast a ballot even though their registration status is in question. After an investigation, the ballot is either verified and counted or invalidated. Critics argue that this practice has led to considerable vote fraud.

faithless elector   An elector in the electoral college who refuses to follow the will expressed by the presidential popular vote and instead casts an electoral vote for another candidate. Most states legally require electors to vote for the candidate to whom they were pledged, although the Constitution allows them discretion.

fat cat   A term typically used to describe big political contributors who seek political influence or favors in exchange for money. According to *Safire's Political Dictionary*, the expression goes back to the late 1880s when the use of high-pressure tactics on contributors was called fat-fry-ing. A leading Republican fund-raiser during that era wrote a letter urging his colleagues to "fry the fat out of the manufacturers."

Federal Election Campaign Act (FECA)   The 1971 law that created contemporary campaign finance rules. The act replaced the old—and widely ignored—Federal Corrupt Practices Act of 1925.

Federal Election Campaign Act of 1974   The amendment to the Federal Election Campaign Act (FECA) that established campaign contribution limits on individuals and political action committees, as well as expenditure limits on presidential candidates who accepted public financing.

Federal Election Commission (FEC)   The commission created by Congress in the 1974 Federal Election Campaign Act. The FEC monitors compliance with federal election laws. Its authority was limited by *Buckley v. Valeo* in 1976. Campaign organizations and political action committees are required to disclose their contributions and expenditures to the FEC. Those records are public documents that are open to public scrutiny.

federal political committee   When an organization or group makes federal contributions or expenditures (or a combination of both) exceeding $1,000 per year, it becomes a political committee and must register with the FEC.

Fifteenth Amendment   The amendment to the U.S. Constitution, ratified in 1870, that officially granted the right to vote to black males.

filing   The official declaration of intentions to run for office made by prospective candidates. Many states limit the number of candidate filings by requiring that candidacy petitions be signed by a specified number of registered voters. The prospective candidate must present the petitions and files with an appropriate official (for instance, the secretary of state or county clerk). In some states, individuals may seek candidacy for local office simply by declaring their intentions before a designated official. In other states, a sum of money must also be deposited.

foreign national   Non-U.S. citizens, including foreign governments, political parties, corporations, associations, partnerships, individuals with foreign citizenship, and immigrants not possessing a green card, all of whom are prohibited from making contributions or expenditures to any U.S. election (federal, state, or local), either directly or through another person. The acceptance of contributions from foreign nationals is also prohibited.

franchise   The right to vote.

front loading   The bunching of presidential primaries early in the season. During a presidential election year, some states or regions schedule their caucuses and presidential primaries early, squeezing the nomination contests into a few weeks. This front loading burdens candidates, forcing them to run in several states at the same time, and it also favors candidates with name recognition and well financed campaign organizations.

full disclosure   A proposed campaign finance reform that would require all candidates to disclose publicly the sources and amounts of all their campaign contributions.

gerrymandering   A process by which electoral district boundaries are drawn to enhance the fortunes of a political party or group or to protect incumbents.

grandfather clause   Used by some Southern states following the Reconstruction era, grandfather clauses were written into state constitutions, bestowing the right to vote or granting immunity from suffrage requirements to those whose ancestors had voted prior to 1867. A major intent of grandfather clauses was to disfranchise black citizens.

hard money   Individual campaign contributions that fall under FEC limits. The maximum limit for so-called hard contributions in 2008 by individuals was $2,300 per election to a candidate and up to $28,500 per calendar year to a national party committee. In odd-numbered years, these limits are increased according to the rate of inflation.

Hare system   *See* single transferable vote and preferential voting.

Hatch Act   *See* Political Activities Act of 1939 (Hatch Act).

hatched   A term used to describe federal government employees whose opportunities for political activity have been limited by the Hatch Act.

Help America Voter Act (HAVA)   Passed in 2002 largely in response to the voting irregularities experienced in the 2000 presidential election, the legislation provided for replacing punch card voting systems with electronic or optical scan devices, establishing administrative standards for voter registration record keeping and election administration, and the formation of the Election Assistance Commission to assist states in the conduct of federal elections.

inaugural committee   Committee charged with raising funds for the president elect. While campaign contributions are regulated by the FEC, donations to pay for a president elect's inaugural are not. Consequently, inaugural committees are not required to publicly identify contributors. President George W. Bush's 2005 inaugural committee raised $42 million from various donors, including corporations. For instance, several companies, including Home Depot, Exxon Mobil Corporation, and Ford Motor Company, gave $250,000 each to underwrite the inauguration celebration.

incumbency effect   The general tendency of voters to support public officials running for reelection, thereby giving these officials an advantage over challengers. The so-called incumbency effect has many explanations, including the tendency of PACs to focus contributions on incumbents and the ability of current officeholders to use the perquisites of office, such as the franking privilege, in their campaigns.

independent expenditures Expenditures by individuals or groups on behalf of a candidate that are not officially coordinated with the candidate's campaign. There is no limit on such expenditues. In 2004 a series of television ads funded through the section 527 group Swiftboat Veterans and POWs for Truth attacked Democratic presidential candidate John Kerry's military record in Vietnam. In 2007 the liberal group MoveOn.org ran a controversial advertising campaign criticizing General David H. Petraeus, President George W. Bush's military commander in Iraq.

indirect initiative An initiative that, after the required number of citizen signatures have been acquired in a petition, goes first to the state legislature for approval and is submitted to voters if the legislature rejects it or suggests a substitute measure.

initiative A process by which citizens may propose a new law and have it placed on the ballot by petition, which requires signatures from 5 to 15 percent of the registered voters.

Iowa caucus The earliest caucus held in the presidential election season, in which delegates to the national political party nominating convention are selected. A presidential candidate who does well in Iowa is taken more seriously than those who fail there. Some reformers argue that the presidential primary and caucus system should be altered so that less populous states like Iowa do not have inordinate influence on the nomination process.

IRS checkoff Taxpayers may mark a box on their federal income tax returns if they wish to have $3 of their tax obligation contributed to the Presidential Election Campaign Fund. Checking the box neither increases nor reduces any refund due. Public funding of presidential elections has occurred since 1976. Originally the voluntary contribution was $1, but it was raised to $3 in 1994. The checkoff has never been very popular with the public, and consequently the fund has been unable on occasion to support full payments of matching funds to candidates in presidential primaries.

issue advocacy ads As defined narrowly by the U.S. Supreme Court, a political ad that explicitly advocates the election or defeat of a political candidate. Consequently, numerous groups and both political parties run issue advocacy ads, which can be financed by unlimited and unregulated independent expenditures. Many so-called issue advocacy ads are thinly veiled attacks on specific candidates. In *Federal Election Commission v. Wisconsin Right to Life, Inc.* (2007) the U.S. Supreme Court broadened the notion of such ads, stating that they come under the limitations of the Bipartisan Campaign Reform Act only if they can definitely be interpreted as appealing for votes for or against a specific candidate.

late money Money that is contributed in the final days or weeks of a campaign and that may indicate a candidate's momentum as election day approaches.

leadership PACs Supposedly independent political action committees that are organized by politicians. Ostensibly they serve as fronts for a candidate's own campaign fund-raising. For instance, Sen. Robert Dole (R-KS) in 1995 disbanded his Better America Foundation, which critics claimed was used to free donors from FEC limits or reporting regulations.

limited voting Employed in voting systems with multimember districts, a type of voting in which each voter has at least one vote fewer than the number of positions to be filled. This voting procedure is used in several cities, including Boston, New York, and Philadelphia. Supporters of this voting system claim that it assists members of minority parties or groups to win elections.

literacy test A reading test. Supposedly a method to determine an individual's fitness as a voter, literacy tests were used primarily to disfranchise black voters in several states. Prospective voters had to answer a set of questions or interpret constitutional passages to the satisfaction of white voter registration officials. Congress suspended literacy tests in the Voting Rights Act of 1965 and prohibited them in subsequent legislation.

long ballot A ballot that is literally long because a large number of offices are subject to election. These ballots may cause confusion among voters and lead to uninformed choices.

macing Levying assessments on public officials' salaries as contributions to campaigns. Prior to reform legislation, political parties would routinely engage in this practice.

majority–minority district A legislative district that is drawn to enhance the opportunities for citizens of a racial or ethnic minority to elect representatives.

malapportionment The circumstance that results when state legislatures draw electoral districts so that district populations are very unequal or when legislatures fail to redraw district lines when significant population shifts have occurred.

matching funds Funds that serve as public financing of candidates in presidential primaries on an optional basis. The federal government matches the first $250 of each contribution to a campaign if candidates observe spending limits imposed by the FEC and raise $5,000 in donations of $250 or less in 20 states. Candidates who accept matching funds must accept limits on spending in the state primaries and caucuses. Candidates who refuse matching funds, such as George W. Bush and John Kerry in 2004 and Hillary Clinton and Barach Obama in 2008, may spend as much as they can raise during the presidential primary season.

McCain-Feingold bill   Campaign finance reform bill proposed Sens. John McCain (R-AZ) and Russell Feingold (D-WI) in the 104th Congress, calling for a ban on soft money and political action committees, closer monitoring of independent expenditures, a prohibition on most bundling, incentives to limit campaign spending such as offering candidates 30 minutes of free broadcast time, raising contribution limits, and banning the use of postal franking privileges for mass mailings by senators and representatives during the reelection seasons.

Missouri Plan   Also referred to as merit selection, a method of selecting state court judges that may take several forms. The most common form includes a nominating commission (usually appointed by the governor and composed of laypersons and persons with legal expertise) that chooses three or more candidates to fill a vacancy on the bench. The governor appoints one of the candidates who serves for a period of at least one year. After this initial term is served, the judicial candidate runs unopposed in a retention election and then serves a normal term of office.

motor-voter bill   *See* National Voter Registration Act (NVRA).

multimember districts   Voters in this type of electoral district elect more than one member to a legislative body.

National Voter Registration Act (NVRA)   The act passed by Congress in 1993 and popularly called the motor-voter bill. NVRA makes voter registration easier for Americans. The law went into effect in 1995 and requires states to allow voter registration by mail or in person when an eligible citizen applies for a driver's license. Voter registration may also occur at state offices that serve the poor or the disabled.

negative advertising   Advertisements used to define candidates' opponents, primarily portraying them in a negative light and attempting to expose weaknesses in their record. Often opponents respond to negative ads by charging their attackers with mudslinging. Negative advertising has been blamed for increased voter cynicism and low voter turnout.

New Hampshire primary   The first primary election in the presidential election year. The New Hampshire primary has become crucial to candidates seeking political and financial support and momentum. Some reformers see the inflated importance of one state's primary as a good reason for changing the presidential primary system. However, so far tradition and the determination of New Hampshire residents to maintain their state's status as the first presidential primary have militated against any attempt to reform the system.

Nineteenth Amendment The amendment to the U.S. Constitution, ratified in 1920, that granted women the right to vote.

nonpartisan election An election that occurs at the local level (for instance, judges, members of a board of education, or positions on a city council) and that allows a candidate to run for office without indicating a political party affiliation.

office block ballot A general election ballot that groups all the candidates under the office for which they are running. It places more emphasis on the office and may discourage straight ticket voting. Those who oppose party voting (or straight ticket voting) consider the office block ballot a desirable election reform.

one person, one vote The principle that no person's vote should count more than anyone else's. When legislative reapportionment occurs, the districts must be apportioned on the basis of population—no one district should be larger than another in population—therefore ensuring that no person's vote counts more than anyone else's. This principle was enunciated in *Reynolds v. Sims*, 377 U.S. 533, 1964.

open primary A type of primary in which voters may determine on election day in which political party's nominating election they will participate.

opportunity district Term used by an attorney in an argument before the U.S. Supreme Court in 1995 in reference to majority–minority districts. Justice Antonin Scalia found the phrase objectionable. Scalia stated that the term "opportunity district" was emotionally loaded and that he much preferred the phrase "majority–minority district."

packing *See* concentration gerrymandering.

participatory democracy A type of democracy in which individuals and groups are directly involved in political decision making. Citizens formulate policy without representatives serving as buffers between them and the political system, such as in New England town meetings.

party boss A political leader who has an extraordinary amount of control over a state or local party organization and who retains power through patronage, graft, and the manipulation of election procedures and voting behavior. The direct primary, civil service reform, and a more literate electorate have diminished bossism.

party column ballot This general election ballot lists all candidates for elective office under their party labels and symbols, making it easier for voters to select a straight ticket, that is, to vote for all candidates from one party by pulling a single lever on the voting machine.

Pendleton Act (Civil Service Reform Act of 1883) The act that created the Civil Service Commission and that introduced considerations of merit into federal hiring and firing policies, thus limiting the patronage the political parties could award to faithful campaign workers. Although initially only 10 percent of the federal workforce was covered under the legislation, by 1933, 80 of federal jobs were awarded on the basis of merit.

plurality system   An electoral system in which a candidate for public office can win an election by receiving more votes than any other candidate, without necessarily securing a majority of votes cast. The plurality winner may not receive a majority of votes if more than two candidates are competing for the position. Those supporting greater minority representation advocate the plurality rather than a majority requirement in primary elections.

political action committees (PACs)   Committees that collect money from their membership and donate it to political candidates and parties. Although not officially recognized until the 1974 Federal Election Campaign Act, PACs have existed since 1943 when the Congress of Industrial Organizations formed a separate committee to avoid the ban on contributions from labor unions. Under current federal law, a PAC may give up to $5,000 to a federal candidate during the primaries and another $5,000 during the general election.

Political Activities Act of 1939 (Hatch Act)   The legislation that forbade political activity by federal employees, limited individual contributions to a political committee to $5,000, and made it illegal for a political committee to spend more than $3 million in any campaign.

political apathy   The failure of an eligible citizen to vote or to take an interest in public affairs. Political apathy may indicate satisfaction with the political process, or it may indicate alienation and despair. Some point to political apathy as a reason for reforming the electoral system and for using get-out-the-vote drives and other mobilization techniques to increase interest and participation.

political editorializing rule   A broadcasting rule stating that, if a broadcaster endorses a political candidate, the Federal Communication Commission requires the broadcaster to give the opposing candidate the right to reply. This is not the same as the abandoned fairness doctrine policy, which required radio and television broadcasters to allow all sides on public issues equal access to public airwaves.

political machine   A local or state political party organization that is characterized by centralized leadership control over member activity and that is highly effective at getting party supporters to the polls on election day. The organization recruits members through patronage and the dispensing of favors. One of the objectives of reform movements such as the Progressives was to minimize the influence of political machines.

poll tax   A tax that was once required of citizens, mostly in Southern states, who wished to register. Ostensibly instituted to pay election costs, it was intended to discourage blacks and poor whites from voting. Although the sum of the poll tax was relatively small, the states that used it could up the ante by requiring an individual to pay back taxes for past elections in which they did not vote—thereby increasing the taxes due. In 1964 the Twenty-fourth Amendment prohibited poll taxes in federal elections. Poll taxes were declared unconstitutional in all elections, federal and state, by the 1966 Supreme Court decision *Harper v. Virginia Board of Elections.*

poll watcher   An individual who observes voting practices and procedures during elections, usually on behalf of a political party or candidate. They attempt to encourage proper behavior and may report irregularities.

precinct   The smallest subdivision used for organizing the vote in elections. Most precincts contain fewer than 1,000 voters and serve as the basic unit for building political party organizations. The introduction of at-large elections lessened the importance of precincts.

preclearance   *See* Voting Rights Acts (VRAs).

preference primary   *See* advisory primary.

preferential ballot   A ballot that is not binding and that may be used in an advisory capacity. For example, in a presidential primary of this type, the voters inform the delegates to the national nominating conventions of their nonbinding preferences.

preferential voting   A voting system in which electors rank candidates from first choice to last. The system is employed in a version of proportional representation. The candidate with the lowest number of first-place votes is declared defeated, and those who designated that candidate as their first choice have their second-choice votes distributed among the remaining candidates. This process continues until all seats have been filled.

presidential primaries   Presidential primaries involve statewide elections that give rank-and-file party members an opportunity to select the delegates to their party's national nominating convention. In the last 40 years these primaries have become increasingly important to the ultimate selection of party candidates. The large financial resources required, the time and energy presidential hopefuls must devote to primaries in individual states, and the tendency of states to schedule primaries much earlier than in past election cycles have led to reform proposals such as holding a few regional presidential primaries.

primary election   An election, held before the general election, whose purpose is to nominate a political party's candidates for office. Primary elections are held for state and federal offices.

Progressive Movement A movement in American politics whose members believed that governing institutions could "progress" if science were applied to public problems. The movement reached its peak in the early 20th century with the creation of the Progressive Party in 1911. The Progressives were a disparate group of reformers who advocated a number of successful reforms, including the civil service system; the direct primary; the initiative, referendum, and recall; and nonpartisan municipal elections.

proportional representation (PR) A system of representation in which the seats in the legislature are allocated according to the voting strength of each party or group. For example, a minor party that receives 10 percent of the popular vote wins roughly 10 percent of the legislative seats. PR has taken many forms, although there are two major types: the list system, in which political parties receive legislative seats in proportion to their popular vote, and the single transferable vote, which employs preferential voting. Two relatively complex forms of the list system are the Sainte-Laguë method and the d'Hondt method, each of which involves successively dividing the total number of votes (V) that a party list won by the number of seats (s) that each party has been allocated so far— [$V/(2s+1)$ in the Sainte-Laguë method and $V/(s+1)$ in the d'Hondt method]—and awarding a seat to the party with the largest result at each stage until all the seats have been allocated.

public financing (general election funding) A public grant available to the presidential nominees of each major party, the amount of which is determined by a cost-of-living adjustment. To receive the funding, candidates must limit their spending to the amount of the grant and not accept private contributions for the campaign (with the exception of paying for legal expenses or spending up to $50,000 of their own personal funds). Minor party candidates may qualify for partial public funding if they receive 5 percent or more of the popular vote in the election. This reform measure applies only to presidential elections. So far, Congress has failed to establish a public financing system for elections to the U.S. House of Representatives and Senate. However, some states have instituted public financing for selected political offices such as the governor, other executive branch offices, and state legislative seats.

push-polling Calls by a candidate's workers to potential voters in the guise of a legitimate public opinion survey but with the actual intent of persuading people to support a particular candidate. Push-polling is generally considered an unethical practice.

reapportionment A new apportionment (or reapportionment) of congressional seats normally occurs every 10 years, based on U.S. Census data. Each state is assigned a new number of congressional seats based on changes in state population. Reapportionment results in redistricting, which is the redrawing of congressional district boundaries. Periodic reapportionment is also required of representative bodies such as state legislatures and county commissions.

recall   Some states allow their voters to recall, or remove, elected officials from office before their terms expire. Typically at least 25 percent of voters in the previous election must sign a petition indicating their desire to remove the official.

redistricting   The redrawing by state legislatures of congressional district boundaries in response to a reapportionment of congressional seats among the states. *See* also reapportionment and malapportionment.

referendum   A procedure by which a law or constitutional amendment proposed by the legislature is submitted directly to the voters for approval.

regional primary   A primary election held by a geographically contiguous group of states on the same day during the presidential primary season. Some reformers have recommended a system of regional primaries organized at the national level to shorten the primary season and lessen the influence of primaries held in less populous states early in the season.

repeating   An illegal practice of voting more than once in the same election. It was used extensively during the era of urban political machines. Accusations occasionally surface today that repeat voting occurs to assist a candidate in winning an election.

repeat voting   *See* repeating.

residence voting   A voting qualification based on where a citizen resides. Lengthy residency requirements were declared unconstitutional by the U.S. Supreme Court in 1972. The Voting Rights Act of 1970 specified that states could require no more than 30 days' residence for citizens to be eligible and vote in presidential elections.

responsible party government   A political principle that places emphasis on party discipline and the accountability of political parties to voters. Political parties give their support to specific objectives and party platforms, and they offer voters "a choice, not an echo." Some reformers argue that significant improvement in the American electoral process requires implementation of this model.

results test   A criterion for determining the acceptability of changes in voting rules that emphasizes the potential discriminatory outcomes of electoral arrangements, rather than the intent of lawmakers. The results test was part of the 1982 revisions to the Voting Rights Act.

retrogression   A decline in minority representation, a phenomenon that, under the Voting Rights Act, should not occur.

Revenue Act of 1971   Legislation that authorized a voluntary $1 checkoff on federal income tax returns in an effort to create public financing of major political party candidates for president.

rotation in office   *See* term limits

runoff election   A follow-up election required by some states, particularly in primaries, if no one candidate receives a majority of votes. Minority candidates and interest group representatives have criticized runoff elections, arguing that minority candidates who may be successful in achieving a plurality in the first election cannot win the runoff election.

short ballot   A ballot containing only a small number of elective offices for voters to fill. Short ballots are advocated as a means of simplifying elections and allowing voters to make more intelligent choices.

short counting   Intentionally misreporting vote totals to benefit a favored candidate. Dishonest election judges or tellers may attempt to employ this type of vote fraud. The appointment of poll watchers to oversee the ballot counting process can discourage short counting.

single-member district   An electoral district that elects only one candidate, based on a plurality of votes, to an office. Voter choices are more restricted than in a multimember district. However, if a system of proportional representation is not used with multimember districts, the single-member district provides greater opportunities for minority representation.

single transferable vote   A type of proportional representation that employs preferential voting and the transfer of second-choice votes from a losing candidate to the remaining contenders.

Smith v. Allwright, **321 U.S. 649, 1944**   A case in which the U.S. Supreme Court ruled that white primaries violated the Fifteenth Amendment. Previously the Court had ruled that political parties or private organizations could exclude anyone they wished, including blacks, from membership. In this case the Court ruled that parties were performing a state function and hence could not exclude anyone from membership.

smoke-filled room   When political bosses reigned supreme, the smoke-filled room became the stereotypical image of anywhere political bargaining and deal making occurred. In days gone by, the bosses would decide whom to nominate to run as candidates under the party label. The phrase definitely carries a sinister, undemocratic connotation.

soft money   Contributions that are not subject to Federal Election Commission limits and that may be used for get-out-the-vote activities, voter registration campaigns, and party-building efforts. Soft money includes funds that are not spent on behalf of a specific candidate for federal office. Considered a loophole in federal election law, soft money enables parties to raise huge amounts of money through contributions to state party committees and the so-called nonfederal bank accounts of the Democratic and Republican National Committees. The Bipartisan Campaign Reform Act of 2002 attempted to limit the role of soft money in campaigns.

solid South Used by V. O. Key Jr., a phrase that refers to the fact that at one time the South voted consistently and uniformly Democratic. Voters in the solid South were overwhelmingly white because discriminatory registration laws and intimidation tactics were used to discourage blacks from voting. The Democratic Party's advocacy of equal rights for blacks is cited as one of the pivotal explanations for why the South is no longer solid.

special election An election held to fill an office that an incumbent has vacated before the term expires, to recall a public official, or to allow voters to decide on public policy issues in an initiative or referendum.

straight ticket voting Voting only for candidates of the voter's political party. The office block ballot discourages, and the party column ballot tends to encourage, straight ticket voting.

targeting A practice that is used by political action committees and that involves identifying particular members of the U.S. Congress for defeat and channeling campaign funds to their opponents.

Tasmanian dodge A form of illegal paper ballot voting in which a bribed voter returns a blank ballot to a candidate's worker, who marks the ballot appropriately and gives it to another voter who casts it and returns from the polls with another blank ballot. In this way, unscrupulous politicians can assure that bribed voters vote as promised. *Also known as* the endless chain.

term limits A restriction on the number of terms a public official may serve consecutively in office. The Twenty-second Amendment, ratified in 1951, limited presidents to two terms or no more than 10 years of service. More recently, many Americans have supported term limits for members of Congress and state legislatures. The term limits movement, which gained momentum in the late 1980s and early 1990s, has lobbied strongly for such limits. The U.S. Supreme Court in *U.S. Term Limits, Inc. v. Thornton* (1995) ruled that states were prohibited by the Constitution from imposing term limits on members of the U.S. House of Representatives and Senate.

Twelfth Amendment The amendment to the U.S. Constitution, ratified in 1804, stipulating that electors vote separately for president and vice president. The development of political parties after 1787 required a change in the original system of electing the president.

Twenty-fourth Amendment The amendment to the U.S. Constitution, ratified in 1964, that eliminated the use of poll taxes in federal elections.

Twenty-sixth Amendment The amendment to the U.S. Constitution, ratified in 1971, that extended the right to vote to citizens between ages

18 and 20. Twenty-one was the legal voting age in most states prior to this amendment.

Twenty-third Amendment   The amendment to the U.S. Constitution, ratified in 1961, that gave residents of the District of Columbia the right to vote in presidential elections, granting the District a number of electoral votes not to exceed that of the least populous state.

two-party system   Because candidates in the United States generally run in single-member districts with a plurality vote required for victory, a two-party system is reinforced. Third parties are discouraged under such electoral arrangements because voters tend to conclude that their votes will be wasted if they vote for candidates who have little chance of winning a plurality of the popular vote.

two-round system   An electoral system in which a second election is held shortly after the first if no candidate for an office receives a predetermined proportion of the vote (often set at a majority). In France, which uses the two-round system, any candidate receiving at least 12.5 percent of the vote in the first round qualifies as a candidate in the second round. If more than two candidates qualify, the candidate receiving a plurality of the vote in the second round is declared the winner.

vote dilution   The result when an effort is made to limit a group's voting strength by reducing its ability to influence or elect public officials of their choice. The dispersal gerrymander is an obvious way to dilute a group's vote strength.

voter registration   A procedure required of prospective voters that is used to establish their identity and place of residence prior to an election so that they are certified as eligible to vote in a precinct. The purpose of voter registration is to diminish opportunities for election day voting fraud. However, some reformers argue that the registration requirement significantly decreases voter turnout when otherwise eligible citizens fail to register.

voter rolloff   A circumstance that occurs when voters quit voting after they have made their selections for the more prominent offices at the top of the ticket. For example, they vote for president, U.S. senator, and governor but do not vote for lesser offices, such as judges, school board officials, and county commissioners. Long ballots may induce voter rolloff. *Also known as* ballot rolloff.

Voting Rights Acts (VRAs)   The Voting Rights Act of 1965 and subsequent amendments approved in 1970, 1975, 1982, and 2006. The Voting Rights Act and its revisions and amendments require preclearance of all proposed changes in voting laws by the attorney general or the federal district court of the District of Columbia if a jurisdiction has a history of low minority electoral participation. The act and subsequent amendments banned literacy tests nationwide and required bilingual voting ballots in 24 states.

Watergate   The term for the break-in at the Democratic National Party headquarters in the Watergate building complex in Washington, D.C., by individuals affiliated with the Committee to Reelect the President and the subsequent cover-up efforts of Richard M. Nixon's administration. Other acts associated with the Watergate scandal included illegal use of the Central Intelligence Agency, the Federal Bureau of Investigation, the Internal Revenue Service, and other governmental agencies for partisan purposes; the employment of dirty tricks during the 1972 election campaign; and the receipt of illegal campaign contributions and their use for purposes unrelated to the campaign. Watergate is partially responsible for triggering campaign finance reform in 1974.

white primary   Instituted in Southern states in the early 20th century, a primary that either forbade or discouraged black participation in primary elections. Because the Democratic Party dominated Southern politics at the time, excluding blacks from the party primary amounted to disfranchisement. *See also Smith v. Allwright.*

Index

About the Authors

Glenn H. Utter, professor and chair of the Political Science Department at Lamar University, was educated at Binghamton University, the University of Buffalo, and the University of London. Utter specializes in modern political theory and American political thought. He wrote *Encyclopedia of Gun Control and Gun Rights* (2000) and *Mainline Christians and U.S. Public Policy* (2007), coedited *American Political Scientists: A Dictionary* (1993, 2002), and cowrote *Conservative Christians and Political Participation* (2004) and *The Religious Right* (1995, 2001, 2007). He has written several articles for political science journals and other scholarly publications.

Ruth Ann Strickland, professor of political science at Appalachian State University, received her PhD from the University of South Carolina. Strickland specializes in judicial process, administrative law, and public policy analysis. She coauthored *The Constitution under Pressure* (1987) and has written numerous articles for political science journals and edited books.

ML   6/08